Library of Public Policy and Public Administration

Volume 11

Around the world there are challenges to the way we administer government. Some of these have to do with brute force that is backed by self-interest. However, there are those intrepid souls who think we are all better than this. This series of monographs and edited collections of original essays seeks to explore the very best way that governments can execute their sovereign duties within the sphere of ethically-based public policy that recognizes human rights and the autonomy of its citizens.

Proposals to the series can include policy questions that are nationally or internationally situated. For example, regional migration from victims of war, terrorism, police integrity, political corruption, the intersection between politics and public health, hunger, clean water and sanitation, global warming, treatment of the "other" nationally and internationally, and issues of distributive justice and human rights.

Proposals that discuss systemic changes in the structure of government solutions will also be considered. These include *corruption and anti-corruption, bribery, nepotism,* and *effective systems design.*

Series benchmark: 110,000-150,000 words. Special books can be somewhat longer.

More information about this series at http://www.springer.com/series/6234

Amitai Etzioni

Happiness is the Wrong Metric

A Liberal Communitarian Response
to Populism

With highest regards.
 - Amitai Etzioni

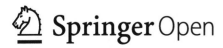 Springer Open

Amitai Etzioni
The George Washington University
Washington, DC, USA

ISSN 1566-7669
Library of Public Policy and Public Administration
ISBN 978-3-319-69622-5   ISBN 978-3-319-69623-2   (eBook)
https://doi.org/10.1007/978-3-319-69623-2

Library of Congress Control Number: 2017958825

Printed on acid-free paper

This Springer imprint is published by Springer Nature
The registered company is Springer International Publishing AG
The registered company address is: Gewerbestrasse 11, 6330 Cham, Switzerland

For the moral wrestlers

Contents

Part VI   Science and Technology

Introduction

When I helped my son carry his belongings to the dorm on his first day of college, he ran into a classmate. The young man asked: "What are you going to major in?" When my son responded "applied math," his classmate said, with considerable condescension, "I am going to do *pure* math!" When I taught sociology at Columbia University, my department prided itself on its strong theory and method classes. It was very reluctant to allow the teaching of applied subjects and steadfastly refused the introduction of a course in criminology. Indeed, those who wanted to teach such classes were relegated to the Teachers College and the School of Social Work and were not allowed to vote in department meetings.

The most prestigious ethics publication in the English language is *Ethics*. A typical issue, for instance, that of April 2017, covers topics such as deontological decision theory, distributive ethics, and understanding how risk factors into deontological theory. There is no similar journal for applied ethics. True, there are some very fine publications that deal with specific applied areas, e.g., the *Hastings Center Report* for bioethics and the *Journal of Business Ethics* for this field. However, no major journals provide a venue to share ideas or public deliberations of applied ethics as a field, a kind of publication most other fields have at least one of. This book attempts to provide some impetus for further development of applied ethics.

Ethics was a sterile and dull subject for decades, which rehashed questions of the kind "How many angels can stand on the head of a pin?" until it was applied to medicine. Here, ethics was able to help a great deal to patients in sorting out their choices, to guide health-care professionals as well as public policy. Moreover, this application is reported to have a salutary feedback effect on ethics.

I myself was first introduced to "basic" ethics when I spent a year studying with Martin Buber (Etzioni 2003). I wrote what at least I consider a learned essay and small book about his work (Etzioni 1998). And when I became involved in communitarianism, that provided more opportunities for reflection on what is the "good" and who and how one determines what it is (Etzioni 2011). However, I found it intellectually more stimulating and most assuredly more of service to struggle with applied ethical issues, as will soon become all too clear. I never bought the notion that academics should not venture outside the ivory tower and that engaging in questions of values and public policy somehow corrupts their academic purity and virtue.

Moreover, like others, I found that applied work enlivened the basic one. Thus, when I tried to sort out when privacy should yield to the common good, for instance, to protect public health, I found it helped me think through more generally how one is to deal with clashes between two core values (Etzioni 1999). Most of what follows is applied.

To some, the term "ethics" evokes values such as veracity, loyalty, and truthfulness. However, the ethics domain is much vaster. It concerns itself with individual rights, social justice, peace, and much else. Cases in kind follow. They all deal with current challenges both in societies and on the global level.

Part I asks how we can determine what a good life is. Many measure it by how happy people are. Happiness in turn is assumed to be derived from high income that enables one to lead an affluent way of life, mainly viewed as being able to consume a lot of goods and services. However, evidence shows that by and large (there are always exceptions when one deals with social science data), once income rises above the level at which people's basic needs can be met, it adds little to their happiness. Other social scientists studied whether what one does gives meaning to life. However, meaning can be gained by joining a gang or ISIS. At least from an ethicist's viewpoint and, as I see it, from most people's personal viewpoint, something is missing, something rather profound, namely, the sense of doing good. It is a sense that leads people to make sacrifices not for self-glorification, not to feel good about themselves, but to service others. I am not writing about saints, but about parents who take care of a severely disabled child, about spouses who take care of their partners with cancer or Alzheimer's, and about volunteers who go into places that are unsafe to help those in danger (see Chap. 1).

The three Abrahamic religions have a clear perception of what human nature is; I call it one of a moral wrestler. Although they differ on the weight they accord–and the ways they depict–the forces that make us stray, they share the basic understanding of human nature. For Catholicism, the original sin plays a greater role than the *yetzer hara* (bad instinct) in Judaism; and neither embraces the Protestant notion of predestination. Islam emphasizes humans' inherent goodness (*fitrah*), which must be upheld against base desires and sinful outside influences. However, all see life as a struggle between doing good and being tempted to violate our sense of what is right; all see room for some form of punishment as well as redemption. Social science by and large, with notable exceptions, has moved away from this view of human nature. This is not true merely for economics but, we shall see, also for psychology, sociology, and anthropology. If we could do more to incorporate the concept of the moral wrestlers into the social sciences, we might be able to learn more about what makes for better human beings and better societies (see Chap. 2).

Part II is dedicated to an examination of human nature. Are we out to maximize ourselves and does society work well when each person focuses on what *they* consider good? On a basic level, this issue has been debated as the difference between homo economicus and *homo sapiens*. Those who adhere to the rationalistic paradigm, the one that treats people as homo economicus, assume that humans have only one kind of motivation: the quest for pleasure. Even when they do good, this is interpreted as seeking esteem or prestige or some other form of "psychic income." As Robert Goodin put it, advocates of homo economicus proceed largely in one of two ways: "One reduces morality to enlightened self-interest, denying that morality has any special place in the decision calculus. Another, while acknowledging that people do internalize moral principles per se, enters them into utility functions as just another consumption good" (Goodin 1980).

In contrast, many other scholars see people as *homo sapiens*, as human beings subject to continuous conflict between the pursuit of pleasure and their moral commitments. The simple line, "I would like to go to a movie, but I ought to visit my friend in the hospital," captures this tension.

Economists tend to assume that one's preferences are given and stable. This allows them to explain changes in behavior largely in terms of variables, such as changes in income and elative prices, and more generally in terms of incentives and disincentives. However, sociologists and psychologists have shown that preferences are formed during socialization and continue to be reformulated during adulthood through factors such as persuasion, leadership, and advertising. Hence, when comparing behavior at two points in time, one must take into account changes in preferences that may well have occurred during the given period. The challenge is that there is no consolidated theory of what factors drive preferences (see Chap. 3).

How do we decide, as members of small communities as well as large ones, as nations, and sometimes even across borders, which moral values to uphold? The processes involved, which I call moral dialogues, are much more common–and effective!–than is often assumed. The details of how moral dialogues take off, evolve, and mature are spelled out in Chap. 4. Suffice here to note that they not only often lead to significant changes in what we consider moral but also affect behavior. For instance, Gallup polling found that in only 18 years, from 1996 to 2014, support for gay marriage more than doubled from 27 to 55%. Once people change their mind as to what is right, they also change their conduct; without that, the police stand over their heads. As far as one can determine, there were no significant shared moral commitments to the environment in 1950. By 2016, "74% of U.S. adults said the 'country should do whatever it takes to protect the environment'" (Anderson 2016). Furthermore, "Seventy-three percent of Americans say they prefer emphasizing alternative energy, rather than gas and oil production, as the solution to the nation's energy problems" (Auter 2016). Ample evidence appears in Chap. 4.

Social science theories have moral effects. If we teach each year many hundreds of thousands of students who take courses in economics and keep telling them publicly that everyone is basically out to enrich themselves, to "maximize" their self-interests, people will become somewhat more selfish than they would be otherwise. Social science theories become popular narratives and these have effects. They can either debase moral behavior to some extent or ennoble it to some. There is reason for concern when one finds that many business schools dedicate very little time–or none at all–to teaching ethics (see Chap. 5).

Part III deals with two major current ethical challenges, both affected by new technological developments. One concerns the massive loss of jobs due to automation, accelerated by applications of artificial intelligence. The other is the rise of right-wing populism, which is driven in part by job loss, globalization, and accelerated societal changes.

Many discussions on the rise of AI-equipped, "smart" machines draw on driverless cars as their lead example. When ethicists first tackled the ethical issues raised by this new technological development, they drew on a "basic" ethical analysis that preceded any applied issue, often referred to as the trolley problems. They concern questions such as imagine a train is rushing down a track; if you do not act, five people are surely to be killed. If you pull a lever, the train will change course and kill only one person. Should you pull the lever (Thomson 1985)? Ethics was the subject of this narrative's many variations, including one that puts you on a bridge above the track, standing next to a fat man. If you throw him overboard, his body will stop the train and so on and so on.

To deal with the issues raised by driverless cars, ethicists applied these narratives to a large variety of imagined situations. For instance, assume a child jumps in front of the car; should the car swerve into the adjacent lane even though it will kill several people there? Hit the brakes and kill the passenger but save the child and so on and so on (Bonnefon et al. 2016).

These narratives provide fine material for academic seminars; for instance, they allow one to explore the difference between sins of commission and those of omission. And to be frank, they make for great topics in Woody Allen-like dinner conversations. However, we shall see when we turn to examine the ethical issues raised by artificial intelligence that they provide a rather misleading way to examine real ethical issues, the kind people and policymakers face (see Part VI). And they do not seem very helpful in exploring a burning issue raised by automation, especially driven by AI: the major forthcoming net job loss. Some refer to it as a job collapse or even job Armageddon.

I write "net" because in previous technological revolutions, jobs were lost but many new and often better jobs were created. (Economists like to scoff at people who, they say, are akin to those who sought to protect the horse and buggy industry when it suffered as a result of the first cars running off the assembly line.) However, we shall see that there is strong evidence to suggest that this pattern–based on very few data points–will not repeat itself. Hence, a major ethical challenge society faces is how to respond to massive net loss of jobs. This is the subject of Chap. 6.

Job loss is but one of the factors that drives the populism that elected Donald Trump president and challenges, to one extent or another, most liberal democratic governments. What propels populism? How can democracies be protected from the onslaught? The answer to these questions, I show below, requires understanding the moral claims made by globalists and by nationalists. Globalists argue for moral positions that hold for all people–human rights; freedom of movement, including across borders (immigration); and free movement of goods across borders (free trade). Nationalists object to all three in the name of the particular values and needs of what they consider their folks, their nation. A close examination of both claims finds that there is a third way that takes us away from a culture war between the two camps to public policies that are morally defensible and mitigate the ill effects of populism. See Chap. 7.

Part IV deals with moral issues raised by individual rights. Rights are not merely a matter of law but are also, in effect, moral claims. They call for respecting individual dignity and liberty and extol the value of protecting citizens from potentially overpowering governments. However, the moral language of individual rights is incomplete. We already see (in Chap. 7 on populism) the importance of bonding and shared moral cultures. These often define what people owe each other, their family members, their community, the nation, and various common goods such as the environment and public health (and to some extent, the global "community"). That we have rights but also responsibilities is a core liberal communitarian idea (Etzioni 1993). Ethical dilemmas arise when our rights and responsibilities come into conflict.

A key case in point is the increasing challenges to free speech in the name of the harm that it imposes on some who are subjected to it, especially on minorities. Recently, there has been a call for safe zones on campuses, safe from ideas that some students find distressing, or warning labels on books for the same reason. Many democracies use the force of the law to limit speech they consider hateful. As I see it, there is a better way, one that involves relying on the moral voice of the community to keep free speech from causing undue harm (see Chap. 8).

We constantly face the minting of new rights. Indeed, much of US history can be told in terms of expiation through rights. Gradually, people without property gained the right to run for office; women gained the right to vote; African Americans' voting rights were much better guaranteed; the rights of disabled people were established; and more recently–there are more rights for those of the same gender to marry. Does this mean that all new rights have the same standing? Have we reached a stage where the minting of more rights undermines their moral standing? One such recent right is the right to be forgotten. In Chap. 9, I suggest that it causes more harm than justice.

The suggestion that people who committed non-violent crimes, especially first offenders, should be shamed instead of jailed raises hackles. "Back to the pillories?" we are asked. Chapter 10 makes the case that shaming is fully morally justified. One should not ignore that people who are "merely" jailed are also shamed. And shaming makes it easier to reintegrate offenders back into the community, while jailing very often has the opposite effect. (True, this holds only for those who share the values of the society at large. For those who view violating the law or norms as a badge of honor, shaming will have little effect) (see Chap. 10).

We have a moral voice, both as individuals and as communities. That is, when we celebrate people for doing good–say Doctors Without Borders for risking their lives to treat patients with Ebola–they feel appreciated. Moreover, such kudos lead others to feel they should consider doing more good themselves, maybe one not as demanding but nevertheless of virtue. And when people violate what we personally, or as members of one community or another, consider good behavior and we gently chastise them, it helps curbing such behavior. The same holds even on the international level. Nations hate to be criticized about the ways they deal with their citizens or with those of other nations, although there are sharp limits to how far they are willing to change their policies in order for these policies to be regarded as morally appropriate. Given the limited leverage moral voices have on the international level, I argue that we have to carefully select the targets of our moral voice. Chastising one regime after the other, for great and not so great violations of what we consider right, squanders whatever effect our moral voice can have. We need moral triage (see Chap. 11).

Part V examines a few key ethical issues raised on the international level. The first centers on the American response to extremism in the Muslim world and asks how policymakers might better craft their messaging. Thus far, voices emanating from the USA have emphasized liberal values, like individual rights, democracy, and free markets, to counter religious extremist rhetoric. I argue that in doing so, we fail to recognize that while most of the Muslim world is not violent, the majority is also not liberal. They are believers who want to see religion play a greater role in public life–I call them "illiberal moderates"–and since they pose as central figures in the fight against violent extremism, we need to speak to them, I claim, on their terms (see Chap. 12).

Part V then turns to the issues of mass atrocities and genocide. I followed these closely ever since a mutual friend introduced me to Samantha Power (who later became US ambassador to the UN during much of the Obama administration), as she was jogging on the banks of the Charles River. When she learned my name, she said with a broad smile, "I hate you!" It turned out that she was a journalist covering the brutal ethnic cleansing in Bosnia, calling in her story under fire to *The Economist*. She was told that her story had to be cut short to make room for a three-page story about communitarian ideas I was championing and which were, at the time, popular with Tony Blair and Bill Clinton. I soon read her Pulitzer Prize-winning volume *A Problem from Hell* in which she documents the history of America's failure to respond to genocide and crimes against humanity. Bill Clinton, who did stop ethnic cleansing in Kosovo, stated that his biggest regret is that he did not in Rwanda (Hughes 2014). Indeed, more and more nations agreed that it was legitimate for foreign powers to interfere in the international affairs of nations if genocide took place. Part V examines how this moral consensus was abused and why the USA did so little–despite Power's urging–to stop the civil war in Syria, the genocide in South Sudan, and the civil war in Libya. It is one of the great ethical questions of the age–as these atrocities continue (see Chap. 13).

Senator John McCain made a compelling case for keeping the promotion of human rights as a core element of US foreign policy, but does not address the fact that while this goal is noble, the means may be foul. There is a vast moral and prudential difference between promoting human rights with nonlethal means (such as public diplomacy, leadership training, cultural exchanges, and even smart sanctions) and coercive regime change. Such changes often lead to very high human and economic costs. These could be considered as a price one must pay for liberty, but they often result in new, very unsavory governments.

Whatever reasons the USA had for invading Iraq, it stayed to make Iraq into a liberal democracy. The human costs for the Iraqis have been horrendous. At least 25,000 people lost their lives and millions lost their homes. The Shia government supported militias acting as death squads against Sunnis, which has driven them to support ISIS. The military is so corrupt that often not enough funds are left for ammunition and food for the troops. In Libya, the humanitarian intervention morphed into a coercive regime change, leading to bloody civil war. The USA ignored that the rebels it considered prodemocratic forces committed many of the same atrocities that Qaddafi's forces did, including ethnic cleansing. Afghanistan, after 16 years of democracy-building, is one of the most corrupt nations in the world; it is a major source of heroin that floods Central Asia and streams into Europe. Terrorism is rampant. The USA has even been unable to stop the institutionalized pedophilia (called *bacha bazi*) of the governing Pashtun elites. One of the many reasons the tragic war in Syria is continuing is that for years, the USA insisted that Assad's departure be a precondition for negotiation.

Coercive regime change also stands in the way of dealing with North Korea, China, and Russia. Recent statements that the USA is out to change the regime in North Korea are sure to make the regime work even harder, if this is possible, to develop its nuclear arms and resist any negotiations. China and Russia feel that their allies are threatened as well as their own regimes.

In short, a strong case for the promotion of human rights needs to be coupled with a discussion on how it will be achieved. Avoiding coercive regime change and relying on nonlethal means seem a morally sound and wise foreign policy (see Chap. 14).

Part VI focuses on the ethical issues raised by artificial intelligence. One may well wonder what qualifies me, a sociologist, to deal with artificial intelligence. The short and long answers are the same. My son Oren (who coauthored the articles in this part) is a leading AI scholar. A father is allowed to gloat, but Google his name or search *The New York Times*, and you will see that he truly is a superstar. Our extended family gets together at least twice a year for a week each time. Long walks and talks during these weeks allow us to understand where the other is coming from, which is essential for work that bridges a highly technical field and ethics.

The ethical issues we addressed in this part concern the fact that AI is making many different kinds of machines–from cars to bombers–increasingly autonomous. That is, they are able to act on their own, way beyond how humans programmed and instructed them. Thus, a driverless car may be programmed to abide by speed limits set by law but note that other cars are speeding and "learn" to speed itself. These recent achievements are the third stage of AI. Like many other technological developments, AI's accomplishments and potential were first overhyped, and then considerable disappointment set in. Now, however, it is reaching a stage in which it changes most everything we do–from surgery to child and elder care.

AI is believed by some to be on its way to producing intelligent machines that will be far more capable than human beings. After reaching this point of "techno-logical singularity," computers will continue to advance and give birth to rapid tech-nological progress that will result in dramatic and unpredictable changes for humanity. Some observers predict that the singularity could occur as soon as 2030.

As we see it, the fact that AI makes machines much smarter and more capable does not make them more fully autonomous. We are accustomed to thinking that if a person is granted more autonomy–inmates released from jails or teenagers left unsupervised–they may do wrong because they will follow their previously restrained desires. In contrast, machines equipped with AI, however smart they may become, have no goals or motivations of their own. It is hard to see, for instance, why driverless cars would unite to march on Washington. And even if an AI pro-gram came up with the most persuasive political slogan ever created, why would this program nominate an AI-equipped computer as the nominee for the next presi-dent? Science fiction writers might come up with ways intelligence can be turned into motivation, but for now, such notions probably should stay where they belong: in the movies.

Instead of slowing down the development of AI, out of fear for where it may lead us, Oren and I hold that humans can keep the ultimate control over ever-smarter machines. How this can be achieved is the subject of five chapters. One asks if and how one can ensure these machines will act ethically (Chap. 15). The discussion then turns to examine the dangers and merits of autonomous weapons (Chap. 16), whether robots should be used in child, elder, and patient care (Chap. 17), and finally issues in bioethics (Chap. 18 and 19).

Part VI begins with a review of the reasons scholars hold that driverless cars and many other AI-equipped machines must be able to make ethical decisions and the difficulties this approach faces. It then shows that cars have no moral agency and that the term "autonomous," commonly applied to these machines, is misleading and leads to invalid conclusions about the ways these machines can be kept ethical. The article's most important claim is that a significant part of the challenge posed by AI-equipped machines can be addressed by the kind of ethical choices made by human beings for millennia. Ergo, there is little need to teach machines ethics even if this could be done in the first place. Finally, the article points out that it is a griev-ous error to draw on extreme outlier scenarios–such as the trolley narratives–as a basis for conceptualizing the ethical issues at hand (Chap. 15).

As technology progresses and autonomous weapons increasingly become a real-ity rather than mere science fiction, an ethical debate has developed surrounding the use of such weapons, which operate with little or no human oversight. Some view the use of autonomous weapons as morally preferable (not to mention strategically advantageous), as they can be used in place of human combatants. Others oppose their use for moral and legal reasons. The article discusses challenges to limiting and defining autonomous weapons and proposes seeking international agreement to ban fully autonomous weapons–those which cannot be recalled–as a first step toward addressing the issues raised and, above all, how to keep these weapons from running amok (Chap. 16).

As artificial intelligence technology seems poised for a major takeoff and changing societal dynamics are creating a high demand for caregivers for elders, children, and those who are infirm, robotic caregivers may well be used much more often. This chapter examines the ethical concerns raised by the use of AI caregivers and concludes that many of these concerns are avoided when AI caregivers operate as partners rather than substitutes. Furthermore, most of the remaining concerns are minor and are faced by human caregivers as well. Nonetheless, because AI caregivers' systems are learning systems, an AI caregiver could stray from its initial guidelines. Therefore, subjecting AI caregivers to an AI-based oversight system is proposed to ensure that their actions remain both legal and ethical (Chap. 17).

A generation after I urged my son Oren to study artificial intelligence, I urged Margaret (who allows me to see myself as her grandfather, actually "saba" in Hebrew) to study biology. I hold that the next great technological revolution will take place as we learn how to recast our bodies the way we are recasting our environment and trying to recast our societies. In Chap. 18, I discuss the unfolding of this active orientation, our engineering ambitions, and the moral issues it raises. The following chapter examines this general issue for development in biology.

Bioethics (and medical ethics) has already addressed numerous moral issues. Should society allow medically assisted suicide? Can patients truly give informed consent? Should there be any limits on women's right to choose? Who gets what and how much of the resources society has set aside for health care? How can we better protect medical privacy in the age of big data? These issues have been subject to a great deal of deliberations and publications. In this book, I deal with one particular dimension of the ethical issues involved: the role of the community. The term "community" is often associated with small, traditional, residential communities, such as villages. However, in the modern era, communities are often nonresidential and based on ethnicity, race, religious background, or a shared sexual orientation. Moreover, people are commonly members of more than one community. Finally, it is often productive to consider communities as nesting within more encompassing communities, such as local ones within a national one. People are hence subject not merely to tension between their personal preferences and the values and norms promoted by their community but are also subject to conflicting normative indications from various communities. For more, see Chap. 19.

Part I
What Makes a Good Life

Chapter 1
Happiness Is the Wrong Metric

1.1 Introduction

Competing social science theories, the policies based on them, and public discourses about improving society draw on different meta-conceptions of human nature. To start with a simple example, if one assumes people are by nature brutish and boorish, we shall look for ways to control them, for a strong authority. If one assumes that they are benign beings, naturally at peace with each other, we shall look for ways to remove forces that distort their good nature. Other such meta-conceptions assume that people seek to maximize pleasure or—are inherently flawed but redeemable. This essay examines recently popular conceptions about human nature and suggests refocusing on a different one.

Among the popular meta-conceptions is the thesis that people are seeking and entitled to seek happiness. The concern with what makes people happy arises within the liberal democratic context. Liberalism, with its focus on individual rights, liberty, and dignity can be viewed as a belief system that was shaped and embraced by people seeking to curb the power of the rulers (feudal lords, monarchs, and later the states) and religious authorities. This is reflected in the question what makes *people* happy rather than, say, the lord of the manor or the Lord of the world.

One widely-shared and powerful interpretation of happiness views individuals as seeking to maximize *their* pleasure and minimize *their* pain. (And that pleasure was associated with command of material goods, needed to gain what is pleasurable.) Related meta-conceptions of human nature have sought to enrich and expand the meaning of happiness by including the gratification a person gains from the happiness of others (e.g. their children) or even from carrying out moral acts (Dunn et al. 2011). Note, though, that in all these expansions of happiness, the happiness of others or service to the common good are achieved by making the person happy. If the children are happy, say about a move overseas, but this does not make the parent happy—the move does not count as contributing to happiness. If making a major donation to a good cause makes the recipients happy, but the contributing person is

© The Author(s) 2018
A. Etzioni, *Happiness is the Wrong Metric*, Library of Public Policy and Public
Administration 11, https://doi.org/10.1007/978-3-319-69623-2_1

not satisfied by the recognition he got or the use of the funds, there is no net happiness gained. Of course, utilitarianism includes concern for the happiness of the greatest number, but this is merely a sum of individual happiness! (Attempts to modify this assumption are discussed below.)

I shall refer to all these various meta-conceptions as those of "satisfiers." They all hold that the individual seeks satisfaction and is self-centered. These approaches also tend to be amoral. Satisfiers do not judge whether some satisfactions or preferences are morally superior to others, nor do they, as utilitarians are wont to do, equate satisfaction with being moral.

The main thesis of this chapter is that sound analysis, good public policies, and proper public discourse assume a rather different meta-conception of human nature. I shall refer to this type of person as a *moral wrestler.* This views the person as subject to an irreconcilable conflict between the quest for happiness (of one kind or another) and—the quest to live up to their moral values; the latter's completion results in a sense of *affirmation.*[1] Much of the dynamic of human behavior reflects this conflict between the quest for pleasure and the quest for affirmation. For now, it suffices to illustrate this point with the simple statement, "I would like to go and see a movie, but I ought to visit my friend in the hospital." To "like" something denotes the pursuit of satisfaction, while "ought" denotes affirming motivation.

Second, this chapter shows that societal structure and culture considerably influence the lifelong struggle between the pursuit of happiness and the quest for affirmation. These collective forces, rather than individuals' preferences and actions, greatly affect whether the quest for affirmation or the pursuit of satisfaction, or a carefully-crafted balance between the two, guides individuals' conduct and societal dynamics. That is, individuals have much less agency than several influential social scientific theories, major ideologies, and the general public assume. It follows that those who seek to understand the components of, and attempt to, form a good life and a good society should grant greater importance to social action, in which individuals act in unison and draw on shared norms and institutions, than to individual agency.

This chapter first briefly outlines the reasons that these age-old issues now deserve special attention, especially in societies with developed economies (Part I). It then reviews the evidence about the growing disconnect between income and happiness, as well as the implications of this trend for the definition of the good life (Part II). The discussion then turns to "higher" sources of satisfaction and their historical relevance (Part III). It then explores the most important reason to reject happiness as a measure of the good life: the good life has a major moral component. It furthermore studies affirmation and the connection between moral behavior and pain and sacrifice (Part IV). The chapter then highlights that preferences are social products that can be collectively modified, for better or for worse (Part V). It closes by discussing the measurements with which to assess the communitarian state of the union, or the balance between the pursuit of pleasure and affirming motivation (Part VI).

---

[1] I first discussed this in my book. See Etzioni (1988).

1.2 Within History

Many of these age-old deliberations on what makes people happy are ahistorical and asociological in the sense that they examine the motivations of individuals as if it matters not whether they lived in ancient Greece or live in contemporary Rome—or, for that matter, in today's New York City, the Swat Valley, or the Amazon River Basin. These deliberations have their place because, indeed, basic human nature is universal; all human beings are motivated by the pursuit of happiness (in part driven by their biological base, although it affects them via cultural filters) and, with the possible exception of psychopaths, all have an "affirming sense" of what they ought to do. However, examining the particularistic, historical, and sociological contexts in which the tension between the quests for satisfaction and affirmation is worked out greatly enriches the analysis. Thus, to urge that people should serve as best they can in whatever position into which they have been cast—as Aristotle (Kraut 2014) argued was ideal—has different implications for the slave than it has for the lord of the manor, and for others who live in different ages and societies.

Since the Great Recession, economic growth, especially in economically developed countries, has been anemic. Unemployment has been high, especially if measures of unemployment include the many people who have ceased to look for work or who work less than they prefer. Wages have stagnated. These conditions have contributed to rising political alienation; a greater variety of extreme and violent expressions such as xenophobia, racism, and anti-Semitism; support for radical right-wing parties and politicians; and some—albeit much less—support for the radical left (UNESCO 2009). Some scholars have posited the existence of a general link between low rates of economic growth and support for right-wing politicians and nationalism (Brückner and Grüner 2010).

It is possible that rates of economic growth will rise again and that the "legitimacy of affluence" (Etzioni 2014) might be restored. However, several leading economists hold that it may well be impossible to return to a high-growth economy (Gordon 2012; Fernald and Jones 2014). Particularly compelling are predictions that account for the fact that the new "industrial revolution" is driven by artificial intelligence—that is, by advanced computers that can replace not only manual labor, but also skilled labor in fields such as medicine and law and education (Brynjolfsson and McAfee 2012; Frey and Osborne 2013). Many lawyers are finding their jobs replaced by computers (Markoff 2011). Industrial jobs currently performed by manufacturing labor, often of the kind protected by unions that offered a gateway into the middle class, will be cut by 22% by 2025 as a result of increased reliance on cheap but technologically advanced robots (Associated Press 2015). Bank tellers are replaced by ATMs; travel agents have been replaced by websites; and large numbers of clerical and other white-collar jobs "once thought to require people" have been lost to improving technologies (Rotman 2013). This trend is now extending to middle class jobs, especially in education and medicine.

Another particularly telling example is the robots that are replacing anesthesiologists. This is a very tedious job, given that 99% of the time the tasks that must be done are routine and boring, but rare failures can be very damaging. Robots do not mind checking the patient's vital signs every split second; they can remain fully mindful of the situation even if the surgery lasts many hours, they do not get distracted, and controlled substances or alcohol do not affect them. In short, robots are ideally suited to replace most anesthesiologists, which would largely eliminate a very well-paying job. (One would expect a human anesthesiologist to supervise several robots, to set their dials, and to deal with alarms in the event that they sound.)

Similar fears of, and opposition to, new technologies arose during previous industrial revolutions, the classic example being the Luddites. However, in earlier cases in which technological advances destroyed old jobs, these novel technologies also created a similar number of new, better-paying and less menial jobs. However, nothing in economic theory suggests that there is an iron law or an identifiable mechanism to ensure these new jobs will materialize following any and all major technological breakthroughs. This time, advanced computers are replacing human labor and eliminating well-paying, desirable jobs, while generating few new ones. Recall that Kodak once employed more than 145,000 people to manufacture its film and camera products and to develop photos at various retail establishments; in 2010, a team of merely 15 individuals created Instagram, which facilitates the exchange of digital photographs (Leslie 2014).

If predictions are correct that new, developed nations will face persistent and growing unemployment, this will affect not merely people's income but also their sense of self, a major source of meaning and structure. *This would lead either to massive alienation and social and political upheaval—or to new characterizations of what makes people happy.*

Moreover, even if economic developments in the foreseeable future do allow for ever higher income and consumption, data suggest that increasing income—above a certain threshold—tends not to increase happiness significantly. For this reason, even if the world could find its way back to high economic growth rates, one must still answer the question whether alternate sources of satisfaction can be found that are not derived from ever-higher levels of income and material consumption. Does affluence provide a satisfactory response to basic questions of the meaning of life, human existence, and purpose? Are humans cast into this world to make and consume products? Or do they aspire to find meaning for their actions in the service of higher purposes, once their basic needs are sated? Religious fundamentalism has offered a highly troubling answer to these questions. What other visions of the good life are compelling and compatible with human nature as that of a *moral wrester*?

Communitarian philosophy provides such an alternate vision. The communitarian movement arose in the 1990s around two main principles. First, the West's increasing focus on the individual had contributed to the neglect of the common good and to an imbalanced society. Second, there is a need to shore up social responsibilities and commitments to society, as well as to form new norms defining what society should expect of its people. Reexamining the role of happiness in crafting a good society reflects this need to restore balance between the self and society by enhancing the common good after centuries during which it was (properly) scaled back (Etzioni 1993, 1996). Most Western societies have yet to achieve this balance.

1.3   The Rising Disconnect Between Income and Happiness

The preponderance of the social scientific literature suggests that once income reaches a certain threshold, additional income creates little additional satisfaction. On the whole, social science's findings, which have well-known limitations and do not all agree, seem to support this notion of diminishing happiness returns on income except for the poor and nearly-poor. Frank M. Andrews and Stephen B. Withey found that one's socioeconomic status has a meager effect on one's "sense of well-being" and no significant effect on one's life satisfaction (Andrews and Withey 1976). A survey of over 1000 participants, who rated their sense of satisfaction and happiness on a 7-point scale and a 3-point scale, concluded that there was no correlation between socioeconomic status and happiness; in fact, the second-highest socioeconomic group was consistently among the least happy of all seven brackets measured. In addition, Jonathan Freedman discovered that levels of reported happiness do not vary greatly among the members of different economic classes, with the exception of the very poor, who tend to be less happy than others (Freedman 1978).

In a 1973 study, Richard Easterlin reported on a phenomenon that has since been labeled the "Easterlin Paradox" (Easterlin 1973, 1974). At any given time, an increase in income generates more happiness; however, in the longer run (10 years or more) happiness fails to increase. For example, between 1962 and 1987, the Japanese per capita income more than tripled, yet Japan's overall happiness remained constant over that period (Easterlin 2005). Similarly, in 1970, the average American income could buy over 60% more than it could in the 1940s, yet average happiness did not increase (Easterlin 1973). A survey of those whose income had increased over a 10-year period revealed that these individuals were no happier than those whose incomes had stagnated (Myers and Diener 1996). Many social scientists have presented similar evidence. For example, David G. Myers and Ed Diener found that while Americans' per-capita disposable (after-tax) income in inflation-adjusted dollars almost exactly doubled between 1960 and 1990, almost the same proportion of Americans reported that they were "very happy" in 1993 (32%) as they did in 1957 (35%)(Myers and Diener 1995). Although economic growth has slowed since the mid-1970s, Americans' reported happiness has been remarkably stable (nearly always between 30% and 35%) across both high-growth and low-growth periods (Myers and Diener 1995).

In the late 1990s and early 2000s, a number of scholarly articles called Easterlin's findings into question. Some scholars, specifically Ruut Veenhoven and Michael Hagerty, argued that Easterlin's methodology was flawed, having found that both happiness and income had increased in the second half of the twentieth century (Veenhoven and Hagerty 2006). A 2008 paper by Betsey Stevenson and Justin Wolfers found a similar correlation between income growth and happiness (Stevenson and Wolfers 2008).

In 2010, Easterlin and his associates responded to Stevenson and Wolfers' challenge by pointing out the short-term nature of the data and by citing the examples of China, South Korea, and Chile to contradict claims that a positive correlation exists between long-term GDP growth and happiness (Easterlin et al. 2010). All three countries have very high growth rates, but none of them showed a statistically significant increase in happiness. The authors wrote, "With incomes rising so rapidly in these three different countries, it seems extraordinary that there are no surveys that register the marked improvement in subjective well-being that mainstream economists and policy makers worldwide would expect to find" (Easterlin et al. 2010).

The one important exception to these findings is the evidence that increasing the incomes of the poor significantly enhances their happiness. The populations of countries with average annual incomes greater than $20,000 are significantly happier than those in countries with average annual incomes of less than $20,000, as Richard Layard's 2005 book *Happiness: Lessons from a New Science* shows[2] (Layard 2005). A 2010 study by Daniel Kahneman and Angus Deaton identified the point after which there is less correlation between additional income and additional happiness: $75,000 (Kahneman and Deaton 2010). The study found that while a positive relationship existed between income and life evaluation,[3] higher income did not improve emotional well-being[4] (See Kahneman and Deaton 2010). Hence, whereas life evaluation rises steadily with increases in income, emotional well-being does not progress once an annual income of $75,000 is reached.[5] Some authors continue to maintain that "absolute income has a large impact on happiness across the income spectrum" (Haybron 2011). However, the preponderance of the evidence suggests that income above a certain level does not buy much additional happiness. Thus, the legitimacy of affluence is questionable, regardless of whether high economic growth is achievable and sustainable. The data should not be understood to suggest that up to a given level of income, more income makes one more satisfied, and that after that level, income adds nothing to one's satisfaction. It suggests that the higher one's income, the less additional income adds to satisfaction, and that once it reaches the cutoff point, it may cease to add any further satisfaction.

One reason high wage-earners derive less happiness from additional income is that the goods that high income allows one to buy are reported not to have absolute value in terms of the happiness they provide. Rather, they are judged relative to other goods available. Indeed, this is the explanation Easterlin himself offers, namely that individual happiness seems to be determined by one's income relative to others, rather than one's absolute income. One interpretation of this claim is the familiar concept of "keeping up with the Joneses"—an expression that captures the use of goods in a status competition among members of the community. Goods are

---

[2] Layard used happiness data from three major long-term public opinion surveys (the Eurobarometer for Western Europe, the General Social Survey for the United States, and the World Values Survey for Eastern Europe and developing nations) to calculate an average happiness measure for each country, which was compared to average income per capita.

[3] That is, their thoughts about their life.

[4] That is, "the frequency and intensity of experiences of joy, stress, sadness, anger, and affection that make one's life pleasant or unpleasant."

[5] The two figures ($20,000 per year and $75,000 per year) are not directly comparable. The first measures a nation's average income; the second comments on individual income.

used as visible markers of one's standing in this never-ending race. This explains why an increase in a nation's collective wealth often fails to increase reported happiness. If practically everyone has three televisions and two cars, owning three televisions and two cars may buy little pride relative to others. Moreover, even very wealthy people can always find someone who earns more than they do. The same factor also seems to explain why people in small towns are happier than those in big cities. Daniel Gilbert writes of New York City, "No matter how hard you try, you really can't avoid walking by restaurants where people drop your monthly rent on a bottle of wine and store windows where shoes sit like museum pieces on gold pedestals. You can't help but feel trumped" (Gilbert 2006).

The argument so far has been that technological and economic changes are challenging societies that have built their social contracts and legitimacy of their regimes on the pursuit of happiness defined mainly by gaining pleasure from material goods ("affluence"). Social and political upheavals will result from these societies' inability to provide their citizens with ever-higher levels of command of material goods.

Even if high rates of economic growth returned, the diminishing correlation between additional income and additional satisfaction at high incomes means that they would be unlikely to produce the kind of satisfaction that people seek and that supports a harmonious society and stable polity. Whether other sources of nonmaterial, non-income sources of satisfaction can fulfill this role is addressed in the next section.

1.4   Maslow and "Higher" Satisfactions

1.4.1   The Hierarchy Revisited

Among the social scientists that draw on a richer theory of human nature than the one embraced by hedonists, Abraham Maslow and his theory about a hierarchy of human needs stand out. Maslow holds that a set of needs motivates all human behavior; these needs exist in a hierarchy, such that the most "prepotent" need that remains unsatisfied is most active, or most strongly drives behavior (Heylighen 1992). As more prepotent needs are gratified, higher needs exercise greater influence over the individual's behavior (Lollar 1974, p. 40), although it is not necessary for a prepotent need to be fully gratified before higher order needs affect behavior (Sengupta 2011, p. 103).

Maslow identified five fundamental categories of needs. Ranked from most basic to highest-order, these are physiological needs, safety-security, love and belonging, esteem, and self-actualization (Lester 1990, p. 1187). *Physiological needs* include the "chemicals, nutrients, or internal (e.g. exercise/health) or environmental (e.g. temperatures) conditions necessary for the body to survive" (Taormina and Gao 2013, p. 157). This need is satisfied as long as the individual is not so physiologically deprived as to be in bodily danger; the underlying imperative of physiological needs is biological survival (Groves et al. 1975, p. 65). *Safety-security* needs are the absence of threatening stimuli—including but not limited to "wild animals, criminal assault, disease, war, anarchy, natural catastrophes, […] the lack of such things as job security, financial security, [and] medical insurance" (Taormina and Gao 2013, p. 157). The need for *love and belonging* is predicated on the finding that the absence of affective bonds with other human beings causes stress responses that people experience as loneliness and depression (Taormina and Gao 2013, p. 158). *Esteem* involves the need to be valued by others and to feel intrinsically that one has contributed to the world. The highest need is *self-actualization.*[6]

Self-actualization, considered the highest need, is defined as achieving the fullest use of one's talents and interests—the need "to become everything that one is capable of becoming" (Hagerty 1999, p. 250). As implied by its name, self-actualization is highly individualistic and reflects Maslow's premise that the *self is "sovereign and inviolable" and entitled to "his or her own tastes, opinions, values, etc"*(Aron 1977, p. 13). That is, self-actualization refers to an *individual* need for fulfillment (Hagerty 1999, p. 250). The particular form *self-actualization* takes varies greatly from person to person. In some individuals "it may take the form of the desire to be an ideal mother, in another it may be expressed athletically, and in still another it may be expressed in painting pictures or in inventions" (Koltko-Rivera 2006, p. 303). Indeed, some have characterized self-actualization as "healthy narcissism" (Pauchant and Dumas 1991, p. 58).

Some of the characteristics of a self-actualized individual outlined by Maslow in latter writings include references to moral considerations. Maslow acknowledges that for some people, self-actualization may include, for example, being a good mother (Maslow 1943, p. 382). However, Maslow's first and commonly-cited definition of self-actualization does not contain a moral imperative.

For the purpose of the following discussion, it suffices to group Maslow's needs into three main "layers" or categories. Physiological needs and security comprise *basic creature comfort needs*, which are closest to inborn biological urges; the second layer is made up of love and belonging and esteem; and the third layer, the pinnacle, of self-actualization.

To reiterate, these are merely a few of the many findings about the satisfying effects of gratifying higher order needs. These sources of satisfaction have several common attributes. First, *they take place within the third, communal sector*. Much public discourse has focused for the last two centuries on the merits of the private sector versus the public sector—of the role of markets versus the role of the government. As a result, much less attention has been paid to the role of the third sector— the one that encompasses nuclear and extended families; friendships; educational, religious, and political activities; volunteerism; many thousands of not-for-profit

---

[6] Maslow's later work included a sixth need: *self-transcendence*, or "seek[ing] to further a cause beyond the self and to experience a communion beyond the boundaries of the self." This sixth need involved a specific cognitive activity he called "being-cognition," which was present in mystical, aesthetic, and other transcendental experiences in which the person "c[a]me to identify with something greater than the purely individual self" (Koltko-Rivera 2006).

organizations, and much more. Much of social life—everything from bringing up children to supporting those who have lost a loved one—takes place in this third sector. It is here that norms are formed and often reinforced through informal social controls rather than formal incentives or legal coercion. In this sense, the three sources of satisfaction examined in the preceding paragraphs are all communitarian.

Another common attribute is that *all these examples are basically not capital intensive, and hence are not based on one's income or job.* People who have lasting, meaningful, and affective relationships find them to be a major source of mutual satisfaction, which can be achieved with very little material costs. Chess played with plastic pieces is as enjoyable as chess played with figures carved out of ivory; there is no evidence that the Lord better hears prayers from a leather-bound prayer book than from one made of recycled paper; and one does not need a BMW to drive to a picnic. One can spend time with one's spouse and children, attend religious services, or volunteer without spending much money.

True, all these activities can be corrupted. One can try to achieve love by seeking more income to buy ever-more expensive goods, or one can ground one's esteem in one's ability to out-earn another. But there is no inherent connection between income and the ability to engage in higher pursuits the way income is needed for creature comforts. Unless prevented by a commercial culture, people love spending time with their parents more than they love expensive toys, prefer spousal intimacy over objects, and would rather participate in community public service instead of donating. (None of this should be read to suggest that people up to a certain income threshold are preoccupied with addressing their basic creature needs, but that after that threshold they turn to pursuing higher satisfactions. Maslow's theory indicated that gradually, as basic needs are more sated, people invest more of themselves in serving their higher needs.)

Finally, most importantly for all that follows, *the activities that serve higher needs may be pro social but nevertheless tend to be amoral.* Because this distinction is crucial and often overlooked, it deserves some elaboration. The reason that these communitarian activities are a source of satisfaction lies in human nature, which craves affective bonding (what Maslow calls "love"), positive approval ("esteem"), and meaning (a key element of "self-actualization"). Hence, people for whom the social structures and cultural and political regimes in which they function allow them to have more opportunities to meet these cravings tend to be less alienated and more satisfied (as well as have healthier and longer lives). This is the reason that numerous observers assume that communities are good in the moral sense of the term, and that societies in which communities are intact are better than societies in which communities have been undermined and people are atomized (Kornhauser 1960). These "mass societies" are held to be full of rebellious, violent, and mentally maladjusted people (Kornhauser 1960).

All of these observations ignore that communities that provide all of these higher sources of satisfaction can coalesce around very negative values. A gang, a Nazi community, or a community of card-carrying KKK members can provide similar satisfaction to their members as do the Rotary Club, a branch of the Fabian Society, or a community of violinists. One must determine whether the activity from which a person draws higher satisfactions is a moral one. Just as people with strong muscle tone are healthier than those with weak muscle tone but this does not determine whether these muscles are used to kill someone or build a home for the homeless— so too are those who are members of communities better off than those who are isolated, but their communities may promote values observers would consider anathema. The same point applies to the "social capital" that some use to refer to bonding and communal relationships. People who have social capital are more satisfied than those who lack it (Putnam 2000), but one should not ignore the uses of this capital. Another way to express this fundamental point is the statement that behavior that is prosocial is not necessary moral.

It follows that some social structures and political regimes may make people happier but not better. Satisfaction is the wrong metric if it is not coupled with an assessment of the extent to which the structures and regime that satisfy also promote a good life and community. As far as individuals are concerned, there are happy criminals and singing nuns, miserable inmates and gloomy nurses. Contrary to what hedonists hold, their satisfactions should not be judged to be equal.

1.4.2 Within History: Capping Versus Denial

Showing that seeking higher satisfaction leads to greater satisfaction overall does not mean favoring an austere or ascetic life of denial. Asceticism, the practice of denying one's physical or psychological needs in pursuit of higher-order goals, often spiritual in nature, has appeared in virtually all religions at one point or another (Encyclopaedia Britannica Online 2002). Examples of asceticism exist today, such as Christian and Jain monks and nuns. However, most sects that fully embraced asceticism as a basic tenant of their community either failed completely or became much less austere. For example, the Israeli kibbutzim, collective communities founded by Jews who emigrated from Russia in the early 1900s, originally emphasized that a life of simplicity, materially speaking, "would encourage the realization of the full potentialities of human nature" (Spiro 2004, p. 559). Members were instructed "to seek gratification only within a restricted range of personal needs" (Leviatan et al. 1998, p. 3). At their consumption peak, kibbutzim fully financed members' trips abroad, and a growing basket of products (Ashkenazi and Katz 2009, p. 577). Similarly, the Amana community in Iowa traces its roots to German dissidents of Lutheranism known as Pietists, who sought to protest "the ceremony and pomp of the established churches" (Hoehnle 2001, p. 3). The community eventually established itself in the United States as a group that avoided all luxuries and decorative arts and held 11 church services per week (Abramitzky 2011). However, young members eventually resisted church restrictions on modern conveniences deemed "worldly" by elders and many left the church (Hoehnle 2001, p. 5). What remained changed drastically—epitomized by the incorporation of the Amana Society in 1932 (Hoehnle 2001, p. 16), a joint stock corporation that eventually owned, among other things, the very successful Amana Refrigeration, Inc.

People need to be able to attend to their basic creature comforts in order to be satisfied. Only once these lower-order needs are reasonably satisfied does investing more of oneself in higher pursuits lead to greater overall satisfaction. This important observation has been ignored to their peril by many communities in different societies and historical moments. These communities—including the Montanists and the Essenes—shortchanged their basic needs in favor of more strenuous dedication to higher pursuits, making asceticism the central feature of their culture. Most of them failed entirely or exist today in greatly diminished form.

Other sects changed their cultures to pay greater attention to basic needs. In the 1960s, the importance of attending to basic needs was demonstrated by the number of members of the "counter-culture"—who, in the United States and northwest Europe, tried to live on cheap wine and handouts, to sleep on mats, and otherwise follow a "simple" life—who soon gave up on the ascetic dimensions of their culture. There is no denying basic human needs or the quest for pleasure that comes from serving them adequately.

Serving these basic needs turns from a "healthy," satisfying pursuit to an obsession, though, when consumption turns into what might be called consumerism— when people continue to invest themselves in seeking ever *more* material goods than they need to satisfy their basic needs, and when people employ material goods to gain love or esteem.

If developed societies could develop a culture of capping that would guarantee everyone sufficient income to provide for their basic creature needs—but otherwise would center life on higher pursuits—that culture would provide for less alienation and less anti-social behavior. This is particularly true if the predictions made above about the challenges posed by new technical developments turn out to be true. The more people who can make ends meet because the income they need is capped, the fewer who will seek second jobs or work overtime; all of this will leave work for those who have not yet reached their cap. And the people who spend more of their life in higher pursuits will feel not deprived, but rather satisfied, which will help societies adapt to the new technical reality of less demand for labor.

In addition, quite obviously, a life that combines a cap on consumption and greater dedication to higher pursuits would be much less taxing on the environment than consumerism and the level of work needed to pay for it. This is the case because higher pursuits require relatively few resources and cause less pollution. Much less obvious are the ways capped culture combined with increased focus on the pursuit of higher satisfactions would serve social justice. Social justice entails transferring wealth from the disproportionately wealthy to those who are underprivileged. Such reallocation of wealth has been limited in large part because those who command the extra assets tend also to be politically powerful. Promoting social justice by organizing those with less and forcing those in power to yield has had limited success in democratic countries and has led to massive bloodshed in others. However, one must expect if those in power were willing to embrace the capped culture, they would be more ready to share than otherwise. This thesis is supported by the behavior of middle-class people who are committed to the values of giving and tending to the "least among us"—a value prescribed by many religions and by left liberalism.

To review the argument so far: The current conditions in which developed countries find themselves whether pursuing ever-higher incomes and consumption of material goods will continue to be possible—and people be able to drive meaning out of those jobs to be available after robots take over many of the best ones. Data furthermore show that ever-higher incomes may not buy ever-higher levels of satisfaction, but people who have already met their basic needs can increase their overall satisfaction by pursuing higher needs (higher in Maslowian terms). This chapter shall next show that although this understanding of human nature and society is much more valid than one that centers exclusively on material consumption and pleasure-seeking, it still ignores one substantial motivator of human behavior—moral commitments. Without this dimension, the conceptual apparatus for understanding much of interpersonal and social dynamics is extremely deficient. Above all, it leads to giving the pursuit of happiness too much prominence and undermines the moral commitments that are essential for making a good life and a good society.

1.5   Affirmation, Living Up to Moral Commitments

This part of the chapter presents evidence that people are motivated in part by their quest to live up to their moral commitments. Lacking a better term, I shall refer to this kind of motivation as affirmation. We shall see that this motivation cannot be reconstituted as another source of satisfaction, most importantly because it typically entails pain. Moreover, if viewed as one source of satisfaction among many others, we shall lose major insights into the dynamics of human behavior that result from the conflict between satisfaction and affirmation. To illustrate first very briefly: if one states that "I would *like* to go to a movie but *ought* to visit a friend in the hospital", and reads this as not different from "I would like to go a movie or a dinner"—one has lost much of what social science needs to study.

1.5.1   Introspection

Compare two senses. One is the feeling one has after considerable pleasure—a great meal, a relaxing massage, listening to your favorite tune. Now compare this to the sense one has after doing something considered to be a moral duty—spending a long night with a very sick friend, spending a weekend with a colicky baby, fasting for 24 h. Nobody will doubt that the activity *per se* is not pleasurable, but many satisfiers argue that the second kind of act also results in pleasure: the pleasure of having done what one ought to do. However, if one compares the two kinds of satisfaction, those that arise from acts that are inherently pleasurable and those that arise from moral behavior—it becomes clear that these are very different kinds of satisfaction.

These differences stand out even more when the moral behavior is truly demanding. Giving bone marrow is a painful operation that can save another's life; it is painful and exhausting to carry a cross up a steep mountain in the heat of the desert, as people do at Mount Sinai; and attending to a spouse who has a terminal illness is emotionally and mentally exhausting.

1.5.2 Affirmation Defined

Social science suffers from a surfeit of technical terms; I hence am reluctant to add one more. However, the current use of language is deceptive. By referring to both kinds of motivations and senses as "satisfaction," the difference between the two disappears, and the wording, in effect, affirms the hedonistic reductionist assumption that all acts that seem moral are actually self-serving and motivated by the pursuit of pleasure. Even if one wishes to argue that there is no profound difference between the two kinds of acts—denoting the two kinds of motivations and acts under comparison is necessary before collapsing them. Referring to acts that are motivated by a sense that one should live up to one's moral commitments as "affirmation" rather than as "satisfaction" enables this discussion. (A similar attempt is made when people discuss pure or authentic altruism [see May 2011] in contrast to inauthentic "altruistic" behavior motivated by self-interest [see Feigin et al. 2014]).

The term "obligation" should be avoided in this context, because obligations are externally-imposed commitments, while those that drive moral behavior are internally-derived; they are what the person holds he ought to do. Finally, one might be inclined to refer to this behavior as virtuous (see Schwartz 2010); however, to reiterate, the fact that someone is driven by what he considers his moral commitment does not mean that these acts are moral. A jihadist who labors to kill as many infidels one afternoon as he can may feel that he is engaging in moral behavior. The term "virtuous" should be reserved for those acts that serve incontestable values, those whose moral standing is self-evident (see Etzioni 1998, 2006).

For this chapter, I do not draw a distinction between the quest for affirmation as a source of motivation ("push"), and the sense of accomplishment ("pull").

1.5.3 Affirming Behavior Is Painful, Not Pleasurable

In sharp contrast to the thesis that acts motivated by attempting to live up to moral commitments are but another source of satisfaction, one ought to note that practically all affirming behavior is in effect painful, or deprives one of pleasure. Fasting, donating an organ, attending to the sick, speaking truth to power, and so on are all cases in point. As Connie Rosati argues, moral behavior is "widely believed to conflict, frequently and sometimes severely, with what an agent most values or most prefers to do." Even if one gains some amount of pleasure as a limited side effect when one lives up to one's moral commitments, the main effect is pain. It is as if moral systems are built on the assumption that there is no reason to spend the limited moral capital that society commands on motivating people to take steps they are motivated to take anyhow because they are pleasurable, and that society should instead invest this limited capital in motivating people to do things they otherwise would not be inclined to do because they are not pleasurable.

One further notes that the pursuit of satisfaction tends to take care of itself (although society should take care to ensure that the pursuit of satisfaction is not perverted), while affirmation tends to decay if left to its own devices. Hence, there is a strong social interest in promoting the factors that reinforce and strengthen affirmation, which make people and societies more moral than they would be otherwise.

I find observations of the spouses of Alzheimer patients to be particularly illuminating. As far as I can determine through personal observation, most spouses stay with their afflicted partner instead of walking away or institutionalizing them early in the course of the disease. (There seems to be little quantitative data on this point.) Satisfier reasoning would assume the spouse acts according to an implicit "exchange of service" contract, in which the healthy spouse attends to their ill partner in the expectation that the favor will be repaid in kind. Hence no affirming is involved; merely a mutually beneficial exchange. However, this interpretation cannot be used in this case (or for many other terminal illnesses) because Alzheimer patients do not recover, and hence one knows that their care will not pay back. A satisfier may argue at this point that another reason people attend to their ill spouses is because of psychic income: the healthy spouse derives satisfaction from the gratitude of the ill spouse. However, Alzheimer's patients often do not provide such income, and indeed after a while cease to recognize their caregiver. Finally, satisfiers may fall back on reputation or a "warm glow" as a payoff. However, given the very great challenges associated with caring for an Alzheimer's patient, including the costs and pain that treating such patients engenders, reputation or a warm glow could hardly compensate for it to the extent that the act of care-giving could be considered "self-interested." There seems no other explanation than the one several such spouses gave when asked: they felt strongly that staying with their ill partner was the right thing to do. Those who question whether moral commitment alone can motivate such self-sacrifice should note that such a sense leads mothers to run into burning houses to save their children, inspires people to volunteer to risk their lives and fight for the country, and encourages people to risk their health by donating organs. I am not arguing that they gain no benefits from such acts, but that these are small compared to the sacrifice, and that it is the quest for affirmation that makes up the difference. Indeed, as we have seen, the stronger one's sense of affirmation, the more likely one is to do what one considers the right thing.

1.5.4 Self-Centered Reductionists

Satisfiers have gone to great lengths to argue that all that people seek is happiness, defined as pleasure, or some other source of satisfaction. The hedonistic version of utilitarianism forms the foundation of modern economic theory (Stigler 1987, p. 52). Economists often associate utility with conceptions of material goods and, hence, with income. For example, Libby Rittenberg and Timothy Tregarthen define utility as the "satisfaction" that "people derive from the goods and services they consume and the activities they pursue," which means that it is "ultimately" land, labor, and capital, the economy's factors of production, that create utility (Rittenberg and Tregarthen 2011, p. 54). In a money economy, therefore, "every level of wealth provides a certain amount of utility" (Mankiw 2011, p. 285).

Economists argue that they moved away from this definition of utility. Some hold that it is being replaced with the notion that utility is whatever the person prefers; it does not have to have a particular content. Thus Gary Becker's approach rebutted earlier economists' "assumptions of self-interest," he replaced them with the idea that "individuals maximize welfare, as they conceive it, whether they be selfish, altruistic, loyal, spiteful, or masochistic" (Wolfers 2014). What the theory requires is a common denominator so that the value of various items can be set in the terms of that "utility." (In an early discussion of the subject I used the term P, I, and X utility to denote the difference (Etzioni 1988). They stand for Pleasure, Interdependency, and "empty" utilities.) However, in effect, many economists and other social scientists who hold to similar assumptions continue to rely on utility as happiness.

Satisfiers have gone to great lengths to defend their view of what drives people. Gift-giving, for example, seems to contradict psychological hedonism because it involves a voluntary reduction of one's own utility in order to benefit another. Hedonists have responded by arguing that gift giving is often driven by "cooperative egoism," with those who give gifts expecting reciprocal gifts, reputation, status, approval, or some future benefit (see Hammond 1975). And, they held, to the extent that gift giving occurs in the absence of expected rewards, for example in the case of anonymous gift giving, hedonists argue that the giver enjoys a "warm glow" from the act of gift giving itself (see Andreoni 1990). (Note that no evidence is presented that if a person donated say $100,000 to charity, he gained $100,000 worth of warm glow. It is assumed that the amount is the same—say the reductionists—because why would he have donated the money otherwise? This and thousands of other such statements illustrate how a theory can defend itself from reality and the extent people will go to assume all behavior is self-serving in one way or another.

An anecdote involving British philosopher Thomas Hobbes provides an early expression of this thesis: when asked why he had given money to a beggar, Hobbes replied that "he made his donation with the sole intent of relieving his own misery at the sight of the beggar" (Aubrey 1898, p. 352).

Likewise, given the fact that participation in religious activities cannot be explained merely by an "expected stream of 'benefits'" over an individual's lifetime, Corry Azzi and Ronald Ehrenberg introduced the ideas of a "salvation motive" to secure "afterlife consumption" (Azzi and Ehrenberg 1975). Put simply, reductionists claim, individuals spend money and time on religion in this life with the expectation that they will be rewarded handsomely after death. Needless to say, the evidence for the nature and size of these rewards is not extensive….

To dismiss the role of moral commitments in decision making, satisfiers go to great lengths to explain "surprising" behavior. One example is the prevalence of tipping at restaurants. Tipping does not make sense from a reductionist perspective, particularly given that it is not legally required and that people tip the same regardless whether they intend to return to the restaurant in the future (Kahneman et al. 1986). As a result, reductionists have tended to regard tipping as "mysterious or seemingly irrational behavior" (Lynn 2006). Michael Lynn and Andrea Grassman, for example, explain the prevalence of tipping at restaurants as a way to "to buy social approval and equitable relationships" (Lynn and Grassman 1990). Reductionist theories in the field of psychology similarly try to debunk moral behavior. Elliott Sober points out that it is "easy to invent egoistic explanations for even the most harrowing acts of self-sacrifice," for while such arguments may seem "forced," they are difficult to falsify without being able to read minds. For example, one "fixture" in the debate about egoism is the soldier who throws himself on a grenade to save his comrades—though seemingly a purely selfless act, psychological egoists argue that the soldier "realizes in an instant" that acting with cowardice would condemn him to a lifetime of guilt and shame that would be worse than death (Sober 2000). In other words, the soldier acts in his own self-interest to achieve "a better life, in terms of welfare" or utility (Shaver 2014). However, this line of argument raises a host of difficulties for egoism. The soldier might insist he is acting morally or out of duty, in which case the egoist must argue that he is lying or deluded.

Similar reductionist arguments have proposed a "bequest motive" to explain "excessive" saving (Jurges 2001), as well as a "taste for altruism" on the part of nonprofit employees, who are said to "derive well-being from participating in the enterprise, and are thus willing to accept a lower wage" (McGinnis 2011). Some have even argued that suicide represents a utility-maximizing behavior for an individual whose "total discounted lifetime utility […] reaches zero" (Hamermesh and Soss 1974; see also Becker 2012).

If one assumes that all acts are motivated by the pursuit of pleasure and the avoidance of pain, one can only conclude that saints "must be" masochistic, deriving net pleasure rather than pain from their sacrifices. If one abandons the reductionist assumption and allows for other factors to explain behavior, acts of self-sacrifice and altruistic behavior—of affirming value commitments in general—becomes much easier to explain: people are sometimes compelled by moral considerations to "do the right thing" even if they do not expect to derive any pleasure from such actions.

Much more important, *most* people, *most* of the time are pursuing both pleasure and affirmation. They differ a great deal in the extent that they are dedicating themselves to one kind of pursuit or the other, and the same person—and community and society—changes in that way over time. Understanding what makes some societies more self-oriented and pleasure-seeking, and others more dedicated to affirmation is a major subject for social science, personal deliberations, and public discourse and policy. Collapsing the two kind of pursuits into one means losing the conceptual tools this kind of analysis requires. One must abandon reductionist theories of human behavior in order to study why, having received training in medicine, for example, some people join Doctors without Borders, others become plastic surgeons, and still others work on biological weapons.

Adam Smith famously argued in *The Wealth of Nations* that the market as a system relies on each actor's pursuing his *self*-interest:

> It is not from the benevolence of the butcher, the brewer or the baker that we expect our dinner, but from their regard to their own interest. We address ourselves not to their humanity but to their self-love, and never talk to them of our own necessities but of their advantages (Smith 1776, p. 14).

If there is no fundamental difference between "self-love" and love for others, Smith's whole thesis vanishes. If people can derive pleasure directly from serving others, their community, and their values, there is no need for the invisible hand to direct individualistic pursuits to serve the common good. Even the distinction between profit and loss becomes unnecessary, as one man's loss is often another's gain. On the grounds of sound conceptualization, it seems best to separate the quests for self-satisfaction from efforts to adhere to one's values, i.e. from affirming behavior.

1.5.5   Evidence of Affirming Behavior

A considerable body of *experimental* data provides evidence of the power of affirmation. Experiments show that many people mail back "lost" wallets to strangers with cash intact (Homstein et al. 1968; see also Hunter 2013). Widely replicated studies found that more than 70% of people returned lost letters addressed to "Medical Research Associates" or a household address (Milgram et al. 1965; Curtis and Curtis 2011). While some might argue that such studies represent "trivial" forms of self-sacrifice, people have been shown to make much greater sacrifices for others. For example, Shalom Schwartz found that a "strikingly high proportion" of people (59%) expressed willingness to donate bone marrow to strangers, a more "costly" form of self-sacrificing behavior, whereas only 5% refused to at least have their blood tested for compatibility.

Research on altruism casts further light on the role affirmation plays in human behavior. Though most economic models make the reductionist satisfier assumption that all behavior derives from self-interest, prominent economists throughout history, including Adam Smith, Kenneth Arrow, Paul Samuelson, and Amartya Sen have acknowledged that in reality "people often do care for the well-being of others and that this may have important economic consequences" (Fehr and Schmidt 2006). Since the 1970s, a large body of work has investigated whether altruistic behavior is purely self-interested, and experiments have indicated, to the contrary, that genuine altruism does motivate some altruistic behavior. For example, John

Dovidio et al. found, in an experiment designed to demonstrate egoistically motivated altruism, that "participants helped a person in need more when the helping act
relieved the person's main problem than when it solved an unrelated problem," leading them to change their minds and argue that altruistic motivation did exist (Dovido
et al. 1990). Likewise, an experiment by Daniel Batson et al. showed that people's
tendency to help others in pain with whom they empathized was unaffected by the
difficulty of helping, suggesting that altruistic rather than egoistic motivations were
involved (Batson et al. 1981). As a result of such research, recent reviews of the
literature conclude that reducing all motivation to rational self-interest is untenable:
"Some people, some of the time, do help other people out of altruism" (Piliavin
2009; see also Jeffries et al. 2006; Feigin et al. 2014). Put another way, while individuals sometimes help others in the hope of winning long-term gains for themselves, at other times altruism is a form of affirmation that individuals pursue even
at the expense of their own pleasure.

Critics argue that studies that merely ask people how they *would* behave do not
provide firm predictions of behavior. However, studies of *actual affirming* behavior
itself reach the same conclusion. For example, Latane and Darley and Piliavin et al.
found that high proportions of people did assist researchers pretending to be in distress (Latane and Darley 1970; Piliavin et al. 1969). Even in poor urban areas, where
a lack of social capital or physical resources is thought to discourage altruism, a vast
majority of residents reported witnessing affirming behavior including "saving the
life of someone who was in danger; taking permanent custody of, or providing temporary care for, the children of neighbors; providing housing for homeless individuals and families; intervening to protect others from crime or violence; and providing
money, food, clothes, guidance, and encouragement to others" (Mattis et al. 2009).

Throughout history, we find people who risk their lives for others and for causes,
from Christians who saved Jews in Nazi Germany to Freedom Riders who challenged segregation in the American South. Such behaviors are not adequately
explained by self-satisfying motivation (Steele et al. 2008). Christopher J. Einolf
and others have found that "people with extensive moral obligations are more likely
than people with constricted obligations to engage in volunteer work and charitable
giving" (Einolf 2010). Note that in such studies the value comments and the moral
acts that affirm them are measured independently from one another, and the higher
the level of commitment, the more likely one is to act morally. Some illustrative
evidence follows.

1.5.6 Even in Economic Behavior

In addition to cases of altruism and self-sacrifice, affirming behavior is surprisingly
evident in behaviors normally considered as self-satisfying. For example, economists explain the level of savings as an increasing function of one's income and the
value one places on consumption after retirement, as well as the interest rate.
However, these factors explain only part of the variance in the amount saved, with a

large part determined by "non-economic factors such as religion, geography, ideology, culture" (Kessler et al. 1993). For example, Guiso et al. demonstrate that religious belief correlates significantly with thriftiness (Guiso et al. 2003). Of such non-economic factors, relevant moral considerations include a moral aversion towards indebtedness, the sense that one ought to help one's children "start off in life," and the sense that saving is moral in and of itself. Max Weber's thesis in *The Protestant Ethic and the Spirit of Capitalism* was that "worldly Protestant asceticism" valuing frugality and hard work was associated with the emergence of capitalism in Europe (Weber 1930, p. 115). Paul Webley and Ellen K. Nyhus likewise show that "saving and thrift have traditionally been valued greatly and have been seen as positive, indeed as highly moral" (Webley and Nyhus 1999).

In the United States, a decline in the sense of moral value of saving has coincided with a dramatic decline in the saving rate. Over the latter half of the twentieth century, thrift declined as a dominant value as advertising that promoted consumerism, and American culture increasingly "centered on spending and pleasure" (Tucker 1991; Yarrow 2014; see also Pate and Day 2015). This in part manifested in greater public acceptance of buying on credit. After "waves of financial innovation" began in the 1980s, "total consumer credit card debt rose from $211 billion to $876 billion" between 1989 and 2006, and "the proportion of indebted households carrying over $10,000 in credit card debt rose from 3% to 27%," leading the savings rate in the U.S. to enter a "30-year decline" (Oxford Economics 2014; see also Carroll et al. 2012; Sweet et al. 2013).

Since the 1970s, a high negative value has been attributed to public debt, or the deficit. While the actual effects of the deficit on economic performance is a complicated one, the public accepted that it is a violation of moral commitments to children, and a sign of living above one's means. These moral values have a great effect on voting and were used to justify the curtailing of numerous social programs and in some years, defense spending.

Along the same lines, the "standard economic model of rational and selfish human behavior" predicts that people will act with honesty or dishonesty "only to the extent that the planned trade-off favors a particular action" (Mazar et al. 2008; see also Hechter 1990). In this view, people behave honestly only when "trust is enforced in the marketplace through retaliation and reputation." However, a study by Jeremy Frimer and Lawrence Walker found that "communal values" did in fact predict honest behavior (in this case returning the difference of an overpayment), while "self-interested" values predicted dishonest behavior, except in cases where the two motives could be reconciled (Frimer and Walker 2009).

Satisfiers do *not merely* claim that there is an element of pleasure (or self-interest) in all seemingly altruistic behavior, but also that such behavior is wholly self-interested. The Public Choice school, which emerged in the 1970s has had a "prevailing influence" on the discipline of public administration and much influence on several others (Baimyrzaeva 2012, p. 37). Public choice theory applied to politics the economist's assumption that individuals are selfish rational actors (Shughart 2008; see also Mueller 1986). In other words, even collective action, according to satisfiers, is merely the result of individuals seeking to maximize their utility. Thus Public Choice predicts that voter turnout will be low, given that the minimal impact of any one vote makes voting "irrational" (Shughart 2008; see also Downs 1957a, b); that members of a community will "free ride" by neglecting to contribute to public goods (Kim and Walker 1984), and that politicians seek votes in order to acquire "the income, power, and prestige that go with office" (Downs 1957a) for themselves rather than the voters. In reality, a majority of eligible Americans do vote in presidential elections, and voting rates are highest among wealthy working age and educated people who should be most sensitive to the time cost and "irrationality" of voting (See Bipartisan Policy Center 2012). Behavioral experiments show that rather than "free ride," individuals "allocate a large percentage," typically "50% or more," to public goods in early experimental rounds, and "still allocate a substantial percentage" in later rounds (Tresch 2008, p. 157), a finding borne out in the real world by contributions to public broadcasting, for example.

The reason for these failures is that Public Choice fails to take into account the role of affirmation. For example, despite experimental designs emphasizing "the monetary importance of the situation," researchers found that "normative factors such as fairness" had a strong influence on people's decision to contribute to public goods rather than free ride (Marwell and Ames 1979). Another study found that a "sense of civic duty based on affiliation with the society as a whole" to be the "key variable accounting for the participation of the many citizens" without strong partisan or interest group affiliations (Knack 1992).

In short, there is very considerable evidence, from different realms of social life, including in the private and public sector, (data based on experiments, attitude surveys, and statistics about actual behavior) that moral commitments are one significant factor that motivates people, which leads to affirming action—and entails pain.

1.5.7 Codetermination

The thesis that affirmation plays a key role in people's choices and actions does not rule out the quest for satisfaction as a motivation, but rather holds that affirmation is another important source of motivation. This thesis holds (1) that both pleasure and moral commitments significantly influence human behavior, and (2) that the relative influence of the two kinds of motivation varies between historical and societal conditions, and between different individuals under the same conditions. It follows that theories of behavior and society, as well as measurements of collective well-being, must take into account the forces that shape both factors, and the relative strength of these factors.

One particularly illuminating study by Harold Grasmick and Donald Green shows the relative importance of deterrence and moral commitments in curbing crime (Grasmick and Green 1981). The authors asked respondents whether they had committed various criminal and immoral acts in the past and if they thought they would do so in the future. They then asked respondents to "estimate the chances you would be arrested by the police if you did each of these things," in line "with the utilitarian perspective" that "measures of perceived certainty of punishment must be from the viewpoint of the respondent." In order to account for the fact that the same punishment may have a different impact on different people, they also asked "how big a problem that punishment would create for your life." Finally, in an effort to measure moral commitment the authors asked respondents to rank a series of criminal acts in order of how wrong they considered them to be (never, seldom, sometimes, usually, and always). All three independent variables correlated significantly. Moreover, moral commitment was correlated more strongly with reported past and estimated future criminal acts (−0.42 and −0.55, respectively) than were the perceived certainty of arrest (−0.34 and −0.24, respectively) or the perceived severity of punishment (−0.27 and −0.30, respectively). That is, *both deterrence and moral commitments discouraged illegal acts.* This finding supports highlights the importance of morality, in addition to material incentives and coercion, for a functioning society and economy (see Drakulich and Crutchfeild 2013; Arrow 2006; Phelps 1975, p. 5).

Along the same lines, the literature on tax compliance has found that people's decision to pay (or evade) their taxes has as much to do with their moral obligation as a citizen as with the fear of punishment. However, this economic model in fact "greatly overpredicts noncompliance"—just as a purely egoistic individual would lie, cheat, and steal, he would also evade his taxes. Instead, studies of tax compliance found that "incorporating noneconomic motivations, such as a moral preference for honest reporting, does reduce predicted noncompliance" to more realistic levels (Andreoni et al. 1998). In particular, people's "personal norms," including "altruistic orientation," community values, cooperation, honesty, and religious beliefs, as well as their "social norms," the attitude of one's "professional groups, friends and acquaintances" toward tax evasion, all have a significant influence on tax compliance. Likewise, the "perceived fairness of taxation," including the both the "perceived balance of taxes paid and public goods received" and the "perceived justice" the enforcement regime, is strongly related to tax compliance (Hofmann et al. 2008).

Research has also found that "social interventions" based on "leveraging social concerns" can be more effective than material incentives in encouraging cooperative behavior. In trying to encourage water conservation in drought-affected California, the traditional economics-based approach of raising water prices did little to discourage water use. On the other hand, the simple act of emailing homeowners a comparison of their water use to that of their neighbors was as effective as a 10% price increase (Yoeli et al. 2015). This case, however, shows the continuing prevalence of reductionist assumptions.

1.6   Preferences Socially Made, Can Be Socially Reconstructed

Increasingly, a considerable number of social scientists, some say most, recognized the limits of psychological hedonism as a foundation for theories of choice—but not because they discovered the moral dimension. They were particularly concerned with the fact that statements about happiness were "based entirely on the internal subjective feelings of the individuals in question," which "were not objectively observable" (Hands 2009, p. 635). This led to a focus on relative or "ordinal" measures of utility, which did not depend on hedonistic assumptions (Baumol 2002). Paul Samuelson, for example, put forward the theory of "revealed preferences," according to which "consumers' preferences can be revealed by what they purchase under […] different income and price circumstances" (Roper and Zin 2013). According to Daniel Kahneman and Richard Thaler, the concept of "utility as an aspect of experience," in which "people choose the options that they will most enjoy," "essentially disappeared from economic discourse" during the twentieth century, with economists moving to a model of "decision utility" focusing on whether preferences are "consistent with each other and with the axioms of rational choice" (Kahneman and Thaler 2006).

According to this approach, the person's feelings are immaterial; only the fact that his or her preference guided their choice matters. An often cited example is the preference of a person who sought to climb a mountain and did so climb; it matters not, say those who follow this line of analysis, if having reached the top of the mountain he felt happy, satisfied, disappointed, or empty; he got what he chose. It is worth noting, however, that economics textbooks continue to use "pleasure" and "happiness" interchangeably with utility, suggesting that this conceptual shift is very far from complete (see Frank 2007, p. 6; Pindyck and Rubinfeld 2009).

In response, one notes that it surely matters; the climbers who are unhappy, one would predict, are less likely to climb again. Moreover, the theory still does not encompass moral preferences, or if it does, it treats them as one kind of preference among many others, and thus collapses a distinction that is crucial to many sound analyses of human behavior.

The theory is also tautological, because researchers determine both what the subject's actions and preferences are from the same observation. To say that, "if he climbed the mountain, it must be because he preferred it," adds nothing to our understanding of the subjects. It is like multiplying every number by one. Philip Murkowski adds that revealed preference theory is "either a tautology if defined at a point in time," or "entirely toothless if time is allowed to pass," since "violations could be discounted as changes in tastes" (Mirowski 2006). Richard Thaler and Cass Sunstein argue that assuming people "make choices that are in their best interest" is "either tautological, and therefore uninteresting, or testable," but if one does try to test it, the assumption is shown to be "false—indeed, obviously false" (Thaler and Sunstein 2003). And Amartya Sen faults revealed preference theory for neglecting "the fact that man is a social animal and his choices are not rigidly bound to his own preferences only" (Sen 1982, p. 66).

One further notes that the theory of revealed preferences, like much of mainstream Western (so called neoclassical) economic theory and related fields (such as law and economics and Public Choice political science), is isometric with liberal-libertarian assumptions. They hold liberty to be the prime value, and that the individual should be free to make choices which should be interfered with only if they seriously harm others. (Some would add, harm the common good; others deny that there is such a thing). This idea is of course at the foundation of democratic theory (according to which voters drive public policy) and consumer sovereignty (according to which customers drive the economy by voting with their dollars). The reason I say "isometric" is because many who base their academic or policy analysis on the preference theory do not personally subscribe to the liberal-libertarian ideology or are even aware that their world draws on its assumption. Nevertheless, these strong normative assumptions are part and parcel of the preference theory, because its core assumption is that what does and should drive a good economy, polity, and society is what people prefer. All this is greatly undermined once one finds out that people's preferences are largely not theirs but implanted.

This is the case because if the personal preferences did not reflect the true, inner person but were introduced or implanted by some external agent into the person, then that agent would in effect control their behavior. If this were the case, there would be no reason to treat these preferences as an expression of free will, and one would have to evaluate the values of the particular pursuits that an agent made people prefer.

I move next to show, for those who do not take it for granted, that much of what people prefer is implanted. True, most, if not all people, can eke out a measure of freedom and choice, but it is much less than satisfiers and followers of the preference theory assume. There is hence nothing immoral about limiting the pursuit of pleasure (e.g. speeding, driving while drunk) in order to make room for affirming action, especially in periods and societies where it is neglected.

The assumption concerning autonomous preferences conflicts with the empirical findings of the study of persuasion through advertising and other forms of manipulation by marketing. This has led defenders of the theory to argue that advertising serves merely an informative function. In reality, advertising often focuses more on influencing its audience subconsciously[7] than on providing information (Lee 1997). Advertisements often appeal to emotions, irrational fears, and cognitive biases as a way of "manufacturing need, (Phillips 2011)" inducing preferences for the goods they seek to market rather than merely producing goods to satisfy existing prefer-

---

[7]"Advertising in contemporary society is generally regarded as having two central and correlative functions, that of informing and that of persuading consumers. The informative function is likely to be stressed by defenders of the advertising practice, for by providing information to consumers about products, services, and prices advertising allows the consumer to make reasoned choices about the things on which he/she will spend his/her money" (Santilli 1983, p. 27)

"The overwhelming bulk of advertising in American mass media is designed to promote the sale of products and services" (Pearlin and Rosenberg 1952, p.5).

ences. Women did not feel that they had to pay for a painful procedure to remove hair from their private parts until the industry convinced them that a 'bush' was embarrassing (Herzig 2015). Consumers felt no need to purchase mouthwash until they were convinced that without it their dental hygiene routine was incomplete.

Faced with the preceding observations, economists argue that economic theory "needs" the assumption that preferences reflect the true inner self in order to assess the contribution of the economy to general welfare. The economy is assumed to function well when it provides the goods preferred by people at prices such that supply equals demand. Individuals are thought to vote with their purchasing dollars so as to guide the economy toward that blessed state of equilibrium, which is considered the "holy grail" of neoclassical economics (Berger 2009, p. xii). If preferences can be manipulated by social pressures or advertising, then an economy that satisfies those preferences would appear not to serve the people but, rather, the manipulators who affect the preferences. Such a revelation would require economists to study the relative power of persuasion and political power exercised by various elites.

True, acknowledging the reality of manipulation and the initial formation of preferences by a variety of social forces, as well as their continuous reshaping does not prevent one from noting that there are limits to the extent to which people can be manipulated. One telling example is that of the USSR. It tightly controlled its educational system and shaped cultural productions such as movies, television, and books in line with its ideology, while limiting access to other cultures. It further provided strong incentives for conformity and strongly disincentivized dissent. Nonetheless, after 70 years, the regime was unable to suppress religion, family loyalties, and aspirations for liberty, leading to its collapse. There have been many thousands of attempts in the West alone, from the Israeli Kibbutzim to American "hippie" communes to various religious orders, to form cultures and communities dedicated to an ascetic life. All of these, too, failed to maintain their culture of denial for most members. These failures demonstrate that the extent to which preferences can be shaped against basic underlying human needs is limited (Etzioni 1971). Indeed, if it were possible to manipulate people without limits, as suggested in *1984*, it would be possible to make slaves sing in appreciation of their servitude. The historical record clearly demonstrates otherwise, but only over the longer run, and for basic human needs rather than for specific preferences. (And those must be studied to determine who and what shaped them rather than take them as given.) Once it has been established what these basic needs are, it becomes possible to assess the contributions of the economy to the general welfare without disregarding that preferences to a significant extent are inauthentic in the sense that they do not express the true, underlying needs of the person but rather mirror the manipulators. However, in the longer run, regarding basic human needs such as the quest for a measure of autonomy, for dignity, and for affective bonds—people do prevail (Etzioni 1968).

Although there are many variations (Maccoby 1992), the basic sociological and psychological understanding of the process of and factors influencing preference formation goes as follows: Children are born with biological urges but their mode of satisfaction is very open ended. They have basic needs to meet but are not born with a specific need for Cokes and french fries, or snails and red wine, or hummus, olives and nargila. These preferences reflect the particular cultures and communities they are born into and raised. In particular, children's initial preferences are formed through complex processes of socialization involving identification, habituation, and explicit and implicit persuasion. Children acquire their preferences by imitating their parents and other adults; they are persuaded by them, and are influenced by their narratives. However, preference formation is not limited to the home; children learn from schools, peer groups, media, and other sources besides their parents. And these processes of socialization never end; thus colleges and professional schools play a role in the preference formation of their students, and after graduation, people continue to be influenced by peer groups and leaders and are averse to changing their preferences. Children gradually develop an ability to modify their preferences on their own, but when all is said and done, individuals' preferences are, broadly speaking, largely the product of socialization, *and* only to some extent of individual reflection and desires.

In short, despite these many and important differences about how preferences are formed, the evidence is overwhelming that they are not inborn the way biological urges are, but rather reflect the particular cultures and subcultures in which the child is raised; that is, preferences are socially shaped. Research also shows that they are constantly reshaped through peer pressures, exposure to leadership, and advertising. Individuals have a degree of freedom, but it is much smaller than hedonists assume.

It follows that these preferences should not be granted the kind of strong normative standing to which they would be entitled if they truly reflected free will. It also stands to reason that, given that corporations and various interest groups and ideological camps constantly labor to reshape preferences, there is no reason for those who represent the common good or the public interest not to do the same, e.g. by discouraging people from smoking.

Above all, that those who seek to better the human condition by encouraging them to reduce their obsession with material consumption once their basic needs are well and securely met, to exercise more, and to share more, would be more effective if they focused not on changing individuals, but rather on changing cultures and social and political structures, which shape preferences. This in turn requires collective action, of those who seek changes to ally themselves with others, and above all form a social movement. History shows that movements such as the civil rights movement, the environmental movement, those of national liberation and many others—are the forces most able to withdraw the legitimacy of an old regime and invest the freed legitimation in the formation of a new one (see Etzioni 2013).

1.6.1 Well-Being: Much Better But Not Good Enough

Carol Graham made the following points:

> There is a big difference in the idea of happiness/well-being as an object of policy (as, for example, Jeff Sachs and the Bhutanese espouse) and its usage as a metrics, as a tool of analysis to help us understand the intersection between income and non-income determinants of well-being (as well as their causal properties). Indeed, many of the most serious scholars in the field, like Danny Kahneman, Arthur Stone, and others who I served with on

a National Academy of Sciences panel on well-being metrics and policy, shy away from the term happiness as it confounds momentary contentment with life satisfaction and other deeper dimensions of well-being.

She continued:

There is also increasing consensus among scholars of well-being that there are two distinct dimensions: a. Hedonic or experienced well-being, which includes contentment, pain, plea-sure, sadness, and so on. b. Evaluative well-being, which is more complex and captures individuals views of their lives as a whole. This latter dimension implicitly includes Aristotle's eudemonia, which is individuals' capacity to lead purposeful or meaningful lives (which includes a moral dimension.)[8] (See also Graham and Nikolova 2015; Stone and Mackie 2013)

In response I draw on the difference in the literature between subjective well-being (as reported by those studied) and objective well-being. Subjective well-being is surely a much more meaningful and richer concept than that of happiness. Studies of happiness in the hedonic/experiences sense assess how satisfied a person is at a given moment by asking questions such as "how happy are you" and "did you smile fre-quently yesterday." In contrast to those seeking to understand well-being, use ques-tions such as "how satisfied are you with your life in general" and "do you feel that you have purpose or meaning in life" (with possible responses on a ten-point scale).

However, this concept raises two questions. First, a relatively minor one, whether all or even most people have a clear and stable conception of the purpose of their lives and its meaning—and to what extent they formulate such notions mainly in response to the questions asked, and whether when asked again, under different cir-cumstances, they would not provide rather different answers. (By the way, this mea-surement would make young people come off as less well than older ones because many young ones are less clear about their purpose/meaning than older ones).

Second, there can be little doubt that people who state that they have a purpose and a meaningful life may be jihadists, gang leaders, produce ads to promote the purchase of cigarettes, or sell subprime mortgages. I see no correlation between being a good human being and leading a purposeful and meaningful life. To get at the moral dimension one would need to ask people what they did during the last weekend; what they would do if everyone in their group did free ride: how improper they consider keeping cash in a found wallet; how they rank inequality versus eco-nomic growth; and other such questions.

Objective well-being can include moral assessments—and anything else those who study the connection wish to include. Examining such studies shows that defi-nitions of objective well-being reflect the values of the researchers, not their sub-jects. Thus, some students of objective well-being assume that people who live in a society that has a lower environmental footprint than others are more just, and are at peace with others who are better off. Others—if they have higher income, pay fewer taxes, and are freer from government regulations. That is, this concept moves us in the right direction but still faces two challenges: (a) it mixes moral and non-moral determinants of well-being, preventing us from measuring the moral factor, and (b)

---

[8] Quoted with permission.

it ignores the moral positions of the subjects and instead draws on implicit, not accounted for, values of the researcher.

In short, studies of well-being move well beyond those of happiness but leave room for a distinct and explicit study of how moral people are by their lights and those of explicitly spelled out and accounted for values of others. And what determines how moral people are.

1.7 Say It with Figures

This chapter next turns to examining various measurements for assessing the state of individuals and societies—above all, how satisfied people are and how satisfying societies are. There is considerable literature on the subject. The goal of this section is not to review it, but rather to select a few key measurements, to suggest that some are preferable to others, and to hold that all of them lack a key element. The section begins with those measurements that are particularly deficient and compares them to those that are more satisfactory. However, this development is logical rather than historical; that is, no neat progression exists over time from poorer to better definitions and measurements, and all of them are still used.

1.7.1 Happiness: Asked and Answered

A very elementary measurement widely used to study happiness is to simply ask people whether they are happy. A typical survey of this kind asks, "Are you happy?" For example, an annual study of Europeans asks: "Taking all things together, how would you say things are these days—would you say you're very happy, fairly happy, or not too happy these days" (Di Tella et al. 2003)? A similar study, conducted in the United States from 1972 to the present, asks: "Taken all together, how would you say things are these days—would you say that you are very happy, pretty happy, or not too happy" (General happiness 2016; Frey and Stutzer 2002, p. 405; Di Tella et al. 2003)? Indeed, much of the economics literature on happiness relies on such self-reporting of happiness (Xefteris 2012, p. 291), as have other attempts to report on and analyze happiness, such as the Pew Research Center's study of parenthood and happiness (Parker 2014).

Aside from assessing the state of individuals, measurements such as gross national happiness (GNH) have been introduced to assess various social groups and whole societies. Common to many of these attempts is an underlying philosophy of classical hedonistic utilitarianism, which holds that societies ought to maximize "the sum-total of happiness" (Tannsjo 2007, p. 81). These measurements are based on the number of individuals who state that they are happy, rather than on the basis of some collective or emergent property, such as the extent to which the environment is protected (Tella and MacCulloch 2006, p. 26).

Because a considerable number of economists and quite a few other social scientists assume that pleasure is derived from the consumption of material goods, and because they are uncomfortable with subjective measurements such as self-reporting, they favored income or GDP as objective measurements of happiness for individuals and societies, respectively. This kind of measurement fails on the grounds already discussed—that is, higher levels of income are often not associated with increased happiness.

1.7.2 Life Satisfaction

Questions about happiness (e.g. "Did you smile today?") have been criticized on the grounds that they are like snapshots that capture a person's feelings at a single point in time. Others ask people questions about "life satisfaction." They ask people to what extent their life so far measures up to their expectations and resembles their envisioned "ideal life" (Van Hoom 2007). The most widely-used standard set of questions is the Satisfaction with Life Scale (Alexandrova 2005 p. 303). Other standard surveys for measuring life satisfaction include the World Values Survey and the Eurobarometer Surveys (Frey and Stutzer 2002 p.405).

An often-cited study of life satisfaction is the OECD Better Life Index, which asks people to "evaluate their life as a whole rather than their current feelings." The countries with the highest life satisfaction in 2014 were Denmark, Iceland, and Switzerland, while the countries with the lowest life satisfaction were Estonia, Greece, Hungary, Portugal, and Turkey (OECD n.d.). This particular index also tracks details about 11 dimensions that the study's architects deemed "essential" to a good life: housing, income and wealth, jobs and earnings, education and skills, environmental quality, civic engagement, health, subjective well-being, social connections, work-life balance, and personal security (Gurría 2015).

1.7.3 Well-Being

In medicine, the term "well-being" is used to argue that physicians and other healers should not limit themselves to curing a person's presenting illness, but rather should treat the person's general condition. This general condition may include a person's psychological state, or ability to carry out the activities that makes his life a satisfying one (see McLeod 2015). A similar concept is applied to societies by those who study satisfaction. Students of well-being hold that studies of people should not be limited to whether they are happy, but rather should include other factors. Data on subjective well-being is usually obtained through self-reports. A popular multi-item scale is the Positive and Negative Affect Schedule (PANAS) (Van Hoom 2007). This measurement of happiness has been published annually since 2012 by the World Happiness Report (Helliwell et al. 2015, p. 3).

Others measure well-being by using measurements that reflect various objective factors that the researchers hold correlate with well-being, including how well the environment is protected (Bevc et al. 2007), the level of inequality (Hajdu and Hajdu 2014), and so on. Objective measurements of well-being include national income as a baseline and incorporate adjustments to account for non-market factors such as income inequality or climate change (Sirgy et al. 2006, p. 381). The concept of gross national happiness (GNH) was applied in Bhutan in 1972 by then-king Jigme Singye Wangchuck; the concept was not initially conceived of as a metric, but rather as a general philosophy intended to "balance" the values of Western capitalism with "the historical foundations and tenets of Bhutan's traditional culture and polity" (Givel 2015, p. 108). It refers to aggregate happiness of all human beings as a cohesive unit, happiness that specifically "take[s] into account the needs of others," and is specifically anti-materialist; one president of the Center for Bhutan Studies held that the goal of GNH is to "create conducive conditions for happiness in which individual strivings can succeed" (Bates 2009, p. 4). GNH is defined as "the degree to which citizens in a country enjoy the life they live," and is now measured in Happy Life Years (HLY) (Veenhoven 2004). Thirty-three qualitative indicators of GNH can broadly be broken into four "pillars" of "equitable economic development, culture and religious preservation, environmental protection, and good governance." Happy Life Years for various countries range from 63 in Switzerland to 21 in Moldavia (Veenhoven 2004).

The concept of well-being allows those who measure it to pack it with whatever they value as a determinant of well-being. They tend though to take into account neither the level of moral behavior, nor the fact that citizens of societies such as Nazi Germany or Imperial Japan at their peak were quite satisfied and that those in London during the Blitz were quite miserable.

1.7.4   Measuring Moral Behavior

Whatever measurement is used to assess people's satisfaction, whether this is based on their own statements or divined from the factors researchers assume (ought to) make them happy, the communitarian approach here developed requires adding a major measurement—one that would assess the extent to which the members of a society live up to a set of values. Theoretically, one could measure the extent to which they live up to their particular society's set of values. Such a score, however, would be of limited merit because it would be high for societies that set low standards for themselves or values that are considered to be of little virtue in the eye of the observer. Religious extremist societies, such as the ISIS caliphate, are one such example of a society that would score high on such a measurement of the extent to which a society lives up to its own values. Instead, such a measurement should be based on adherence to a universal set of values, such as measured by rates of child abuse, corruption, and volunteerism in a given society (Etzioni 2011). Because there is only moderate consensus about what these universal values should be, different observers might use different measurements. A value affirming index might be comprised of several already-available measurements, such as those next cited, augmented by some new ones if need be.

One element of the index would be the level of *corruption*. A review of efforts to develop such an indicator, by Paul M. Heywood and Jonathan Rose, finds that there is a "gap" between the conceptualization of corruption and its measurement (Heywood and Rose 2014, p. 528). Nonetheless, organizations such as Transparency International have striven to establish a ranking of countries based on self-reported perceptions of corruption (Corruption Perceptions Index) in among each country's citizens. According to the 2014 index, Denmark has the lowest perceptions of corruption, while Somalia has the highest perceptions of corruption. (The United States falls seventeenth on the list.) (Corruption Perceptions Index 2014).

Another measurement is that of the level of *child abuse* in various countries. UNICEF ranked in 2013 the overall well-being of children in developed countries based on five indicators, of which some sub-indicators are exposure to violence, bullying, and national homicide rate; according to this ranking, the Netherlands has the best overall child well-being, while Romania has the worst (Adamson 2013). Germany had the least amount of physical fighting among children, while Spain had the most; Italy had the least bullying of children, while Lithuania had the most; and Iceland had the lowest homicide rate, while Lithuania had the highest (Adamson 2013). In 2006, the United Nations conducted a worldwide study of violence against children; although country-level data is not publicly available, the study found that millions of children are subjected to violence and homicide, forced labor, rape, sexual assault, and more annually. Homicide statistics for children are twice as high in low-income countries as in high-income countries, the study found, and many countries have failed to implement meaningful legislation that criminalizes violence against children in accordance with the United Nations Declaration on the Rights of the Child (United Nations 2006). The World Health Organization also keeps (non-comprehensive) statistics on what is officially called child maltreatment; according to statistics borrowed from the WorldSAFE Project, mothers reported that they hit their children with an object in the past 6 months at the rate of 4% in Chile, 26% in Egypt, 36% in India, 21% in the Philippines, and 4% in the United States (WHO n.d.).

Others measure the rate of *domestic violence* in countries worldwide. For example, the World Health Organization tracks violence against women, including intimate partner violence, on a regional basis; the lifetime prevalence of physical and sexual intimate partner violence against women was 36.6% in Africa, 29.8% in the Americas, 37.0% in the Eastern Mediterranean, 25.4% in Europe, 37.7% in South-East Asia, and 24.6% in the Western Pacific (WHO 2013).

Another metric is the degree to which the country's *tax code* is "progressive"— that is, taxes the wealthy and corporations at higher rates than the poor, or, to use an alternate definition, at rates higher than their share of income.

A study of *volunteerism* rates by a leading expert on the subject, Lester M. Salamon, ranked countries in terms of volunteerism as a share of GDP for 36 countries and found that Sweden ranked highest, while Mexico ranked lowest; the

United States came in fifth, after Sweden, Norway, France, and the United Kingdom (United Nations 2011, p. 21). Other organizations such as the Charities Aid Foundation (CAF) have measured the likelihood of helping strangers, charitable giving rates, and volunteerism in various countries; the CAF created a metric called the World Giving Index based on these three variables and ranked countries worldwide accordingly. The top 20 countries for each indicator are shown in the figure below (Charities Aid Foundation 2014).

Top 20 countries in the World Giving Index, with score and participation in giving behaviours

	World Giving Index ranking	World Giving Index score (%)	Helping a stranger score (%)	Donating money score (%)	Volunteering time score (%)
Myanmar	1	64	49	91	51
United States of America	1	64	79	68	44
Canada	3	60	66	71	44
Ireland	4	60	64	74	41
New Zealand	5	58	69	62	44
Australia	6	56	65	66	37
Malaysia	7	55	63	60	41
United Kingdom	7	55	61	74	29
Sri Lanka	9	54	56	56	50
Trinidad and Tobago	10	54	75	49	37
Bhutan	11	53	54	63	43
Netherlands	12	53	54	70	34
Indonesia	13	51	48	66	40
Iceland	14	50	52	70	29
Kenya	15	49	67	43	37
Malta	16	49	43	78	25
Austria	17	48	57	57	29
Denmark	18	47	55	62	23
Iran	19	46	62	52	24
Jamaica	20	45	73	26	35

Only includes countries surveyed in 2013.

Data relate to participation in giving behaviours during one month prior to interview.

World Giving Index scores are shown to the nearest whole number but the rankings are determined using two decimal points.

These examples suffice to illustrate a few of the elements that might be included in a value affirming index that draws on the values observers consider to be universal. Some surely might add measurements of democratization and human rights as defined by the United Nations and measured by Freedom House, or other such assessments. Once such an index has been developed, it will be possible to score societies or communities as satisfied but morally deficient, or as austere but virtuous, or as austere and morally deficient, or as satisfied and virtuous and so on. Some more suitable labels may be found, but these do well as a first approximation. Such measurements had best grant greater weight to the value affirming index to measurements of satisfaction, because it does not take much effort to encourage people to seek self-satisfaction—but it requires a great deal of socialization, encouragement, and support to make them more virtuous. Above all, these measurements are best used to study development over time, to determine not only what makes people richer, happier, or more satisfied, but also more moral human beings living in more moral societies.

References

Abramitzky, R. 2011. On the (lack of) stability of communes: An economic perspective. In *Oxford handbooks online*.

Adamson, P. 2013. *Child well-being in rich countries: A comparative overview*. Florence: UNICEF.

Alexandrova, A. 2005. Subjective well-being and Kahneman's 'objective happiness. *Journal of Happiness Studies* 6 (3): 301–324.

Andreoni, J. 1990. Impure altruism and donations to public goods: A theory of warm-glow giving. *The Economic Journal* 100 (401): 464–477.

Andreoni, J., B. Erard, and J. Feinstein. 1998. Tax compliance. *Journal of Economic Literature* 36 (2): 818–860.

Andrews, F.M., and S.B. Withey. 1976. *Social indicators of well-being: Americans' perceptions of life quality*. New York: Plenum Press.

Aron, A. 1977. Maslow's other child. *Journal of Humanistic Psychology* 17 (2): 9–24.

Arrow, K. 2006. The economy of trust. *Religion & Liberty* 16 (3): 3, 12–13.

Ashkenazi, M.H., and Y. Katz. 2009. From cooperate to renewed kibbutz: The case of kubbutz 'galil' Israel. *Middle Eastern Studies* 45 (4): 577.

Associated Press. 2015. Robots replacing human factory workers at faster pace. *The Los Angeles Times*.

Aubrey, J. 1898. In *"Brief lives": Chiefly of contemporaries, set down by John Aubrey, between the years 1669 & 1696*, ed. A. Clark. Oxford: At the Clarendon Press.

Azzi, C., and R. Ehrenberg. 1975. Household allocation of time and church attendance. *Journal of Political Economy* 83 (1): 27–56.

Baimyrzaeva, M. 2012. *Institutional reforms in the public sector: What did we learn?* Bingley: Emerald Group Publishing.

Bates, W. 2009. Gross national happiness. *Asian Pacific Economic Literature* 23 (2): 1–16.

Batson, C.D., B.D. Duncan, P. Ackerman, T. Buckley, and K. Birch. 1981. Is empathic emotion a source of altruistic motivation? *Journal of Personality and Social Psychology* 40 (2): 290–302.

Baumol, W.J. 2002. s. v. utility and value. *Encyclopædia Britannica Online*. http://www.britannica.com/. Accessed 9 June 2015.

Becker, G. 2012. *The Becker Posner Blog*.

Bentham, J. 1789. *An introduction to the principles of morals and legislation*. Oxford: Clarendon Press.

Berger, S. 2009. *The foundations of non-equilibrium economics: The principle of circular and cumulative causation*. London: Routledge.

Bevc, C.A., B.K. Marshall, and J.S. Picou. 2007. Environmental justice and toxic exposure: Toward a spatial model of physical health and psychological well-being. *Social Science Research* 36 (1): 48–67.

Bipartisan Policy Center. 2012. 2012 voter turnout report.

Brückner, M., and H.P. Grüner. 2010. *Economic growth and the rise of political extremism: Theory and evidence.* CEPR Discussion Paper No. DP7723, http://www.uni-kassel.de/. Accessed 26 June 2015.

Brynjolfsson, E., and A. McAfee. 2012. *Race against the machine: How the digital revolution is accelerating innovation, driving productivity, and irreversibly transforming employment and the economy.* Lexington: Digital Frontier Press.

Carroll, C., J. Slacalek, M. Sommer. 2012. *Dissecting saving dynamics: measuring wealth, precautionary, and credit effects.* IMF Working Paper.

Charities Aid Foundation. 2014. *World giving index 2014: A global view of giving trends.* https://www.cafonline.org/pdf/CAF_WGI2014_Report_1555AWEBFinal.pdf.

Curtis, B., and C. Curtis. 2011. *Social research: A practical introduction.* London: Sage Publications.

Di Tella, R., and R. MacCulloch. 2006. Some uses of happiness data in economics. *The Journal of Economic Perspectives* 20 (1): 25–46.

Di Tella, R., R.J. McCulloch, and A.J. Oswald. 2003. The macroeconomics of happiness. *The Review of Economics and Statistics* 85 (4): 809–827.

Dovido, J.F., J.L. Allen, and D.A. Schroeder. 1990. The specificity of empathy induced helping: Evidence for altruism. *Journal of Personality and Social Psychology* 59: 249–260.

Downs, A. 1957a. An economic theory of political action in a democracy. *Journal of Political Economy* 65 (2): 135–150.

———. 1957b. *An economic theory of democracy.* New York: Harper.

Drakulich, K.M., and R.D. Crutchfield. 2013. The role of perceptions of the police in informal social control. *Social Problems* 60 (3): 383–407.

Dunn, E.W., D.T. Gilbert, and T.D. Wilson. 2011. If money doesn't make you happy, then you probably aren't spending it right. *Journal of Consumer Psychology* 21 (2): 115–125.

Easterlin, R. 1973. Does money buy happiness. *The Public Interest* 30: 3–10.

———. 1974. Does economic growth improve the human lot? Some empirical evidence. In *Nations and households in economic growth: Essays in honor of Moses Abramovitz,* ed. P.A. David and M.W. Reder. New York: Academic Press, Inc.

———. 2005. Diminishing marginal utility of income? Caveat Emptor. *Social Indicators Research* 70: 243–255.

Easterlin, et al. 2010. The happiness-income paradox revisited. *PNAS* 107 (52): 22463–22468.

Einolf, C.J. 2010. Does extensivity form part of the altruistic personality? An empirical test of Oliner and Oliner's theory. *Social Science Research* 39 (1): 142–151.

Etzioni, A. 1968. Basic human needs, alienation and inauthenticity. *American Sociological Review* 33: 870–885.

———. 1971. *The active society: A theory of societal and political processes.* New York: Free Press.

———. 1988. *The moral dimension.* New York: The Free Press.

———. 1993. *The spirit of community.* New York: Simon and Schuster.

———. 1996. *The new golden rule.* New York: Basic Books.

———. 1998. The implications of human nature. In *The new golden rule: Community and morality in a democratic society,* ed. A. Etzioni, 160–188. New York: Basic Books.

———. 2006. Self-evident truth (beyond relativism). In *Universalism vs. relativism: Making moral judgements in a changing, pluralistic, and threatening world,* ed. D. Browning, 19–32. Lanham: Rowman & Littlefield.

———. 2011. On communitarian and global sources of legitimacy. *The Review of Politics* 73 (1): 105–122.

———. 2013. The bankruptcy of liberalism and conservatism. *Political Science Quarterly* 128 (1): 39–65.

———. 2014. *The new normal: Finding a balance between individual rights and the common good.* New York: Transaction Publishers.

Fehr, E., and K.M. Schmidt. 2006. The economics of fairness, reciprocity and altruism – experimental evidence and new theories. In *Handbook of the economics of giving, altruism and reciprocity*, ed. S.C. Kolm and J.M. Ythier, 615–691. Amsterdam: Elsevier.

Feigin, S., G. Owens, and F. Goodyear-Smith. 2014. Theories of human altruism: a systematic review. *Annals of Neuroscience and Psychology* 1 (1): 1–19.

Fernald, J.G., and C.I. Jones. 2014. The future of US economic growth. *American Economic Review* 104 (5): 44–49.

Frank, R.H. 2007. *Microeconomics and behavior*. 7th ed. New York: McGraw Hill.

Freedman, J.L. 1978. *Happy people: What happiness is, who has it, and why*. New York: Harcourt Brace Jovanovich.

Frey, C.B., and M. Osborne. 2013. *The future of employment: How susceptible are jobs to computerisation?* Paper presented for the Machines and Employment Workshop. Oxford University.

Frey, B.S., and A. Stutzer. 2002. What can economists learn from happiness research? *Journal of Economic Literature* 40 (2): 402–435.

Frimer, J.A., and L.J. Walker. 2009. Reconciling the self and morality: An empirical model of moral centrality development. *Developmental Psychology* 45 (6): 1669–1681.

General happiness. 2016. *General social survey*. Chicago: NORC, University of Chicago. https://gssdataexplorer.norc.org/variables/434/vshow. Accessed 1 June 2015.

Gilbert, D. 2006. *Stumbling on happiness*. New York: Random House. quoted in Senior, J. (2006, July 17). Some dark thoughts on happiness. New York Magazine.

Givel, M.S. 2015. Gross national happiness in Bhutan: Political institutions and implementation. *Asian Affairs* 46(1): 102–117.

Gordon, R. 2012. *Is U.S. economic growth over? Faltering innovation confronts the six headwinds*. Cambridge, MA: Center for Economic Policy Research.

———. 2014. *The demise of U.S. economic growth: Restatement, rebuttal, and reflections*. NBER Working Paper No. 19895.

Graham, C., and M. Nikolova. 2015. Bentham or Aristotle in the development process? An empirical investigation of capabilities and subjective well-being. *World Development* 68: 163–179.

Grasmick, H.G., and D.E. Green. 1981. Deterrence and the morally committed. *The Sociological Quarterly* 22 (1): 1–14.

Groves, D.L., H. Kahalas, and D.L. Erickson. 1975. A suggested modification to Maslow's need hierarchy. *Social Behavior and Personality* 3 (1): 65–69.

Guiso, L., P. Sapienza, and L. Zingales. 2003. People's opium? Religion and economic attitudes. *Journal of Monetary Economics* 50 (1): 225–282.

Gurría, A. 2015. Going beyond GDP—The OECD's better life index. *OECD Insights*.

Hagerty, M.R. 1999. Testing Maslow's hierarchy of needs: National quality-of-life across time. *Social Indicators Research* 46: 249–271.

Hajdu, T., and G. Hajdu. 2014. Reduction of income inequality and subjective well-being in Europe. *Economics: The Open-Access, Open-Assessment E-Journal* 8(2014–35): 1–29.

Hamermesh, D.S., and N.M. Soss. 1974. An economic theory of suicide. *Journal of Political Economy* 82 (1): 83–98.

Hammond, P. 1975. Charity: Altruism or cooperative egoism? In *Altruism, morality, and economic theory*, ed. E.S. Phelps. New York: Sage Found.

Hands, D.W. 2009. Economics, psychology and the history of consumer choice theory. *Cambridge Journal of Economics* 34 (4): 633–648.

Haybron, D. 2011. Happiness. In *The Stanford encyclopedia of philosophy*, ed. E.N. Zalta.

Hechter, M. 1990. The attainment of solidarity in intentional communities. *Rationality and Society* 2: 142–155.

Helliwell, J., R. Layard, and J. Sachs. 2015. *The initial World Happiness report reviewed the scientific understanding of the measurement and explanation of subjective well-being*. World Happiness report 2015. New York: Sustainable Development Solutions Network.

Herzig, R.M. 2015. *Plucked: A history of hair removal*. New York: NYU Press.

Heylighen, F. 1992. A cognitive-systemic reconstruction of Maslow's theory of self-actualization. *Behavioral Science* 37 (1): 39–57.

Heywood, P.M., and J. Rose. 2014. 'Close but no cigar': The measurement of corruption. *Journal of Public Policy* 34 (3): 507–529.

Hoehnle, P. 2001. Community in transition: Amana's great change, 1931–1933. *The Annals of Iowa* 60: 1–34.

Hofmann, E., E. Hoelzl, and E. Kirchler. 2008. Preconditions of voluntary tax compliance: Knowledge and evaluation of taxation, norms, fairness, and motivation to cooperate. *Zeitschrift Für Psychologie/Journal of Psychology* 216 (4): 209–217.

Hornstein, H., A.E. Fisch, and M. Holmes. 1968. Influence of a model's feelings about his behavior and his relevance as a comparison other on observers' helping behavior. *Journal of Personality and Social Psychology* 10: 220–226.

Hunter, M. 2013. Wallet drop: World's least honest cities. *CNN*.

Jeffries, V., B. Johnston, V. Lawrence, T. Nichols, S.P. Oliner, E. Tiryakian, and J. Weinstein. 2006. Altruism and social solidarity: Envisioning a field of specialization. *The American Sociologist* 37 (3): 67–83.

Jurges, H. 2001. Do Germans save to leave an estate? An examination of the bequest motive. *The Scandinavian Journal of Economics*. 103 (3): 391–414.

Kahneman, D., and A. Deaton. 2010. High income improves evaluation of life but not emotional well-being. *Proceedings of the National Academy of Sciences of the United States of America* 107 (38): 16489–16493.

Kahneman, D., and R.H. Thaler. 2006. Anomalies: Utility maximization and experienced utility. *The Journal of Economic Perspectives* 20 (1): 221–234.

Kahneman, D., J.L. Knetsch, and R.H. Thaler. 1986. Fairness as a constraint on profit seeking: Entitlements in the market. *The American Economic Review* 76 (4): 728–741.

Kessler, D., et al. 1993. Savings behavior in 17 OECD countries. *Review of Income and Wealth* 39 (1): 37–49.

Kim, O., and M. Walker. 1984. The free rider problem: Experimental evidence. *Public Choice* 43 (1): 3–24.

Knack, S. 1992. Civic norms, social sanctions, and voter turnout. *Rationality and Society* 4 (2): 133–156.

Koltko-Rivera, M.E. 2006. Recovering the later version of Maslow's hierarchy of needs: Self-transcendence and opportunities for theory, research, and unification. *Review of General Psychology* 10 (4): 302–317.

Kornhauser, W. 1960. *The politics of mass society*. New York: Routledge.

Kraut, R. 2014. Aristotle's ethics. In *The Stanford encyclopedia of philosophy*, ed. E.N. Zalta.

Latane, B., and J. Darley. 1970. *The unresponsive bystander: Why doesn't he help*. New York: Appleton-Century Crofts.

Layard, R. 2005. *Happiness: Lessons from a new science*. New York: Penguin.

Lee, L.W. 1997. Persuasive advertising and socialization. *International Journal of Business and Economics* 4: 203–214.

Leslie, I. 2014. Kodak vs Instagram: This is why it's only going to get harder to make a good living. *The New Statesman*.

Lester, D. 1990. Maslow's hierarchy of needs and personality. *Personality and Individual Differences* 11 (11): 1187–1188.

Leviatan, U., H. Oliver, and J. Quarter. 1998. *Crisis in the Israeli Kibbutz: Meeting the challenge of changing times*. Westport: Praeger.

Lollar, D. 1974. An operationalization and validation of the Maslow need hierarchy. *Educational and Psychological Measurement* 34 (3): 639–651.

Lynn, M. 2006. *Tipping in restaurants and around the globe: An interdisciplinary review*. Cornell University, SHA.

Lynn, M., and A. Grassman. 1990. Restaurant tipping: An examination of three 'rational' explanations. *Journal of Economic Psychology* 11 (2): 169–181.

Maccoby, E. 1992. The role of parents in the socialization of children: An historical overview. *Developmental Psychology* 28: 1006–1017.

Mankiw, G. 2011. *Principles of microeconomics*. 6th ed. Boston: Cengage Learning.

Markoff, J. 2011. Armies of expensive lawyers, replaced by Cheaper software. *New York Times*.

Marwell, G., and R.E. Ames. 1979. Experiments on the provision of public goods. I. Resources, interest, group size, and the free-rider problem. *American Journal of Sociology* 84 (6): 1335–1360.

Maslow, A.H. 1943. A theory of human motivation. *Psychological Review* 50: 370–396.

Mattis, J.S., et al. 2009. The social production of altruism: Motivations for caring action in a low-income urban community. *American Journal of Community Psychology* 43: 71–84.

May, J. 2011. Psychological egoism. In *Internet encyclopedia of philosophy*.

Mazar, N., O. Amir, and D. Ariely. 2008. The dishonesty of honest people: A theory of self-concept maintenance. *Journal of Marketing Research* 633 (45): 633–644.

McGinnis, J. 2011. The young and the restless: Generation Y in the nonprofit workforce. *Public Administration Quarterly* 35 (3): 342–362.

McLeod, T.C.V. 2015. Addressing psychological concerns to practice whole-person health care. *Journal of Athletic Training* 50 (3): 229–230.

Milgram, S., L. Mann, and S. Harter. 1965. The lost-letter technique: A tool of social research. *The Public Opinion Quarterly* 29: 437–438.

Mirowski, P. 2006. Wong's foundations after 25 years. In *The foundations of Paul Samuelson's revealed preference theory: A study by the method of rational reconstructioned,* ed. S. Wong.

Mueller, D.C. 1986. Rational egoism versus adaptive egoism as fundamental postulate for a descriptive theory of human behavior. *Public Choice* 51 (1): –3, 23.

Myers, D.G., and E. Diener. 1995. Who is happy. *Psychological Science* 6 (1): 12–13.

———. 1996. The pursuit of happiness. *Scientific American* 274 (5): 70–72.

OECD. n.d. *Better life index*. http://www.oecdbetterlifeindex.org/topics/life-satisfaction/. Accessed 2 June 2015.

Oxford Economics. 2014. *Another penny saved: The economic benefits of higher US household saving*.

Parker, K. 2014. Parenthood and happiness: It's more complicated than you think. *Pew Research Center*.

Pate, K. and P. Day. 2015. *Reflections on the CFED thrift book event*. Corporation for Enterprise Development.

Pauchant, T., and C.A. Dumas. 1991. Abraham Maslow and Heinz Kohut: A comparison. *Journal of Humanistic Psychology* 31 (2): 49–71.

Pearlin, L.I., and M. Rosenberg. 1952. Propaganda techniques in institutional advertising. *Public Opinion Quarterly* 16(1): 5–26.

Phelps, E.S. 1975. *"Introduction," altruism, morality, and economic theory*. New York: Russell Sage Foundation.

Phillips, K. 2011. The manufactured wants and unmet needs of young America. *Forbes*.

Piliavin, J.A. 2009. Altruism and helping: The evolution of a field. *Social Psychology Quarterly* 72 (3): 209–225.

Piliavin, I., J. Rodin, and J.A. Piliavin. 1969. Good Samaritanism: An underground phenomenon? *Journal of Personality and Social Psychology* 13: 288–299.

Pindyck, R., and D. Rubinfeld. 2009. *Microeconomics 7 ed*. Upper Saddle River: Prentice Hall.

Putnam, R. 2000. *Bowling alone: The collapse and revival of American community*. New York: Simon & Schuster.

Rittenberg, L., and T. Tregarthen. 2011. Principles of macroeconomics. N.p.: Saylor Academy

Roper, J.E., and D.M. Zin. 2013. Revealed preference theory. *Encyclopædia Britannica Online*. http://www.britannica.com/EBchecked/topic/1952214/revealed-preference-theory. Accessed 9 June 2015.

Rotman, D. 2013. How technology is destroying jobs. *Technology Review*.

Santilli, P. 1983. The informative and persuasive functions of advertising: A moral appraisal. *Journal of Business Ethics* 2(1): 27–33.

S. v. "Asceticism". 2002. *Encyclopaedia Britannica Online*. https://www.britannica.com/topic/asceticism. Accessed 17 September 2015.

Schwartz, S. 2010. Basic values: How they motivate and inhibit prosocial behavior. In *Prosocial motives, emotions, and behavior: The better angels of our nature*, ed. M. Mikulincer and P.R. Shaver, 221–241. Washington: American Psychological Association Press.

Sen, A. 1982. *Choice, welfare and masurement*. London: Basil Blackwell.

Sengupta, S.S. 2011. Growth in human motivation: Beyond Maslow. *Indian Journal of Industrial Relations* 47 (1): 102–116.

Shaver, R. 2014. "Egoism". *Stanford encyclopedia of philosophy*. http://stanford.library.usyd.edu.au/entries/egoism/. Accessed 23 June 2015.

Shughart, W.F.I.I. 2008. Public choice. In *The concise encyclopedia of economics*, ed. D.R. Henderson. Indianapolis: Liberty Fund, Library of Economics and Liberty.

Sirgy, M.J., A.C. Michalos, A.L. Ferriss, R.A. Easterlin, D. Patrick, and W. Pavot. 2006. The quality-of-life (QOL) research movement: Past, present, and future. *Social Indicators Research* 76 (3): 343–466.

Smith, A. 1776. *The wealth of nations, modern library edition*. New York: Random House.

Sober, E. 2000. Psychological egoism. In *The Blackwell guide to ethical theory*, ed. H. LaFollette, 129–148. Oxford: Blackwell.

Spiro, M.E. 2004. Utopia and its discontents: The kibbutz and its historical vicissitudes. *American Anthropologist* 106(3): 556–568.

Steele, W.R., et al. 2008. The role of altruistic behavior, empathetic concern, and social responsibility motivation in blood donation behavior. *Transfusion* 48 (1): 43–54.

Stevenson, B., and J. Wolfers. 2008. Economic growth and subjective well-being: Reassessing the Easterlin paradox. In *Brookings papers on economic activity*.

Stigler, G. 1987. *The theory of price*. New York: Macmillan Publishing Company.

Stone, A.A., and C. Mackie. 2013. *Subjective well-being: Measuring happiness, suffering, and other dimensions of experience*.

Sugden, R. 2005. Correspondence of sentiments: An explanation of the pleasure of social interaction. In *Economics and happiness: Framing the analysis*, ed. L. Bruni and P.L. Porta. New York: Oxford University Press.

Sweet, E., A. Nandi, E. Adam, and T. McDade. 2013. The high price of debt: Household financial debt and its impact on mental and physical health. *Social Science & Medicine* 91: 94–100.

Tännsjö, T. 2007. Narrow hedonism. *Journal of Happiness Studies* 8 (1): –79.

Taormina, R.J., and J.H. Gao. 2013. Maslow and the motivation hierarchy: measuring satisfaction of the needs. *American Journal of Psychology* 126 (2): 155–177.

Thaler, R.H., and C.R. Sunstein. 2003. Libertarian paternalism. *The American Economic Review* 93 (2): 175–179.

Transparency International. 2014. *Corruption perceptions index 2014: Results*. http://www.transparency.org/cpi2014/results. Accessed 2 June 2015.

Tresch, R.W. 2008. *Public sector economics*. New York: Palgrave Macmillan.

Tucker, D.M. 1991. *The decline of thrift in America: Our cultural shift from saving to spending*. Santa Barbara: Greenwood Publishing Group.

United Nations. 2006. *Report of the independent expert for United Nations study on violence against children*. http://www.unicef.org/violencestudy/reports/SG_violencestudy_en.pdf.

———. 2011. Taking the measure of volunteering. In *State of the world's volunteerism report 2011*, 21.

United Nations Educational, Scientific, and Cultural Organization. 2009. *Fact sheet on the impact of economic crisis on discrimination and xenophobia*.

Van Hoorn, A. 2007. *A short introduction to subjective well-being: Its measurement, correlates and policy uses*. Working Paper. Nijmegen Center for Economics.

Veenhoven, R. 2004. *Happy life years: A measure of gross national happiness*. Centre for Bhutan Studies and GNH Research.

Veenhoven, R., and M. Hagerty. 2006. Rising happiness in nations 1946–2004: A reply to Easterlin. *Social Indicators Research* 79: 421–436.

Weber, M. 1904. Die protestantische Ethik und der Geist des Kapitalismus. English edition: Weber, M. 1930. In *The Protestant ethic and the spirit of capitalism* (trans: Parsons, T.). New York: Scribner.

Webley, P., E.K. Nyhus. 1999. *Representations of saving and saving behavior*. University of Exeter. http://people.exeter.ac.uk/. Accessed 26 June 2015.

Wolfers, J. 2014. How Gary Becker transformed the social sciences. *The New York Times*.

World Health Organization. 2013. Global and regional estimates of violence against women: Prevalence and health effects of intimate partner violence and non-partner sexual violence.

———. n.d. Child abuse and neglect by parents and other caregivers. In *World report on violence and health*, 63.

Xefteris, D. 2012. Formalizing happiness. *Journal of Happiness Studies* 13 (2): 291–311.

Yarrow, A. 2014. *Thrift: The history of an American cultural movement*. Amherst: University of Massachusetts Press.

Yoeli, E., S. Bhanhot, G. Kraft-Todd, D. Rand. 2015. How to get people to pitch in. *The New York Times*.

Chapter 2
Bring Back the Moral Wrestler

The three Abrahamic religions—Judaism, Christianity, and Islam—share a basic conception of human nature. Human beings are morally flawed. People are able to tell right from wrong, but they keep straying. They are assumed—by their very nature—to engage in a life-long wrestle between the better angels of their nature and their debased self. The three religions differ on the weight they accord—and the ways they depict—the forces that make us stray. For Catholicism the original sin plays a greater role than the *yetzer hara* (bad instinct) in Judaism; and neither embrace the Protestant notion of predestination. Islam emphasizes humans' inherent goodness (*fitrah*), which must be upheld against base desires and sinful outside influences. However, all see life as a struggle between doing good and being tempted to violate our sense of what is right. And all believe that we can do better, that is in one form or another of redemption.

In the modern era, social sciences sought to explain human behavior in empirical, secular terms. Each social science has its own conception of human nature; indeed, each has several and changing views of what leads people to make the choices they render. In the process, we gained both a richer conception of human nature but also a less clearly etched one. This chapter suggests that social sciences need to pay more mind to what makes for winning moral wrestling, and to bring the moral wrestler back into focus.

I should note that the traditional view of human nature did not die. First of all, because religion did not fade away—contrary to the expectations of the Enlightenment—but continues to have a major influence on our lives, especially when we deliberate about what is right versus wrong. Second, because our civil secular culture adopted the key religious concepts about human nature. For instance, we examine the moral implications of the stewardship of the environment—for example, when activists point to their calling. However, these conceptions compete, both in personal lives and in making of public policy, with secular understanding of human nature promulgated by social sciences.

Before I proceed to outline the various issues raised by the ways social science explores human nature and its implication for moral wrestling, I cannot stress

© The Author(s) 2018   41
A. Etzioni, *Happiness is the Wrong Metric*, Library of Public Policy and Public Administration 11, https://doi.org/10.1007/978-3-319-69623-2_2

enough that there is no one agreed conception concerning the subject at hand in any of the social sciences, even in neoclassical economics, which seems to be the social science with the highest level of consensus. Hence all statements that follow merely suggest that some members of a given social science guild have contributed to a particular take on moral wrestling—without implying that all or even most members of the discipline subscribe to the given viewpoint.

2.1 Homo Economicus: Not a Wrestler

Economics is considered by academics as the queen of the social sciences, the most prestigious of the lot. It carries more weight in the public and private spheres than all the other social sciences combined. It is not an accident that the White House has a Council of Economic Advisers, but all suggestions to create a Council of Social Advisers have been rebuffed. Of the 19 public policy schools in the US, at least 18 are dominated by economists. In the private sector, MBAs—whose training is more based on economics than on other disciplines—outrank other social scientists.

Economists (to reiterate, many but by no means all or even most) draw on a meta-conception of human nature, often referred to as homo economicus. People are assumed to seek to maximize their *self*-interest, which at least initially was equated with satisfaction drawn from the consumption of goods and services. It is a view that can be referred to as materialistic hedonism. This thesis is often expressed by the use of the term "utility." The original concept of utility, as developed late in the eighteenth century by Jeremy Bentham (1789), is narrow: All actions are directed toward gaining pleasure or avoiding pain.[1] Happiness, satisfaction, and pleasure are treated as synonyms (Gottheil 2013, p. 121). Utilitarian philosophy views pain and pleasure not only as sources of motivation, but also of ethical guides: "It is for them [pain and pleasure] alone to point out what we ought to do" and determine the "standard of right and wrong" (Bentham 1789). Along similar lines, John Stuart Mill (1863) wrote that "actions are right in proportion as they tend to promote happiness; wrong as they tend to produce the reverse of happiness," with happiness defined as "pleasure and the absence of pain." When British philosopher Thomas Hobbes was asked why he gave a coin to a beggar, Hobbes replied that "he made his donation with the sole intent of relieving his own misery at the sight of the beggar" (Aubrey 1898, p. 352). Adam Smith (1776) famously argued in *The Wealth of Nations* that the market as a system relies on each actor pursuing his *self*-interest:

> It is not from the benevolence of the butcher, the brewer or the baker that we expect our dinner, but from their regard to their own interest. We address ourselves not to their humanity but to their self-love, and never talk to them of our own necessities but of their advantages. (p. 14)

---

[1] Jeremy Bentham, *An Introduction to the Principles of Morals and Legislation* (Oxford: Clarendon Press, 1789), accessed June 9 2015 at http://caae.phil.cmu.edu ("By utility is meant that property in any object, whereby it tends to produce benefit, advantage, pleasure, good, or happiness, (all this in the present case comes to the same thing); or (what comes again to the same thing) to prevent the happening of mischief, pain, evil, or unhappiness to the party whose interest is considered.").

The hedonistic version of utilitarianism forms the foundation for much of modern economic theory (Stigler 1987, p. 52). Economists often associated utility with conceptions of material goods and, hence, with income. For example, Libby Rittenberg and Timothy Tregarthen define utility as the "satisfaction" that "people derive from the goods and services they consume and the activities they pursue" (Mankiw 2011, p. 285).

Economists have gone to great lengths to defend their view of what makes people choose. Gift-giving, for example, seems to contradict hedonism because it involves a voluntary reduction of one's own utility, in order to benefit that of others. Economists have responded by arguing that gift-giving is often driven by "cooperative egoism," with those who give gifts expecting reciprocal gifts, reputation, status, approval, or some future benefit (Hammond 1975). And to the extent that gift-giving occurs in the absence of such expected rewards, for example in the case of anonymous gift-giving, economists argue that the giver enjoys a "warm glow" from the act of gift-giving itself (Andreoni 1990).

Likewise, given the fact that participation in religious activities cannot be explained merely by an "expected stream of 'benefits'" over an individual's lifetime, Corry Azzi and Ronald Ehrenberg (1975) introduced the ideas of a "salvation motive" to secure "afterlife consumption." Put simply, they claim, individuals spend on religion in this life with the expectation that they will be rewarded handsomely after death. Needless to say, there is very little evidence to support this proposition.

To avoid exploring the role of moral values in decision making, several economists have gone to great lengths to explain "surprising" behavior. One example is the prevalence of tipping at restaurants. Tipping does not make sense to these economists, particularly as data reveals that people tip about the same amount regardless of whether they intend to return to the restaurant in the future (Kahneman et al. 1986), i.e. those who tip cannot expect to gain anything in return. Tipping is hence regarded as "mysterious or seemingly irrational behavior" (Lynn 2006). Similarly, some economists have postulated that there is a "bequest motive" to explain "excessive" saving (Jurges 2001), as well as a "taste for altruism" on the part of employees of not for profit enterprises, who are said to "derive well-being from participating in the enterprise, and are thus willing to accept a lower wage" (McGinnis 2011).

Often, when gains in income or assets or material goods cannot explain behavior—for instance, somebody giving up a high salary and comfortable life in a suburb to volunteer to treat Ebola patients in Africa, as a Doctor without Borders—such behavior is explained as reflecting one form or another of psychological income (esteem, prestige, or self-rewarding). That is, behavior which seems to be driven by moral values or concern for others or the common good, is held to be self-serving. More about this below.

Quite a few economists have moved away from this definition of utility. Some replaced this with the notion that utility is whatever the person prefers; it does not require a particular content. Thus, Gary Becker's approach rebutted earlier economists' "assumptions of self-interest"; he replaced them with the idea that "individuals maximize [their own] welfare, as they conceive it, whether they be selfish, altruistic, loyal, spiteful, or masochistic" (Wolfers 2014). There still is little room for moral wrestling, as wellbeing of the self (sometimes extended to include that of one's immediate family) governs. However, as long as moral behavior is treated as one's "taste," it disappears in the wash because it is dumped in with all the other preferences. There is no difference, even according to this updated conception of human nature, between volunteering and watching TV, making a donation and removing cash from the passing plate, fighting for one's nation, and avoiding the draft.

Economists rarely explore the conception of a good society. Instead they refer to the social welfare of people. Economies are considered to provide more welfare the more wealth the economy produces is distributed in ways that satisfy more of the preferences of more people (i.e. the greatest happiness of the greatest number). The trouble with this conception—which avoids moral judgment, most importantly of whether any given distribution of economic assets is just—is that it takes for granted that the preferences of people reflect their true will and self. However, once one notes that preferences are affected by advertising and other forms of persuasions, one realizes that any given distribution of wealth needs to be morally assessed.

These concepts, aside from not providing a sound basis for studying moral wrestling, have side effects: Data show that those who embrace them act less morally than others. This was demonstrated when two social scientists organized a game that allowed people to free ride; that is, benefit from the group's efforts without doing their share of the work. Twelve groups participated in the game. In eleven, most participants did rather little free riding; in the twelfth group most everyone did. Turns out, it was full of graduate students in economics (Marwell and Ames 1981).

2.2   Homo Sapiens as Clueless

Over the last decades, a major branch of psychology, referred to as behavioral economics, set out to prove economists wrong and proffer a rather different conception of human nature. Several of these psychologists use the term *Econs* for homo economicus, and *Humans* for homo sapiens. Their findings and their implications have been summarized in a best-selling book, *Thinking, Fast and Slow* by the Nobel Laureate psychologist Daniel Kahneman (2011).

The main finding of behavioral economics, supported by robust evidence from both experiments and field studies, is that people have hardwired, innate, cognitive biases. These lead them to systematically misperceive facts and draw wrong conclusions from them. Because they fear loss more than losing a gain, they see a $1000 salary cut as a much bigger deal than not getting a $1000 raise. They view spending $100 as a major outlay if they just spend $20 on something else, but not if their last purchase cost $300. They do not get around to putting money into a retirement account, even when often reminded, and even if there are strong economic advantages to doing so. And they still are fooled by marketers who charge $3.99 for an item, which people see as costing $3 rather than $4. And so on and so on. Moreover, even people with high IQs, after being trained in statistics, do not function significantly better. That is, their intellectual defects are so strong, education and training cannot do much to remedy these innate, hardwired intellectual flaws (Kahneman 2011).

Richard Thaler is another towering behavioral economist. He served as the President of the American Economic Association and is on the short list of those expected to receive a Nobel Prize in economics in the near future. He wrote a book entitled *Misbehaving* (2015). One may think that he is a behavioral economist who makes deviating from what is considered moral behavior his topic. Actually, for Thaler, "misbehaving" is an ironic term. It happens when people behave—as he finds people very often do—in ways that conflict with the ways economics assume people will behave. We "misbehave" when we act on the basis of poorly collected, poorly analyzed, misunderstood information, from which we draw the wrong conclusions—far from the rational way many economists assume people will act. We stumble through life like drunken sailors.

Behavioral economics as a school has not applied its findings to improve our understanding of moral wrestling. It has focused on trying to convince mainstream economics of the need to adapt its models to the fact that people are, to put it succinctly, not rational creatures. In short, behavioral economics finds that people are clueless but has precious little to say about the ebbs and flows of moral wrestling, above all about what makes us better than we would be otherwise.

2.3 Be Happy

A group of social scientists, drawn from a variety of disciplines, studies what makes people happy. We have seen that a very elementary measurement widely used to study happiness is to simply ask people whether they are happy. For example, an annual study of Europeans asks: "Taking all things together, how would you say things are these days—would you say you're very happy, fairly happy, or not too happy these days?" (Di Tella et al. 2003, p. 810–811). A similar study asks: "Taken all together, how would you say things are these days—would you say that you are very happy, pretty happy, or not too happy?" (Frey and Stutzer 2002, p. 405). Indeed, much of the literature on happiness relies on such self-reporting of happiness (Xefteris 2012, p. 291), as do reports by the prestigious Pew Research Center on parenthood and happiness (Parker 2014).

Questions about happiness (e.g. "Did you smile today?") have been criticized on the grounds that they are like snapshots that capture a person's feelings at a single point in time. Hence, several social scientists turned to ask people questions about "life satisfaction." For example, an often-cited study of life satisfaction is the OECD Better Life Index, which asks people to "evaluate their life as a whole rather than their current feelings." Such wording of the questions respondents are asked may indeed be superior to "did you smile today," but does not get one any closer to studying moral wrestling and what makes for better wrestling.

Most recently, happiness studies sought to broaden their scope by focusing on the question of whether people feel that their life has "meaning." Having a meaningful life is considered more meaningful, than just being happy. However, this concern is also morally neutral. Gang members and Jihadists feel that their lives are as meaningful or more than those who work in most factories and offices.

2.4   It Is All in Our Genes

James Q. Wilson (1993), a renowned political scientist, believed that people have an innate sense of fairness. Studies show that very young toddlers have a sense of empathy. Evolutionary biologists hold that people are sympathetic to others because this moral predisposition was an advantage in the early days when people had to share the spoils of what they hunted and were safer as a group. Those who were not sympathetic got less food and security, and hence they—and their genes—were less likely to survive. A review of the sociobiological argument that people have an altruistic gene will serve to examine other such claims.

This argument can be advanced basically in one of two forms. In one, the gene determines the moral positions of the actor, i.e. moral people are born, not fashioned. However, one cannot help but wonder, given the rapid changes in the extent to which people are altruistic, how these changes could be accounted for by genes, which are set for one's lifetime. For instance, initially, when the German chancellor welcomed a million refugees into Germany, her policy was very widely supported by the German people. However, following a few incidents—sexual assaults during an Oktoberfest, a machete attack—the German people turned out to be much less sympathetic to the same refugees. Such changes, which are very common, are incompatible with the notion that people have genes that make them moral in one way or another. If, on the other hand, one considers genes merely as predispositions—then all the key questions about moral wrestling remain unanswered. What are the factors that make people heed their genetic predisposition versus disregard it? Nurture it or fight it? In short, it does not seem that we will find in the genes a scientific basis for or an understanding of what makes some people better moral wrestlers than others, or changes their achievements over time.

The softer social sciences—anthropology, sociology, and psychology—did better in providing secular and empirical understanding of moral wresting. In the process, though, we shall see, they opened a Pandora's Box.

2.5   Anthropology Liberates: But Engenders Cultural Relativism

Ruth Benedict had and has a major effect on the conception of human nature. Benedict (1934) in *Patterns of Culture* described the values of the Kwakiutl of the Pacific Northwest, the Pueblo of New Mexico, and the Dobu culture of New Guinea, and in a later work that of the Japanese. She stressed that although to Western eyes the moral values of these different societies (or tribes) may seem strange, if not objectionable, each made sense once they were understood within the context of the moral culture of the various societies.

Viewed in the context in which her works and those of other leading anthropologists (especially Franz Boas and Margaret Mead) were published at the time—in the mid-twentieth century—they served as a major antidote to cultural imperialism, to the arrogant but widely-held notion among colonizing nations that they were called upon to bring light to the primitives. At the same time, by arguing that the values of the different cultures were merely different rather than some being morally superior to others, she and her colleagues in effect promoted moral relativism.

True, some social scientists tried to save the day by maintaining that these anthropological positions amounted merely to 'methodological relativism,' the need for unbiased studying of cultures different than those of the social scientist who did the study. However, their findings were often cited and commonly used to support philosophical relativism, the suspension of moral judgment, which takes the oomph out of moral wrestling. Once one takes the position that x believe in monogamy but y believe in polygamy, and that x has no basis on which to tell y that x's choice is more moral than that of y—one pulls the rug out from under all cross-cultural moral claims. And because the same is true for subcultures within each society, these intra-societal judgments are also left without a firm foundation.

Seeking an exit, various social scientists have argued that some values are held by all cultures, and hence could serve as a solid foundation for moral judgments. However, it turns out that even the most elementary moral value, thou shalt not kill, is not universally shared. Of course many cultures approve killing outsiders—whether they are Nazis, Communists, or infidels. However, many cultures also strongly lionize killing some of their own, for instance in so-called honor killings, in which fathers and brothers kill their daughters or sisters if they bring shame on the family. No exit here.

2.6 Sociology: Collectivizing the Wrestle

A major sociological insight is that what makes people more or less moral human beings, how well they wrestle, is The System: the power structure, the economy, and the culture. People abuse drugs, commit crimes, and walk out on their children mainly not because of their "bad character" but because they have been economically deprived, socially disadvantaged, politically disempowered, or otherwise alienated. The main moral wrestling does not take place within the person but with society. For instance, social movements—such as the women's rights, civil rights, and gay rights movements—made American society a less immoral place. Banks, deregulated, which then sold subprime mortgages to millions of people and evicted them when they could not pay, and resisted reforms that were supposed to protect future millions from a similar fate, are not so much the work of "bad" people, but of a flawed system. The moral wrestler does not need better character education but political reforms, driven by societal changes in the distribution of power and assets, and parallel changes in the values fostered by the collective culture.

Sociologists (and social psychologists) added, on the personal level, the study of "socialization," the process through which newborn children are turned from animals into social creatures. This is achieved as the newborns bond with their caregivers (often their parents), who in turn draw on these bonds to implant moral values in those in their care. When these children grow older, they are exposed to other sources of values—in school, on TV, and in social media, through peer pressure, and in places of worship. In the process, these growing children slowly develop their own value profile. These are then reinforced by what sociologists call "informal social controls," the approval and disapproval of others with whom people have meaningful social bonds, mainly their extended families, friends, and other community members.

One may wonder what all this has to do with moral wrestling. Sociologists find that children are just as likely to be "socialized" into a Nazi culture as into a liberal one, into the values of a KKK community as into a progressive one. Nowhere is the basic moral neutrality of this core sociological conception of human nature more in evidence than in the way sociologists treat the concept of being a deviant. In traditional cultures, people whose conduct differed from the one prescribed by the prevailing social values were labeled deviants. Lumped together in this category were gay people, political dissidents, mental patients, women who smoked or worked outside the home, and criminals. They were all stigmatized and subjected to various correctional efforts and punishments.

Sociologists argue that these people were merely committed to a different set of values. Albert Cohen (2008) writes: "It is commonplace that normative rules vary enormously from one social system to another. It follows that no behavior is deviant in itself but only insofar as it violates the norms of some social system." Here sociology has made a major contribution to the liberal moral culture, to tolerance; it informs people that one who is considered deviant is actually just different. And—that one who was considered deviant yesterday will not be viewed so today or tomorrow. In other words, sociology does embrace moral relativism not only on the societal but also on the personal level. It follows that some people may be more conformist than others but it does not make them better people, morally speaking. Accordingly, one can make people conform more but this does not make them better moral wrestlers, more able to figure out what is right, and more able to live up to their moral obligations.

2.7 Clinical Psychology: From Freud to Morally Neutral

Like all great texts, the work of Sigmund Freud can be read in different ways. However, for the purposes at hand, one basic and often shared interpretation will suffice. Freud, in effect, incorporated in a secular conception the age old, religious conception of a moral wrestler. Accordingly, by Freud, people are struggling between the pulls of their debased self (the id) and the commands of the moral voice (the super ego). Sometimes, and under some conditions, one side prevails, and sometimes the other. Moreover, people construct out of this give and take their own personality (ego). And although the urges of the id can be channeled into pro-social behavior (through sublimation), such conversion is never fully successful. The id gnaws; moral wrestling is never ending (Moreover, the sublimation exacts its own psychological costs, captured in *Civilization and its Discontents* [Freud 1930]).

Clinical psychology has a number of different schools and gurus. By and large, though, they tend to help the person liberate him or herself from the moralistic demands of their society and follow his or her own star. Thus, Philip Cushman (1990) finds that clinical therapeutics see the ideal individual as one who has gained a "masterful self", who can "function in a highly autonomous, isolated way," and is "self-sufficient" (p. 604). That is, free from the restraints morality demands society puts on people's desires. Therapy liberates people from the demons of their past and leaves them free to follow whatever they deem good.

Jerome Frank (1978) sees psychotherapies as sharing a value system that accords "primacy to individual self-fulfillment," such as, "maximum self-awareness, unlimited access to one's own feelings, increased autonomy and creativity" (p. 6–7). Although Frank recognizes the benefit of self-realization, he warns against modern psychotherapy's focus on promoting personal happiness as its main focus. Frank points out that the literature of psychotherapy accords little attention to virtues and values such as "the redemptive power of suffering, acceptance of one's lot in life, adherence to tradition, self-restraint and moderation" (Frank 1978, p. 7). There is much to be said for freeing people from their inner demons, reflecting the defective ways in which they were brought up. However, psychotherapy tends to exorcise at the same time the moral dictates promoted by society. Those do deserve critical examination and reform, but people should not be left in a moral vacuum, especially if one seeks to understand under what conditions we become better moral wrestlers.

2.8 Social Psychology: Powerful Narratives

Psychology is fragmented into fields that are as different from one another as poetry is from a car manual. Some psychologies are concerned with other matters than human nature, let alone moral wrestling. For example, comparative psychology focuses on animal behavior, in the expectation that studies on rats, dogs, or monkeys, for example, will yield valuable insights about human behavior. Biological psychology and cognitive psychology are also otherwise occupied. Even abnormal psychology studies "mental, emotional and behavioral aberrations" but not moral ones. In a typical textbook, *Introduction to Psychology* by James W. Kalat, which runs 616 pages and provides an overview of the various schools of psychology— two pages deal with moral variables. And these deal with moral reasoning and not moral motivation and commitments.

Quite a few psychologists have adopted self-centered, self-satisfying, hedonistic perspectives. Some have even argued that suicide represents a utility-maximizing behavior for an individual whose "total discounted lifetime utility [...] reaches zero" (Hamermesh and Soss 1974).

All the preceding statements refer to various sub-disciplines of psychology, their dominant texts and concepts, and many followers. However, each of these psychologies has individual scholars who made contributions to the study of moral wrestling, like Jonathan Haidt. Also, there is an important but small group of psychologists who study moral emotions, including Joshua Knobe, Stephen Darwall, and June Tangney. However, their work is not widely known and surely has not affected most of psychology as a review of even the most recent textbooks reveals.

A major contribution psychology had and is making to our understanding of moral wrestling are several very powerful narratives that grew out of experiments psychologists have conducted. Although these are works of scientific research rather than ethical deliberations, they resulted in major narratives that are helping people in their moral wrestling. For example, during the 1960s, psychologist Stanley Milgram (1963) conducted an experiment on people's obedience to authority figures after he learned about Nazi war criminal Adolf Eichmann's defense in the Nuremberg trials that he was "just following orders." In the study, people were instructed to pull switches that they believed delivered painful shocks to other participants. Sixty-five percent of participants delivered the maximum shock, a powerful indication of people's susceptibility to unethical leadership.

Philip Zimbardo carried out a prison experiment at Stanford that investigated the extent to which people's bad behavior can be attributed to their assigned social roles (Haney et al. 1973). In this study, participants were randomly assigned roles as guards or as inmates in a simulated prison. The "guards" quickly became aggressive and abusive, and the "inmates" began to develop emotional disorders so severe that the 2-week study had to be ended after only 6 days. The findings created a powerful cautionary tale about people's tendency to conform to social expectations, whatever their moral content. Since then, the findings of these and other such psychological studies have been cited in numerous essays and classrooms about ethics; in sermons by ministers, priests, and rabbis; and made into a movie. They are often used to warn people about the dangers of rising demagogues—and the need to be prepared to disobey orders that violate basic moral principles. Such narratives are a powerful tool of moral education. They make people into better moral wrestlers.

2.9   In Conclusion

Religion provides a conception of human nature and human fate in which the struggle between good (moral) intentions and the forces that work to prevent them from being followed—plays a key role. The Enlightenment led to a quest for a secular, evidence-based conception of human nature. Economists advanced a conception that has little room for moral wrestling. Behavioral economists backed the view of the person as intellectually limited, but the moral implications of these shortcomings remain to be spelled out. Social biology fashioned genetic explanations that treat moral behavior as either pre-determined or as needing explanation from other branches of social sciences. Anthropology made a major contribution when it liberated the moral wrestler from the association with white supremacy, but left him without a firm moral grounding. Sociology collectivized the moral wrestling, a major contribution. Many psychologists avoid the subject, but some psychological studies do provide powerful insights into the moral nature of people and the struggle between their debased self and their nobler parts.

In short, some social sciences are blind to a critical element of human nature and of the good society. They add little to the understanding of the forces that make individuals more versus less moral. Indeed, some seem to unwittingly undermine the lifelong moral wrestling that is a defining characteristic of human nature. Other social sciences do improve our understanding of moral wrestling—however, in the process they have undermined the very foundations of moral judgments. It seems that the place to look for new grounds on which to understand the forces that can make people better may be in the works of those individual social scientists who do not conform to the norms of their disciplines.

References

Andreoni, J. 1990. Impure altruism and donations to public goods: A theory of warm-glow giving. *The Economic Journal* 100 (401): 464–477.

Aubrey, J. 1898. In *Brief lives*, ed. A. Clark. Oxford: Clarendon Press.

Azzi, C., and R. Ehrenberg. 1975. Household allocation of time and church attendance. *Journal of Political Economy* 83 (1): 27–56.

Benedict, R. 1934. *Patterns of culture*. New York: Houghton Mifflin.

Bentham, J. 1789. *An introduction to the principles of morals and legislation*. Oxford: Clarendon Press. Retrieved from http://caae.phil.cmu.edu. Accessed 9 June 2015.

Cohen, A.K. 2008. Deviant behavior. In *International encyclopedia of the social sciences*. Retrieved from http://www.encyclopedia.com/social-sciences/applied-and-social-sciences-magazines/deviant-behavior.

Cushman, P. 1990. Why the self is empty. *American Psychologist* 45 (5): 599–611.

Di Tella, R., R.J. McCulloch, and A.J. Oswald. 2003. The macroeconomics of happiness. *The Review of Economics and Statistics* 85 (4): 809–827.

Frank, J.D. 1978. *Psychotherapy and the human predicament*. New York: Schocken.

Freud, S. 1989. *Civilization and its discontents*. New York: W.W. Norton & Company. (Original work published 1930).

Frey, B.S., and A. Stutzer. 2002. What can economists learn from happiness research? *Journal of Economic Literature* 40 (2): 402–435.

Gottheil, F. 2013. *Principles of economics*. 7th ed. Boston: Cengage Learning.

Hamermesh, D.S., and N.M. Soss. 1974. An economic theory of suicide. *Journal of Political Economy* 82 (1): 83–98. Retrieved from http://www.becker-posner-blog.com. Accessed 26 June 2015.

Hammond, P. 1975. Charity: Altruism or cooperative egoism? In *Altruism, morality, and economic theory*, ed. E.S. Phelps. New York: Sage Found.

Haney, C., C. Banks, and P.G. Zimbardo. 1973. Interpersonal dynamics in a simulated prison. *International Journal of Criminology and Penology* 1: 69–97.

Jurges, H. 2001. Do Germans save to leave an estate? An examination of the bequest motive. *The Scandinavian Journal of Economics* 103 (3): 391–414.

Kahneman, D. 2011. *Thinking, fast and slow*. New York: Farrar, Straus and Giroux.

Kahneman, D., J.L. Knetsch, and R.H. Thaler. 1986. Fairness as a constraint on profit seeking: Entitlements in the market. *The American Economic Review* 76 (4): 728–741.

Lynn, M. 2006. *Tipping in restaurants and around the globe: An interdisciplinary review*. Cornell University, School of Hospitality Administration. http://scholarship.sha.cornell.edu/articles/99. Accessed 26 June 2015.

Mankiw, G. 2011. *Principles of microeconomics*. 6th ed. Boston: Cengage Learning.

Marwell, G., and R. Ames. 1981. Economists free ride, does anyone else? *Journal of Public Economics* 15: 295–310.

McGinnis, J. 2011. The young and the restless: Generation Y in the nonprofit workforce. *Public Administration Quarterly* 35 (3): 342–362.

Milgram, S. 1963. Behavioral study of obedience. *The Journal of Abnormal and Social Psychology* 67 (4): 371–378.

Mill, J.S. 1863. *Utilitarianism*. London: Parker, Son & Bourn, West Strand. Retrieved from www.utilitarianism.com. Accessed 9 June 2015.

Parker, K. 2014. *Parenthood and happiness: It's more complicated than you think*. Pew Research Center. http://www.pewresearch.org/fact-tank/2014/02/07/parenthood-and-happiness-its-more-complicated-than-you-think/.

Smith, A. 1937. *The wealth of nations*. New York: Random House. (Original work published 1776).

Stigler, G. 1987. *The theory of price*. New York: Macmillan Publishing Company.

Thaler, R.H. 2015. *Misbehaving*. New York: W.W. Norton.

Wilson, J.Q. 1993. *The moral sense*. New York: The Free Press.

Wolfers, J. 2014. How Gary Becker transformed the social sciences. *New York Times*. https://nyti.ms/2vtVjCN.

Xefteris, D. 2012. Formalizing happiness. *Journal of Happiness Studies* 13 (2): 291–311.

Part II
Human Nature

Chapter 3
Crossing the Rubicon

Neoclassical economists have treated preferences as given and stable. This assumption allows these economists to explain changes in choice behavior over time or across different markets largely in terms of differences in income and prices. However, as we shall see, there are strong reasons to hold that preferences change over time and differ from one culture (and subculture) to another. Hence, this chapter argues that one needs to include in the study of choice behavior the forces that form preferences in the first place and those that reshape them over time. Moreover, these forces cannot be studied by relying upon the concepts and basic assumptions upon which economists rely. It hence seems necessary to "cross the Rubicon" that divides economics from the other social sciences such as sociology and psychology. These disciplines study many non-economic variables that account for the formation of and changes to preferences, but have not formed a consolidated theory of the forces that drive preferences and of the interactions among these and economic variables. If the turf on the economics side of the Rubicon—in which only preferences are found—is frozen and barren, on the non-economics side one is easily lost in the jungle.

Part I of this chapter examines the original position of many neoclassical economists on this matter and their various attempts to adapt economic theories to account for the observation that preferences are dynamic rather than stable. It concludes that the neoclassical paradigm employed by mainstream economics and its allied disciplines (Mäki 2009, pp. 352–353)—as well as the modified versions that followed—do not adequately explain changes in preference. Part II outlines the basic conceptualizations used by psychologists and sociologists to study preferences, and reveals the absence of a consolidated theory.

This chapter draws on "Crossing the Rubicon: Including Preference Formation in Theories of Choice Behavior" in *Challenge* 57 (2), (March/April 2014): 65–79.

3.1   From Given and Stable to Internally Modified

The definition of "preferences" is subject to some deliberation and debate.[1] However, a widely-used definition in economics is a ranking of possible choices prior to any consideration of resource constraints. Hausman (2011), for example, defines the concept as "total subjective comparative evaluations"—that is, a ranking of options based on all relevant information about value (p. 10), including social expectations and anticipated pleasure. Preferences are said to be "revealed" by the choices people make. However, critics held that this definition makes preferences tautological, because there are two observations based on the same data point. Whatever the person buys shows both his preference and what he actually got, hence there is no way of telling if he had a preference prior to the act of buying that influenced his choice. Thus economists write that a person who never consumed wine suddenly bought a bottle of wine—which shows that he must have had a preference for wine. In this kind of formulation, adding the term preference adds nothing to our understanding of choice behavior.

This flaw can be corrected if one presumes that preferences entail at least some measure of consistency over time, a choice predisposition. To return to the example just cited, one would say that the particular person's preference is not to consume wine and would seek to understand what made him act against his preference.

The field of economics has largely ignored the study of preference formation, as reflected by the consensus among economists that utility and preferences are "purely introspective" and subjective, and therefore beyond the scope of economic modeling (Keita 2012, p. 77). Above all, they assumed that economic agents were closed systems when making choices and that their preferences were stable (Martins 2011, p. 253). Stigler and Becker (1977) capture this quintessential neoclassical perspective in their famous quote: "One does not argue over tastes for the same reason that one does not argue over the Rocky Mountains—both are there, will be there next year, too, and are the same to all men" (Rizvi 2001, pp. 141–142). In short, economists either simply ignored preferences or deemed it "not useful for economics" (Rizvi 2001, pp. 141–142) to assume that preferences are changeable or to study their formation—sometimes referred to as "opening the preferences" (Etzioni 1985). Those economists who did recognize that preferences may be changeable did not advocate that preference formation be considered "part of the corpus of orthodox theory" because such a study would detract from the study of "logical action" in economics and thus "belong[ed] to sociology" (Drakopoulos 2012, pp. 541, 542). Economists thus largely ignored or left the study of preference formation to other disciplines, particularly those that adhere to paradigms other than the neoclassical one preferred by economics.[2] Moreover, several leading economists, particularly

---

[1] Economics' treatment of how people make decisions *based on* their preferences—that is, "rationally"—is a separate subject not discussed in this chapter. Rational choice theory has been itself subject to a whole range of criticisms.

[2] The question of what form preferences take, however, was very much a subject of economic inquiry. The discipline struggled for some time to describe preferences without having to model

law and economics scholars, led by Becker, have extended the application of preference-free analysis[3] to explain *non-economic* choices such as the selection of a mate (Frank 2011; Cigno 2011; Becker 1973), the decision to lead a life of crime (Matsueda et al. 2006, pp. 95–97; Becker 1968), the choice to have children (Becker 1993; Ermisch 1988), and even to choices involving religious behavior (Blasi 2009) and suicide (Chen et al. 2010; Hamermesh and Soss 1974).

The stability, exogeneity, and universality assumptions that substituted for an empirically-based theory of preference formation are crucial for neoclassical economics; if preferences are in flux due to social factors—such as leadership, persuasion, cultural changes, and social movements—and psychological factors that vary among individuals and societies,[4] neoclassical predictions about choice behavior become subject to a long series of caveats that limit their relevance (Martins 2011, p. 253). For instance, one can no longer predict what people will buy mainly on the bases of changes in prices and their income if their purchases are also affected by changes in what the culture considers proper items to consume or if people's relevant emotions are manipulated by advertising.

3.1.1 The Economists' Treatment of Preference Formation

Faced with mounting evidence that preferences are changeable, neoclassical economics has adapted the neoclassical paradigm in three major ways via the following approaches.[5]

Originally and in many current treatments, economists have not been concerned with preferences one way or the other, but have studied the effects of changes in income, prices, or some other economic factor on choice behavior. Thus, if saving increases between Time 1 and Time 2, economics will seek to determine the extent to which this change may be due to increased income of the population or to increased yields on savings.

---

the complicated "black box" processes by which they were formed. Economists largely concluded—following Samuelson—that choices "revealed" preferences. This revealed preference theory escaped the problem of preference formation's being a psychological and social phenomenon by relying instead on positivist, empirical data. This helped the discipline describe preferences for the purposes of economic inquiry, but offered no insight into how they were actually *formed*.

[3] Some recent articles that generally adhere to the idea that human behavior can be entirely explained by economic factors have relaxed the definition of cost, income, and utility, for example by suggesting that failure to follow socially prescribed behaviors leads to "costs" like guilt and increased stress.

[4] Or if preferences are "fuzzier" than they are clear and fixed. "This set of assumptions – and the precise conception of preferences it employs – is therefore essential to all neoclassical modeling" (Norton 1994, p. 312) and preferences are "marked by a certain amount of fuzziness and although their actual choices are perforce 'exact,' they are nonetheless the outcome of fuzzy preferences" (Basu 1983).

[5] Although this list is not comprehensive, it represents a sort of sketch of the ways in which the discipline has responded to the problem of modeling variable preferences.

Some economists recognize preferences, and accept that preference rankings are affected by values and a wealth of other "motivators," but see no need or reason to study what shapes and reshapes these preferences. They treat them as given and stable, and start their analysis with these preferences in place. Thus these economists recognize that, for various reasons, the Japanese have a much stronger preference for saving than Americans and even that this difference may be due to their culture rather than due to some factors modeled by economists. However, their analysis simply places whatever these preferences are at Time 1, and presumes that any that changes occurred in saving after that are due to changes in income and yield or other such economic factors—but not due to changes in preferences for saving, say due to changes in the culture. For instance, the strong emotional and political reaction to rising public deficits and debt reflect a conservative normative shift rather than clear economic consequences.

A merit of a study by Charness and Rabin (2002) is that it does find that people tend to prefer choices characterized by fairness, equal distribution, social welfare, and treating people the way they "deserve" to be treated. Moreover, they study the implications of these preferences for particular economic situations. However, they do not attempt to describe how propensities for fairness and so forth developed in the first place.

Other economists acknowledge that one needs to study the forces that shape preferences. However, they delegate these tasks to other social sciences. For instance, Dietrich and List (2013) hold that an individual's preferences "depend on certain 'motivationally salient' properties of the alternatives over which the preferences are held." They hold that each alternative has characteristics, that individuals prefer particular characteristics, and that understanding those preferred characteristics explains preference formation and change. Individuals focus on some properties more than they do on others, and the set of such properties is known as their "motivational state." This motivational state "solves" the problem of understanding how competing motivators interact to form preferences. Dietrich and List then point out that "the question of which properties are motivationally salient for an agent in a given context [...] is a psychological issue, which our formalism by itself cannot settle" (p. 615).

Other economists assert that preferences can be studied by using economic concepts and models. For example, behavioral economics has consistently found that human beings are risk-averse, such that people prefer avoiding losses to obtaining gains of similar size. Some economists have hence concluded that preferences are reference-dependent—that is, one's economic "status quo" influences one's economic preferences—and have held that they can thus be modeled, perhaps without recourse to the other social sciences.[6]

---

[6] "By directly constructing reference-dependent utility from consumption utility and assuming that the reference point is endogenously determined as rational expectations about outcomes, our theory provides an algorithm for translating a 'classical' reference-independent model into the corresponding reference-dependent one." When describing the situations to which the model might not apply, no mention is made of alternative factors that complicate their model (Kőszegi and Rabin 2006: 1155).

Although many variations on the idea that preferences are a product of one's economic environment exist, two main theories have developed within economics literature, specifically within the literature dealing with consumption. The first, intrinsic habit formation, holds that individuals' past consumption influences their future consumption preferences (Rozen 2010, p. 1341). To stay with our example: how much one seeks to save in the future is presumed to be affected by how much one saved in the past. The second, preference interdependence, sometimes referred to as "keeping up with the Joneses" or as "extrinsic habit formation," holds that the consumption patterns of others influence an individual's consumption preferences (Kapteyn et al. 1980, p. 125). That is, one's acquaintances' savings influence one's own savings.

Some attempt to combine both approaches and provide a unified theory of endogenous preference formation which holds that "an individual's welfare [preference] function is *identical* to the distribution of consumption patterns the individual has observed over time. This includes both his own consumption and the consumption [of] others in his social reference group" (Kapteyn et al. 1980, pp. 151–152).

One notes that the assertion that preferences are affected by economic factors does not contradict the fact that preferences are partially determined by *non-economic* factors—and thus, that any economic model of preference formation that limits itself to economic variables is partial.

Finally, economists sought to treat norms (defined as a specification of normative values), which play a major factor in shaping preferences according to psychologists and sociologists, as part of the environment. That is, the economic agents include the costs of violating them or the benefits from abiding by them in their rational analysis of their decision making. Psychologists and economists responded by arguing that norms (and the informal social controls that help enforce them) work on a subconscious level ("below the radar screen") and hence cannot be subjected to this kind of decision making and modeled in that way. Moreover, norms are internalized and become part of the self.

There seems to be no area of human choice in which the discrepancy between the neoclassical assumptions of preferences (including all the various adaptations) and the empirical evidence are further apart than in the study of persuasion, in particular of persuasive advertising. Adherents of the neoclassical approach to preferences have gone to great lengths to maintain their assumptions. "The classical economic theory of markets with perfect competition and rational agents is a deductive theory that requires almost no contact with empirical data once its assumptions are accepted" (Simon 1959, pp. 254–255)—a form of analysis that, supported by abstract models and mathematical proofs, helps to protect the economic theory from seemingly incompatible empirical evidence about choice behavior. Economists hence maintain that advertising—which is widely found to appeal to people's emotions, irrational fears, and cognitive biases to persuade individuals to purchase products[7]—is merely informative. However, evidence shows that a great deal of

---

[7] "Obviously there is a lot of pandering to System 1 in advertising. I don't know if you have in mind the ads that encourage you to trade so as to beat the market and become rich. Those ads are clearly

advertising does next to nothing to increase individuals' knowledge about a subject (Lee 1997),[8] and instead seeks to sway them subconsciously.[9] Moreover, studies support the popular assertion that advertising is primarily about "manufacturing need" (Phillips 2011)—that is, firms do not produce goods in response to people's preferences but, instead, induce preferences for the goods they seek to market. Individuals never "needed" deodorant until deodorant manufacturers convinced them that their odors were "bad" ones that required correction. Appeals to impulses are antithetical to the idea of an informative advertisement intended to help "rational" consumers carefully reason about which product best suits their actual needs. In short, advertising demonstrates that the economic perspective on preference formation is far from complete—and that attempts to maintain it are guided by what Daniel Kahneman calls "theory-induced blindness" (Kahneman 2011).

In brief, the discipline of economics has historically "lack[ed] an empirical theory about the content of individual preferences" (Witt 1991, p. 563), and attempts to resolve this deficiency have so far been unsatisfactory. All of these observations— and the criticisms of these observations—show that a plausible theory of choice behavior must incorporate the social and psychological factors that initially form and continuously modify preferences, and must provide a specific model of how they do so.

3.1.2   The Ultimate Caveat

Faced with the preceding observations, economists argue that economic theory "needs" stable preferences not merely in order to assume that changes in behavior can be explained to a satisfactory level by economic variables, but also in order to assess the contribution of the economy to general welfare. The economy is assumed to function well when it provides the goods preferred by people at prices such that

---

directed at overconfident people, and are intended to enhance their overconfidence. Most of the advertisement is addressed to System 1, not to System 2. There is very little information in advertising, and anybody who watches programs with loads of advertising, such as the Super Bowl for example, would be hard put to find any information about any product. It is very striking—there is none. It's all appealing to different types of emotions" (Kahneman 2012, p. 10).

[8] To cite one example, using a sampling of individuals in non-battleground states during the 2000 presidential election, Huber and Arceneaux (2007, p. 957) found that people are not usually made more informed by political advertisements; they are simply persuaded *without* becoming more knowledgeable about the policy subjects or candidates under consideration.

[9] "Advertising in contemporary society is generally regarded as having two central and correlative functions, that of informing and that of persuading consumers. The informative function is likely to be stressed by defenders of the advertising practice, for by providing information to consumers about products, services, and prices advertising allows the consumer to make reasoned choices about the things on which he/she will spend his/her money" (Santilli 1983, p. 27).

"The overwhelming bulk of advertising in American mass media is designed to promote the sale of products and services" (Pearlin and Rosenberg 1952, p. 5).

supply equals demand. Individuals are thought to vote with their purchasing dollars so as to guide the economy toward that blessed state of equilibrium, which is considered the "holy grail" of neoclassical economics. If preferences can be manipulated by culture or corporations, by social pressures or advertising, then an economy that satisfies those preferences would appear not to serve the people but, rather, the manipulators who choose the preferences. Such a revelation would require economists to study the relative power of persuasion and political power exercised by various elites, a far cry from economics. Moreover, it calls into question the very fundamental precept that people are free agents, and undermines the value of liberty.

However, it is possible to acknowledge the reality of manipulation and the (re) formation of preferences by a variety of social forces while noting that there are limits to the extent to which people can be manipulated.

The cultural theory of preference formation posits something similar: that individual preferences come about when a person determines his or her group identities, and then observes the norms associated with those groups. Certain options are socially validated by those with whom an individual identifies, which leads her to adopt preferences for those options using heuristics and schemas (Wildavsky 1987, pp. 9–10). The responsive communitarian framework, to which this author subscribes, suggests that human beings are "multiple" beings, capable of acting in line with their internalized social norms (*superego*) and their pursuit of pure pleasure (*id*) (Etzioni 1988, pp. 11–12). The grand challenge facing the non-economic social sciences is that of determining how and to what degree each of these multiple selves, social norms, and processes of social validation contributes to specific preferences.

Thousands of studies examine various elements of the general process of preference formation. However, they have not yielded reached a consensus regarding which variables to study or about the relationship among them, that is, have not been consolidated into an overarching theory of preference formations and dynamics. Instead, a thousand flowers bloom. Various studies that stress the role of broad categories of variables relevant to preference formation and change include biological (Witt 1991) and neurological (Simion 2005) factors and processes, cognitive patterns and heuristics, social norms (Bicchieri 2010, p. 297; Binmore 2010, p. 142), demographic characteristics, structural positions, and a host of cultural factors. There are also numerous differences of scholarly opinion about how socialization occurs; for example, not all psychologists agree that children attach to and attempt to emulate their primary caregiver in a single way, and there is no consensus about the relative influence exercised by each individual in a child's life (Maccoby 1992). Additionally, because many of these processes and social factors influence preferences subconsciously—they operate "under the radar"—social scientists further disagree about how to model them objectively, without resorting to imprecise subjective ways of evaluating their influence.

A full survey of the non-economic approaches to preference formation and the hundreds and thousands of precise variables thought to play a part is beyond the scope of this chapter. Suffice it to say that the non-economic disciplines have not yet presented a *consolidated* theory of preference formation. Furthermore, as was previously demonstrated, the relatively unified theory provided by economics has disintegrated in recent years due to empirical challenges and failure to take into consideration a host of social and psychological variables that influence preference formation.

It is additionally beyond the scope of this chapter—and perhaps beyond the scope of human science—to present such a comprehensive, consolidated theory. The task of presenting a formal, universal theory is further complicated by the sheer variety of human experience. However, the lesson to be taken from these observations is simple: human preference formation cannot be reduced to a defined set of economic factors. Instead, it must be acknowledged that an indefinite number of environmental, biological, neurological, and—above all, because how we are socialized determines to a large degree how we respond to the environmental, biological, and neurological conditions of our existence—*sociological* variables, through processes that are not yet precisely described, account for vastly more variance in preferences than do economic factors. By taking a step back and considering the big picture rather than remaining wedded to a single discipline's assumptions, it becomes possible to sketch out a rough framework for how preferences might be formed and change, and hence the non-economic factors that ultimately affect choice behavior.

Developing such a big picture theory would have three main benefits. First, it would go a long way toward helping to organize the sprawling literature on human preference and choice. Once a general framework is established, it will be much easier to understand how each study relates to the others, which, in turn, may help scholars to understand how the thousands of variables they disparately describe interact with each other. Second, it will facilitate a "crossing of the Rubicon" between economic and non-economic disciplines that will ultimately yield a still-incomplete but wiser, interdisciplinary approach to preference formation divorced from the "theory-induced blindness" and jockeying for influence that is characteristic of today's theories. Third, such a framework would be much better for policy-makers, who need a way of thinking about preferences that is universally applicable—not because it is a comprehensive theory of everything with models that are theoretically elegant but clumsy and unwieldy in the real world, but because of its flexibility and the ability to "plug in" variables in the appropriate location when needed.

References

Basu, K. 1983. Fuzzy revealed preference theory. *Journal of Economic Theory* 32: 212–227.

Becker, G.S. 1968. Crime and punishment: An economic approach. *Journal of Political Economy* 76: 169–217.

———. 1973. A theory of marriage: Part I. *Journal of Political Economy* 81: 813–846.

———. 1993. *A treatise on the family*. Cambridge, MA: Harvard University Press.

Bicchieri, C. 2010. Norms, preferences, and conditional behavior. *Politics, Philosophy, and Economics* 9: 297–313.

Binmore, K. 2010. Social norms or social preferences? *Mind & Society* 9: 139–157.

Blasi, A.J. 2009. A market theory of religion. *Social Compass* 56: 263–272.

Charness, G., and M. Rabin. 2002. Understanding social preferences with simple tests. *The Quarterly Journal of Economics* 117: 817–869.

Chen, J., Y.J. Choi, K. Mori, Y. Sawada, and S. Sugano. 2010. Socio-Economic studies on suicide: A survey. *Journal of Economic Surveys* 26: 273–284.

Cigno, A. 2011. The economics of marriage. *Perspektiven der Wirtschaftspolitik* 12: 28–41.

Dietrich, F., and C. List. 2013. Where do preferences come from? *International Journal of Game Theory* 42: 613–637.

Drakopoulous, S.A. 2012. The history of attitudes towards interdependent preferences. *Journal of the History of Economic Thought* 34: 541–557.

Ermisch, J. 1988. Economic influences on birth rates. *National Institute Economic Review* 126: 71–92.

Etzioni, A. 1985. Opening the preferences: A socio-economic research agenda. *The Journal of Behavioral Economics* 14: 183–198.

———. 1988. *The moral dimension: Toward a new economics*. New York: Free Press.

Frank, R.H. 2011. Supply, demand and marriage. *New York Times*.

Hamermesh, D.S., and N.M. Soss. 1974. An economic theory of suicide. *Journal of Political Economy* 82: 83–98.

Hausman, D.M. 2011. Mistakes about preferences in the social sciences. *Philosophy of the Social Sciences* 41 (1): 1–25.

Huber, G.A., and K. Arceneaux. 2007. Identifying the persuasive effects of presidential advertising. *American Journal of Political Science* 51: 957–977.

Kahneman, D. 2011. *Bias, blindness, and how we truly think (Part 2)*. Bloomberg.com.

———. 2012. The human side of decision making: Thinking things through with Daniel Kahneman, PhD. *The Journal of Investment Consulting* 13: 5–14.

Kapteyn, A., T. Wansbeek, and J. Buyze. 1980. The dynamics of preference formation. *Journal of Economic Behavior and Organization* 1: 123–157.

Keita, L. 2012. Revealed preference theory, rationality, and neoclassical economics: Science or ideology. *Africa Development* 37: 73–116.

Kõszegi, B., and M. Rabin. 2006. A model of reference-dependent preferences. *The Quarterly Journal of Economics* 121: 1133–1165.

Lee, L.W. 1997. Persuasive advertising and socialization. *International Journal of the Business of Economics* 4: 203–214.

Maccoby, E.E. 1992. The role of parents in the socialization of children: An historical overview. *Developmental Psychology* 28: 1006–1017.

Mäki, U. 2009. Economics imperialism: Concept and constraints. *Philosophy of the Social Sciences* 39: 351–380.

Martins, N. 2011. Can neuroscience inform economics? Rationality, emotions, and preference formation. *Cambridge Journal of Economics* 35: 251–267.

Matsueda, R.L., D.A. Kreager, and D. Huizinga. 2006. Deterring delinquents: A rational choice model of theft and violence. *American Sociological Review* 71: 95–122.

Norton, B.G. 1994. Economists' preferences and the preferences of economists. *Environmental Values* 3: 311–332.

Pearlin, L.I., and M. Rosenberg. 1952. Propaganda techniques in institutional advertising. *The Public Opinion Quarterly* 16: 5–26.

Phillips, K. 2011. The manufactured wants and unmet needs of young America. *Forbes*.

Rozen, K. 2010. Foundations of intrinsic habit formation. *Econometrica* 78: 1341–1373.

Rizvi, S.A.T. 2001. Preference formation and the axioms of choice. *Review of Political Economy* 13: 141–159.

Santilli, P.C. 1983. The informative and persuasive functions of advertising: A moral appraisal. *Journal of Business Ethics* 2: 27–33.

Simion, C. 2005. Orienting and preference: an enquiry into the mechanisms underlying human decision making. Dissertation, California Institute of Technology.

Simon, H.A. 1959. Theories of decision-making in economics and behavioral science. *The American Economic Review* 49: 23–53.

Stigler, G.J., and G.S. Becker. 1977. De gustibus non est disputandum. *The American Economic Review* 67: 76–90.

Wildavsky, A. 1987. Choosing preferences by constructing institutions: A cultural theory of preference formation. *American Political Science Review* 81: 4–21.

Witt, U. 1991. Economics, sociobiology, and behavioral psychology on preferences. *Journal of Economic Psychology* 12: 155–171.

Chapter 4
Moral Dialogues

4.1 Introduction

Moral dialogues are social processes through which people form new shared moral understandings. These dialogues typically are passionate, disorderly, and without a clear starting point or conclusion (in contrast to elections or debates in a legislature). However, moral dialogues often do lead to profound changes in the moral positions of those who are engaged in them. Although moral dialogues never change the values of all those involved, they often, as we shall see, change the moral positions of a sufficient number of people so that actions and policies that previously had little support (e.g. environmental protection), and actions and policies considered morally inappropriate by many (e.g. same-sex marriage) gain widespread moral approval.

Moreover, we shall see that when moral dialogues mature, the new shared moral understandings that arise have profound sociological effects well beyond changes in values and norms and attitudes. These new or changed moral understandings are embedded in new laws or lead to significant changes in law and more importantly, they lead to major changes in voluntary behavior. For instance, the shared understanding that we have a moral obligation to the environment led to the founding of a new government agency (the Environmental Protection Agency); scores of new laws and regulations; and considerable changes in voluntary personal behavior including recycling, preferences for sustainable sources of energy (a factor in purchasing cars, appliances, and solar panels), donations, and voting. True, these changes were also affected by other factors, especially changes in economic incentives. However, the restructuring of these incentives reflects in part changes in shared moral understanding. This chapter focuses on the dynamics and effects of moral dialogues that lead to significant changes in shared moral understandings (SMU).

The analysis combines two methods. It follows historians by studying the development of various moral dialogues over time in a particular community or nation, in a given period. It follows sociologists in that it seeks to identify recurring social factors that moral dialogues draw on to bring about new SMU. These elements are

© The Author(s) 2018
A. Etzioni, *Happiness is the Wrong Metric*, Library of Public Policy and Public Administration 11, https://doi.org/10.1007/978-3-319-69623-2_4

next listed and then studied. That is, the chapter summarizes what is known about moral dialogues and develops an analytical framework for future research.

To study moral dialogues one needs to start with a baseline, to show where the shared moral understandings were before the moral dialogues changed them (Sect. 4.1). Next the chapter examines the sociological dialogue starters that lead to the initiation of moral dialogues (and their differences from historical 'firsts') (Sect. 4.2). The next section deals with the attributes and dynamics of moral dialogues. These include a review of intensive, interlinked multiple group discussions—which we shall call "megalogues"—that are required for moral dialogues to take place on a large scale (Sect. 4.3); the distinct attributes of moral dialogues as compared to rational deliberations and culture wars (Sect. 4.4); and the crucial role of dramatization (Sect. 4.5). The chapter then turns to show that moral dialogues that reach closure have significant sociological consequences. These are revealed in changes in shared values, laws, and behavior, when one compares the end state to the baseline (Sect. 4.6).

Following these sections is a case study to illustrate the various elements in one specific historical development, the change in SMU about same-sex marriage (Sect. 4.7). The importance of moral dialogues for community building is briefly discussed (Sect. 4.8). The chapter closes by pointing to a particularly challenging question— how is one to determine whether socially shared moral understandings, which basically reflect moral consensus—are indeed moral? (Sect. 4.9).

This chapter leaves for future discussion the study of the effects of external structural factors on moral dialogues, such as differences in political and economic power, social inequality, race, and gender. The chapter seeks to introduce moral dialogues as distinct from reasoned deliberations, expressions of emotions, and culture wars and leaves the important effects of structural factors on moral dialogues, a major subject all by itself, to a separate examination.

One can readily envision moral dialogues within a family or a small community but may well wonder if a society that encompasses many millions of people can engage in a moral dialogue. We shall see below that such society-wide dialogues take place by linking millions of local conversations (between couples, in neighborhood bars, in coffee houses, car pools, next to water coolers at work, and so on) into a society-wide moral give and take.

In his book on democratic citizenship, *Citizen Speak*, Andrew Perrin describes the social interactions in which moral dialogues occur, though he does not use this term. He writes:

> In everyday political life, citizens do have the opportunity to deliberate, though not in the laboratory conditions of Ackerman and Fishman, nor in the dramatic street battles of social movements. They can deliberate with friends, colleagues, fellow students, neighbors, members of organizations they belong to, anonymous others through letters to the editor, talk radio, Internet chat, and more...I have called these contexts political microcultures. (Perrin 2006, pp. 7–8)

However, Perrin seems to wonder if such deliberations could lead to the equivalent of a shared moral understanding. In the face of conflicting values, he questions whether they might result in compromise rather than consensus (2009, p. 48).

Since the advent of modern media, especially following the rise of social media, moral dialogues occur even on a transnational level. The suggestion that the "people of the world" can have moral dialogues may seem at first like one of those dewy-eyed notions held by naive idealists. Indeed, even in national dialogues, not all citizens participate, and the resulting understandings are not shared by everyone. Millions are preoccupied with basic needs, set back by a lack of education, or under the influence of mind-numbing substances, and in parts of the world run by authoritarian regimes.

However, the attentive public (Miller 2010), deemed as those who are publicly aware and engaged, is growing, as education and access to the media are spreading through many parts of the world. Thus, the citizens of countries as different as Russia, China, Iran, and Saudi Arabia have more access to transnational communications than they had in 1980. Hence, the reach of transnational moral dialogues is rising.

The effect of transnational moral dialogues is reflected in new shared understandings regarding land mines, trading in ivory and antiques, whale hunting, norms against proliferation of nuclear weapons, armed intervention in the internal affairs of other nations, the responsibility to protect (against genocides), human trafficking, and—to a lesser extent—in support of human rights and climate protection.

Before I can proceed, I must note a meta point that underlies much of the following: escaping the curse of dichotomies. A good part of public discourse and quite a few philosophical and social science deliberations draw on dichotomies. For instance, for the last two centuries the people of many nations have been engaged in debates between those who champion the private sector and those who champion the public sector; between the merits of the market compared to those of the government; between liberals and conservatives. These debates typically ignore a very large amount of social "business" conducted in the third sector, that of communities, voluntary associations, ethnic and religious groups, hundreds of thousands of not-for-profit corporations, and millions of families. This observation is particularly relevant for much that follows because moral dialogues occur largely in the third sector.

The curse of dichotomies is equally evident in the analysis of behavior as either rational or irrational, and of dialogues as either evidence-based, drawing on facts and logic ('cold'), or as passionate ('hot'), and hence irrational. Such dichotomies are particularly seductive because they do not tax the memory, are strongly favored by the mass media (which only rarely give voices to third positions), and allow one to split ambiguities and project positive traits and attributes on one element of the dichotomy and negative ones on the other.

Last but not least, dichotomies greatly simplify analysis. This is the case because if one shows that one option of the only two which dichotomy-based analysis recognizes is valid or good, then there is no need to study the other. Its evaluation logically follows. Thus, if one sees time as divided only into days and nights, if something did not occur during the day, then one need not study anything to determine that it occurred at night. It logically follows. Thus, once critics of the rational model, homo economicus, showed that people do not command the intellectual qualities the model presumes—specifically that people cannot process information the way the model requires—it followed logically that people are irrational, poor decision makers, in simple English, "fools" (Akerlof and Shiller 2016). And if dialogues are not based on reason, they are assumed to be dominated by emotions. Other scholars have noted this dichotomy and maintain that it is outmoded. For instance, Jeff Goodwin et al. (2001) write that "[m]obilization theorists shared little with their predecessors except a dichotomized opposition between rationality and emotion, which led them to deny emotions altogether in the politics they studied. Today...we can begin to see emotions in a new light" (p. 10). According to Goodwin et al. (2001), the "opposition of emotions and rationality" is "misleading" (p. 15); emotions can play a part in rational action. Similarly, a good part of what follows seeks to break out of this kind of dichotomous analysis and show that people often are non-rational but not necessarily irrational, and that dialogues can focus on moral issues, which have a passionate element but also a reasonable one, albeit a particular kind of reasoning.

Moral dialogues tend to follow a set pattern. I choose my words carefully. Not all moral dialogues follow all the stages next outlined. The pattern should hence be viewed as an ideal type (Encyclopedia Britannica 2016). It serves as an analytic matrix for the study of various specific dialogues and the comparison of one to others. In presenting the pattern (some would call it 'natural history'), I draw on illustrations from American experience, although its presence in other societies and transnational dialogues is self-evident.

4.2   Baselines

To assess the effects of any given moral dialogue, one must establish what the shared moral understanding was before the dialogue took place. For instance, to assess the effects of moral dialogues on our moral obligations to "mother earth," about our stewardship of the environment, one must start by noting that in the 1950s, there was no shared sense of such a moral responsibility. People dumped garbage in lakes and streams, drove cars that emitted a great deal of pollutants and used coal as a major source of energy, without any concern about their environmental implications. In the same period, racial segregation was legally enforced and widely supported. Women were expected to be homemakers and submissive. Gay people were considered sinners and deviants. Smoking in public raised no moral issues. Researchers can readily find some academics, clergy, or visionaries that made a moral case against any one of these established mores. However, they did not start moral dialogues and did not have a significant effect on the nationwide shared moral understanding.

4.3 Sociological Dialogue Starters

Moral dialogues often start with the articulation of what might be called a "moral brief," akin to what lawyers file before they argue a case before the Supreme Court. It typically includes a criticism of the prevailing moral culture and society and a substantive statement of what a new shared moral understanding (SMU) should contain. One should note in this context that some protest movements and organizations mainly provide a criticism of the prevailing order but contain little content—or only exceedingly vague content—about the core values to replace the old one. They are more disruptive than transformative. Major changes in SMU require that briefs also include statements about the new SMU to replace the old one. (It is a point that was not fully taken into account by several groups that brought down old regimes during the Arab Spring.)

Betty Friedan provided such a brief for a moral dialogue about women's rights and status in her 1963 book *The Feminine Mystique*. Rachel Carson provided such a brief for the environmental movement in her book *Silent Spring*, published in 1962. Ralph Nader did the same for the consumer protection drive in his book *Unsafe at Any Speed*, published in 1965. Other moral dialogues were started by a declaration, like Martin Luther's 95 theses, which prompted the Protestant Reformation. A Harvard committee provided a brief for changing the definition of death to one that occurs when there is a "brain death." Sometimes moral dialogues are triggered by an event rather than a brief, such as the Three Mile Island accident, which started a dialogue about nuclear safety. However, in all the cases examined, a brief followed.

In examining moral briefs, it is important to distinguish between historical starters ('first') and sociological take-off points. When a book or trial or event leads to a new moral dialogue, historians will often point out that rather similar ones have already been published or have taken place before. For instance, before *The Feminine Mystique*, other books on the topic had been published, including *The Second Sex* by Simone de Beauvoir in 1949. However, these previous starters were false starts; they did not start major moral dialogues that could lead to new SMU. For the purpose of studying changes in SMU, one must focus on those briefs and events that served to initiate the kind of dialogues and societal changes next described; that is, those that were followed by a dialogue that took off rather than remained grounded.

Some studies refer to the selection of dialogue starters as "agenda setting," the process through which people attribute a higher importance to some issues as compared to others. According to H. Denis Wu and Renita Coleman (2009), "For more than thirty years, the main concept in agenda setting theory has been the transfer of issue salience, or how media emphasis of certain issues raises their importance for the public" (p. 776). A common finding is that the media largely determines the issues the public focuses on.

James Jasper (1998) describes what here is referred to as 'starters,' using the term "moral shocks." According to Jasper,

'Moral shocks,' often the first step toward recruitment in social movements, occur when an unexpected event or piece of information raises such a sense of outrage in a person that she becomes inclined toward political action, whether or not she has acquaintances in the movement. The triggers may be highly publicized public events such as a nuclear accident, or personal experiences such as the death of a child. They may be sudden, like an accident or public announcement, or they may unfold gradually over time, as in the realization by Love Canal's residents that they were living over a toxic waste dump. Similarly, the shock may come from a plan for something new or from new information about something existing, which has already done unseen damage (p. 409).

The content of the brief, how well it is argued and presented, or the nature of the starting events, is often not the most important factor determining whether they will serve merely as a historical first or will lead to a sociological take-off. Much more important is whether or not the sociological conditions that would allow the changes to take off are in place. Thus, for instance, briefs for liberal democracy in societies of the kind the US found in Afghanistan in 2003 are unlikely to lead to a take-off (Etzioni 2015). Kristin Luker's (1985) book *Abortion and the Politics of Motherhood* illustrates how a change in sociological conditions allowed for a moral dialogue to take off. Luker writes that

the pro-choice activists started out being considerably more liberal than many Americans, but within a very short period of time, American public opinion had moved much closer to the pro-choice position. It is tempting to argue that the pro-choice people simply "persuaded" a great many fellow Americans to accept their point of view. To some extent they probably did; certainly the mere fact that they made the abortion issue a subject for public debate allowed many more people to become familiar with it and to form personal opinions about the merits of the case. It seems likely, however, that American public opinion was shaped more significantly by the large-scale social changes going on at the time—changes in the status of women, changes in traditional sexual morality, and an increasing concern with poverty (p. 226).

Similarly, looking at the feminist movement, it seems that *The Feminine Mystique* led to take-off not necessarily because it was better argued or had more evidence than previous books on the same subject, but because it was published after many women worked in factories and some participated in the military during WWII and were thus open to suggestions that they are able and entitled to play roles other than homemakers (among other factors). The question of which sociological developments set the stage for this and other take-offs, and those which failed, is not explored in the following discussion because it requires a major study in and of itself.

Some starters that launch moral dialogues are events rather than briefs. For instance, Rosa Parks refusing to give up her seat and move to the back of the bus is widely recognized as a starter of the civil rights movement, among others (Morris 1999). The brief for the movement followed later, especially in the speeches of Martin Luther King Jr., above all in "I Have a Dream." This case illustrates my hypothesis that for moral dialogues to take off and reach their destination (a new SMU), all the elements are needed, but the sequence may differ from one dialogue to another.

Finally, one should note that many moral dialogues take off but then lose altitude and need to be relaunched if they are to lead to a new SMU. For instance, dialogues about inequality in the US are following this pattern. Google Trends data shows the popularity (relative to all other Google searches) of certain search terms. Interest in "social inequality," for instance, is lacking a definitive spike; instead it consistently wavers.

Moreover, some moral dialogues that do take off never produce a new or changed SMU. For instance, briefs that called for the formation of a global government, in particular the 1947 Montreux Declaration by the World Federalists as part of the World Movement for World Federal Government (The Montreux Declaration 1947), initiated a measure of moral dialogues but these petered out without gaining a new SMU.

4.4 Megalogues

For a starter brief or event to lead to a new SMU, it must be followed by processes that would lead a large number of people to reexamine their moral values, give up what they long believed was right, and accept a new set of values as morally valid.

Some advocates of moral causes believe that if the president would make a powerful speech or conduct 'fireside chats' as President Roosevelt did, this would lead to a new SMU and change the direction of the nation. President Kennedy's speech that urged Americans not to ask what their country can do for them but what they can do for their country is credited with engendering a historical change; however, although the speech is often quoted, there is precious little evidence that, by itself, it had much of an effect. President Carter tried to make Americans treat the saving of energy as a test of their moral fortitude in his famous malaise speech—with mainly negative effects. President Obama spoke eloquently for many causes, especially for finding common ground, but the nation became more polarized. Such speeches can serve as sociological dialogue starters, but they must be followed by dialogues for them to have the sought-after societal effects. People who adhere to a moral value do not change their position because of just one speech, however eloquent.

Instead, when a topic takes off, or 'gets hot,' it becomes the subject of extensive discussion in personal settings (over dinner, in bars, firehouses) and in local meetings of voluntary associations and clubs (Rotary, PTA, places of worship). These, in turn, are amplified and linked through national organizations during their meetings (such as AIPAC, League of Women Voters, NAACP, Sierra Club, Conference of Catholic Bishops, National Council of Churches, etc.), and through the media (call-in shows, commentaries, and debates on TV and radio) and social media.

To illustrate, in 2015–2016 a subject that was only sporadically discussed in previous years became a focus of a nationwide moral dialogue in the US, namely the rights of transgender people. Google Trends data shows that the relative popularity of the search term "transgender bathrooms" in the United States was low for over a decade and then experienced a sharp increase after 2015.

4.5 Distinct Attributes

Moral dialogues differ sharply from both expressions of emotions and from rational deliberations. In effect, they constitute a hybrid that has qualities of its own, different from the composite elements. Moral statements contain emotions in contrast to sheer statements of facts or logic. At the same time, these statements contain justifications—that is, they are intellectually accountable—in contrast to emotions. When one discloses that one hates or loves or declares any other emotion, it suffices to state 'because this is what I feel' (*de gustibus non est disputandum*) (Stigler and Becker 1977). In contrast, if one states that a given condition is immoral, say not fair, one is expected to spell out the reasons and give a basis for this statement. And one may be challenged with arguments that such a statement is inconsistent with previous ones, or violates a general ethical position to which the person subscribes, or with still other arguments—and one is expected to justify one's moral judgment or modify it. This is what I mean to be held accountable.

The discussion next turns to elaborate these points, comparing the three kinds of expression (rational, emotional, and moral) and the related group processes.

Moral statements differ from rational statements that are focused on facts, as well as from logical conclusions that can be drawn from these facts. People are invested emotionally in moral statements, and hence when new facts arise or new arguments are made based on evidence, people will not change their positions readily. True, much has been written to point out that facts and values cannot be completely separated and they often bleed into each other. Still, there is a clear difference between what have been called *is* versus *ought* statements. Reasoned deliberations are about *is*, moral dialogues about *ought*.

To illustrate, one may argue whether or not the death penalty is justified on empirical-logical, rational grounds by comparing crime rates in states that have versus do not have death penalties. Or, before and after such sentences were carried out in states that either dropped or adopted this penalty. In contrast, if one holds that it is morally wrong for the state to deliberately take a life, statistics about the effects on crime rates will matter little (or only if one can show that the result leads to a higher loss of lives).

Quite a few previous discussions of the attributes of dialogues suffer from the curse of dichotomies. The main case in point is the growing recognition that the assumption that people are rational creatures, able to collect and process the information needed to make rational choices, is a false one (Sen 1977; Thaler 2015). It is assumed ipso facto that therefore people are irrational, unable to make sensible judgments, because the analysis started from a binary position. If not A then it must be B. Actually, as Talcott Parsons pointed out long ago, there is a whole third realm, that of the non-rational. This realm includes 'other worldly' matters, which deal with questions and views about the afterlife, deities, the meaning of life, why we were born to die, and with the selection of moral values, especially when two or more of these values are in conflict.

The same holds for group deliberations. Thus, according to James Kuklinski and his associates, "In a democratic society, reasonable decisions are preferable to unreasonable ones; considered thought leads to the former, emotions to the latter; therefore deliberation is preferable to visceral reaction as a basis for democratic decision making" (Kuklinski et al. 1991; Dryzek 2008). James Q. Wilson (1990) writes about "the contrast [James] Madison draws between opinions and passion, since opinion implies a belief amenable to reason whereas passion implies a disposition beyond reason's reach" (p. 559).

Moral values and deliberations are either ignored or explicitly 'reduced' to irrational emotions. According to Ernest R. House, "Values might be feelings, emotions, or useless metaphysical entities" (House 2005, p. 2). Cheryl Hall (2007) notes that an "endemic problem for deliberative theory stems from the supreme value it places on calm rational discussion, to the exclusion of both emotionally laden speech and passionate protests" (p. 81). Some advocates of deliberative democracy have suggested supplementing deliberation "with more obviously emotional forms of communication" (Hall 2007, p. 82). However, Hall argues that deliberative democracy is "more reliant on passion than either advocates or critics acknowledge," criticizing the assumption that reason and passion must be in opposition in deliberation. All these statements assume a dichotomous world, limited to 'cold' rational deliberations or 'hot' emotions.

Jonathan Haidt (2012), in his nuanced analysis, still holds in the end that people are basically driven by emotions, and make up post hoc reasons to justify them. Thus, if one seeks to persuade them, one must appeal to their emotions. If this would be true, moral arguments would make no difference, ethical deliberations would have no effect.

The stark opposition between rational and emotional group processes does not recognize a third realm of moral statements and dialogues—in which people engage each other's values. Reasoning concerning moral differences, the kind of deliberations ethics texts provide, are different from the reasoning involved when one deals with facts. True, the two realms bleed into each other. Nevertheless the distinction stands. Thus, to argue against the death penalty because one believes that the state should never deliberately take a person's life falls into the first category, while the argument that the death penalty is not effective in suppressing crime falls into the second.

The following serves as an illustration of this third realm of moral statements. For generations, Americans have been strongly opposed to governments running high deficits. Indeed, many American states and municipalities are legally required to balance their budget each year. This position is mainly based on moral values, such as 'one should not live beyond one's means,' and not 'burden our children with debts' and that it is morally wrong to be in debt. It is sinful. In German, the same word is used to describe guilt and debt. The actual harm deficits cause is a rather complex question and there is considerable evidence that balancing the budget each year (rather than over a cycle of recessions and prosperity) is a poor policy.

I am not arguing that rational deliberations and moral dialogues do not affect each other. However, when one examines particular dialogues one can, as a rule, readily determine which statements are mainly moral versus largely factual, and see differences in give and take between those that are evidence-centered and those focused on moral issues.

We can gain some insight into the issue from mental experiments. A father finding out that his young son smoked may merely yell at him, demanding that he stop (sheer emotion) or—strongly express, in emotive terms, his concern for his son's health, and also explain the risks involved to him and others around him. For the purposes of moral dialogues, it matters not in this case if the argument that the father made was merely a rationalization that followed his emotions or one he developed on the basis of information he garnered and understood. What matters is if his son is less likely to be swayed when exposed to sheer emotion as compared to emotion accompanied by reasoning. Moral dialogues, it follows, draw on both emotional expressions and reason. Otherwise they are shouting matches, guilt trips, or expressions of blind love, shame, and other such emotions.

Some accord a great role to the media as a moral persuader. For instance, when it shows a graphic picture following an earthquake or typhoon, millions of donations flow to the people in the devastated area, based on the emotions the picture evokes. However, on closer inspection, one notes that the picture does not so much shape one's moral disposition as direct where it is applied. One can determine this by noting that large donations will come from Americans because voluntary donations are part of the American moral tradition. In some other countries, the same pictures will lead to greater demands on the government to act. And in still others, very few donations will be forthcoming. Bernard Cohen (1963) made this point well when he observed that "[the press] may not be successful much of the time in telling people what to think, but it is stunningly successful in telling its readers what to think about" (p. 13).

In further deliberating on the question at hand, one can draw on firsthand experience in moral deliberations. Thus, when we serve on a committee that considers whether or not to disclose to the public or the authorities some unethical conduct or acts that might be illegal—for example, bullying or unconfirmed reports about inappropriate advances made by a coach—we note that our emotions are surely engaged but that we also take into account moral arguments.

Moral dialogues resolve differences and are thus able to lead to new SMU in their own ways, a far cry from relying on new empirical evidence. One often-used procedure in moral dialogues is to appeal to an overarching value that the various parties to the sorting out process share. Robert Goodin (1989) in effect is using this rule when he seeks to pave the road for a community that must sort out a course between the rights of non-smokers and those of smokers. At first, this may seem as a typical clash between two values: the rights of one group versus those of another. However, Goodin points out that both groups are committed to the value that one's liberty does not allow that person to violate the "space" of the other. In popular terms, my right to extend my arm stops when my fist reaches your nose. Goodin argues that value applied because non-smokers, in their non-smoking, do not penetrate the smokers' space, while smokers do violate non-smokers' space in public situations, thus non-smoker rights should take priority. Using such arguments, American communities reached the SMU that lies at the foundation of the new restrictions on smoking in numerous public spaces. (The fact that these new regulations met very little opposition shows that they were based on a thoroughly shared moral understanding, unlike Prohibition.)

Another procedure is to bring a third value into play when two diverge or clash. For instance, those who recently tried to restore the Black-Jewish coalition of the 1960s in the United States argue that both groups share a commitment to liberal causes. Additionally, attempts to create an interfaith coalition pointed to the shared commitment to fight poverty, as the participants struggled to work out a joint position (Lerner and West 1995). Groups that strongly support pro-life public policies and those that strongly support pro-choice ones agreed to work together to improve the care of children, which both groups cherish.

"Culture war" is a term that was used originally between social conservatives and liberals about issues such as abortion and divorce (Stein 2001). More generally, it is used to refer to "a conflict between groups with different ideals, beliefs, [or] philosophies" (OED 2016). It implies persistent, unresolved value differences such as between Protestants and Catholics in earlier eras, Shias and Sunnis, and secular and Ultra-Orthodox Jews more recently. One may view culture wars as failed moral dialogues, in part due to higher levels of emotional involvement compared to moral dialogues. However, one should note the findings of an excellent study by historian Stephen Prothero (2016) which show that, over time, even these dialogues (sometimes referred to as culture wars) often lead to new SMU, for instance about same sex-marriages, the use of contraception, and divorce. This may even be true about gun control; however, in this realm shared moral understandings have not yet reached a level where they can lead to significant changes in voluntary behavior or the law.

4.6 Dramatization

So far the analysis of moral dialogues has focused on communications; on members of a community, however small or large, exchanging moral viewpoints, discussing moral issues with one another, reexamining their moral positions, and reaching (often) common ground. One should not ignore, however, that all such dialogues also contain acts that serve to dramatize the moral issues under discussions, such as sit-ins, demonstrations, occupying administrative buildings on campuses and corporations, sit-downs in traffic lanes, and spilling blood on fur coats (by animal rights activists). Court cases such as the Scopes Trial, Congressional hearings regarding Joseph McCarthy, and the confirmation of Justice Clarence Thomas also serve to dramatize the issues.

These dramatizations serve two main purposes. One is to nurture the dialogues. Following dramatizations, especially those with novel rather than merely routinized elements, one finds a spike in dialogues. A case study is presented later in the chapter. The importance of dramatization has risen since the advent of TV. Pictures are highly evocative while verbal dialogues rarely lend themselves to dramatic footage. Hence, dramatizations are a particularly effective means to promote moral dialogues, to keep the issues under discussion in the public eye, and to evoke participation.

Second, dramatizations engage people's emotions, while verbal give and take relates more to intellectual accountability elements. Dramatization thus helps ensure that people who may be swayed by an argument will also refigure their emotional commitments accordingly.

4.7 Closure

Many moral dialogues lead not only to significant changes in the moral positions of millions of individuals—which are essential for bringing about changes in prevailing SMU or to form new ones—but also engender significant changes in behavior and laws. When moral dialogues are advanced successfully, they lead to the formation of new shared moral judgments or to changes in moral positions (values, norms, and attitudes). For example, as far as one can determine, there was no significant shared moral commitments to the environment in 1950. By 2016, "74% of U.S. adults said the 'country should do whatever it takes to protect the environment'" (Anderson 2016). Furthermore, "Seventy-three percent of Americans say they prefer emphasizing alternative energy, rather than gas and oil production, as the solution to the nation's energy problems" (Auter 2016).

To reiterate, even when successful, the change in SMU encompasses merely a large segment of the people who engaged in these dialogues; there always remain some who do not change their moral position. Moreover, some moral dialogues fail, e.g. between the pro-choice and pro-life groups. Many take off, slow down, and are relaunched before a significant level of SMU is reached (e.g. the dialogue on inequality). However, when these dialogues take off and mature—they change the moral positions of large segments of the populations, often ending with new moral majorities.

More importantly, the great significance of SMU is that they lead to voluntary changes in behavior—well beyond changes in attitudes. Thus, people who acknowledge that they have a moral obligation to the environment are much more likely than others to recycle, use recycled paper, bike and walk, buy low-emission cars that use fuel efficiently, support public policies that protect the environment, use solar panels, and so on. True, these behaviors are also affected by changes in economic incentives and legislative acts. However, for reasons next outlined, it makes a very great difference (a) if the changes in behavior are mainly voluntary, due to changes in what people consider the right behavior—versus mainly due to economic and legal incentives and (b) if the changes in incentives and laws are supported by SMU or not.

To call attention to the role of SMU in engendering significant voluntary changes in behavior, is not to suggest that the social change effected by SMU cannot be supplemented or manipulated when combined with economic and legal incentives or disincentives and social arrangements such as "nudges" (Thaler and Sunstein 2008).

The role of SMU in affecting behavior rather than just attitudes is of great significance and hence deserves some elaboration. In a very extensive study of what motivates people, a study whose findings were replicated and augmented many times, Amitai Etzioni (1961) showed that people can be motivated to engage in pro-social behavior that they would not have engaged in otherwise, in three ways. They can be coerced; motivated by economic incentives or disincentives; or convinced of the moral rightness of changing their behavior. The study shows that people resent being coerced, and will try to deviate from forced patterns of behavior whenever they believe they can get away with it. Hence compliance will be costly, unreliable, and far from satisfactory.

People who are paid to behave—read a book (Warren 2012), come to class (Haynes and Birnbaum 2008), work, etc.—will be less alienated than those who are coerced, but also seek to gain the incentives while giving as little as possible in return because their preferences are not compatible with what they are paid to do.

In sharp contrast, people who find that what they are asked to do is morally compelling will feel ennobled when they carry out their tasks and will seek to carry them out well, even if they are not supervised. (Those in hybrid situations will act accordingly; e.g. the feelings and behaviors of physicians paid to take care of their patients but also convinced that they are doing good, will fall somewhere between those only responding to economic incentives and those who feel morally compelled.)

There are those who hold that each person is out to pursue their self-interests, and famously, that an invisible hand will ensure that as a result, the economy will thrive and all will do well. Whether this is true or not for the economy need not to be examined here; however, this certainly does not hold true for society. The problem of social order, as Dennis Wrong (1923, 1994) put it, is that people need to be motivated to engage in pro-social behavior. However, no society can provide for a sufficient number of police, accountants, or border patrol agents, etc. to coerce a satisfactory level of pro-social behavior. Moreover, such enforcement is costly, as the US discovered when it incarcerated people en masse, spending more on prisons than on higher education, trying but failing to curb substance abuse. Last but not least, such enforcement faces the often-cited challenge: who will guard the guardians? Many enforcement agents are corrupt and engage in anti-social behavior themselves.

In contrast, to the extent that most people do most times much of what needs to be done—go to work, take care of their family, pay taxes, avoid polluting, and so on—because they hold that the expectations that they will act responsibly are legitimate, compliance will be high, costs will be low, and inclination to rebel, minimal. An interesting example is tax compliance. It has been shown that if people believe that taxes are fair and legitimately used, they pay more of the taxes owed (Lewis 1982, pp. 5–6).

When SMU are formed, they enable a society to limit coercive enforcement and rely much more on self-regulation. For example, when public smoking bans were enacted, they caused little opposition and resulted in general compliance because they followed public education (especially on secondhand smoke risks) and moral dialogues (Etzioni 1996, p. 146). On the other hand, Prohibition failed miserably because public consensus on the issue was lacking; the law was not backed up by a shared moral understanding (Etzioni 1996, p. 143).

Although the main benefits of new SMU (or the reworking of an old, obsolete one), we have just seen, is an increase in voluntary adherence to social norms that define pro-social behavior, SMU also lead to new laws and regulations or to changes in them. That is, the new SMU tend to become legally embedded and reinforced. This is the case because (a) many social functions cannot rely only on moral persuasion and voluntary compliance (or—economic incentives). (b) Even if relatively few people ignore the social norms and such behavior is ignored, it is likely to unravel voluntary compliance over time because those who adhere to the norms will feel that they are being taken advantage of or treated unfairly and feel like "suckers." Thus, if a growing number of people speed or park illegally with impunity, more and more will follow. Hence, mature SMU are best expressed not only in changes in voluntary behavior but also embedded in laws. Thus, the rise in the SMU that we have a stewardship over the environment led to the formation of the EPA and scores of laws limiting pollution. The rise in SMU that African Americans were treated unfairly led to Affirmative Action, the formation of EEOP, and court cases banning several forms of segregation, among other such moves.

Those who tend to favor enacting moral changes should note that in many cases gaining new SMU precedes the enactment of laws that express and undergird the values agreed upon. Dialogue about women's rights advanced before Title IX became the law of the land. The same is true about gay rights before the Supreme Court ruling that made same-sex marriage legal across the country, and before legal segregation was struck down.

4.8   Case Study

4.8.1   Baseline

The moral dialogue about same-sex marriages is a subset of a much more encompassing moral dialogue on homosexuality, a dialogue not here examined. In 1970, no US state allowed same sex marriages. Even civil unions for same-sex couples did not exist as an alternative. According to the Supreme Court, it was not even a substantial federal question (implying that same-sex marriage was not something to be considered), a statement the Court made in 1972 when refusing to hear a case on the issue. Over a decade later in 1986, as a result of the Supreme Court's decision in *Bowers v. Hardwick*, states maintained their ability to criminalize gay sexual relations (2016). In 1996, the Defense of Marriage Act (DOMA) was passed with 79% approval in the House (HR 3396 1996a) and 85% approval in the Senate, (HR 3396 1996b) which declared that for federal purposes, marriage was between one man and one woman (Cole 2016, p. 28). It was signed by President Clinton, whose statement on DOMA declared that "I have long opposed governmental recognition of same-gender marriages and this legislation is consistent with that position" (Clinton 1996). In terms of public opinion, a 1996 Gallup poll found that 68% of respondents thought same-sex marriage should not be valid (Gallup 2016). Data from the Pew Research Center taken from the same year shows a similar figure of 65% (Pew Research Center 2015).

4.8.2 Sociological Dialogue Starters

There were several "historical starters," such as the 1993 case in which the Hawaii Supreme Court suggested that it may be unconstitutional to reject same-sex marriage (Schmalz 1993). However, this prompted a backlash, and "[b]y 2001, thirty-five states had passed laws limiting marriage to a union of one man and one woman [including Hawaii]" (Cole 2016). One should not mistake this legislation as a reflection of a new shared moral understanding but rather a codification of the status quo, which was previously seen as unnecessary. Vermont's recognition of same-sex civil unions in 2000 can be viewed as a "sociological starter" though it provided an alternative to same sex marriage rather than a redefinition of marriage.

A take-off point was reached when Massachusetts was the first state to legalize gay marriage in 2004 (Belluck 2004). As such, because of the DOMA provision denying federal benefits to same-sex couples, it put state and federal law at odds (Cole 2016, p. 82). The decision in Massachusetts prompted a backlash of state constitutional amendments banning same-sex marriage (Cole 2016, p. 49). California voted for Proposition 8 in 2008, which banned same-sex marriage in the state. But "...advocates could show the nation that allowing gay and lesbian couples to marry had no negative consequences" (Cole 2016, p. 51).

4.8.3 Billion-Hour Buzz

The legalization of same-sex marriage by Massachusetts in 2004, with the media portraying happy gay and lesbian newlyweds, helped to trigger a national debate on the subject. For instance, a search of *New York Times* articles containing the phrase "gay marriage" from 2000 through the end of 2003 turns out about 230 results, while from 2004 through the end of 2007 there are over 1500.

In 2004, 2005, and 2006, proposed amendments to the Massachusetts state constitution were discussed at "constitutional conventions." "Each convention generated extensive local and national media coverage, and drew large crowds of demonstrators on both sides." Ultimately no amendments were made, and same-sex marriage remained legal (Cole 2016, pp. 48–9). During this time, marriage equality remained a salient issue across the country. In order to get a sense of public opinion after Proposition 8 in California, there were focus groups, roundtables, and 30 groups created a combined survey (Cole 2016, p. 70).

In Maine, same-sex marriage was legalized in 2008, repealed by voters in 2009, and then was supported on a ballot measure in 2012. To prepare for the 2012 referendum, a new type of canvassing was introduced, one that involved "in-depth conversations, in which the canvasser asked open-ended questions designed to invite respondents to share their experiences." Over 200,000 such conversations took place, and it is estimated that these conversations changed the stance of 12,500 Maine voters (Cole 2016, pp. 68–70). One of the televised political ads in Maine at the time closed with the statement: "This isn't about politics. It's about family and how we as people treat one another" (Cole 2016, p. 74).

Television played a key role in moral dialogues on marriage equality. The portrayal of gay and lesbian characters in the media has increased (Associated Press 2014), and there is evidence that this had an impact on public opinion. "According to a 2012 Hollywood Reporter poll, 27% of people who had changed their minds about gay marriage from anti- to pro- in the last decade said that they made their decision after watching gay characters on shows like Modern Family and Glee" (Dockterman 2015).

When President Obama came out in support of same-sex marriage in 2012, it had a significant impact on the amount of conversation taking place (Hitlin and Tan 2012). On blogs there was more than a 60% increase in statements on same-sex marriage after Obama's announcement, and the number was even greater on Twitter (Hitlin and Tan 2012). "For the week of May 7–11 [2012], Obama's comment on May 9 in favor of same-sex marriage was the No. 1 topic on blogs and the No. 3 subject on Twitter." Furthermore, "there have been nine previous weeks [since 2009] when the subject [same-sex marriage] was among the most discussed on blogs or Twitter" (Hitlin and Tan 2012).

In 2013, the Human Rights Campaign (HRC) introduced an image of a pink equal sign against a red backdrop in support of marriage equality as part of a social media campaign in connection with the Supreme Court's consideration of *Hollingsworth v. Perry* and *United States v. Windsor*, two cases that had implications for marriage equality. The logo went viral, with many people replacing their Facebook profile picture to one that included it, prompting news headlines such as "How the Red Equal Sign Took Over Facebook…" (Kleinman 2013). HRC provides the following description of phenomenon of the red logo:

> The red marriage equality logo first appeared on HRC's Facebook page at 2 p.m. on March 25, 2013. Within 24 hours, HRC's Facebook post to encourage digital activists to change their social media profile pictures to a red and pink version of its ubiquitous logo received 189,177 shares, 95,725 likes, appeared over 18 million times in Newsfeeds, created upwards of 10 million impressions worldwide, and inspired countless memes. Facebook recorded a 120 percent increase in profile photo updates, and they deemed the effort the most successful campaign in their history (McCarty 2014).

Pew Research Center did a study of news coverage both leading up to and during the Supreme Court hearings; the study looked at 500 stories about marriage equality during an 8-week timeframe, concluding that the coverage indicated "strong momentum for same-sex marriage" (Hitlin et al. 2013). Although this number is by no means inclusive of every relevant news story during the selected timeframe, it serves to give an idea of the extent to which marriage equality was being discussed. Pew also noted that the "Gay Voices" microsite of the *Huffington Post* "produced so much coverage that it was examined separately from the rest of the news media" (Hitlin et al. 2013).

4.8.4 Dramatization

The movement for same-sex marriage used court cases to dramatize the issues at the heart of the moral dialogue. Protests keep attention on the issue. For example, after Proposition 8, protests were widespread in California (Associated Press 2008), which kept the issue in the media. 2500 protesters gathered at the Sacramento Capitol, and other large protests occurred outside of religious institutions that had supported the measure to ban same-sex marriage (Associated Press 2008). Same-sex marriage was also supported in pride parades in many cities. In 2013, DOMA was ruled unconstitutional by the Supreme Court decision in *United States v. Windsor* (2016), which furthered the momentum of the pro-same-sex marriage movement.

4.8.5 Closure

In June 2015, the US Supreme Court decision in *Obergefell v. Hodges* recognized a constitutional right to same-sex marriage which applies to all 50 states. However, some states still have laws on the books that ban same-sex marriage and now seek to obstruct it in other ways. A month prior to the decision, a Gallup poll showed that 60% of respondents thought same-sex marriage should be legal (Gallup 2016). The tide had turned, and Justice Kennedy recognized that Americans had reached a new shared moral understanding. He wrote that "new insights and societal understandings can reveal unjustified inequality within our most fundamental institutions that once passed unnoticed and unchallenged" (Cole 2016, p. 92).

4.9 Community Building and Power Structures

When moral dialogues mature, they also serve as a major source of community building and nurturing. Communities are not merely places where people bond and have affection for one another, but they are also places where they have a shared moral culture, and share values from which specific norms are derived (Etzioni 1996). However, these moral cultures are continually challenged by technological, economic, and international developments among others. Moral dialogues serve to recast these cultures in response. These dialogues also serve to shore up as well as revise the core values needed to prevent communities from disintegrating as a result of various factions pursuing their own subset of values.

Social scientists and social philosophers long worried that the social transformation that accompanied the industrial revolution, that entailed moving most people from villages, which were communities, into cities, in which people were "atomized," caused people to lose their essential social moorings. The thesis is often referred to as a shift from *Gemeinschaft* to *Gesellschaft* (Tönnies 1887/1955). True, we since learned that one can find communities in industrial societies, for instance in ethnic neighborhoods such as Chinatown, Spanish Harlem, the Village, and in gated communities, in which many millions of Americans live (Blakely 2012). However, there is still considerable evidence that a large number of people are missing the social bonds that are essential for their flourishing, hence, the call for rebuilding communities. Moral dialogues are one major process for such a communitarian reconstruction.

Major liberal scholars hold that each person should define the good and the state should be morally neutral. Hence some suggested that the state should stop issuing marriage licenses altogether and leave the various religions' functionaries and civic bodies to determine what marriage is. Moreover, liberals feared that even if the state remains morally neutral, as long as the society forms strong SMU, these will be embedded in laws (Gutmann 1985, p. 319).

In contrast, communitarians pointed out that social order requires a core of shared values. Some of the reasons have already been cited, regarding the need for much of the order to rest on voluntary compliance. Other reasons are that in order for various factions (that have different interests and different values) to be able to form shared public polices and to limit conflicts from turning into unresolved standoffs if not violence, society needs a core of substantive values, as well as a belief in procedures to resolve differences. SMU are the process that can keep these essential core values intact, or allow them to adapt rather than unravel in times of change.

I refer to a set of "core" values because the difference between core and other values is crucial for several reasons. First, much attention has been paid in recent years to the polarization of American politics reflected in more and more people identifying themselves with either a conservative or a liberal position and fewer and fewer as somewhere in the middle—as well as a growing adamancy in the positions held by both camps. Polarization is viewed as a key reason the government is in gridlock and held in low regard by the overwhelming majority of the American people. From a communitarian viewpoint the main question is whether the polarization concerns secondary values and hence differences can be settled by appealing to core values—or is holistic, leading to irreconcilable differences. If the breakdown of moral consensus is holistic, either moral dialogues will fail to lead to SMU, or they will restore the needed consensus by leading to the formation of a new core of shared values.

The same difference is also highly relevant to the ways immigrants and minorities are treated. The US long recognized the value of diversity and pluralism, but holds that these are best bounded by a shared framework. This issue comes into sharp relief when the treatment of immigrants is debated. France seeks complete assimilation. In the US, some advocates called for bleaching out all traces of previous moral commitment to one's country of origin and its culture. At the opposite extreme, a British commission concluded that due to the diversity of the UK, the government should not promote a national identity (Parekh 2000). There are numerous intermediary positions. Particularly relevant for the discussion at hand is an approach that might be referred to as Diversity within Unity. It holds that there is no reason to oppose or see as threatening the social order if various members of society pray to different Gods, maintain distinct sub-cultures, and secondary loyalties to their country of origin—as long as their first loyalty is to their new country, they accept the democratic regime as the way to resolve differences, learn the nation's language or languages (while, if they wish, maintaining their original one), and abide by the laws (but these laws ought to tolerate differences, say, in the ways animals are slaughtered and marriages are performed) (Etzioni 2007, pp. 186–92).

SMU serve to sort out which moral values fall into the diversity category and which into the unity one. Above all, they help to recast the whole framework when societal changes call for it to be recast. And SMU serve to sort out what are considered core values and what are diverse ones that enrich rather than threaten the social order.

A major subject that is not treated in this chapter because it requires its own major study is the role of power in structuring communications in general and moral dialogues in particular. It is sufficient to note that not all people have equal access to the media (e.g. the digital divide); the media is owned and managed in ways that favor some groups and viewpoints over others; and whether or not the results of dialogues are implemented is clearly affected by the prevailing power structure.

One should note, though, that moral dialogues differ in their relation to power from other communications and deliberations. I advance the hypothesis that in effect these dialogues favor those who otherwise are less privileged. As it stands, appealing to values is often the strongest societal change resource to which they have access. Indeed, a study of American history, I hypothesize, would show that major societal changes that came about—were the result of social movements in which the formation of new SMU played a key role. These include the movements that championed civil rights, women's rights, the protection of the environment, gender equality, and the progressive movement. In all of these movements, moral dialogues played a key role. (All of these examples, to reiterate, are hypotheses yet to be studied.)

4.10 Relativism?

The term 'moral' implies that one approves of the act so judged. However, there is no a priori reason to hold that just because the overwhelming majority of the people of a given community come to a SMU, that the content of this understanding will be in line with what a particular person will consider moral. For example, the majority of Americans used to hold that separate but equal was a fair SMU (reflected in the 1896 Supreme Court decision in *Plessy v. Ferguson*). Another example is the Defense of Marriage Act, which held that for the purposes of federal law, marriage is between a man and a woman, as well as gave states the right to decide whether or not to recognize same-sex marriages that had taken place outside their jurisdiction. Many will not find these SMU to be moral.

In short, moral dialogues are just that—dialogues about what the majority considers moral—not what is moral by some ethical theory or any theory of one's standards. One must hence keep in mind that whatever SMU communities or societies or transnational bodies reach—which have all the functional merits I discussed earlier, such as making society more peaceful, functional and effective—they may nevertheless be immoral by your or my standards, the Bible, Kant, Rawls, utilitarianism, Aristotelianism, or virtue ethics. Those troubled by the substance of any SMU are hence called upon to continue to reexamine them and, if found objectionable, work to change the SMU through moral dialogues (Etzioni 2011, p. 105).

References

Akerlof, G.A., and R.J. Shiller. 2016. *Phishing for phools: The economics of manipulation and deception*. Princeton: Princeton University Press.

Anderson, M. 2016. For Earth Day, here's how Americans view environmental issues. *Pew Research Center*.

Associated Press. 2008. *In California, protests over gay marriage vote*. http://www.nytimes.com/2008/11/10/us/10protest.html.

———. 2014. *Number of gay and lesbian TV characters growing, says GLAAD*.

Auter, Z. 2016. In U.S., 73% now prioritize alternative energy over oil, gas. *Gallup*.

Belluck, P. 2004. Massachusetts arrives at moment for same-sex marriage. *New York Times*.

Blakely, E. 2012. In gated communities, such as where Trayvon Martin died, a dangerous mindset. *Washington Post*.

Clinton, W.J. 1996. Public papers of the Presidents of the United States, Book 2. July 1 to December 31, 1996. United States Government Printing Office. Washington: 1998, 1635.

Cohen, B. 1963. *The Press and foreign policy*. Princeton: Princeton University Press.

Cole, D. 2016. *Engines of liberty: The power of citizen activists to make constitutional law*. New York: Basic Books.

Dockterman, E. 2015. These shows helped shape America's attitudes about gay relationships. *Time*.

Dryzek, J.S. 2008. Democratization as deliberative capacity building. *Comparative Political Studies* 42 (11): 1379–1402.

Encyclopædia Britannica Online. 2016. *Ideal type*. Accessed 9 May 2016, http://www.britannica.com/topic/ideal-type.

Etzioni, A. 1961. *A comparative analysis of complex organizations*. New York: Free Press of Glencoe.

———. 1996. *The new golden rule*. New York: Basic Books.

———. 2007. *Security first*, 186–192. New Haven: Yale University Press.

———. 2011. On communitarian and global sources of legitimacy. *The Review of Politics* 73 (1): 123–128.

———. 2015. COIN: A study of strategic illusion. *Small Wars & Insurgencies* 26 (3): 345–376.

Gallup. 2016). *Marriage*. http://www.gallup.com/poll/117328/marriage.aspx.

Goodin, R.E. 1989. *No smoking: The ethical issues*. Chicago: The University of Chicago Press.

Goodwin, J., J.M. Jasper, and F. Polletta, eds. 2001. *Passionate politics: Emotions and social movements*. Chicago: The University of Chicago Press.

Gutmann, A. 1985. Communitarian critics of liberalism. *Philosophy and Public Affairs* 14 (3): 308–322.

H.R. 3396 (104th): Defense of Marriage Act. 1996a. https://www.govtrack.us/congress/votes/104-1996/h316.

———. 1996b. https://www.govtrack.us/congress/votes/104-1996/s280.

Haidt, J. 2012. *The righteous mind: Why good people are divided by politics and religion.* New York: Pantheon Books.

Hall, C. 2007. Recognizing the passion in deliberation: Toward a more democratic theory of deliberative democracy. *Hypatia* 22: 81.

Hardwick, Bowers V. 2016. *Chicago-Kent College of Law at Illinois Tech. Oyez.*, n.d. June 9. https://www.oyez.org/cases/1985/85-140.

Haynes, D., and M. Birnbaum. 2008. DC tries cash as a motivator in schools. *Washington Post.* http://www.washingtonpost.com/wp-dyn/content/article/2008/08/21/AR2008082103874.html.

Hitlin, P., and S. Tan. 2012. In social media, support for same-sex marriage. *Pew Research Center.*

Hitlin, P., M. Jurkowitz, and A. Mitchell. 2013. News coverage conveys strong momentum for same-sex marriage. *Pew Research Center.*

Hodges, Obergefell V. 2016. *Oyez.* Chicago-Kent College of Law at Illinois Tech, n.d. June 9. https://www.oyez.org/cases/2014/14-556.

House, E.R. 2005. Unfinished business: Causes and values. *American Journal of Evaluation* 22 (3): 313. Cited in: Harris, R.A. 2005. A summary critique of the fact/value dichotomy. virtualsalt.com, 2.

Jasper, J.M. 1998. The emotions of protest: Affective and reactive emotions in and around social movements. *Sociological Forum* 13 (3): 397–424.

Kleinman, A. 2013. How the red equal sign took over Facebook, according to Facebook's own data. *The Huffington Post.*

Kuklinski, J.H., E. Riggle, and V. Ottati. 1991. The cognitive and affective bases of political tolerance judgments. *American Journal of Political Science* 35: 1–27.

Lerner, M., and C. West. 1995. *Jews and Blacks: Let the healing begin.* New York: G.P. Putnam's Sons.

Lewis, A. 1982. *The psychology of taxation.* New York: St. Martin's.

Luker, K. 1985. *Abortion and the politics of motherhood.* Berkeley: University of California Press.

McCarty, M. 2014. One year out, the little red logo that transformed the marriage equality narrative. *Human Rights Campaign.*

Miller, J.D. 2010. Attentive public. In *Encyclopedia of Science and Technology Communication*, ed. S.H. Priest, 73–75. Thousand Oaks: SAGE Publications. https://doi.org/10.4135/9781412959216.n27.

Morris, A.D. 1999. A retrospective on the civil rights movement: Political and intellectual landmarks. *Annual Review of Sociology* 25: 517–539.

OED. 2016. *Culture, N.* Oxford University Press. http://www.oed.com/view/Entry/45746?redirectedFrom=culture+war. Accessed 23 May 2016.

Parekh, L.B. 2000. *The future of multi-ethnic Britain: Report of the Commission on the Future of Multi-Ethnic Britain.* London: Profile Books.

Perrin, A.J. 2006. Citizen speak: The democratic imagination in American life. Chicago: The University of Chicago Press.

Pew Research Center. 2015. *Gay marriage.* http://www.pewresearch.org/data-trend/domestic-issues/attitudes-on-gay-marriage/.

Prothero, S. 2016. *Why the liberals win the culture wars (even when they lose elections).* New York: Harper Collins.

Schmalz, J. 1993. In Hawaii, step toward legalized gay marriage. *New York Times.*

Sen, A.K. 1977. Rational fools: A critique of the behavioral foundations of economic theory. *Philosophy & Public Affairs* 6 (4): 317–344.

Stein, A. 2001. Revenge of the shamed: The Christian right's emotional culture war. In *Passionate politics: Emotions and social movements*, ed. J. Goodwin, J.M. Jasper, and F. Polletta. Chicago: The University of Chicago Press.

Stigler, G., and G. Becker. 1977. De gustibus non est disputandum. *The American Economic Review* 67 (2): 76–90.

Thaler, R.H. 2015. *Misbehaving: The making of behavioral economics*. 1st ed. New York: W.W. Norton & Company.

Thaler, R.H., and C.R. Sunstein. 2008. *Nudge: Improving decisions about health, wealth, and happiness*. New Haven: Yale University Press.

The Montreux Declaration. 1947. Available at: http://www.cvce.eu/content/publication/1999/1/1/adf279f7-80a4-4855-9215-48a5184328aa/publishable_en.pdf.

Tönnies, F. 1955. *Community and association* (Gemeinschaft und gesellschaft). C.P. Loomis (Trans.). London: Routledge and Kegan Paul (Original work published 1887).

United States V. Windsor. 2016. *Oyez*. Chicago-Kent College of Law at Illinois Tech, n.d. June 9, 2016. https://www.oyez.org/cases/2012/12-307.

Warren, J. 2012. Should we pay kids to read? *The Atlantic*.

Wilson, J.Q. 1990. *Interests and deliberation in the American Republic, or why James Madison would have never received the James Madison Award*. PS: Political Science and Politics, 559.

Wrong, D.H. 1994. *The problem of order: What unites and divides society*. New York: The Free Press. (Original work published 1923).

Wu, H.D., and R. Coleman. 2009. Advancing agenda-setting theory: The comparative strength and new contingent conditions of the two levels of agenda-setting. *Journalism and Mass Communication Quarterly* 86 (4): 775–789.

Chapter 5
Moral Effects of Teaching Economics

Neoclassical economics has been criticized for being unrealistic, generating poor predictions, and engendering flawed public policies. This chapter examines a fourth charge: that teaching the subject has a morals-debasing effect. The charge holds that neoclassical economics' focus on self-interest, pleasure, and, hence, consumer goods—what critics refer to as its hedonism and materialism—renders those influenced by its teachings less moral and more anti-social. This issue has been particularly relevant in recent years, when a societal focus on individualism and deregulation are said to have contributed to the near-global financial and economic crisis that has led hundreds of millions of people—across the world—to lose their jobs, homes, and life savings.

5.1 Typical Findings

One of the first experiments to test the "debasement" hypothesis is one conducted by Marwell and Ames (1981). In this study, the social scientists designed a prisoner's dilemma-type game where participants were given an allotment of tokens to divide between a return-generating private account and a public fund. If every player invested all of their tokens in the public fund, they would all end up with a greater return than if they had all put their money into their respective private accounts. However, if a player defected and invested in the private account while the other players invested in the public fund, she would gain an even larger return. In this way, the game was designed to promote free-riding: the socially optimal behavior would be to contribute to the public fund, but, with respect to game theory, the dominant strategy would be to defect.

This chapter draws on "The Moral Effects of Economic Teaching" in *Sociological Forum* 30 (1), (March 2015): 228–233. I am indebted to Jesse Spafford for research assistance on this chapter.

Marwell and Ames found that most subjects divided their tokens nearly equally between the public and private accounts. Economics students, by contrast, invested *only 20%* of their tokens in the public fund, on average. This tendency towards free-riding was accompanied by a divergence between the moral views of the economists and non-economists. While three-quarters of non-economists reported that a "fair" investment of tokens would necessitate putting *at least* half of their tokens in the public fund (with 25% reporting that only putting *all* of the tokens in the public fund would qualify), over a third of economists didn't answer the question or gave "complex, uncodable responses" (Marwell and Ames 1981, p. 309). The remaining economics students were much more likely than their non-economist peers to say that "little or no contribution was 'fair,'" or to indicate that notions of fairness influenced their decisions (Marwell and Ames 1981, p. 309).

Following Marwell and Ames, a broad range of studies have found economics students to exhibit a stronger tendency towards anti-social behaviors relative to their peers. For example, Carter and Irons (1991) had both economics students and non-economics students play the "ultimatum" game—a two-player game where one player is given a sum of money to divide between the two. The other player is then given a chance to accept or reject the offer; if she accepts it, then each player receives the portion of money proposed by the offerer, if she declines, then neither player gets any money. Carter and Irons found that, relative to non-economics students, economics students were much more likely to offer their partners small sums, and, thus, deviate from a "fair" 50/50 spilt.

Similarly, Frank et al. (1993) found that economics majors were significantly more likely than their peers to defect in a standard prisoner's dilemma game—with a much higher proportion of economics students justifying their choice simply in terms of the rules of the game rather than via appeal to notions like "fairness." Further, these social scientists found that such anti-social behavior persists outside of the laboratory: they conducted a survey revealing that economics professors were both twice as likely to give *no* money to charity than were their peers and were "among the least generous in terms of their median gifts to large charities" (Frank et al. 1993, p. 162).[1]

Finally, these researchers had both economics and non-economics students fill out two "honesty surveys"—one at the start of the semester and one at the conclusion—regarding how likely they were to either report being undercharged for a purchase or return found money to its owner. The authors found that, after taking an economics class, students' responses to the end-of-the-semester survey were more likely to reflect a decline in reported hypothetical honest behavior than students who studied astronomy. While 23.3% of exiting astronomy students were recorded as being less likely to report a billing error where they were undercharged, 38.25% of exiting economics students were recorded as being less honest in this respect. And while 10% of astronomy students recorded less-honest responses regarding whether or not they would return found money, 27.2% of economics students reported that

---

[1] The authors received 576 completed surveys from professors chosen randomly from professional directories. Sevety-five of these surveys were filled out by economists.

they were less-likely to return the money than they were at the start of the semester (Frank et al. 1993, p. 169).[2]

Other studies supported these key findings. Frey et al. (1993) report that economics students are less likely to consider a vendor who increases the price of bottled water on a hot to be acting "unfairly." Cadsby and Maynes (1998) find that economics and business students are more prone to defect, even in games that have been tweaked to create an efficient equilibrium that can be reached by cooperating in addition to the one reached by defection. Selten and Ockenfels (1998) find that economics students who played a lottery game were willing to commit less of their potential winnings to fund a consolation prize for losers than were their peers. Frank and Schulze (2000) find that economics students were significantly more corruptible in that they were more likely to accept bribes than other students. A survey conducted by Gandal et al. (2005) find that economics students valued personal achievement and power more than their peers while attributing less importance to social justice and equality. Rubinstein (2006) reports that economics students were much more likely to favor profit-maximization over promoting the welfare of workers when faced with a business dilemma. Faravelli (2007) finds that economics students were significantly less likely to favor egalitarian solutions to problems than their peers outside of economics. Haucap and Just (2010) find that a survey of economists revealed they were more likely than their peers to consider the allocation of scarce resources in accordance with who can afford to pay the price set by supply and demand to be a fair method of rationing and distributing resources. And, Bauman and Rose (2011) report that economics majors are less likely to donate to local social programs.

5.1.1 Selection Effect?

One may ask whether studying economics is a *cause* of moral debasement. The findings cited so far could reflect not an indoctrination effect of teaching economics—but a *selection effect* whereby students prone to immoral behavior are more likely to choose to study economics than more moral students. Carter and Irons (1991), for example, note that selfish behavior exhibited in the ultimatum game was already present in entering economics first-years, contending that "economists are born, not made" (Carter and Irons 1991, p. 174). The general consensus among researchers is that, if there is an indoctrination effect, it ought to manifest itself in the form of students with greater exposure to economics expressing more pronounced anti-social behavior.

Frey et al. (1993) note no difference in evaluations of the fairness of a price increase between beginner and advanced economics students, thus endorsing the

---

[2]The percentages of economics students listed here are averages calculated by the author under the assumption that the two economics classes surveyed by the authors were identical in size. They are, thus, approximations rather than exact representations of the collected data.

selection hypothesis. Frank and Schulze (2000) find that older and younger economics students are equally corruptible, suggesting a selection effect rather than indoctrination. And, Gandal et al. (2005) find that entering economics students' tendency to endorse more self-interested normative values did not intensify after completing a year or economics education—findings that provide "support for a self-selection process" (Gandal et al. 2005, p. 1237).

In contrast, a set of other studies *do* find evidence of an indoctrination effect. Frank et al. (1993) report that, while defection—i.e. playing a "dominant" strategy that will leave a player better-off independent of her opponent's strategy but, if chosen by both players, will leave her worse-off than if both had chosen a different strategy—by non-economics students in the prisoner's dilemma game steadily declines with education, the rate of defection for economics students remains constant. More convincing is the researchers' analysis regarding how honesty surveys reveal an indoctrination effect. Their study compared the percentage of students who expressed more "dishonest" attitudes after exiting an economics course with the percentage of astronomy students who exhibited a similar moral slide—their finding being that economics students were significantly more likely to experience such moral decline. More importantly, however, the researchers *also* compared the results from the students of *two different economics classes*. One class was taught by a professor who focused upon game theory and prisoner's dilemmas with an emphasis on "how survival imperatives often militate against cooperation." The other was taught by a professor who did not focus on these topics. The result? Although the entering economics students for both classes reported similar levels of dishonesty scores at the start of the class, but by the end, those in the class with a focus on game theory reported significantly higher levels of dishonesty scores than their peers. Such results show that it is *not* just selection that is responsible for the reported increase in immoral attitudes.

Later studies support this conclusion. Faravelli (2007) finds that there are measurable ideological differences between lower-level economics students and upper-level economics students that are similar in kind to the measured differences between the ideology of economics students as a whole and their peers. He finds that upper-level students are even less likely to support egalitarian solutions to distribution problems than lower-level students, suggesting that time spent studying economics does have an indoctrination effect.

Finally, Bauman and Rose (2011) compare donations to social programs over time relative to exposure to economics and find a combination of selection and indoctrination effects: while senior economics and younger majors who had taken far fewer classes were equally unlikely to give money to social causes—suggesting selection rather than indoctrination is to blame—*non-majors* who were exposed to economics *were* less likely to donate money than their peers who did not take economics courses. This suggests that, although those drawn to economics already have more "debased" orientation compared to their peers, exposure to economics adds a debasing effect.

5.1.2   Qualifications

It should be noted that the debasing effect is often significant but far from total. There are areas of attitudes that will not be affected by exposure to economics. Thus, even in games like the prisoner's dilemma, the economics students' tendency to defect disappears when given the opportunity to interact with their fellow player beforehand and make promises to cooperate once the game has begun—a finding originally reported by Frank et al. (1993) and later replicated by Hu and Liu (2003). In addition, other studies such as Seguino et al. (1996) and Frey and Meier (2003) fail to find evidence of economics producing the particular anti-social behavior under consideration. Others find such evidence, but without the results crossing the threshold of statistical significance (see, for example, Ahmed [2008] and Ahlert et al. [2013]).

Few studies find that the study of economics correlates with *pro*-social behaviors. Yezer et al. (1996) find that economics students are more likely to deliver a found letter filled with cash to the recipient listed on the envelope than are non-economics students. And Laband and Beil (1999) find that professional economists are less likely to cheat on their association dues than are political scientists and sociologists.

5.2   In Conclusion

The fact that even taking one course in neoclassical economics may make people less moral may reflect the fact that the course merely reinforces pre-existing inclinations toward such a position. The problem is not that students are exposed to such views, but that there is no "balancing" course taught in typical American colleges, in which a different view of economics is presented. Moreover, while practically all such classes are characterized by the neoclassical viewpoint, in classes that embrace a different view—e.g. social philosophy, political science, and sociology—a great variety of approaches are advanced, thereby leaving students with a consolidated debasing exposure and a cacophony of conflicting pro-social views.

The fact that those who become professional economists are more affected is most likely not merely due to much more exposure to the neoclassical message, but also to the fact that these students join a peer group and subculture that undergirds these views.

Finally, one should note that not all economists will agree that what is considered here "debasing" is actually debasing. Some share with libertarians the conservative, laissez-faire view that, if everyone will follow their own self-interest and seek pleasure, the invisible hand will ensure that the greatest happiness for the greatest number is realized. Some even go so far as to argue that greed is good. If anybody doubted that this viewpoint is mistaken, the economic developments since 2008 should have disabused them of this notion.

5.2.1 When It Comes to Ethics, B-Schools Get an F

Ever since Enron, business schools—the training grounds for corporate managers—have been forced to face the fact that they often fail to produce honest executives. Why they have failed is a complex and revealing tale, one that I can relate from personal experience, having taught ethics at Harvard Business School (HBS) from 1987 to 1989—the years many of today's current corporate officers were in training.

HBS, which deserves particular scrutiny as the school to which many others look when they design their own curriculums, had little in the way of formal ethics teaching in 1987. And that was typical. A 1988 survey of MBA schools found that only one-third had a required ethics class (Schoenfeldt et al. 1991).

It was in 1987 that John S.R. Shad, then chairman of the Securities and Exchange Commission, made a personal donation of some $20 million to HBS to support the teaching of ethics. On April 21, 1989, after months of contentious debate, an initial proposal was put up for a faculty-wide vote. As a visiting professor, I was sitting in the bleachers, and I witnessed a memorable scene. Reactions ranged from distrust to outright hostility. One economist argued that "we are here to teach science." Another faculty member wanted to know, "Whose ethics, what values, are we going to teach?" And a third pointed out that the students were adults who got their ethics education at home and at church. By the meeting's end, the project had been sent back to the drawing board.

Debates continued over whether ethics should be a required course or a separate elective or, alternatively, whether the topic should be integrated into all classes. A member of the marketing department mused that if the latter policy were adopted, his department would have to close because much of what it was teaching constituted a form of dissembling: selling small items in large boxes, putting hot colors on packages because they encourage people to buy impulsively, and so forth.

A finance professor was also concerned about its effects on his teaching. Students later told me that they learned in his course how you could make a profit by breaking implicit contracts. Say, for instance, that you acquire controlling shares in a company such as Delta, where workers used to work harder and pose fewer demands than at other airlines because of an informal understanding that they had lifelong employment. The finance course would explain that once you take over, you could announce that you are not bound by any such informal arrangements. While such a change might be deemed a prudent move for the company, it could also bring personal gain to the new management: your stock jumps (because your labor costs seem lower, absent commitments to carry workers during a downturn) and, bingo, you cash in your stock options and move on.

In the following years, an ethics course was taught at HBS, but it was ghettoized—a minor requirement to be gotten out of the way as quickly as possible. These days, students take a required "mini" course on ethics upon arrival, and there is a required first-year course titled "Leadership and Organizational Behavior." And that's it. It's the same at other schools. One student at Stanford B-school, which had a similar program, described his ethics class as "like going to church on Sunday."

The George Washington University School of Business and Public Administration, where I once taught, has an elective on moral reasoning (the art of clarifying what your values are, rather than educating you on how to develop higher moral standards). And the University of Michigan, which has an activist student group that pushed its B-school to be mindful of social policy, requires only that students take one class in ethics or in law. Many other schools do less.

In my own Harvard Business School ethics classes, students resisted my argument that executives should take ethical considerations into account (Etzioni 2003). They held, as they had been taught, that a company focused entirely on efficiency would drive a second one, more concerned with ethics, out of business. Ethics, they told me repeatedly, were something a corporation simply cannot afford. Only if being moral bought the corporation "good will"—with a value that could be calculated and demonstrated—should the corporation take ethical considerations into account.

Many business school professors choose to steer clear of teaching morality, pointing out, with some justification, that while it is relatively clear what economics dictate and even what the law dictates, what is "ethical" is far from obvious. What appears ethical to one person is not to another, they say, and what is ethical under some conditions is not under others.

This equivocation was driven home to me during a crisis that erupted when I was at HBS. A professor instructed his class to read a case study about Braniff, an airline then headed toward bankruptcy: After a customer heard that Braniff was in financial trouble, he called the head of the company and said that he wanted to purchase a large number of tickets. But, the customer wanted to know, would the company be up and flying a few months hence? The head of Braniff, the story goes, responded that he was not sure. The students argued that the CEO should have lied, that he endangered the shareholders' equity by being candid, and that he was representing the shareholders, not the customers. The professor teaching the class was at a loss, and he asked an associate dean how to proceed.

Unsure himself, the dean arranged for a faculty conference to discuss the question. Those present made numerous arguments to justify lying. Business, some said, was like poker: If you play, you know that bluffing will take place. Others took a utilitarian line, arguing that there are no absolute values and that what is moral depends on the consequences of one's actions and on what their utility (or benefit) is. Based on this rationale, the CEO should have lied. To do otherwise might have caused the already troubled airline to collapse, causing harm to the shareholders, employees, and creditors. Still others took a market-driven approach to truth-telling: People who are found to be lying will lose customers while those who are trustworthy will gain them—making truth-telling a good idea in this case. Only two faculty members insisted that telling the truth is an absolute moral value and that the CEO should therefore avoid lying (Applbaum 2000).

The result was unfortunate. The professor returned to his classes, as many others did, with a reinforced sense that teaching ethics was a tricky business and that one should not take a firm position in favor of one value or another: It all depends....

An Aspen Institute study of about 2000 graduates of the top 13 business schools found that B-school education not only fails to improve the moral character of the students, it actually weakens it (Aspen Institute 2008). The study examined student attitudes three times while they were working toward their MBAs: upon entering, at the end of the first year, and upon graduating. Those who believed that maximizing shareholder values was the prime responsibility of a corporation increased from 68% upon entrance to 82% by the end of the first year.

In another study, students were asked if, given a 1% chance of being caught and sent to prison for 1 year, they would attempt an illegal act that would net them (or their company) a profit of more than $100,000, more than one-third responded "yes" (Roderick et al. 1991).

In light of the recent corporate scandals, some B-schools will surely attempt to strengthen ethics education. They should recruit more faculty members to teach ethics. And ethics courses should be approached not as a way to circumvent challenges by outsiders (such as the consumer protection movement or advocates of the poor) but as a moral obligation any decent person heeds. The ethics requirements set by the Association to Advance Collegiate Schools of Business, which is responsible for the accreditation of B-schools, should be more straightforward: No MBA student should graduate without having taken at least one full-term course in a class aimed at heightening students' ethical standards. At least.

References

Ahlert, M., K. Funke, and L. Schwettmann. 2013. Thresholds, productivity, and context: An experimental study on determinants of distributive behavior. *Social Choice and Welfare* 40: 957–984.

Ahmed, A. 2008. Can education affect pro-social behavior? Cops, economists and humanists in social dilemmas. *International Journal of Social Economics* 35: 298–307.

Applbaum, A.I. 2000. *Ethics for adversaries: The morality of roles in public and professional life.* Princeton: Princeton University Press.

Aspen Institute. 2008. *Where will they lead? MBA student attitudes about business & society.* https://assets.aspeninstitute.org/content/uploads/files/content/docs/bsp/SAS_PRINT_FINAL. PDF.

Bauman, Y., and E. Rose. 2011. Selection or indoctrination: Why do economics students donate less than the rest? *Journal of Economic Behavior & Organization* 79: 318–327.

Cadsby, C.B., and E. Maynes. 1998. Choosing between a socially efficient and free-riding equilibrium: Nurses versus economics and business students. *Journal of Economic Behavior & Organization* 37(2): 183–192.

Carter, J.R., and M.D. Irons. 1991. Are economists different, and if so, why? *The Journal of Economic Perspectives* 5: 171–177.

Etzioni, A. 2003. *My brother's keeper.* Lanham: Rowman & Littlefield.

Faravelli, M. 2007. How context matters: A survey based experiment on distributive justice. *Journal of Public Economics* 91: 1399–1422.

Frank, B., and G.G. Schulze. 2000. Does economics make citizens corrupt? *Journal of Economic Behavior & Organization* 43: 101–113.

Frank, R.H., T. Gilovich, and D.T. Regan. 1993. Does studying economics inhibit cooperation? *The Journal of Economic Perspectives* 7: 159–171.

Frey, B.S., and S. Meier. 2003. Are political economists selfish and indoctrinated? Evidence from a natural experiment. *Economic Inquiry* 41: 448–462.

Frey, B.S., W.W. Pommerehne, and B. Gygi. 1993. Economics indoctrination or selection? Some empirical results. *The Journal of Economic Education* 24: 271–281.

Gandal, N., S. Roccas, L. Sagiv, and A. Wrzesniewski. 2005. Personal value priorities of economists. *Human Relations* 58: 1227–1252.

Haucap, J., and T. Just. 2010. Not guilty? Another look at the nature and nurture of economics students. *European Journal of Law and Economics* 29: 239–254.

Hu, Y., and D. Liu. 2003. Altruism versus egoism in human behavior of mixed motives. *American Journal of Economics and Sociology* 62: 677–705.

Laband, D.N., and R.O. Biel. 1999. Are economists more selfish than other "social" scientists? *Public Choice* 100: 85–101.

Marwell, G., and R.E. Ames. 1981. Economists free ride, does anyone else? *Journal of Public Economics* 15: 295–310.

Roderick, J.C., H.M. Jelley, J.R. Cook, and K.A. Forcht. 1991. The issue of white collar crime for collegiate schools of business. *Journal of Education for Business* 66 (5): 387–290.

Rubinstein, A. 2006. A sceptic's comment on the study of economics. *The Economic Journal* 116: C1–C9.

Schoenfeldt, L.F., D.M. McDonald, and S.A. Youngblood. 1991. The teaching of business ethics: A survey of AACSB member schools. *Journal of Business Ethics* 10 (3): 237–241.

Seguino, S., T. Stevens, and M.A. Lutz. 1996. Gender and cooperative behavior: Economic man rides alone. *Feminist Economics* 2: 1–21.

Selten, R., and A. Ockenfels. 1998. An experimental solidarity game. *Journal of Economic Behavior & Organization* 34: 517–539.

Yezer, A.M., R.S. Goldfarb, and P.J. Poppen. 1996. Does studying economics discourage cooperation? Watch what we do, not what we say or how we play. *The Journal of Economic Perspectives* 10: 177–186.

Part III
Job Loss & Right Wing Populism

Chapter 6
Job Collapse on the Way to New Athens

A significant number of analysts have shown that automation, especially the kind driven by Artificial Intelligence, is destroying many jobs and is expected to eliminate many more in the near future, including many middle class jobs. This development in turn is held to raise social and political tensions and to raise moral issues. A common response is the observation that such creative destruction always follows technical advances, but that these very advances lead to the formation of new and better jobs—jobs that entail less menial work and that pay better. However, there is some evidence that this may well not be the case this time. The chapter examines these assessments in part I.

Several treatments have been offered to deal with the net job loss, should it occur, which some refer to as job collapse or even job Armageddon. These include education reforms as well as training and retraining programs, which are reviewed and assessed in part II. Providing income security to all members of society, whether or not they work, to mitigate the social and political effects of job losses, is reviewed and assessed in part III. Various other suggestions have been made to cope with this challenge posed by automation (part IV). The chapter finds that none of the suggested treatments will suffice and hence calls for a fundamental change in culture and the economy, outlined in part V.

This chapter draws on "Job Collapse on the Road to New Athens" in *Challenge* 60 (4), (2017): 327–346. I am indebted to David Kroeker-Maus and Anne Jerome for research assistance on this chapter.

A. Etzioni, *Happiness is the Wrong Metric*, Library of Public Policy and Public Administration 11, https://doi.org/10.1007/978-3-319-69623-2_6

6.1 Job Collapse

6.1.1 Jobs Already Lost Due to Automation

Automation is reported to have already destroyed a great number of jobs. 88% of the jobs lost in manufacturing between 2000 and 2010 were attributable to productivity growth, which in turn is largely due to automation and advances in information technology (Hicks and Devaraj 2017). The net number of manufacturing jobs that disappeared in the US during this period was roughly 5.6 million.

Reports from specific industries illustrate the kind of jobs lost. An oft-cited example is that of Eastman Kodak which, at its peak, employed 145,300 people. In 2012, the company declared bankruptcy, not because photography had decreased in popularity, but because the advent of digital cameras eliminated the need for skilled technicians who made photography chemicals and paper.

In 2015, the 11 largest banks in the US and Europe announced 100,000 job cuts, amounting to more than 10% of their total workforces. John Markoff notes that, although the introduction of ATMs did not eliminate the need for bank tellers, it did eliminate thousands of back office jobs for less-visible clerical workers (Markoff 2016).

The legal profession is experiencing the effects of the introduction of automating technologies. In 1978, when the Justice Department brought an anti-trust lawsuit against CBS, the discovery process required a "platoon of lawyers," to examine six million documents, at a cost of $2.2 million. In 2011, an E-discovery company was able to analyze 1.5 million documents for less than $100,000.

Data indicate that current law school graduates have a significantly harder time finding a job than in any previous generation: Kyle McEntee, Executive Director of Law School Transparency notes that, "Students who graduated in 2015 started in 2012, the second of five consecutive years of enrollment decline. In that time, the raw number of legal jobs has *also* fallen each year [emphasis added]" (McEntee 2016).

6.1.2 Expected Future Job Losses

There are varying predictions of the number of jobs automation will destroy in the near future. Labor economists Melanie Arntz, Terry Gregory and Ulrich Zierahn suggest that the risk of technological unemployment is relatively low. They argue that previous studies have taken an occupation-based approach to calculating the automatability of jobs, whereas actual automation is task-based. Thus, *specific functions can be automated*, but given the heterogeneity of tasks in many occupations, it is much *less likely that those entire occupations will be automated*. According to Arntz et al.'s calculations, only 9% of jobs across the 21 OECD countries are automatable (Arntz et al. 2016).

Others have noted the risk to professions previously thought to be beyond the reach of automation because they involve tasks thought to be the sole preserve of humans (Kaplan 2015). An oft-cited study by Carl Benedikt Frey and Michael A. Osborne of Oxford calculated in 2013 that 47% of current US employment is at high risk of computerization in the next decade or two (although they stress that their estimate only shows which jobs *could* potentially be automated, not which ones actually *will*) (Frey and Osborne 2013). The professions at the highest risk of computerization, according to Frey and Osborne, include such disparate occupations as telemarketers, tax preparers, watch repairers and insurance underwriters.

Mike Mayo, a banking analyst, expects that "The additional electronification of the security markets should result in an ongoing swap of capital for labour...more machines over people" (Noonan and Arnold 2015). A 2016 study by Deloitte predicted that 114,000 jobs in the legal sector are likely to become automated in the next 20 years (Croft 2016). Legal scholars John O. McGinnis and Russell G. Pearce predict that "Just as computers have progressively replaced humans in complex calculations (people who made such calculations were in fact called computers a hundred years ago), so will machine intelligence replace the legal search function of lawyers" (McGinnis and Pearce 2014). Millions of truck and taxi drivers' jobs are expected to be killed by driverless cars.

There are predictions that the rise of massive open online courses (MOOCs) will lead to a collapse in jobs for academics. Clayton Christensen, a Harvard Business School professor predicted in 2013 that, in 15 years, half of all universities will have gone out of business, as higher education is ripe for technological disruption (Suster 2013). In April 2013, the philosophy department at San Jose State University wrote an open letter to Harvard professor Michael Sandel (whose lectures on justice are one of the most popular online courses), saying "Professors who care about public education should not produce products that will replace professors, dismantle departments, and provide a diminished education for students in public universities" (Hechinger and McDonald 2013). It is odd to consider MOOCs as a way to treat the issue at hand. A handful of MOOCs, produced by a few leading professors and a small media team, can kill hundreds of thousands of teaching jobs, worldwide. The main constraint is that the MOOCs have not formed a suitable business model but that does not seem an insurmountable hurdle. One further notes that a professor who used 12 teaching assistants online found that the one students ranked highest was a robot... (Korn 2016).

A recent study by Daron Acemoglu and Pascual Restrepo found that robots have significant negative effects on wages and employment opportunities. "Even if overall employment and wages recover, there will be losers in the process, and it's going to take a very long time for these communities to recover," Acemoglu concluded (Cain Miller 2017).

6.1.3 Luddite Fallacy?

The fear of technological unemployment is not new; it is at least as old as the Luddites who destroyed mechanical looms in the early 1800s, for fear that increasing mechanization threatened the jobs and livelihoods of workers. Thus, some argue that the fear of automation reducing the overall need for workers is just another example of the 'Luddite fallacy.' Harvard economist Lawrence Katz argues "We never have run out of jobs. There is no long-term trend of eliminating work for people. Over the long term, employment rates are fairly stable. People have always been able to create new jobs. People come up with new things to do" (Rotman 2013).

However, there is some evidence that this time the number of new jobs created will be significantly lower than the number of old jobs destroyed. While the unemployment rate fluctuates, the share of prime-age Americans (i.e. 25–54 years old) who are working or looking for work *has* been trending steadily downward since 2000. And among men in this prime age group, the share of those who are neither working nor looking for work (the latter group not being reflected in the unemployment rate) has doubled since the 1970s. Moreover, the inability to find a job is not limited to older workers whose skills have become obsolete; the share of recent college graduates who are "underemployed" was higher in 2015 than it was in 2000 (Thompson 2015).

Mark Nall, a program manager for NASA, points out:

> Unlike previous disruptions such as when farming machinery displaced farm workers but created factory jobs making the machines, robotics and AI are different. Due to their versatility and growing capabilities, not just a few economic sectors will be affected, but whole swaths will be. This is already being seen now in areas from robocalls to lights-out manufacturing. (Smith and Anderson 2014)

Hod Lipson concluded that "for a long time the common understanding was that technology was destroying jobs but also creating new and better ones. Now the evidence is that technology is destroying jobs and indeed creating new and better ones but also fewer ones" (Rotman 2015).

6.1.4   Net Job Loss?

The main differences among various scholars seem to be about the size of the net job loss rather than whether some loss will occur. A January report from the World Economic Forum entitled "The Future of Jobs," (World Economic Forum 2016) estimates that between 2015 and 2020, 7.1 million jobs will be lost across 15 of the major developed and emerging countries surveyed, but that only 2 million new jobs will be created, resulting in a net loss of 5.1 million jobs.

Martin Ford, in *Rise of the Robots* paints a grim picture of what the book's subtitle labels a "jobless future." He finds that, while previous technological revolutions replaced the jobs they created (for example, the automotive industry replacing the carriage industry), technology is now taking away more jobs than it creates, and that both blue- and white-collar jobs are at risk. Ford notes that, after the 2008 recession, many companies decided that "ever-advancing information technology" would allow them to return to their previous level of output without returning to previous staffing levels. That is, even though the recession caused employees to be laid off, technology made it unnecessary to hire them back after the recovery.

Erik Brynjolfsson and Andrew McAfee observe that the new tech companies are creating more billionaires, but hiring far fewer workers. They offer an anecdotal comparison between Kodak and Instagram: Eastman Kodak, at its peak, employed 145,000 workers, most of them in middle-class jobs. Instagram, which is already valued at several times the value of Eastman Kodak at its peak, employs only 4600 workers (Brynjolfsson and McAfee 2014).

Thompson notes that, "In 1964, the nation's most valuable company, AT&T, was worth $267 billion in today's dollars and employed 758,611 people. Today's telecommunications giant, Google, is worth $370 billion but has only about 55,000 employees—less than a tenth the size of AT&T's workforce in its heyday." And General Motors has only one third the number of employees it had in the 1970s, even though it now produces *more* cars and trucks (Wiseman 2016). This pattern of increasing output and a declining workforce can be seen in the economy more broadly: In 1980 it took, on average, 25 workers to generate $1 million in manufacturing output, but in the US today it takes only five workers (Muro 2016).

Hod Lipson, an engineering professor at Cornell, and expert on AI and robotics, is working on creative robots that are capable of assembling themselves from basic building blocks. Thus, not only could these robots replace human workers, but they would not even create many new jobs in robot assembly.

Some optimists point to the fact that, despite advances in automation, the unemployment rate in the US is low—4.8% as of January 2017. A McKinsey Global Institute study found that, between 2001 and 2009, there were 4.8 million new jobs created in the US that related to interactions and complex problem solving, compared to only 3.4 million jobs related to transactions and production which were lost (Manyika et al. 2012). When one takes into account, however, the number of people who have stopped looking for work, there is less ground for optimism. The Bureau of Labor and Statistics' U-6 measure, which includes both underemployed and those who have given up looking for work, was almost 10% at the end of 2016. Economist Samuel Rines notes that the labor force participation rate has been declining since 2000, and that, although the labor force is not shrinking in absolute terms, "as a portion of the employable population, it is shrinking and will continue to do so." Since 2007, the labor force participation rate has fallen by 3.2% (Rines 2017).

Moreover, many of the new jobs pay less than the lost ones, have fewer or no benefits, provide less job security, and are less meaningful. This is reflected in the growing proportion of contingent labor—freelancers, independent contractors and consultants who are not on a company's payroll. According to numbers from a 2016 study by the Metropolitan Policy Program at the Brookings Institution, the number of gig economy workers has increased the number of payroll employees by 27% more in the last two decades (Wells 2016). A 2015 Government Accountability Office study found that, between 2005 and 2015, the share of contingent workers grew from 30.6% to 40.4% (US Government Accountability Office 2015).[1]

---

[1] It should be noted that the GAO definition of contingent workers includes part-time workers.

Finally, most of the discussions of net job loss treats the US as an island, and are concerned only with the effects of technological unemployment on American society. However, many European countries have double-digit unemployment rates, as high as 18.2% in Spain and 23.0% in Greece (Eurostat 2017). Moreover, in some developing countries where the majority of the population is under 18, the impact of insufficient jobs will be felt even stronger. There are 16 African countries where at least 50% of the population is under the age of 18, and in Afghanistan the percentage is 51.4%. Given that most of these countries already have a shortage of well-paying jobs, the effect of such a huge share of the population entering the workforce in coming years will only exacerbate social tensions.

6.1.5   What Is to Be Done?

A 2016 report released by the Obama White House entitled "Artificial Intelligence, Automation, and the Economy" suggested three policy responses to technological change. The report acknowledges that "Most of these strategies would be important regardless of AI-driven automation, but all take on even greater importance to the degree that AI is making major changes to the economy." Thus, some of the proposals in the White House report merely reflect pre-existing Democratic policy priorities, which are not directly relevant to automation-driven job loss, and thus are not discussed here.

The following three sections analyze the broad policy responses suggested by the White House report and others for addressing large-scale job loss. Each group of solutions will be presented and then evaluated.

6.2   Education and Training for the Jobs of the Future

The White House report favors "expanding the availability of job-driven training and opportunities for lifelong learning." The report points out that early education is an important component, as people with low levels of basic skills are likely to be displaced in an era of AI-driven technological change. The report touts President Obama's Computer Science for All initiative, which "seeks to give all students at the K-12 level access to coursework in computing and computational thinking." And the report calls for increasing access to post-secondary education, and expanding access to training and re-training as well as the availability of job-driven training. Many others write about the importance of education in averting mass technological unemployment. Brynjolfsson and McAfee suggest several steps to restore the US' advantage in primary education, which has declined in the past 50 years. For example, in 1955, high school enrollment levels in the US were twice as high as any European country. But by 2009, American high school students ranked 14th out of 34 countries surveyed in reading, 17th in science and 25th in math. They suggest longer school hours, a longer school year, and higher teacher salaries in exchange for more teacher accountability.

The Frey and Osborne report argues that humans' ability to acquire new skills is what has prevented previous worries about technological unemployment from materializing. Thus, education could help, but the increasing cost of education makes it difficult for many to acquire necessary skills. Hence, the authors suggest that the increasing availability of online education courses could offer a solution.

Jerry Kaplan proposes an approach that would increase access to skills training, albeit one that would require new financial instruments which he calls "job mortgages." Under this scheme, employers would issue non-binding letters of intent to hire people if they acquire specific skills that the employer thinks will be valuable. (Kaplan suggests payroll tax breaks for employers who follow through on their offer.) Training institutions will offer courses to teach the skills that employers seek, and potential employees holding non-binding letters of intent would be able to get a "job mortgage" loan to finance their training. The loans would be repaid from income once the sponsorship recipients started new jobs; if no job materializes, the individual would be held responsible for only 20% of the loan (Kaplan 2015).

6.2.1 An Assessment

6.2.1.1 Education

Reforming education systems is likely to have long-term effects; however, as several observers note, the pace of technological change is rapid and hence skills that school-children learn are likely to be obsolete by the time they enter the workforce. The World Economic Forum report cites an estimate that "65% of children entering primary school today will ultimately end up working in completely new job types that don't yet exist" (World Economic Forum 2016, p. 3). The report also holds that the pace of technological change and the accelerating rate of "creative destruction" casts doubt on the wisdom of transforming universities into glorified vocational schools.

One also notes that a large number and variety of efforts and considerable investments have been made over the last decades in the US to improve the US education system. Public expenditures on education increased from $258 to $534 billion between 1979–1980 and 2012–2013 (US Department of Education 2016). However, National Assessment of Educational Progress (NAEP) test scores remained virtually the same for 17 year-olds between 1971 and 2012, and although the test scores of nine and 13 year-olds showed statistically significant improvement during this time frame, it was only among those ranking in the lower percentiles (Barshay 2013). Thus, while the achievement gap may be closing, the achievement level of top students has been stagnant for 40 years (Barshay 2013).

Furthermore, students in the US are still less qualified than students in many other developed countries, with whom they have to compete. According to the 2015 PISA (Program for International Student Assessment) test results, the US ranks

24th in reading and science, and 38th in math (Desilver 2017). The ranking in 2012 was 17th in reading, 21st in science, and 29th in math.[2]

In short educational reforms, of value in themselves, are hard to come by and may well continue to lag behind the rapidly changing job market.

6.2.1.2   Retraining

Retraining of workers who have lost 'old' jobs to enable them to take on new jobs seems an obvious solution. This idea is supported by the fact that even when unemployment was high, when there was a very ample supply of labor, a considerable amount of high tech jobs could not find American workers able to fulfill these jobs (See Graham 2017)—the workforce is facing a skills mismatch (McKinsey Global Institute 2017). However, there are strong reasons to hold that older workers, who spent a good part of their lifetime in jobs such as coal mining, cannot be retrained to do high tech jobs. And the destruction of jobs is much higher than the high tech openings. Hence even if retraining will work perfectly, it will reduce unemployment but not get at the heart of the matter—a great net loss in jobs. To say it with figures: Assume an economy had 100 jobs, lost 20, and in addition has 3 unfilled because of skill mismatch; so the unemployment rate is 23%. Training can reduce unemployment to 20% but not lower. Training beyond this point will merely lead employers not to hire someone else or to fire someone.

One may argue that the US, in 2017, was nearing full employment and hence the problem posed by automation has been solved or never existed. However, after peaking in 2000 at 67.3% (US Department of Labor 2016) the US labor force participation rate has experienced a general trend of decline; as of 2016 it was at 62.8% (US Department of Labor 2016).

Most importantly, the new jobs are paying much less than the old ones, have fewer or no benefits, and offer much less job security (as one learns from the rapid growth of the gig economy). There is reason to believe that this trend will continue. This kind of employment is almost as alienating as unemployment and is a major source of nationalist populism that endangers political stability of democratic regimes and freer trade.

6.3   Basic Income and Social Safety Nets

To deal with the personal, social, and political effects of persistent unemployment and poor jobs, suggestions have been made to provide people who cannot find work with the means they need to survive.

According to the White House report, "This includes steps to modernize the social safety net, including exploring strengthening critical supports such as unem-

---

[2] Determined from data available at https://data.oecd.org/

ployment insurance, Medicaid, Supplemental Nutrition Assistance Program (SNAP), and Temporary Assistance for Needy Families (TANF), and putting in place new programs such as wage insurance and emergency aid for families in crisis." The White House report also proposes strengthening unemployment insurance, noting that "fewer than one in three unemployed Americans now receive unemployment insurance benefits, and benefits replace a smaller percentage of wages than before for those who do qualify."

Frey and Osborne predict that there will be a rise in "job polarization" as the share of low-wage jobs grows. They thus suggest policies to decrease the "tax wedge" (i.e. the difference between gross pay and take-home pay) for low-wage workers. They outline a number of potential options for accomplishing this, including raising marginal income tax rates on top earners in order to decrease tax rates for low income earners, increasing corporate taxes, or instituting a wealth tax, as proposed by Thomas Piketty (Frey and Osborne 2015).

Brynjolfsson and McAfee endorse Milton Friedman's idea of a negative income tax, which is quite similar to basic income: workers earning below a certain threshold would receive a payment from the government on unused deductions, thus encouraging work, while also ensuring that no one falls below a certain income level (Brynjolfsson and McAfee 2014).

Martin Ford advocates for a "basic income guarantee"—also frequently referred to as universal basic income (UBI) (See Van Parijs and Vanderborght 2017)—which, he notes, has historically had support from conservatives and libertarians, most prominently Friedrich Hayek. The conservative argument is that a basic income guarantee would still allow individual freedom, and would replace less efficient safety net mechanisms such as food stamps, housing assistance, etc. (Ford 2015).

The concept of UBI has attracted the attention and support of a number of Silicon Valley philanthropists. GiveDirectly, a charity that is beta-testing UBI as a solution for extreme poverty by giving all villagers in a designated village in Kenya the equivalent of $22 per month for 12 years, has attracted $24 million in donations from the founders of Facebook, Instagram and eBay (Lowrey 2017). Several countries are experimenting with UBI or running pilot projects; in both Finland (which is testing the UBI with 2000 unemployed citizens [Goodman 2016] and India (where the Finance Ministry is considering it [Zhong 2017], the UBI is seen as a replacement for some or all existing social welfare programs.

6.3.1 An Assessment

There are two differing visions for UBI. The first, and more common, sees the UBI as a replacement for other social welfare programs. Michael Tanner, a Senior Fellow at Cato Institute, notes that prominent libertarians have endorsed a UBI, and that it would provide an "intriguing alternative to our current dysfunctional welfare state" (Tanner 2014). That is, instead of receiving food stamps, housing allowance, Medicaid, and unemployment insurance payments—those unemployed would receive a monthly check, roughly of the same value. This may or may not make them feel less controlled, and able to freely spend their money as they wish. They may use it wisely or for controlled substances, opioids, and liquor. However, it will do little to overcome the income losses due to loss of jobs.

Robert Greenstein of the Center on Budget and Policy Priorities suggests that a UBI that replaced existing social welfare programs would actually increase poverty, if it was not means-tested: "If you take the dollars targeted on people in the bottom fifth or two-fifths of the population and convert them to universal payments to people all the way up the income scale, you're redistributing income upward" (Greenstein 2016). Moreover, the difference in cost-of-living highlights another problem with UBI as a replacement for current safety net programs: it would almost certainly have to be accompanied by some sort of public housing guarantee, as even a UBI that put recipients above the poverty level might still be insufficient to afford housing in many cities.

The second vision of UBI sees it as a complement to other programs. For example, if each American citizen received $10,000 (which would *still* put them below the poverty line), the program would cost nearly $3 trillion dollars, more than *three times the current expenditure on all welfare programs* (Tanner 2014). In 2015, Switzerland held a referendum on a proposal to give a UBI of roughly $2700 per month. The measure was defeated, but *The Economist* calculated that the cost of UBI would have equaled 30% of Switzerland's GDP.

The costs will have to covered by significantly higher taxes elsewhere (most likely on top earners) or a wealth tax, and both of these seem politically very difficult.

A negative income tax would be a way of means-testing the UBI. This may well be more affordable but could give rise to other issues:

> If the benefit is phased out fairly quickly for those with incomes above the poverty level, the program may well be affordable, even cheaper than the current welfare system. But too rapid a phase-out would create a "poverty cliff," where the marginal tax rate for earning additional income would significantly discourage work or other efforts to escape poverty. A more gradual phase-out minimizes this problem, but adds considerably to the expense of the program. (Tanner 2014)

Beyond concerns about the cost of a UBI, others argue that work provides more than just a paycheck. Lawrence Katz has argued that work is a source of status and that it helps to organize people's lives. Brynjolfsson and McAfee write that work is psychologically important and cite Voltaire's aphorism, "Work saves a man from three great evils: boredom, vice and need." A UBI would perhaps ward off the third of those "great evils" but not the other two.

6.4   Others

One proposed solution to net job loss is a job guarantee, similar to the Works Progress Administration that was part of FDR's New Deal. The basic principle is that the government would create make-work jobs to fill the gap left by the private sector, or act as an "employer of last resort." In their book *Only Humans Need Apply*, Thomas H. Davenport and Julia Kirby argue for a job guarantee instead of UBI, citing studies that find that that unemployed people are less happy, and that compensating them does not make them as happy as putting them back to work (Davenport and Kirby 2016). Pavlina Tcherneva suggests a grassroots job guarantee program that would be run by the non-profit sector but funded by the government. She writes "The federal government will allocate grants to nonprofits that are already on the ground and doing many of the jobs that the public and private sectors have failed to do" (Tcherneva 2012).

Several authors focus on other proposals, like the notion of encouraging entrepreneurship and alternatives to traditional employment (such as freelancing and self-employment). Brynjolfsson and McAfee write that entrepreneurship is the best way to create new jobs and opportunity, and that innovation is more likely to take place in startups rather than in incumbent companies. They suggest making the regulatory requirements and business environment more favorable for entrepreneurs. Frey and Osborne suggest that because digital technologies make it cheaper for entrepreneurs to start their own businesses and because self-employed workers report higher levels of satisfaction in their work, self-employment may become the new normal in the future. Thus, they suggest reducing red tape that discourages self-employment. They also propose changing policies that they suggest disincentivize hiring, such as payroll taxes or mandating employer-covered health care insurance. The WEF report writes that policymakers will need to put in place safeguards and regulations that allow employees to transfer their benefits between jobs.

Bill Gates has suggested a robot tax to help slow the pace of automation as well as to finance jobs that require human empathy such as taking care of the elderly or working with kids in schools (Delaney 2017).

6.4.1 An Assessment

A job guarantee scheme could be viewed as preferable to a UBI, as there is some guaranteed direct output, however small, from make-work jobs, whereas the output from UBI is indirect and uncertain. It is important to ensure that make-work programs do not replace jobs that otherwise would be done, lest they simply substitute a private sector job for a government-sponsored one. Also, previous successful job guarantee or "employer of last resort" programs were meant to be counter-cyclical; indeed, the Works Progress Administration was closed after 8 years. Given that the loss of jobs to automation is likely to continue, and perhaps even accelerate rather than abate, short-term job guarantee programs may not prove a viable model for a response to long-term technological unemployment.

Above all, there are considerable costs involved in make-work schemes. A 2000 Government Accountability Office report on Americorps found that the average cost per volunteer was roughly $23,000 (GAO 2000), a cost which most likely has increased in the intervening 17 years. There seems to be no reason to expect such a program on a large scale to be much more politically feasible than a UBI that does not simply replace other public support.

6.5   The New Athens

The recent and expected job loss and the change in the nature of many of the jobs available, as well as the economic slowdown (and rising inequality), are all major factors in the rise of both political alienation and a variety of right-wing attitudes including xenophobia, racism, anti-Semitism, and support for radical right-wing parties and politicians. The same development is often referred to as a populist wave. The question hence arises if one can identify other sources of contentment than that gained from work for people who have achieved a level of income that ensures that they can attend to their "basic" needs, but little more. What other sources of legitimacy can be developed that are not based on a continually rising standard of living?

One step toward developing a rather different perspective on one's economic conditions is to point to data which strongly suggest that once a certain level of income is attained, additional income (and hence the capacity to spend and consume) creates little additional contentment. Social science findings (which do not all run in the same direction and have other well-known limitations) on the whole seem to lend support to the notion that higher income does not significantly raise people's contentment, with the important exception of the poor (See Etzioni 2016).

6.5.1   Historical "Precedents"

In seeking alternatives to job and economic growth-driven happiness, one notes that there were, throughout human history, many cultures and modes of legitimacy that eschewed consumerism and viewed the good life as based on other core values. As Jeffrey Sachs notes, "The essence of traditional virtue ethics—whether in Buddhism, Aristotelianism, or Roman Catholicism—is that happiness is achieved by harnessing the will and the passions to live the right kind of life. Individuals become virtuous through rational thought, instruction, mind training, and habits of virtuous behavior" (Sachs 2013, p. 83). Thus, consider the way happiness is understood within the Buddhist tradition. According to this view, happiness is not mainly a phenomenological state but rather, is "a way of interpreting the world," and, thus, is more akin to a skill or ability than a sensation (Matthie 2000, p. 19).

For centuries, the literati of imperial China came to prominence not through acquisition of wealth, but through pursuit of knowledge and cultivation of the arts. This group of scholar-bureaucrats dedicated their early lives to rigorous study, in preparation for the exams required for government service. They spent years memorizing the Confucian classics. The literati, having passed the imperial exams, were qualified for government service, but instead elected to dedicate their lives to the arts, or retired early in order to follow artistic pursuits. They played music and composed poetry, learned calligraphy, and gathered with like-minded friends to share ideas and discuss great works of the past.

The Ancient Greeks—aside from the Epicureans[3] (Nussbaum 2005)—generally took "happiness" to be not just a feeling but a way of living (Senior 2010). For example, in Aristotle's philosophy, the sort of "happiness" discussed is not hedonistic but, rather, can also be translated as "flourishing" and is based in the manifestation of virtue—a way of being that can be cultivated and involves finding a balance between "excess and deficiency" and experiencing "emotions at the right times and on the right occasions and towards the right persons and for the right causes and in the right manner" (Sachs 2013, p. 84). Indeed, Aristotle believed that happiness is comprised of acting in accordance with excellence, in particular the greatest and richest variety of excellence available (Nussbaum 2005, p. 175). Further, in addition to viewing happiness as including the "activity of soul in accordance with virtue," Aristotle also believes in the concept of having friends and children (Engstrom 1996, p. 104). Thus, Aristotle's conception of happiness is much broader than that of many contemporary thinkers, amounting to "flourishing human living, a kind of living that is active, inclusive of all that has intrinsic value, and complete, meaning lacking in nothing that would make it richer or better" (Nussbaum 2005, p. 171).

For St. Thomas Aquinas, happiness is not a pleasurable psychological state but, rather, the attainment of one's final good (Wang 2007, p. 322). This final good "consists in the vision of God"—meaning that true happiness cannot be attained on Earth but can be only approximated (Wang, p. 323). And though people might get moments of temporary satisfaction after achieving short-term goals, true happiness comes only with the attainment of union with God (Wang, p. 326).

In the 1960s, a counterculture (hippie) movement rose on both sides of the Atlantic Ocean. Its core values were anti-consumerism, communal living, equality, environmentalism, free love, and pacifism. The British iteration of the hippie movement manifested itself in London's underground culture, a "community of like-minded anti-establishment, anti-war, pro-rock'n'roll individuals, most of whom had a common interest in recreational drugs," and many who opted out of mainstream consumerist culture (Miles 2011).

Many of these movements and communities sought to opt out of both the consumption and work system and to form an alternative universe committed to ascetic life, while dedicating themselves to transcendental activities, including spiritual, religious, political, or social elements. They sought to replace capitalism rather than to cap it and graft onto it a different society.

Most important: practically all of these movements and communities failed to lay a foundation for a new contemporary society, let alone civilization, and practically all of them either disintegrated, shriveled, or lost their main alternative features. It seems that most people cannot abide an ascetic, severe, austere life for the

---

[3] Nussbaum notes that throughout almost the entire canon of Western philosophy, almost all schools of thought refuse to identify "happiness" with psychological "pleasure."

longer run. *It hence seems that if the current environment calls for a new attempt to form a society less centered on consumption, the endeavor will have to graft the new conception of a good life onto the old one. That is, not seek to replace consumption but to cap it and channel the resources and energy thus freed to other pursuits.* To proceed, that is, to ask when we know that income can be capped without frustrating basic human needs, a review of Maslow suggests a way.

6.5.2   The Maslowian Exit

Maslow's hierarchy of needs, from basic human necessities to what he calls "self-actualization," might lead one to intuit that as long as the acquisition and consumption of goods satisfies basic creature comforts—safety, shelter, food, clothing, health care, and education—then rising wealth is contributing to genuine human contentment. However, once consumption is used to satisfy the higher needs, it turns into consumerism—and consumerism becomes a social disease.[4]

In historical terms, the turning point came—for Americans with income well above the poverty line—in the decades that followed WWII. Around the time of WWII, economists held that people have fixed needs and that once these were satisfied, people wouldn't consume more; they would save whatever additional income they earned. During the war, however, economists noted that the American productive capacity had greatly expanded. They feared that with the end of the war, the idling of the assembly lines that produced thousands of tanks, planes, and many other war-related materials would lead to massive unemployment (in effect, a return to the kind of depression that the US faced just before WWII)—because there was nothing that the assembly lines could produce that people needed, given that their fixed, peacetime needs were sated. Social scientists thus held that they had to go to creative extremes to protect society from its 'excess' capacity. This conventional wisdom, however, was soon to change when Vance Packard's *The Status Seekers* called attention to the purveyors of large scale advertising, the producers of artificial, unbounded wants (Packard and Abbott 1963).

In the decades that followed WWII, industrial corporations discovered that they could "manufacture" artificial needs for whatever products they were marketing. For instance, first women and then men were taught that they smelled bad and needed to purchase deodorants. Men, who used to wear white shirts and grey flannel suits, learned that they 'had to' purchase a variety of shirts and suits, and that last year's wear was not proper in the year that followed. Soon, it was not just suits but also cars, ties, handbags, sunglasses, watches, and numerous other products that had to be constantly replaced to keep up with the latest trends. Most recently people have been convinced that they have various illnesses (such as restless leg syndrome) that require the purchase of medications.

---

[4] For a lengthy discussion of Maslow's hierarchy, see Chap. 1.

One cannot stress enough that the quest for a new characterization of the good life is a project for those whose creature comforts have been well and securely sated. Urging such a project on individuals, classes, or societies that have not reached that stage of development is to promote what sociologists call 'status acceptance,' to urge the 'have-nots' to love their misery. It is to provide a rationale for those who 'have' all they need and then some—and who deny such basics to others. Such a position hardly comports with any definition of a good life.

To reiterate: Consumption *per se* is not the issue. Maslow does not suggest an austere life, of sacks and ashes or of making virtue out of poverty. Rather, his theory holds that gaining the material resources needed to provide for basic creature comforts is fully legitimate. However, consumption turns into an obsession when—after necessities are provided—people use the means suitable for attending to creature comforts to try to buy affection, esteem, and even self-actualization. It does not take a great deal of work to earn enough to buy what it takes to satisfy basic needs if these are viewed as what a person requires to be well nourished, clothed, housed, and safe—but not to purchase status (or Veblen) goods. Then one can find other sources of contentment and meaning than material goods.

6.5.3 Income and Happiness

Data suggest that once a certain threshold of income is reached, additional accumulation income creates little additional contentment. On the whole, social science findings, despite well-known limitations and variations in approach, seem to support this notion of diminishing returns of happiness relative to income growth—with the important exception of the poor. Findings by Frank M. Andrews and Stephen B. Withey support the notion that one's socio-economic status has a meager effect on one's "sense of well-being" and no significant effect on one's life satisfaction (Andrews and Withey 1976). A survey of over 1000 participants, who rated their sense of satisfaction and happiness on a 7-point scale and a 3-point scale, concluded that there was no correlation between socioeconomic status and happiness; in fact, the second-highest socioeconomic group was consistently among the least happy of all seven brackets measured. In addition, Jonathan Freedman discovered that levels of reported happiness do not vary greatly among the members of different economic classes, with the exception of the very poor, who tend to be less happy than others (Freedman 1978).

Additional evidence suggests that economic growth does not significantly affect happiness (though at any given time the people of poor countries are generally less happy than those of wealthy ones). David G. Myers and Ed Diener reported that while per-capita disposable (after-tax) income in inflation-adjusted dollars almost exactly doubled between 1960 and 1990, almost the same proportion of Americans reported that they were "very happy" in 1993 (32%) as they did in 1957 (35%) (Myers and Diener 1995). Although economic growth has slowed since the mid-1970s, Americans' reported happiness has been remarkably stable (nearly always between 30% and 35%) across both high-growth and low-growth periods (Myers and Diener 1995). Moreover, in the same period (1960–1990), rates of depression, violent crime, divorce, and teen suicide all rose dramatically (Myers and Diener 1995). For much more data and discussion, see Chap. 1.

6.6   The Sisyphean Nature of Affluence

A reason high wage-earners seem to derive less happiness from additional income is that the goods which high incomes allow one to buy are reported not to have *absolute* value in terms of the happiness they provide. Recall the discussion in Chap. 1 of "keeping up with the Joneses"—an expression that captures the use of goods in a status competition among members of the community. Goods are used as visible markers of one's standing relative to others.

The claim also explains why an increase in a nation's collective wealth often fails to increase reported happiness. If what makes people happy is having *more* wealth relative to others, then it follows that happiness is more dependent on whom one compares himself to rather than his absolute income—and one can typically find someone who earns more than he does.

Other social scientists have posited that it is not explicit social competition that is the problem. Rather, people judge the value of a given consumer good based upon a contextual assessment that factors in the goods possessed by their neighbors (Frank 2007). In thinking about the competitive consumption that characterizes "keeping up with the Joneses," one notes that the motives underlying the behavior make explicit reference to one's peers. One doesn't just want a "big" house, but rather, one that is "bigger than that of the Joneses." By contrast, the contextual valuation of goods prevents collective improvements in wealth from generating collective improvements in happiness even absent any feelings of jealousy, envy, or any explicit reference being made to the conditions of others. Instead, the suggestion is that the value one derives from a given consumer good—i.e. the extent to which one considers it to be of "good" or "high quality"—depends upon the goods possessed by one's peers. Thus, one does not need to want a "better" house than one's neighbors to be affected; rather, one might just want a "good" house, but such a judgment is inevitably influenced by similar goods possessed by one's neighbors. To illustrate this point, Robert Frank uses the example of how one would feel about owning a 1979 Chevrolet Nova (Frank 2007, p. 32). The answer to this question, he argues, depends upon *context*: to those living in Cuba, such a car would seem a luxury while those living in the California would likely find such a car embarrassing or unwieldy (Frank 2007, pp. 32–33). Similarly, whether one judges a living space to be "large enough," one's teeth to be in good shape from an orthodontic standpoint, or one's clothes to be "nice," Frank argues that the determination is made by comparing what one has with similar goods possessed by one's peers (Frank 2007, pp. 29–42).

Studies have shown how contextual judgments affect reported subjective well-being: people taking happiness surveys in the presence of someone in a wheelchair rate themselves as 20% happier on average than those in a control group (Strack et al. 1990, pp. 303–314; see Schwarz and Strack 1999). Given this, increasing the total wealth of a given society would not necessarily increase the happiness of its members, as more or "better" consumer goods merely raises the bar for what people judged to be "good"—a rising standard that would leave people perpetually dissatisfied with their material objects, even as the quality and quantity of those goods increased. At the same time, it would also explain why providing money to the poor *would* have a positive effect upon their reported well-being, as such a transfer would improve their material well-being *relative* to the societal standard.

Some might object that relative inequality is not to blame for wealth's limited ability to promote additional happiness but, rather, bolsters happiness by providing high-status individuals with a feeling of achievement and low-status individuals with a sense of possibility whereby they might improve their circumstances. There are many other variants of this argument, with the common theme that relative inequality is, in fact, desirable from the standpoint of psychological well-being (See Ingram and Katic 2012; Hopkins 2008). Addressing these arguments is a task requiring major treatment of what is meant by inequality, well beyond the scope of the current chapter. Here, one should note first that much scholarship has been done to rebut this argument (See Dorling 2010; Wilkinson and Pickett 2011). Second, note that this argument does little to contest the central thesis that increased wealth does not promote significant increases in happiness. Rather, such claims at best serve as an alternative explanation of why the thesis is true, e.g. because the positive effects of inequality matter rather than absolute wealth or because those effects swamp any effect of wealth.

To further explain the disjointed relationship of income and happiness, consider again the idea that human beings as consumers are doomed to run on a "hedonic treadmill" (Stevenson and Wolfers 2008, p. 69), a concept with various interpretations (Kahneman 1999, pp. 3–25). One account suggests that people psychologically acclimate to changes in well-being, gravitating to a set level of happiness regardless of external stimulus. It is this usage that characterizes the results of the study that led to the coining of the term. Conducted by Philip Brickman, Dan Coates, and Ronnie Janoff-Bulman, this study found that people who had won the lottery were no happier than a control group of non-winners (Brickman et al. 1978, pp. 917–927; Senior 2006).

Alternatively, the "hedonic treadmill" is understood as rises in both well-being and aspirations for well-being that offset each other in hedonic terms. A study in rural China found that while rising incomes improved subjective well-being, they also raised income aspirations, which lowered well-being (Knight and Gunatilaka 2012, pp. 67–81). The authors propose that this "partial hedonic treadmill" explains why China's rapid economic growth has not translated into gains in subjective well-being (Knight and Gunatilaka). It would also explain Amartya Sen's findings that subjective well-being in poor countries often surpasses what is found in rich countries, as those living in poor nations will have often adjusted their expectations to match their circumstances, while the citizens of wealthy nations continue to aim for a higher quality of life than they can realistically attain (Sen 1999).

Either way, there is no way to find contentment in the high-growth, high-consumption, high-affluence way of life if one's well-being is determined not by the satisfaction of one's needs, but by what others have gained—or if the more one buys, the more one feels the need to buy.

6.7   True Flourishing: A Communitarian, Postmodern Culture

The cultures that value highly the following activities and purposes are referred to here as "communitarian" because each activity involves forming and nurturing bonds of affinity with others and service to the common good (Etzioni 1996). The term "postmodern" is used because reference is not to earlier communities that often were overwhelming and oppressive (what Erving Goffman called total institutions [Goffman and Helmreich 1961]), but to new, more liberal ones.

There are three major sources of non-materialistic contentment that also provide for a life that reaches beyond the self.

6.7.1   The Contentment of Mutuality

Spending time with others with whom one shares bonds of affinity—children, spouses, friends, members of one's community—has often been shown to make people happier (Sugden 2005, pp. 97–8; Lane 1993; Putnam 1995). Approval by others to whom a person is bonded is the main source of affection and esteem, which is Maslow's second layer of human needs. However, an important point that should not be overlooked is that more is involved in engaging in social relations than making the ego happy. These relationships are based on mutuality, in which two people "give" to each other and "receive" in one and the same act. People in lasting, meaningful, affective relationships find them to be a major source of mutual enrichment, which can be achieved with very little expenditure or material costs.

Derek Bok (2011, p. 19) writes that "several researchers have concluded that human relationships and connections of all kinds contribute more to happiness than anything else." Research demonstrates that those who are socially isolated are "characterized by higher levels of anxiety, negative mood, dejection, hostility, fear of negative evaluation, and perceived stress, and by lower levels of optimism, happiness, and life satisfaction" (Cacioppo and Hawkley 2003). Further studies show that married people are happier than people who are single, divorced, widowed, separated, or cohabiting (Bok 2011, p. 17), and that close friendships can have nearly as strong an impact on happiness as a successful marriage (Bok 2011, p. 19).

6.7.2   Happiness from Community Involvement

Researchers who examined the effect of community involvement (as opposed to merely socializing with friends or family) also found a strong correlation with happiness. One study, which evaluated survey data from 49 countries, found that membership in (non-church) organizations has a significant positive correlation with happiness (Helliwell 2003, pp. 331–360). Bok notes, "Some researchers have found that merely attending monthly club meetings or volunteering once a month is associated with a change in well-being equivalent to a doubling of income" (Bok 2011, p. 20). Other studies have found that individuals who devote substantial amounts of time to volunteer work have greater life satisfaction (Bok 2011, p. 22).

Political participation, too, yields the fruits of bonding and meaningful activities. As one scholar notes, using the terms of an economist: "Citizens do not only gain utility from the outcome of the political process and its material consequences but also from the democratic process itself" (Frey and Stutzer 2000, p. 82). This is particularly true when the political climate is perceived as fair and, thus, even those whose preferred candidates are defeated feel as though they had an opportunity to have their political preferences considered (Frey and Stutzer). Also, researchers have found that adolescents who have a greater commitment to contributing to society or pursuing some meaningful end have positive experiences that are greater in depth and intensity than their less-politically-engaged peers (Magen 1996 p. 237–267).

6.7.3   Contentment from Transcendental Pursuits (Religious, Spiritual and Intellectual)

Extensive evidence indicates that people who consider themselves religious, express a belief in God, or regularly attend religious services are more content than those who do not. Subjects in one study who agreed with the statement "God is important in my life" saw a gain of 3.5 points on a 100-point scale of happiness (Layard, p. 64). (For comparison, unemployment is associated with a 6-point drop on the same scale.) Other studies show that Americans with a deep religious faith are healthier, live longer, and have lower rates of divorce, crime, and suicide (Bok 2011, pp. 21–22).

There is little research on transcendental activities other than religious pursuits. However, the evidence that exists indicates that participation in activities that have profound meaning to the individual is associated with happiness. For example, "Two studies that examined groups that chose to change their lifestyle to achieve personal values such as 'environmental friendliness' and 'voluntary simplicity' found that both experienced higher levels of well-being. Volunteering, and political action—which are inherently communitarian activities—also provide non-consumerist sources of contentment.

Thus, imagine a world in which the whole population—and not just a sliver—live like the Athens free men while robots comprise the working class. Karl Marx, writing at a time when the average working hours were much longer than today, dreamed that "society will produce in 6 hours the necessary surplus, even more than now in 12 hours; at the same time everybody will have 6 hours of 'time at his disposition,' the true richness" (Ollman 1977). With all the developments in technology since Marx's time, it's likely that the workday could be cut in half again, and that everyone would have even more free time—the "true richness"—to form bonds of affinity, become involved in their communities, and find contentment in transcendental pursuits.

6.8   Contributions to Sustainability and Social Justice

If postmodern societies could develop a culture of capping that expects everyone to be able to attain sufficient income to provide for a secure flow of the goods needed to attend to their basic creature needs—but otherwise center life around non-materialistic, social, and transcendental goods—that culture would provide one obvious additional major contribution to higher levels of contentment (and hence less alienation and anti-social behavior), as well as one far from obvious one.

Obviously, a good life that combines caps on consumption and work with a dedication to transcendental pursuits is much less taxing on the environment than consumerism and the level of work needed to pay for it. This is the case because transcendental activities require relatively few scarce resources, fossil fuels, or other sources of physical energy. Social activities (such as spending more time with one's children) require time and personal energy but not large material or financial outlays. (Often those who spend large amounts of money on their kids' toys or entertainment bond less with them than those whose relations are less mediated by objects.) The same holds for cultural and spiritual activities, such as prayer, meditation, enjoying and making music, art, sports, and adult education. True, consumerism has turned many of these pursuits into expensive endeavors. However, one can break out of this mentality and find that it is possible to engage in most transcendental activities quite profoundly using a moderate amount of goods and services. In short, the transcendental society is much more sustainable than consumer capitalism.

6.8.1   Effect on Social Justice

There is reason to conclude that if the culture of a society shifts from one that extols affluence to one that extols communitarian pursuits—major gains for social justice will become much more probable. An obvious reason to expect that this hypothesis will hold true is that the more members of a particular social grouping view each other as members of the same community—the more they are likely to be willing to support reallocations of wealth that reduce inequality in that society. However, there are much deeper and stronger links between a communitarian culture and social justice. Before I can outline those and present relevant evidence, I need to outline the reasons such a culture shift is called for and what it may encompass.

6.8.1.1   Underlying Assumptions

(a) In the near future, a large number of jobs will be lost to smart (AI-equipped) instruments, machines, and robots.
(b) Unlike previous technological revolutions, this one is unlikely to generate a large number of new jobs.
(c) Hence, underemployment will increase and many of those who do find jobs will be paid poorly and have few benefits. Indeed, many will work in the gig economy.
(d) Those who design, produce, and own the smart instruments will increase their wealth, leading to growing inequality.
(e) As a result, most people—who currently expect to improve their economic conditions and be able to bequeath to their children a better life than they had—will be very frustrated.
(f) As a result of these trends—as well as others not explored here—these frustrations will result in growing hostility toward the government, the affluent, minorities, and foreigners. These trends are already visible in Europe and, to a lesser extent, in the US.

These consequences can be mitigated if those who have *their basic needs well sated and secured* find contentment in pursuits that are not labor or capital intensive and hence have low costs. These communitarian pursuits include spending more time cultivating meaningful relationships; in spiritual pursuits widely understood (from religion to meditation); and in community activism. Reference is not to a culture that favors an austere life but one in which one's consumption is capped at a level at which true needs are fully sated but status goods are avoided—and are sated through one or more communitarian pursuits. (To flag the difference between an austere culture and the one just outlined, I refer to the latter one as a capping society, one in which a person's quest for material goods is not minimized but bounded.) (See Etzioni 2013, 2016).

6.8.1.2   Relevance for Attaining a Significantly Higher Level of Social Justice

Much less obvious are the ways the capped culture serves social justice. Social justice entails transferring wealth from those disproportionally endowed to those who are underprivileged. A major reason such reallocation of wealth has been surprisingly limited in free societies is that those who command the "extra" assets tend also to be those who are politically powerful. Promoting social justice by organizing those with less, and forcing those in power to yield some of their assets to those less powerful, has had limited success in democratic countries and has even led to massive bloodshed in others. However, one must expect if those in power were to embrace the capped culture, they would be much more ready to share than otherwise. They will be able to find more contentment without hogging their surplus.

In exploring these arguments with various colleagues and audiences, I found that many readily agreed with all the steps—until the last one. They held that to expect that people who find contentment in communitarian pursuits rather than affluence-maximizing ones, will be more willing to significantly share their wealth with others, was 'unrealistic, utopian or visionary.' The purpose of the following discussion is to support the thesis that a shift from an affluent society to a communitarian one will enable major gains in social justice. The thesis is based on two arguments, one rather familiar and hence only briefly treated, and the other in need of more elaboration and support.

6.8.1.3   The Reallocation Effects of Communal Bonds

Sociologists used to hold that modern society arose as people shifted from being members of small communities (i.e. villages), in which people knew each other personally and had a strong sense of mutual obligations—to a society that encompasses millions, a so-called mass society (i.e. cities), in which all act like free standing individuals, each pursuing their self-interest. They refer to this thesis as a shift from *Gemeinschaft* to *Gesellschaft* (Tönnies 1955). Initially this shift was considered as enhancing human values as villages were considered oppressive and cities as liberating. However, communitarians pointed out that when people cut off their social moorings, they felt isolated and bereft, and acted out in anti-social ways. In response, communitarians called for a restoration of communal bonds, albeit much less encompassing and overpowering than the traditional ones. To the extent that this renewal of bonds has been achieved, most often not as a result of some kind of sociological analysis, but out of people yearning for social bonds, people have been content.

The most telling example in American society of the role of social bonds in supporting a sense of obligation to the less endowed members is that of ethnic groups. Typically, immigrants to the US are absorbed by communities with people of their own kind, in neighborhoods (such as Chinatown, South Boston, Spanish Harlem, Little Havana) and associations (such as Jewish charities, Catholic charities, and many others). Members of these groups shared resources with the new immigrants, provided welfare, housing, work, and otherwise shared some of their goods. (These immigrants gradually acquired other affiliations and memberships, which protected them from being dominated by any one group.) The same holds for many other kinds of communities, including those based on faith, gender, missions, among others. It follows that the more people in the post-affluent society become more communitarian (in the sense of forging new communities or strengthening or renewing their bonds to one community or another), the more reallocation of wealth can be expected.

6.8.1.4 The Role of Normative Content

A case study serves to introduce my next point.[5] John graduated from Columbia University with an MBA and at the same time with a JD from NYU, after studying for 4 years and accumulating considerable debt. He could have had his pick of Wall Street jobs, but instead moved to Chicago to work at an anti-poverty bank, where his salary was a modest one. He married Rachel, who he met at law school. In an era where talented lawyers were in high demand and gained high salaries and bonuses, she instead chose to work for Planned Parenthood, with a similarly modest salary. They did not live a life of poverty but what might be called a version of voluntary simplicity. They were more likely to go out to a pizza joint than a four star restaurant; they did ski but in nearby places; and they put their kids in public schools. Their son became active in high school as an elected head of an activist group that fought to make the school greener, and then he ended up in college. He spent part of his time tutoring a child in a disadvantaged neighborhood and built a home for Habitat for Humanity during his spring break.

Using a highly conservative estimate of the differences in salary bonuses and benefits the couple gained and would have gained if they worked on Wall Street or a major law firm, assuming early retirement at 65, they gave up some 20 million dollars of consumption in order to serve the social goals they believed in, helping those less endowed. Because they believed in what they were doing, they were at least as content as those who worked on Wall Street or major law firms.

There are already—before a transition to a communitarian society—millions of people, upper middle class ones, who choose lives centered on pro-social pursuits and reduced consumption, feeling enabled rather than deprived or coerced. Moreover, most of these people subscribe to religious faith or left liberal belief systems, which both favor reallocation. These are people who embrace beliefs associated with the Social Gospel, liberation theology, Tikkun Olam, and left liberal or social democratic beliefs (Putnam and Campbell 2010; see McKitrick et al. 2014).

Many of the supporters of Bernie Sanders, who called for raising taxes on the rich, were upper middle class young people, whose incomes (or that of their parents) would suffer. But they enthusiastically supported him because they believed in the ideals he was speaking for. They are but the most recent example of the observation that when people of means embrace a reallocation belief, they will be ready to share more than those who do not.

Economists may argue that these kinds of believers gain other satisfactions than those they would derive from consumer goods, such as self-esteem and camaraderie, from these acts, and hence they are not truly altruistic. This matters not, because even if they do agree to share the material surplus because of selfish reasons, these believers are still more willing to share than the non-believers. Hence, the more the communitarian beliefs are embraced, the more social justice one should expect.

---

[5] Identifying details have been changed.

References

Andrews, F.M., and S.B. Withey. 1976. *Social indicators of well-being: Americans' perceptions of life quality*. New York: Plenum Press.

Arntz, M., T. Gregory, and U. Zierahn. 2016. *The risk of automation for jobs in OECD countries: A comparative analysis*. OECD Social, Employment, and Migration Working Papers 189.

Barshay, J. 2013. High school test scores haven't improved for 40 years; top students stagnating. *Education by the Numbers*.

Bok, D. 2011. *The politics of happiness: What government can learn from the new research on well-being*. Princeton: Princeton University Press.

Brickman, P., D. Coates, and R. Janoff-Bulman. 1978. Lottery winners and accident victims: Is happiness relative? *Journal of Personality and Social Psychology* 36 (8): 917–927.

Brynjolfsson, E., and A. McAfee. 2014. *The second machine age: Work, progress, and prosperity in a time of brilliant technologies*. New York: WW Norton & Company.

Cacioppo, J.T., and L.C. Hawkley. 2003. Social isolation and health, with an emphasis on underlying mechanisms. *Perspectives in Biology and Medicine* 46 (3): S39–S52.

Cain Miller, C. 2017. Evidence that robots are winning the race for American jobs. *New York Times*.

Croft, J. 2016. More than 100,000 legal roles to become automated. *Financial Times*.

Davenport, T. H., and J. Kirby. 2016. *Only humans need apply: Winners and losers in the Age of smart machines*. HarperCollins Publishers.

Delaney, K.J. 2017. The Robot that takes your job should pay taxes, says Bill Gates. *Quartz*.

Desilver, D. 2017. US students' academic achievement still lags that of their peers in many other countries. *Pew Research Center*.

Dorling, D. 2010. *Injustice: Why social inequalities persist*. Bristol: Policy Press.

Engstrom, S. 1996. Happiness and the highest good in Aristotle and Kant. In *Aristotle, Kant, and the Stoics: Rethinking happiness and duty*, ed. S. Engstrom and J. Whiting. Cambridge: Cambridge University Press.

Etzioni, A. 1996. *The new golden rule: Community and morality in a democratic society*. New York: Basic Books.

———. 2013. A silk purse out of a sow's ear. *Journal of Modern Wisdom* 2 (4049).

———. 2016. Happiness is the wrong metric. *Society* 53 (3): 289–293.

Eurostat. 2017. *Unemployment statistics*, http://ec.europa.eu/eurostat/statistics-.

Ford, M. 2015. *Rise of the robots: Technology and the threat of a jobless future*. New York: Basic Books.

Frank, R.H. 2007. *Falling behind: How rising inequality harms the middle class*, 29–42. California: University of California Press.

Freedman, J.L. 1978. *Happy people: What happiness is, who has it, and why*. New York: Harcourt Brace Jovanovich.

Frey, C.B., and M. Osborne. 2015. Technology at work: The future of innovation and employment. *Citi GPS: global perspectives & solutions*.

Frey, C.B. and Osborne, M. 2013. The future of employment: How susceptible are jobs to computerization? *Oxford Martin Programme on Technology and Employment*.

Frey, B.S., and A. Stutzer. 2000. Happiness prospers in democracy. *Journal of Happiness Studies* 1 (2000): 79–102.

GAO. 2000. *National service programs: Two AmeriCorps programs' funding and benefits*.

Goffman, E., and W.B. Helmreich. 1961. *Asylums: Essays on the social situation of mental patients and other inmates*. Vol. 277. New York: Anchor Books.

Goodman, P. 2016. Free cash in Finland, must be jobless. *The New York Times*.

Graham, R. 2017. The retraining paradox. *The New York Times Magazine*.

Greenstein, R. 2016. Universal basic income may sound attractive but, if it occurred, would likelier increase poverty than reduce it. *Center on Budget and Policy Priorities*.

Hechinger, J., and M. McDonald 2013. Harvard-for-free meets resistance as US professors see threat. *Bloomberg Technology*.

Helliwell, J.F. 2003. Well-being, social capital and public policy: What's new? *Economic Modelling* 20 (2): 331–360.

Hicks, M., and S. Devaraj. 2017. *Manufacturing in America*. Ball State University Center for Business and Economic Research.

Hopkins, E. 2008. Inequality, happiness and relative concerns: What actually is their relationship? *Journal of Economic Inequality* 6 (4): 351–372.

Ingram, P., and I. Katic. 2012. *Does income inequality matter for life satisfaction?* Presented at the American Sociological Association Annual Meeting.

Kahneman, D. 1999. Objective happiness. In *Well-being: The foundations of hedonic psychology*, ed. D. Kahneman, E. Diener, and N. Schwarz, 3–25. New York: Russell Sage Foundation.

Kaplan, J. 2015. *Humans need not apply: A guide to wealth and work in the age of artificial intelligence*, 201. New Haven: Yale University Press.

Knight, J., and R. Gunatilaka. 2012. Income, aspirations and the hedonic treadmill in a poor society. *Journal of Economic Behavior & Organization* 82 (1): 67–81.

Korn, M. 2016. Imagine discovering that your teaching assistant really is a robot. *The Wall Street Journal*.

Lane, R.E. 1993. Does money buy happiness? *The Public Interest* 32: 58.

Lowrey, A. 2017. The future of not working. *The New York Times Magazine*.

Magen, Z. 1996. Commitment beyond the self and adolescence: The issue of happiness. *Social Indicators Research* 37 (3): 235–267.

Manyika, J., S. Lund, B. Auguste, and S. Ramaswamy. 2012 *Help wanted: The future of work in advanced economies*. McKinsey Global Institute.

Markoff, J. 2016. *Machines of loving grace: The quest for common ground between humans and robots*. New York: HarperCollins Publishers.

Matthie, R. 2000. *Happiness: A guide to developing life's most important skill*. New York: Little Brown and Company.

McEntee, K. 2016. Law grads still face a tough job market. *Bloomberg Law*.

McGinnis, J.O., and R.G. Pearce. 2014. The great disruption: How machine intelligence will transform the role of lawyers in the delivery of legal services. *Fordham Law Review* 82 (6): 3041–3066.

McKinsey Global Institute. 2017. *A future that works: automation, employment, and productivity*. San Francisco: McKinsey & Company.

McKitrick, M.A., J.S. Landres, M. Ottoni-Wilhelm, and A.D. Hayat. 2014. Connected to give: Faith Communities. *Jumpstart Labs*.

Miles, B. 2011. Spirit of the underground: The 60s Rebel. *The Guardian*.

Muro, M. 2016. Manufacturing jobs aren't coming back. *MIT Technology Review*.

Myers, D.G., and E. Diener. 1995. Who is happy? *Psychological Science* 6 (1): 12–13.

Noonan, L., and M. Arnold. 2015. Thousands more bank jobs under threat. *Financial Times*.

Nussbaum, M. 2005. Mill between Aristotle and Bentham. In *Economics and happiness: Framing and analysis*, ed. L. Bruni and P.L. Porta, 173. New York: Oxford University Press.

Ollman, B. 1977. Marx's vision of communism a reconstruction. *Critique: Journal of Socialist Theory* 8 (1): 4–41.

Packard, V., and B. Abbott. 1963. *The status seekers: An exploration of class behaviour in America*. Penguin books.

Putnam, R.D. 1995. Bowling alone: America's declining social capital. *Journal of Democracy* 6 (1): 65–78.

Putnam, R., and D. Campbell. 2010. *American Grace: How religion divides and unites us*. New York: Simon and Schuster.

Rines, S. 2017. America shouldn't expect a job boom anytime soon. *The National Interest*.

Rotman, D. 2013. How technology is destroying jobs. *MIT Technology Review* 16 (4): 28–35.

———. 2015. Who will own the robots? *MIT Technology Review*.

Sachs, J.D. 2013. Restoring virtue ethics in the quest for happiness. In *World happiness report 2013*, ed. J. Helliwell, R. Layard, and J. Sachs, 84–85. United Nations Sustainable Development Solutions Network.

Schwarz, N., and F. Strack. 1999. Reports of subjective well-being: Judgmental processes and their methodological implications. In *Well-being: The foundations of hedonic psychology*, 61–84. New York: Russell Sage Foundation.

Sen, A. 1999. *Development as freedom*. New York: Knopf.

Senior J. 2006. Some dark thoughts on happiness. *New York Magazine*.

Senior, J. 2010. All joy and no fun. *New York Magazine*.

Smith, A., and J. Anderson. 2014. *AI, robotics, and the future of jobs*. Pew Research Center.

Stevenson, B., and J. Wolfers. 2008. *Economic growth and subjective well-being: Reassessing the easterlin paradox*. Brookings Papers on Economic Activity.

Strack, F., et al. 1990. Salience of comparison standards and the activation of social norms: Consequences for judgements of happiness and their communication. *British Journal of Social Psychology* 29 (4): 303–314.

Sugden, R. 2005. Correspondence of sentiments: An explanation of the pleasure of social interaction. In *Economics and happiness: framing the analysis*, ed. L. Bruni and P.L. Porta, 97–98. New York: Oxford University.

Suster, M. 2013. In 15 years from now half of US Universities may be in Bankruptcy. My surprise discussion with Clay Christensen. *Business Insider*.

Tanner, M. 2014. The basic income guarantee: Simplicity, but at what cost? *CATO Unbound*.

Tcherneva, P.R. 2012. Full employment through social entrepreneurship: The nonprofit model for implementing a job guarantee. *Levy Economics Institute* 12(2).

Thompson, D. 2015. A world without work. *The Atlantic*.

Tönnies, F. 1887. *Gemeinschaft und gesellschaft*. English edition: Ferdinand, T. 1955. *Community and association* (trans: Loomis, C.P.). London: Routledge and Kegan Paul.

US Department of Education. 2016. *Expenditures on corrections and education*.

US Department of Labor. 2016. Labor for participation: what has happened since the peak? *Bureau of Labor Statistics Monthly Labor Review*.

US Government Accountability Office. 2015. *Contingent workforce: Size, characteristics, earnings, and benefits*.

Van Parijs, P., and Y. Vanderborght. 2017. *Basic income: A radical proposal for a free society and a sane economy*. Cambridge, MA: Harvard University Press.

Wang, S. 2007. Aquinas on human happiness and the natural desire for God. *New Blackfriars* 88 (1015): 322–334.

Wells, N. 2016. The 'gig economy' is growing and now we know by how much. *CNBC News*.

Wilkinson, R.G., and K. Pickett. 2011. *The spirit level*. Bloomsbury Press.

Wiseman, P. 2016. *Why robots, not trade, are behind so many factory job losses*. Associated Press.

World Economic Forum. 2016. *The future of jobs: Employment, skills and workforce strategy for the fourth industrial revolution*. Geneva.

Zhong, R. 2017. India considers fighting poverty with a universal basic income. *The Wall Street Journal*.

Chapter 7
Nationalist Populism Is Not an Enemy

This chapter attempts to show that liberalism provides an incomplete moral language to address the populism that is rising in many democratic polities. Communitarian conceptions must be included in order to provide a more comprehensive moral language. This addition, however, raises issues because liberal and communitarian conceptions are in conflict with one another to some extent. The chapter suggests ways this conflict can be limited and proposes a liberal communitarian approach as an effective response to the populism that is challenging democratic regimes.

The chapter first briefly explores widely held assumptions about the causes that propel populism (Sect. 7.1). It then outlines the reasons that liberalism[1] cannot provide an adequate response to populism on its own, and that it needs to be combined with communitarianism (Sect. 7.2). The rest of the chapter introduces elements of such a liberal communitarian philosophy (Sect. 7.3). The elements include (a) coping with free trade; (b) an approach to immigration that combines community building, on the local and national level, with the protection of rights and of pluralism; (c) a framing of particularistic rules within the setting of a universal framework of basic rights illustrated by an examination of homeowner associations; (d) compassionate accommodations to the losers of cultural wars; (e) a study of the difference between the right to free speech and morally appropriate speech; and (f) coping with the conflicts between liberal and communitarian principles. One should note from the outset that this approach holds that societies cannot be designed to follow one overarching principle because of differences in needs, interests, and values of their various members. That is, no value can be maximized.

---

[1] There are considerable differences as to the meaning of this term. It is used in this article in reference to the commitment to liberty, human rights, religious tolerance, and free markets, as well as the thesis that the state ought to be morally neutral. This position is sometimes referred to as contemporary liberalism in contrast to the thicker classical liberalism both of which differ from welfare liberalism.

© The Author(s) 2018
A. Etzioni, *Happiness is the Wrong Metric*, Library of Public Policy and Public Administration 11, https://doi.org/10.1007/978-3-319-69623-2_7

The discussion is centered on two recent variants of philosophical positions that have a long and rich history: *globalism,* a subcategory of contemporary classical liberalism—and *nationalism*, a particular form of communitarianism. Thus, global-ism draws on liberal elements but other forms of liberalism do not necessarily share the globalists' positions—for instance, contemporary classical liberalism and wel-fare liberalism. And nationalism is a form of communitarianism because it views the nation as the major community (whether real or imagined)—a thesis other com-munitarians do not necessarily share—for instance, those who see their main com-munity as their confessional or ethnic one.

7.1 Populism: Definition and Causes

The hallmarks of populism include a demagogue who appeals to the masses in highly emotive terms, attacking the institutions of civil society, offering ready-made solutions for society's complex challenges, and promising to deliver those solutions. Cas Mudde (2004) characterizes populism as a "thin ideology," one that provides an ideological framework, according to which good people are being abused by a cor-rupt elite. (He contrasts it with pluralism, which accepts the legitimacy of many different groups and sets of values.) Similarly, Jan-Werner Müller (2016) argues that populism is anti-pluralist; he also adds that populists are always critical of elites, and that populism is a form of identity politics. The rise of populism in many democratic polities in the 2010s is often attributed to a nationalistic reaction to the ascent of globalization, whose champions hold many of the same positions as contemporary liberals. They favor open societies—open to the flow of goods, people, and ideas. They are universalists who view all people as endowed with the same *human* rights, and as rational deliberative people, able to make their own reasoned decisions.

Globalization, scholars hold, is opposed by current waves of populism that are propelled by nationalists. These are individuals and groups that are parochial (or particularistic), who view their commitments to their local and national communi-ties as trumping global considerations. They are depicted as opposed to the spread of rights ('deplorable') (Chozik 2016) and to immigration (especially of people whose culture and ethnicity differs from the national one); as people who adhere to the traditional values of their communities and hence oppose liberalism; and as protectionists (limiting access to the markets of their nation) (Lind 2016; Haidt 2016). For globalists, "national boundaries are increasingly obsolete and perhaps even immoral…progressive pundits and journalists increasingly speak a dialect of ethical cosmopolitanism or globalism—the idea that it is unjust to discriminate in favor of one's fellow nationals against citizens of foreign countries," according to Michael Lind (2016). George Monbiot (2005) adds,

> When confronted with a conflict between the interests of your country and those of another, patriotism, by definition, demands that you should choose those of your own. Internationalism, by contrast, means choosing the option which delivers most good or least harm to people, regardless of where they live. It tells us that someone living in Kinshasa is of no less worth than someone living in Kensington, and that a policy which favours the interests of 100 British people at the expense of 101 Congolese is one we should not pursue.

Drawing on these definitions, a considerable number of observers view globalists as enlightened, progressive, and on the right side of history, and nationalists as seeking to preserve a traditional, anachronistic, and unjust social order. Pankaj Mishra (2016) sees in Trump's America—and in Europe, India, and Russia—whole countries that "seethe with demagogic assertions of ethnic, religious, and national identity." These movements threaten "the great eighteenth-century venture of a universal civilization harmonized by rational self-interest, commerce, luxury, arts, and science." Nationalists reject the wisdom of the great thinkers of the Enlightenment, Mishra writes, and instead follow the authoritarian philosophy of Jean-Jacques Rousseau.

Another line of analysis sees the rise of populism as being caused in part by globalization, because it undermines both local and national communities. That is, globalization helped engender the forces that oppose it. Scholars who follow this line of analysis often draw on the studies of the rise of fascism to explain the recent rise of populism in liberal democracies. This argument is premised on the observation that as people moved from villages to the cities, they lost many of the social bonds that provided them with emotional security. (Recall Tönnies' 1957 terms for communal and associational societies, *Gemeinschaft* and *Gesellschaft*.) Those social bonds, however, had protected them from the Siren calls of would-be demagogues, because individuals who were well anchored in communities relied on each other and on their communal leaders (heads of families, religious figures, and other authority figures) to resist outsiders' appeals. Once the society of communities turned into a mass society—a society composed of individuals who lost much of their social moorings[2]—they became susceptible to demagogues. This was particularly said to be the case when their economic conditions deteriorated. The conditions in pre-Nazi Germany are often cited. These included massive unemployment, hyperinflation, and loss of dignity (emanating from humiliation following Germany's defeat in WWI and the punishing terms imposed on it by the nations who won the war). Racial nationalism is said to have provided Germany with a new sense of community, meaning, and dignity. "As the political and social fragmentation of the Weimar period imparted a sense of apocalyptic collapse for many Germans, the Nazi millennial worldview in turn conferred a sense of oneness via its racial concept of a unified Volk (race or people), a community of shared blood," writes David Redles (2010, p. 31).

When this analysis is applied to contemporary populism, it suggests, in the terms already introduced, that what we are witnessing is a nationalist reaction to the rise of globalization. Large segments of the population are reported to have experienced job loss (because freer trade led to jobs moving to developing countries), most of those who are employed gained little or no increases in real income, all involved experienced growing income insecurity and inequality, as well as a loss of dignity (associated with the loss of traditional jobs such as coal mining). The same people are also found to be reacting to growing diversity due to immigration, and to cultural

---

[2]A reviewer of a previous drafted noted here that the transition Tönnies points to is not from social relations to atomization but merely a change in the kind of relations people have, from communal to associational. This is indeed the case, but the point is that these are not thick enough.

changes which are the result of extensions of individual rights (e.g. legalization of gay marriages). The affected people view the rise of diversity both as undermining their social standing and as a loss of shared core values and habits.[3] And they feel that they are snubbed by globalist elites.

Globalists do not ignore the communitarian causes of populism; however, they tend to view them as the pathological reactions of people seeking to hold on to the past and to traditional social structures that are discriminatory, authoritarian, and historically indefensible in view of the unstoppable rise of globalization. They tend to see nationalists as misinformed, misled, or captured by the emotive appeals of demagogues. Moreover, globalists often view the weakening of particularistic bonds—including the weakening of commitments to local or national communities—as liberating. They draw on writings such as those by Peter Singer (1972), who argues that one should treat all children as one treats one's own (p. 229). And on the work of Martha Nussbaum's (1996) *For Love of Country*, which argues that we should view ourselves as citizens of the world. History, in other words, is seen as a march from particularism to universalism, from close local and national communities toward a global one.

Globalists, like many liberals, have no room for communities in their moral and philosophical vocabulary. They see people as free-standing individuals, endowed with rights by the mere fact that they are human and not because they are members of this or that community or nation. They hold that people are free (or ought to be free) to move across borders. Above all, each person ought to be free to choose their own definition of the good and not be hindered because their habits, tastes, or values differ from those of others. Diversity and pluralism trump the restrictive demands for conformity of various communities and their core values.

7.2 The Essentiality of Communities

The globalists miss what Aristotle already observed—that human beings are social animals. Individuals need bonding with others to flourish. A considerable number of studies show that when people are cut off from their social moorings, when they are isolated—in prison cells, in high rise buildings (especially the elderly), or in psychological experiments—they show many signs of diminished cognitive and emotive capacity. Scores of other studies show that they thrive when they are involved in lasting meaningful relations with others (see Helliwell 2003; Fratiglioni et al. 2000). That is, communal bonds—which are *prima facie* particularistic, because all communities, including families, local communities, and nations, exclude most people—are an essential part of that which constitutes an individual.

---

[3]Yuval Levin notes that both conservative and liberals are nostalgic for a bygone era: liberals miss the 60s and the Great Society, conservatives miss the 1980s and both are nostalgic for the 1950s, but for different reasons. See Levin (2016).

The absence of sufficient communal bonds is a major reason people feel detached, alienated, and powerless and either withdraw or act out in antisocial ways, including joining gangs and militias (to find community) or abusing drugs and alcohol, or each other.

Identity too is profoundly tied to communities, and thus to particularistic bonds. As Joseph de Maistre put it, "There is no such thing as *man* in the world. In the course of my life, I have seen Frenchmen, Italians, Russians etc.; I know, too, thanks to Montesquieu, that one can be a Persian. But as for *man*, I declare that I have never met him in my life; if he exists, he is unknown to me" (Berlin 1991, p. 100). Michael Sandel (1998) puts it well when he writes that we cannot understand ourselves but "as the particular persons we are—as members of this family or community or nation or people, as bearers of this history, as sons and daughters of that revolution, as citizens of this republic" (p. 179).

Strong involvement of people in their particularistic communities, rather than in some kind of universal social grouping, is highlighted by the fact that millions of people are willing to die for their nation but very few for the United Nations (or even the EU). Globalists might argue that the fact that identity is tied to nations is one reason for wars and the world's great difficulties in coping with global problems. However, these are not feelings that most people have; on the contrary, most find such globalist ideas strange, if not alien. It follows that seeking to deprive people of their national sources of identity and bonding fosters nationalism and populism (at least as long as they neither develop nor are provided with other sources of identity and bonding they find compelling). A colleague noted at this point: "If they didn't have 'national sources of identity' but they had jobs and dignity, is it really that there'd still be populism? That strikes me as unlikely." In response, one notes that most of those who voted for Trump (and for other populist leaders in other societies) had jobs and the dignity they confer. They seem to have felt nevertheless that globalists' demands (real and imagined) assaulted their identity and community (Hochschild 2017; Goldstein 2017).

Furthermore, one cannot ignore that communities form the individuals that are the mainstay of liberalism. Infants are born with human potential; however, they will not even learn to walk upright or communicate with words unless they are 'socialized,' studies show. Parents, families, local communities (as captured in the phrase, "it takes a village") forge individuals, not global systems. And when these communities falter, so does the education of the people within them. To put it differently, the rational, free agents that liberalism sees are the product of communities (some as small as families, others as large as nations, with the smaller ones nestled within the more encompassing ones). One cannot grow one without the incubation provided by the other. (David B. Wong [1988] adds that to learn to be duty-bound and to act in a universalistic way, one first must have relationships of trust with others, i.e. particularistic relations.)

When children become adults, they still need communities to foster a social order that is pluralistic, tolerant, and civil, i.e. a liberal order. Communities provide the informal social controls that uphold norms by chiding violations and praising compliance. The more effective they are, the less need there is for the state to employ coercive means to maintain social order (Wrong 1994). In short, the liberal polity assumes a communitarian society—the kind of society nationalists champion.

True, communities can be overpowering and oppressive. Historically, most communities were indeed too thick and many are still found in parts of the world as different as Singapore and Saudi Arabia. And national communities are prone to conflict with each other because there is only a limited sense of obligation toward the other. However, communities in democratic societies tend to be much 'thinner,' because people can leave communities that they find too 'thick' (Walzer 1994) and often are members of more than one community (e.g. work and residence) and hence are less psychologically dependent on any one community.

A sounder globalist philosophy will seek modes of social design that foster thin communities rather than promote individualism to the extent that it entails attacking communities, especially nations, as troublesome relics of the past. This is accomplished by combining globalist (universalistic, liberal) principles with nationalist (particularistic communitarian) ones. In other words, if one places at one end of the normative spectrum globalist liberalism and at the other end authoritarian communitarianism, the middle ground of the spectrum is liberal communitarianism. It provides both the antidote to populism (by undergirding communities) and to authoritarianism (by incorporating liberal principles). The challenge is to find ways to develop a normative framework that will incorporate the values of globalization with those of nationalism, and find ways that their contradictions can be limited, while recognizing that a measure of conflict and tension between these two core elements of liberal communitarianism is inevitable. This approach is outlined next.

Yuval Levin (2016) dedicated a book to the subject that he calls communitarian liberalism. M. Daly (1994) writes: "Most liberals and a good many communitarians would like the liberal ideals of equality and freedom to be integrated with community commitments in all aspects of American society & families, educational institutions, businesses, health care institutions, religions, and political institutions. Such integration would realize the communitarian ideal of a democratic community" (p. xix).

This philosophy has been summarized in popular terms by David Brooks (2016), who wrote: "I suspect the coming political movements will be identified on two axes: open and closed and individual and social...Donald Trump is probably going to make the G.O.P. the party of individual/closed...The Democrats are probably going to be the party of social/closed...I've been thinking we need a third party that is social/open." Such a party, according to Brooks, would "support the free trade and skilled immigration that fuel growth. But it would also flood the zone for those challenged in the high-skill global economy—offering programs to rebuild community, foster economic security and boost mobility" (Brooks 2016).

An important counter to the line of argumentation laid out so far is that the mass society thesis is mistaken, that communities have far from disappeared. Residential communities abound and there are a large number of non-residential communities, such as the gay community and various ethnic and racial ones. In response, I note that (a) some segments of the population have lost communal bonds. Freer trade and automation force people to relocate to where the new jobs are, leaving their communal bonds and institutions behind. As often, if they develop new communal bonds, a shift in the labor markets requires them to relocate again. For instance, people moved from West Virginia to Montana when coal declined and gas production increased, only to be forced to move again when prices for energy collapsed but the auto industry revived.

(b) Granted, an important correction to the mass society is called for. A good part (arguably the major segment) of populists are in traditional communities that are antagonistic to globalization. Much has been written about the reasons why these communities are antagonistic. Causes are said to include fragmentation of the news, gerrymandering, self-segregation, and political polarization.

For the purpose at hand, it matters little whether people feel that they are losing their communities or that the values of their communities are under attack. Either way they react antagonistically. One may argue that many traditional values ought to be attacked. However, as I see it, a head on confrontation is not the most effective way to change values, and the social costs of such confrontations are high. Progressive observers often argue that when we deal with drug addicts or felons, we should approach them in a therapeutic way, seeking to rehabilitate them and reintegrate them into society. There seems no reason nationalists should be treated more severely.

No less important is the sense that both those who lost their local communities and those who are members of antagonistic ones hold that their national community is under attack by globalists' conceptions of supra-nationalism. These include respect for the UN, the International Criminal Court, and international law generally, among other institutions perceived as detracting from sovereignty.

A globalist suggested to the author that people can satisfy their communitarian needs in families or some other small communities—and should avoid investing themselves in the nation. However, one notes that because of geographic mobility people are losing many of their bonds with their extended families; that the nuclear family is declining (as fewer people marry, stay married, or marry later and have fewer children); and that other communities are hollowed out, leaving the nation as a major focus of bonding and identity. True, many of the problems national governments find difficult to cope with are regional or global in nature (including wars, terrorism, climate change), and would be much easier to manage if people treated humanity as one imagined community, the way they now treat their nation. However, to make claims as if such a global community is currently in place feeds populism rather than helps to curb it.

7.3 Elements of Liberal Communitarianism

If one seeks to reduce populism, violence, prejudice, and xenophobia, then communities must be nurtured as they change, rather than be overridden. The discussion next turns to examine ways the conflict between globalists and nationalists can be reduced. The examination covers major areas of contention: the clash between the advocates of free and fair trade; the debate about limiting the free movement of people (immigration); the objections to communities that are insular and excluding;

free speech that is sensitive to community values; and the minting of new rights and community adjustments. The section closes with a discussion of the ways the two conflicting principles can be accommodated, using the relations between privacy as a human right and national security as a case study.

7.3.1   Limiting Free Trade?

When globalists champion free trade, they stress that it enriches all those involved, making for less costly consumer products as each nation focuses on what it is best equipped to produce, a condition referred to in popular terms as win-win. Actually the ethical situation that free trade entails is illustrated by a familiar challenge raised in reference to utilitarianism, i.e. when one asks how many Christians one may throw in the arena to contend with lions, if a very large number of Romans are going to enjoy the spectacle. The point is that sacrificing even a small number of lives cannot be justified even if it enhances the happiness of a much large number. The Christians of free trade are the hundreds of thousands of workers, in coal, steel, and other sectors, who lost their jobs as a result. Economists respond that most jobs were lost due to automation and other technological developments and not to trade. True, but nonetheless, since 2000 at least five million manufacturing jobs in the US were lost to trade (Long 2016). Free traders do not deny this loss but respond that it can be handled through Trade Adjustment Assistance (TAA), which uses public funds to retrain the displaced workers and find them new jobs.

This response fails on two accounts. First of all, so far TAA has been unable to help most of these displaced people. Many of those involved cannot be retrained; it is hard to make steel workers into computer programmers. And many of the new jobs available are low paying, with few or no benefits, especially when compared to the jobs lost. And flipping hamburgers at McDonald's or selling T-shirts at Target does not provide the meaningful jobs coal miners, steel workers, and others previously took pride in.

Furthermore, free trade champions ignore the effects of free trade on people's essential communitarian needs. They often fail to understand people who are reluctant to move from West Virginia to Montana, say, when the coal industry is declining but the gas industry is growing. They do not take into account that people lose their communal bonds when they move—that they leave behind friends they can call on when they are sick or grieving. Their children miss their friends and everyone in the family is ripped away from the centers of their social lives: school, church, social club, union hall, or American Legion post. And when these people finally bring their families along and form new communities, changes in free trade often force them to move again. Thus, after a boom in Montana, prices of oil and gas fall, and so many of the workers who moved there now need to relocate again. In this way, free trade churns societies, exacting high social costs by undermining communities.

These high social costs do not mean that nations should stop trading with one another; rather, it means that those who are concerned about the social effects of new trade treaties are not know-nothing rednecks but people with valid concerns. These might be addressed by much greater investments in TAA. It could provide those who cannot be retrained—often the older workers—early retirement or jobs in an infrastructure corps. At best, ramped up TAA programs should not require workers to relocate, because relocations increase costs and undermine communities.

Finally, one notes that all countries impose some limitations on trade in the name of national security, consumer safety, protecting farmers, and quite a few other concerns. Hence, to add some limits, especially if they are time limited, to allow groups especially hard hit to have time to adjust, is not a sign that dark populism won but that that measures often taken in the past by 'free' trade partners have been extended.

7.3.2 Limiting Immigration?

Globalists favor the free movement of people across national borders. They strongly support the Schengen Agreement, which removes border controls among many European nations. They strongly supported Angela Merkel, the German chancellor, when she opened the doors to more than a million refugees. And they view Trump's call for building a wall on the Mexican border and restriction on immigration from Muslim countries as typical right-wing, xenophobic, reactionary, nationalist policies.[4]

Actually, there exists a tension between open-ended immigration, especially of people from different cultures, and sustaining communities. Communities benefit from a measure of stability, continuity, and a core of shared values. Social psychologist Jonathan Haidt (2016) views mass immigration as the trigger that set off populism in many nations. He concludes that it is possible to have moderate levels of immigration from "morally different ethnic groups"—so long as they are seen to be assimilating into the host culture—but high levels of immigration from countries with different moral values, without successful assimilation, will trigger a backlash. Haidt suggests that immigration policies ought to take into account three factors: the percentage of foreign-born residents at any given time; the degree of moral difference between the incoming group and the members of the host society; and the degree to which assimilation is being achieved. Globalists do not approve of this approach. They embrace a libertarian perspective toward immigration, and the "core principle of libertarianism," as Jacob Hornberger (2016) writes, "is that freedom entails the right to live your life anyway you want, so long as your conduct is peaceful." Thus, "There is only one libertarian position on immigration, and that position is open immigration or open borders." One may suggest that the idea of open borders is just a theoretical position; that nobody truly believes in unlimited immigration. However, this position describes exactly what took place in the EU when several nations joined the Schengen Agreement, which allows free movement of

---

[4] For a fuller treatment of reactionary thinking, see Lilla (2016).

people across national borders. The resentment that followed is a major reason for Brexit. (A reviewer of a previous draft noted here "But the major immigrant group to the UK is *Polish*. They're not 'morally different'. So this wouldn't have met the Haidt criterion!" As I see it, whom people consider sociologically different is in the eye of the beholder. Indeed, often people seek to avoid and even exclude from their communities people who are rather similar to themselves, such as Sunni and Shia of the same nationality, or Japanese and Koreans.)

Brookings' William Galston (2016) cites public opinion polls that show that Americans have become more concerned about the United States becoming a majority non-white country. In 2016, 21% of Americans said that such a majority would "bother" them, up 7 percentage points from 2013. Furthermore, "Fifty percent of all Americans acknowledged being bothered when they came into contact with immigrants who spoke little or no English." Galston reminds his readers that in an earlier era, when the United States implemented immigration restrictions and caps, immigration fell significantly and "'ethnics' from central and southern Europe were gradually assimilated into white America, a process that many scholars believe contributed to the relatively placid and consensual politics of the postwar decades."

Some nationalists hence call for at least a 'pause' on immigration, especially from Muslim nations. Globalists continue to favor immigration and a short pathway to citizenship for millions of undocumented immigrants. A liberal communitarian will focus on accelerated integration of immigrants, first by properly defining what such integration entails (which, we shall see, makes accelerated integration more achievable) and by taking specific measures to advance it.

To proceed, a liberal communitarian approach benefits from drawing on a strategy that might be referred to as "diversity within unity," which can help lower social tensions in countries that accept large numbers of immigrants while tolerating particularistic diversity—by not seeking full assimilation into the culture of the new homeland. The United States has in effect followed such a strategy with considerable success, compared to the more assimilationist European countries, as well as to Japan and South Korea.

Assimilation, in its strongest form, requires that immigrants abandon their distinct cultures, values, habits, and connections to their country of origin in order to integrate fully into the culture of their new country. France stands out as an archetype of this approach. For many years, it was regarded as discriminatory to even recognize the country of origin or religion of a French citizen. In this spirit, France passed a law in 2004 banning all religious symbols from public schools. The law is so far-reaching, and has been interpreted so broadly, that several schools have demanded that female Muslim students not wear long dresses (Mayet 2015). Towns and cities have banned 'burkinis,' bathing attire that follows Muslim prescripts for covering women in public (Auffray and Equy 2016). Schools in several French towns have decided to stop serving pork-free meals at schools (Chrisafis 2015). This anti-communitarian approach is provoking tension because immigrants are required to give up values and behaviors that are central to their identity. Furthermore, such excessive homogenization is not necessary to obtain a sound state of community. The high level of alienation in immigrant and minority communities in France—and the corresponding alienation of the majority—reveal that this approach is not working and is indeed counterproductive.

In contrast, diversity within unity is a combination of partial assimilation and community building along with a high level of tolerance for differences in others, for pluralism and respect for individual rights. It presumes that all members of a given society will respect and adhere to certain core values and institutions that form the basic shared framework of the society. (This is the unity component.) At the same time, every group in society, including the majority, is free to maintain its distinct subculture—those policies, habits, and institutions that do not conflict with the shared core. (This is the diversity component.) Respect for the whole and respect for all are the essence of this approach; when these two come into conflict, then respect for the national community (which itself may change over time) is to take precedence.

Among the core values are adherence to the law, acceptance of democracy as the way to resolve differences and create public policy, and belief in civility in dealing with others. Religion, a core value for many European societies, need not be a unity value. However, a measure of patriotism should be expected, especially when loyalty to the new, host nation clashes with commitments to the nation of origin. (Thus, if the United States were to go to war with another country, our immigrants from that country would be required to support our effort.) Under diversity within unity, all immigrants are expected to learn the national language but are welcome to keep their own and speak it with their children as a secondary language. They are free to follow their own rituals but also expected to partake in the national ones, such as pledging alliance to the flag.

In recent years, much attention has been paid to the level of immigration, which many of Trump's supporters view as far too high and some social scientists hold is overwhelming American communities and their core values. The level of immigration communities can tolerate, however, is affected by the pace and scope of integration. In other words, higher levels of immigration will have less anti-communitarian effects when integration is more effective.

To illustrate: in the United States, there is a great shortage of classes to teach English to adult immigrants. Obviously, a strong command of the language is an essential element of acculturation. Moreover, the language classes also serve as opportunities to introduce immigrants to American values and lifestyles, as well as to form personal contacts between immigrants and established residents who teach these classes. One could call for a new massive federal program to provide English and civics classes to immigrants. However, this is a mission particularly suited to volunteers. To teach English and to share values does not require a degree from a teaching college. Volunteers are more likely to be members of local communities than civil servants.

In short, the stress that large scale and diversifying immigration poses for local and national communities, which is one cause that drives populism, can be mitigated if one follows the liberal communitarian approach. It seeks diversity within unity rather than assimilation and favors accelerated integration. It follows, though, that to the extent that this approach cannot be implemented, immigration will need to be capped if populism is to be reined in.

7.3.3   Limiting Communities

Many millions of Americans live in a gated community of one form or another, many of which are called homeowner associations.[5] These are criticized by globalists as violating universal rights (see McKenzie 1994). Furthermore, the "spatial segregation [resulting from gated communities] has been criticized as troubling and a continuation of many of the historically discriminatory social policies of the past such as racial and socio-economic segregation, redlining, and discrimination" (Morgan 2013). But gated communities are places that provide their members with varying levels of community, mostly far from thick ones. Liberal communitarianism calls for a two-layered approach to these communities. They should not be allowed to violate basic rights, discriminate, ban books, suppress speech, infringe upon the freedom of religious expression, and so on. If they do, after proper warning, these communities should be compelled by fines or denial of public funds, and if these measures do not suffice, forced to comply. However, in all other matters, these communities should be welcome to form their own policies, to fashion particular rules that only their members will be required to follow. These may include rules concerning the appearance of their communities (homes, lawns), certain types of behavior by their members (loud music after midnight), places they may park their cars, and scores of other matters, expressing the particular preferences of the members of these communities.

In short, particularism can be well tolerated as long as it is occurring within the limits of rights enumerated in the Constitution and its Bill of Rights as interpreted by the courts, augmented with considerations based on a globalist framework, that of universal human rights.

Critics argue that even if communities do not violate rights they nevertheless are insular, isolating, and thus undermine the societal fabric. To conclude that to avoid such effects, one should take measures to curb the development of communities, one ignores the critical role thick relations play in human life—that is, that they are essential to avoid mass societies and their ill consequences, including populism. A communitarian response is to note the need to form bridging social bodies that are comprised of communities rather than individuals (Putnam 2000), and to nestle local communities within more encompassing communities—but not to agitate against the basic building block of solid communities (albeit ones that observe rights).

---

[5]The Community Associations Institute estimates that 68 million Americans common-interest communities, including homeowners' associations, condominium communities and cooperatives. See https://www.caionline.org/AboutCommunityAssociations/Pages/StatisticalInformation.aspx

7.3.4 New Rights, More Empathy

Until recently, media reports and narratives about transgender people treated them mainly as outliers. They were typically discussed as people with individual struggles and peculiar needs. Questions were raised about the age at which transgender surgery should be considered ethical, and what factors led individuals to seek to change their assigned gender, and other such personal considerations.

As of 2012, transgender people have been increasingly referred to as a group and as one that has distinct rights. Public leaders and elected officials started to associate gay and lesbian rights with those of transgendered people, increasingly using the term LGBTQ. For instance, during the 2016 presidential race, Hillary Clinton's campaign stated she had "plans to protect the rights of women, workers, minorities, and the LGBTQ community" (Clinton 2016).

In 2013, California passed a law allowing transgender students to use bathrooms aligned with their identity rather than their gender at birth. In 2015, the Charlotte City Council voted to expand the city's nondiscrimination ordinance to allow people to use bathrooms that correspond with their gender identity. In March 2016, however, House Bill 2 (HB2), also known as the Public Facilities Privacy and Security Act, was passed by the General Assembly in North Carolina, to pre-empt the Charlotte bill. HB2 requires people to use public restrooms (the law does not apply to private universities or businesses) in accordance with the sex listed on their birth certificate.

In response, the US Department of Justice asserted that HB2 is a violation of federal civil rights law, including under Title VII, which protects against workplace discrimination on the basis of race, color, religion, sex or national origin, and Title IX, which protects against sex-based discrimination in education. In May 2016, it notified North Carolina of HB2's violation of the Civil Rights Act. In response, North Carolina filed a lawsuit against the DOJ. A few hours later, the DOJ filed a lawsuit against North Carolina. The Obama Administration announced that it was considering withholding federal aid to North Carolina for schools, highways, and housing (Apuzzo and Blinder 2016).

In February of 2017, the Trump Administration retracted the federal guidelines issued by the Obama Administration, which stated that students had the right to use the restroom that corresponds to their gender identity. Oral arguments before the Supreme Court for the case of Gavin Grimm, a transgender high school student from Virginia prevented from using the boys' restroom at school, had been scheduled for March 2017. However, after the Obama-era guidelines were removed, the Supreme Court decided to remand the case to the Fourth Circuit.

From a globalist, human rights viewpoint the minting of a new right, through an extended interpretation of Titles VII and IX, is but one more step in a long progressive development of rights. Indeed, much of American history can be told as an expansion of rights, beyond those understood as enumerated in the Bill of Rights in its original form. These include extending the right to vote and to run for office to people without property; extending the same to women; ending slavery and providing African Americans both a de jure and a de facto right to vote; forming the right to privacy; extending rights to people with disabilities, and extending the right to marry to gay couples.

From a liberal communitarian viewpoint these developments went a long way to correct an imbalance, to correct a social world in which values that prescribed obligations were strongly etched but protections of the individual were weak. However, communitarians raised the question whether extending these developments serves both the individual and the community well, and if there other ways to respond to newly recognized needs and articulated grievances. Communitarians point to three considerations: the effect of the inflation of rights; the merit of communal treatments; and the need for adaptation and empathy. These points are next illustrated.

In the early 1990s, communitarians pointed out that there was a strong tendency toward minting new rights (Etzioni 1993, pp. 5–6). In Santa Monica, California, men were found dealing drugs in women's restrooms near public beaches and parks. To combat the abuse, the city council passed an ordinance that prohibited men and women from using the opposite sex's facilities unless they were in urgent need (which was defined as a line of three or more in front of them). A local activist, Gloria Allred, saw in the ordinance a violation of a woman's right to urinate in any public facility, at any time. Referring to a similar ordinance in Houston, Texas, she stated: "Little did I know that such a nightmare might soon be reenacted in this fair city." Ms. Allred warned: "This is the first step down a long dark road of restricting women's rights in the name of public safety" (Reinhold 1991).

Death-row inmates at San Quentin have sued to protect their reproductive rights to provide artificial insemination. An attorney in the case reports that "these inmates believe that they are being subjected to cruel and unusual punishment because not only are they being sentenced to die, but future generations of their family are being executed also..." (Seligman 1992).

Lisa Dangler, a mother in Yorktown, New York, sued the local school district for not admitting her son into the high school honor society. She argued that his rejection reduced his chances of being accepted by a select college and medical school. She further claimed that he was being punished because the Danglers were outspoken critics of the school—and hence his rejection was actually a violation of the family's right of free speech. A jury rejected her suit. The presiding judge stated that if the jury had ruled in Ms. Dangler's favor, he would have overturned the verdict. He added: "By attempting to elevate mere personal desires into constitutional rights and claiming denial of their civil rights whenever their desires are not realized, these persons are demeaning the essential rights and procedures that protect us all" (New York Times 1991).

The American Bankers Association took out a full-page ad in *The Washington Post* (when Congress was considering putting a cap on the interest banks may charge credit card holders) that bore the headline, "Will Congress deny millions of Americans the right to keep their credit cards?" (American Bankers' Association 1991).

These examples illustrate that one can trivialize rights by claiming that whatever one seeks—is due to one because it is a constitutionally protected right, and hence should be enforced by courts, and if need be, by the full force of the federal government. Like with other currencies, such an inflation of rights undermines the value. In a *New York Times* editorial entitled "Tempest in a Toilet," Frank Bruni (2016) asks rhetorically, "What species of sentry or manner of inquisition would assess the external and internal anatomy of the bathroom-bound? Shall we divert government spending to this? We skimp on money to repair America's infrastructure, but let's find funds to patrol America's lavatories." He notes that male sexual predators going into women's restrooms (the concern of many who advocate for bathroom bills) would already be breaking other laws against lewdness, harassment, and molestation. Bruni writes "I understand the anxiety that many Americans feel. I get their confusion. I'm not immune to it myself...Let's navigate these waters calmly. Let's flush away the nonsense" (Bruni 2016).

David Benkoff (2015) writes,

> The Bathroom Battle can be easily resolved if respectful people focus on practicalities rather ideology [*sic*]. Options include communal showers with individual stalls, alternative private bathrooms for gender nonconforming children, and special hours for changing and showering. The idea that such accommodations will draw negative attention to transgender kids is frankly silly. Do we really think kids don't already know which of their peers is transitioning?

I am not arguing that the transgender people's quest for using the facilities they prefer is a trivial one, but ask whether it should be treated as a constitutionally protected right or if there is some other way to address it.

Communitarians point to the value of drawing on communal treatments of new issues rather than rushing to involve the courts. Communitarians see an advantage in alternative dispute resolutions (and integrative justice) such as arbitration and mediation over using courts, especially for 'lighter' offenses. Good divorce lawyers urge couples to work out their differences about custody of children and distributions of assets rather than rely on lawyers and courts. These recommendations are based on the realizations that the advocacy model characteristic of American courts tends to increase antagonism between the parties and make amiable, civil community-building outcomes much less likely. In this model there are only two sides, and each side presents its interpretation of the facts in the way that most strongly supports its position. The advocacy model assumes that the clash of two strong one-sided views will lead to a just conclusion, reasonable judgments and sound public policies. This is rarely the case.

In the case at hand, various accommodations were proposed to deal with the special bathroom and locker needs of transgender people. For instance in 2015, Illinois's largest school district offered a separate room to a transgender student as a place where she could change. This proposal was rejected by the US Department of Education (Eldeib and McCoppin 2015). Harper Jean Tobin, policy director at the National Center for Transgender Equality, noted in response to the proposal, "It's a very different thing to say 'Here's the facility. Here's how everyone else can use the facility, except you. We've determined there's something wrong with you that you cannot use the facility in the same way that everyone else can'" (Eldeib and McCoppin 2015).

This is similar to what the Gloucester County Public Schools opted for in the case of Gavin Grimm: offering him use of a unisex restroom in the nurse's office. The ACLU argues that such a policy is unacceptable because it singles out transgender students and subjects them to different treatment (American Civil Liberties Union 2014). In 2015, a transgender high school student in Missouri began using the girls' locker room to change for gym class, rejecting the school's offer of a separate, single-occupancy facility (Grinberg 2015).

One major reason given for the rejection of these accommodations is that what transgender people seek is a full recognition of their new sexual identity; the biological females want to be treated as males, and the biological males as females. Providing them with accommodations in which they can relieve themselves or change in private, without being stared at or subject to comments, does not meet this aspiration. The question then is not whether transgender people have a right to an accommodation, but whether their desire to have their chosen gender identity fully affirmed is a constitutionally protected right.

The answer, I suggest, lies in two parts: the size of the harm and the feelings of others. One needs differ in the scope of the harm transgender people seek to address. The civil rights movement fought for the de facto right to vote, to abolish discrimination in jobs and housing, and to fight many other forms of discrimination that inflicted serious harms on those subjected to them. The same cannot be said about those subject to what are called microaggressions, as the term itself implies. I am not suggesting that these should be ignored, but only that the harm involved is of a different order. It follows that issues of relatively low harm are particularly suitable to be addressed socially rather than legally. Assessed in this way, the desire of transgender people to fully pass does not rank as high as, for example, the desire of gay people to marry. The argument is not that the feelings of transgender people should be ignored or taken lightly, but that they may not be best handled by elevating their protection to the level of a constitutional right, protected by the full forces of the federal government.

Once an issue is framed in legal terms, it is difficult to see how the issue might have benefited from less coercive treatments, at least as a first and second cut. The following new concern, shared by some members of the LGBTQ community, may serve as a way to explore the point at hand because it deals with an issue that has not been turned into a question of rights so far.

The issue is a quest for a gender-neutral language; for example, the use of Mx. as a gender-neutral honorific. Mx. is favored as an option for transgender individuals or anyone who does not want a gender-specific identification of themselves (Petrow 2016). "I think Mx. should be adopted as the standard form of address for everyone, because the real promise of the transgender movement was not the freedom to figure out ways to become more fully male or fully female, but rather freedom from gender entirely. Loosening the gender grip on language is a step in that direction," writes Wake Forest University Professor Shannon Gilreath (Petrow 2016). In 2014, the Vancouver school board introduced a policy to recognize gender-neutral pronouns (xe, xem, and xyr for third person, plural, and possessive, respectively) for students who do not identify as male or female (Kenwood 2014). A web-designer who uses zie and hir (to replace he/she and his/her) notes that people "seem to want to prioritize rigid linguistic rules over people's well-being and self-identification. It's funny because language is ever-evolving along with people, and I find it counterproductive to be so inflexible because of 'linguistic challenges'" (Donato 2014).

Another instance of gender-neutral language is reference to parents generally, rather than using the terms "mother" and "father." For example, the application for federal student aid uses such terminology. According to their website, "The FAFSA questions use gender-neutral terminology for married parents ('Parent 1' and 'Parent 2' instead of 'mother' and 'father')." In 2011 the State Department had planned to replace the words "mother" and "father" with "parent 1" and "parent 2," a move that was welcomed by LBGTQ advocates.

One may favor or oppose such moves, but they are much less of a concern as long as it left to public dialogue to agree which honorific one ought to use. Such dialogues led in the past to the shift from referring to women by their husbands' names (e.g. Mrs. John Doe), to referring to them by their own name—and to wide acceptance of the honorific Ms. Such developments would be much more contentious if the law required a change in honorific and leveled penalties against those who used the 'wrong' one. This does not mean that coercive means have to be avoided in general, but that society is better served if it relies on them more sparingly and takes into account that feelings on both sides are going to be ruffled.

The feelings of others need to be taken into account, at least to the extent of allowing people time to adapt to the cultural changes involved. The resistance to the new transgender bathroom regulation is rooted in part in the sense among nationalists that their way of life and their communities are being uprooted.[6] I do not argue that such feelings should be given a veto power over public policies that promote justice. I suggest that it is prudential to help people overcome their prejudices and adjust to the changing world order.

Nationalists are losing the culture wars, as abortion remains legal, divorce has been normalized, and gay marriages have been approved by the highest court in the land. At the same time, immigrants bring ways of life that conflict with theirs. And economic conditions prevent nationalists from maintaining the standard of living they were used to. The Charlotte ordinance seems to be, for many of them, the straw that broke the camel's back, although one may well argue that they feel that it has already broken, repeatedly, before. As Arlie Russel Hochschild (2016) points out,

> For the Tea Party around the country, the shifting moral qualifications for the American Dream had turned them into strangers in their own land, afraid, resentful, displaced, and dismissed by the very people who were, they felt, cutting in line…Liberals were asking them to feel compassion for the downtrodden in the back of the line, the 'slaves' of society. They didn't want to; they felt downtrodden themselves. (pp. 218–219).

To list these deprivations experienced by nationalists, their sense that their ways of life are being assaulted, is of course not to justify their prejudices. However, it suggests that, morally speaking, one should treat them as good people with utterly

---

[6]A reviewer here noted: "when that way of life is the subordination of minorities it's pretty hard to feel like this is harm..."

objectionable positions rather than as inherently bad people—that is, as irredeemable. (Liberal communitarianism should borrow from religions that hold that we are all God's children, and that one should hate the sin but love the sinner.) And it follows that if globalist policies are to gain ground, they will have to help nationalists to transition rather than condemn and further humiliate them. In other words, empathy is needed both for moral and prudential reasons. One should treat all people with dignity, even if one strongly disagrees with their viewpoints. (Needless to say, if they act on these viewpoints, such actions should be treated as any other violation of the law, or more severely, when they are expressions of hate, as the law calls for.)

One may argue in response that "these people," sometime referred to as "white trash" or "rednecks"—or more indirectly as uneducated, working class whites—cannot be reached. However, the record shows that people in all parts of America have changed their minds over the years, following moral dialogues, on these issues. For instance, Gallup polling found that in only 18 years, from 1996 to 2014, support for gay marriage more than doubled from 27% to 55% (McCarthy 2014).

Empathy is a major moral value, essential for communitarians. Globalists might benefit if they consider what they would feel if the government issued regulations that violate values and habits that they hold in high regard. The argument advanced here is not based on moral equivalency. It grants that a regulation that bans a particular prejudice has the moral high ground, one not accessible to a regulation that limits a right. However, in both cases, those affected feel challenged and threatened. To reiterate, extended dialogues, which provide time to grieve and time to adapt, are justified on both moral and prudential grounds.

Liberal communitarianism, by acknowledging from the start that there are inherent conflicts in healthy societies, favors compromises, especially when the rights advanced are newly minted, the sacrifices asked are relatively small for one side, and the pain for the other is considerable. In this case, however, all compromises were rejected. These included a suggestion that transgender pupils be able to use the faculty facilities in schools; or that separate, gender-neutral facilities reserved for transgender people be added. However, transgender people are reported to feel that such accommodations would defeat their purpose to pass fully, single them out unnecessarily, and subject them to unequal treatment. This raises the question of how far a right extends.

One notes that by mid-2017 there were signs that some globalists were realizing that attacking nationalism head on may not be justified, and certainly not prudent. They hence indicated that what they objected to was 'ethnic nationalism' or 'white nationalism.' As a next step they drew a distinction between patriotism, which is viewed positively, and the nationalism they perceive as troubling (Rather 2017). For instance, E.J. Dionne, Jr. (2017) reports that "nationalism rankles, partly because of its association with the evils of Nazism and fascism." American patriotism, on the other hand, "is not a loyalty to blood or soil. It is an embrace of a series of powerful propositions," a quality "central to our identity."[7]

---

[7] Dionne adds that "Mona Charen of the Ethics and Public Policy Center had it exactly right when she argued: 'Patriotism is enough—it needs no improving or expanding.' She called nationalism 'a

7.3.5 Free Speech: Legal Rights and Moral Rightness

Globalists, as champions of rights, tend to view the world through a legalistic lens, and lean toward promoting rights through legislation and law enforcement (Glendon 1991). Communitarians pay more attention to values that are expressed through norms and promoted through informal social controls. Both have their place; as in other matters, it is a question of balance. When it comes to free speech, American globalists (unlike Canadians and Europeans) tend to view free speech as the most fundamental right of all, and are particularly inattentive to said balance.

For instance, they believe that the right of free speech allows the Westboro Baptist Church to add to the agony of parents who have to bury their children killed in the wars in the Middle East by shouting at them that their children died because America tolerates homosexuality. The Supreme Court ruled in *Snyder v. Phelps* that this behavior is protected under the First Amendment. However, from a liberal communitarian viewpoint this behavior is morally abhorrent, and should be strongly condemned by public leaders, clergy, editorials, and so on. Moreover, the Court has often tolerated rather extensive limitations in speech in terms of TPM (time, place, and manner), including upholding Los Angeles' ban on posting fliers on public property, given the city's interest in "preventing visual clutter, minimizing traffic hazards, and preventing interference with the intended use of public property" (Members of City Council 1984). It upheld permit requirements that limit marches on public streets in order to protect "public convenience" (Cox 1941) rather than speech. The Court also upheld a ban on picketing outside residential homes in order to protect the "wellbeing, tranquility, and privacy of the home," an "important aspect" of protecting "unwilling listeners" from the intrusion of objectionable or unwanted speech (Frisby 1988).

In short, it seems quite clear that the Court is willing to allow the most profound sensibilities of the majority of Americans to be offended (e.g. by flag burning), to let their emotions and values be assaulted (e.g. when they bury their fallen soldiers), to tolerate speech that promotes hate in the most vile terms, and even to allow speech that may well incite violence or riots—but bans speech that may disrupt the slumber of some suburbanites or upset the tranquility of the downtown business community.[8]

To put it more generally: more attention needs to be paid to the crucial difference between the right to state the most offensive things—to use the N-word, deny the Holocaust, advocate for the Islamic State—and the rightness of saying these things. It is the difference between a constitutional right to free speech and what a community considers morally appropriate speech. People are not only citizens with a whole

demagogue's patriotism' more likely to be converted 'into something aggressive.'" Furthermore, "columnist Jonah Goldberg caught something important when he wrote that 'nationalism is ultimately the fire of tribalism, having too much of it tends to melt away important distinctions, from the rule of law to the right to dissent to the sovereignty of the individual.'"

[8] See, e.g. Johnson, 491 U.S. at 399; Phelps, 562 U.S. at 459–60; R.A.V., 505 U.S. at 381; Rock Against Racism, 491 U.S. at 790; Cooper, 336 U.S. at 87.

array of rights, but also members of various communities made up of people with whom they reside, work, play, pray, take civic action, and socialize. These communities, in effect, inform the members that if they must engage in offensive speech—which, granted, is their right—they must understand that one or more of these communities to which they belong might in turn express its dismay and may well follow it with social withdrawal, denial of business, or other social measures. Nothing in the First Amendment promises that free speech will be cost-free. As a result, fewer people will engage in offensive speech unless they have a strong reason to proceed.

In effect, American society in this matter is much closer to a liberal communitarian balance than globalists have it. It grants ample room for unpopular speech, despite repeated claims that it has been suppressed. But American society also seeks to exact consequences for offensive speech. For example, when Lawrence Summers, then the president of Harvard University, suggested that the underrepresentation of women in the sciences somehow reflected their shortcomings, a storm of protest ensued. He argued that he was misunderstood and tried to make amends, but in the end the outcry contributed to his resignation from the job (Finder et al. 2006). Journalist Chris Hedges was disinvited from giving a lecture at the University of Pennsylvania after publishing an article arguing that the strategy of the Islamic State—its terrorism, ethnic cleansing, and religious fundamentalism—"mirrors the quest for a Jewish state eventually carved out of Palestine in 1948" (Haaretz 2014). The Philadelphia Eagles fined player Riley Cooper for using a racial slur at a concert, and the NFL suspended referee Roy Ellison for cursing at a player during a football game (Maske and Jones 2013). As a result, people maintain the right to say most anything they want to say but are also encouraged to take into account the sensibilities of their fellow community members,

To understand why this liberal communitarian balance is crucial, one needs to pay more attention to a deep social structure that is often overlooked. To outline it requires a brief digression into human nature. A study that built on the findings of several hundred empirical works found that there are only three ways to motivate people to engage in behavior that they would not engage in otherwise: force them (threaten to tow their car if they park in the hospital fire lane); pay them (as they are paid on the job); or convince them of the merit of doing what must be done (encourage them to volunteer) (Etzioni 1975). People who are coerced often resent the imposition and tend to do as little as they can get away with. Those who are paid would often rather be doing something else. However, people who are persuaded will do their new chores happily; they want to do them! True, they may not be pure altruists. They often heed the voice of the community because they are social creatures who crave the approval of others and try to avoid their disapproval. What most people overlook is the very significant amount of social transactions that are carried out in this third way. Communities set norms of conduct that define what people are expected to do, and undergird them by little else but a stream of kudos and appreciations as well as mild censorship. Thus, most of what people do for their children, their elders, their friends and neighbors, and for their community is neither coerced nor paid for but fueled by communal norms and informal social controls and mutuality.

A liberal communitarian society will seek to resolve conflicts first and foremost through moral dialogues and resort to coercive enforcement only when these fail. Moral dialogues are social processes through which people form new shared moral understandings. These dialogues typically are passionate, disorderly, and without a clear starting point or conclusion (in contrast to elections or debates in a legislature) (Etzioni 1998).

It was just over 19 years from the day President Clinton signed the Defense of Marriage Act, which defined marriage as between a man and a woman, to the day the Supreme Court approved same-sex marriage at the federal level. In those years, millions of Americans shifted sides. True, there are still millions who did not embrace the new norm, and they will face the new legal reality. However, a considerable time was given to try to sway them. In the case of transgender rights, a very new public policy issue as far as public discourse is concerned, people were given very little time to learn the issues and to be convinced of the values of the suggested changes.

Compassionate and prudent liberals will embrace the principle that when policy changes are planned for a democracy, it is not enough to garner enough votes or get a court to rule. One also needs to engage the public in a moral dialogue that will help it to see the value of the suggested shift. The employment of coercive means is justified only after such dialogues fail.

7.3.6 Coping with Conflicts of Liberal and Communitarian Principles

So far, combining liberal and communitarian principles has been attempted mainly by dividing the relevant turf. When the absorption of immigrants was examined, we found that the elements of unity can be communitarian and those of diversity, or pluralism, liberal. In studying homeowner associations, we saw that individual rights can provide a framework within which communities can follow their particularistic preferences. Moral persuasion (which communitarians favor) best precedes law enforcement (when rights are challenged). However, there are situations in which the two principled approaches come into direct conflict. Here, instead of assuming that one value takes precedence over others—for instance that liberty trumps other values, unless one can make a compelling case that liberty must be curbed—a liberal communitarian assumes that there are two set of values of equal standing: rights and the need for thick, lasting, meaningful relationships. If one can draw on the notion that one value trumps others, one must ask what criteria one uses when two values of the same standing come into conflict.

The way a liberal communitarian would deal with this is next illustrated by studying the clash in one major public domain, between security (a common good) and privacy (a human right).

Three criteria help specify the liberal communitarian approach to this domain (Etzioni 1999). First, a liberal democratic government will limit privacy only if it faces a well-documented and large-scale threat to the common good (such as to public safety or public health). The main reason this threshold must be cleared is because modifying legal precepts endangers their legitimacy. Thus if the Supreme Court reversed itself often, it would have little credibility left. Changes, therefore, should not be undertaken unless there is strong evidence that change in the law (or public policy) is needed.

Second, if the finding is that the common good needs shoring up, one had best seek to establish whether this goal can be achieved without introducing new limits on the rights involved, such as privacy. For instance, one might provide medical records to researchers for the sake of public health without undermining privacy by removing personally identifying information (such as names, addresses and social security numbers) from those records. Third, to the extent that privacy-curbing measures must be introduced, they should be as nonintrusive as possible. For example, many agree that drug tests should be conducted on those directly responsible for the lives of others, such as school bus drivers. Some employers, however, resort to highly intrusive visual surveillance to ensure that the sample is taken from the person who delivers it. Instead, one can rely on the much less intrusive procedure of measuring the temperature of the sample immediately following delivery.

Furthermore, one must realize that any balance a liberal communitarian society achieves between individual rights and the common good is historically contextualized. It must be adapted as technological, international, and domestic developments take place. For example, the balance between rights and the common good changed after the September 11, 2001 attacks against the United States. One can argue over the severity of the threat terrorism now poses, and how severely the United States should react while seeking to protect the nation from future attacks. Few would disagree that some adaptation was called for after 9/11. Both rigid adherence to standards of a previous era (e.g. trying to deal with transnational terrorists as if they had all the rights of soldiers, and can be fought only in the areas in which the US declared war) and suspending the most basic rights to serve security (e.g. allowing torture) are unnecessary and defeat the purposes they are meant to serve. They also undermine the legitimacy of the governments involved and thus feed populism. Finally, a liberal communitarian holds that deliberations should focus both on the extent of this recalibration and on ensuring that corrective measures are neither excessive nor irreversible as historical conditions change again.

7.4   In Conclusion

Globalization (the free flow of goods, people, and ideas) combined with the promotion of human (i.e. globally applicable) rights is a factor that accounts for the rise of populism. In response, extolling the virtues of liberalism will not suffice. What is missing is recognition of the importance of communities, as small as families and as large as nations, for people's flourishing and their ability to resist demagogues. Hence, communitarian considerations are needed for both analysis and policy making. They help understand how communities that are under attack can be maintained and shored up. However, given that communities can be oppressive, they need to be leavened with liberal principles: hence the merit of a liberal communitarian philosophy. While in such a combination, both liberal and communitarian principles protect each other from undervaluing one core element of what makes for free and open communities, one cannot ignore that the two sets of principles cannot be fully reconciled. The chapter provides several major examples of ways that liberal and communitarian principles can be combined and their differences curbed.

References

American Bankers Association ad. 1991, November 17. *Washington Post*, A13.

American Civil Liberties Union. 2014, December 18. *Complaint to United States Department of Justice against Gloucester County Public Schools on behalf of Gavin Grimm*. Available at: https://acluva.org/wp-content/uploads/2014/12/141218-dojcomplaintltrGRIMM.pdf.

Apuzzo, M., and A. Blinder. 2016, April 1. North Carolina law may risk federal aid. *New York Times*.

Auffray, A., and L. Equy. 2016, August 19. Le burkini interdit dans une quinzaine de communes. *Liberation*

Benkoff, D. 2015, November 10. Both sides in the transgender 'bathroom battle' are wrong. *Daily Caller*.

Berlin, I. 1991. Joseph de Maistre and the origins of fascism. In *The crooked timber of humanity: Chapters in the history of ideas*, ed. H. Hardy. New York: Alfred A. Knopf.

Brooks, D. 2016, November 11. The view from Trump tower. *New York Times*.

Bruni, F. 2016, April 23. Tempest in a toilet. *New York Times*. https://www.nytimes.com/2016/04/24/opinion/sunday/tempest-in-a-toilet.html.

Chozik, A. 2016, September 10. Hillary Clinton calls many Trump backers 'deplorables,' and GOP pounces. *New York Times*.

Chrisafis, A. 2015, October 13. Pork or nothing: How school dinners are dividing France. *The Guardian*.

Clinton, C. 2016, October 29. *Chelsea Clinton Campaigns in Michigan*. https://hillaryspeeches.com/tag/equality/

Cox v. New Hampshire. 1941. 312 U.S. 569, 574.

Daly, M. 1994. In *Introduction to communitarianism: A new public ethics*, ed. M. Daly. Belmont: Wadsworth Publishing Company.

Dionne, Jr., E.J. 2017, April 17. Why we don't call it nationalists' day. *Washington Post*.

Donato, A. 2014, November 25. He and she, ze and xe: The case for gender-neutral pronouns. *Plaid Zebra.*

Eldeib, D., and R. McCoppin. 2015, October 15. Feds reject school district's plan for transgender student, locker room. *Chicago Tribune*.

Etzioni, A. 1975. *Comparative analysis of complex organizations*, Revised ed. New York: The Free Press.

———. 1993. *The spirit of community*. New York: Simon & Schuster.

———. 1998. *The new golden rule: Community and morality in a democratic society*. New York: Basic Books.

———. 1999. *The limits of privacy*. New York: Basic Books.

Finder, A., P.D. Healy, and K. Zernike. 2006, February 22. President of Harvard resigns, ending stormy 5-year tenure. *New York Times*.

Fratiglioni, L. et al. 2000. Influence of social networks on occurrence of dementia. *The Lancet*.

Frisby, V. Schultz. 1988. 487 U.S. 474, 484.

Galston, W. 2016, November 22. Immigration reaches critical mass. *Wall Street Journal.*

Glendon, M.A. 1991. *Rights talk: The impoverishment of political discourse.* New York: The Free Press.

Goldstein, A. 2017. *Janesville: An American story.* New York: Simon & Schuster.

Grinberg, E. 2015, September 5. Bathroom access for transgender teen divides Missouri town. *CNN.*

Haaretz. 2014, December 28. Journalist Chris Hedges disinvited from U. Penn over Israel-ISIS comparison.

Haidt, J. 2016, July 10. When and why nationalism beats globalism. *American Interest.*

Helliwell, J.F. 2003. Well-being, social capital and public policy: What's new? *Economic Modelling* 20: 331.

Hochschild, A.R. 2017. *Stranger in their own land.* New York: The New Press.

Hornberger, J. 2016, August 25. There is only one libertarian position on immigration. *Future of Freedom Foundation.*

Kenwood, J. 2014, June 19. Vancouver school board adopts progressive transgender policy. *Vice News.*

Levin, Y. 2016. *The fractured republic: Renewing America's social contract in the age of individualism.* New York: Basic Books.

Lilla, M. 2016. *The shipwrecked mind: On political reaction.* New York Review of Books.

Lind, M. 2016, May 22. This is what the future of American politics looks like. *Politico.*

Long, H. 2016, March 29. U.S. has lost 5 million manufacturing jobs since 2000. *CNN.*

Maske, M., and M. Jones. 2013, November 22. NFL umpire Roy Ellison suspended for incident with Redskins' lineman Trent Williams. *Washington Post.*

Mayet, F. 2015, March 31. Laïcité à Montpellier: Des jupes longues font débat au collège des Garrigues. *Midi Libre.*

McCarthy, J. 2014, May 21. Same-sex marriage support reaches new high at 55%. *Gallup.*

McKenzie, E. 1994. *Privatopia: Homeowner associations and the rise of residential private government.* New Haven: Yale University Press.

Members of City Council of L.A. v. Taxpayers for Vincent. 1984. 466 U.S. 789, 789.

Mishra, P. 2016, August 1. How Rousseau predicted Trump. *New Yorker.*

Monbiot, G. 2005, August 8. The new chauvinism. *The Guardian.*

Morgan, L.J. 2013. Gated communities: Institutionalizing social stratification. *The Geographical Bulletin* 54 (1): 24.

Mudde, C. 2004. The populist zeitgeist. *Government and Opposition* 39 (4): 541.

Mulhall, S., and A. Swift. 1992. *Liberals and communitarians.* Cambridge: Blackwell.

Müller, J.W. 2016. *What is populism?* Philadelphia: University of Pennsylvania Press.

New York Times. 1991, November 23. Mother scolded for suit over son's honors.

Nussbaum, M.C. 1996. In *For love of country?* ed. J. Cohen. Boston: Beacon Press.

Petrow, S. 2016, August 3. Civilities: Is it time to include 'Mx.' in the mix with 'Ms.' and 'Mr.'? *Washington Post.*

Putnam, R.D. 2000. *Bowling alone: The collapse and revival of American community.* New York: Simon & Schuster.

Rather, D 2017, April 12. Interview by Ana Marie Cox. *New York Times Magazine.*

Redles, D. 2010. The Nazi old guard: Identity formation during apocalyptic times. *Nova Religio: The Journal of Alternative and Emergent Religions* 14 (1): 24.

Reinhold, R. 1991, November 15. In land of liberals, restroom rights are rolled back. *New York Times.*

Sandel, M. 1998. *Liberalism and the limits of justice.* 2nd ed. New York: Cambridge University Press.

Seligman, D. 1992, February 10. Keeping up. *Fortune.*

Singer, P. 1972. Famine, affluence, and morality. *Philosophy & Public Affairs* 1 (3): 229.

Tönnies, F. 1957. *Community and society (Gemeinschaft und Gesellschaft)* (Trans. and ed.: C.P. Loomis). East Lansing, MI: University of Michigan Press. (Original work published in 1893)

Walzer, M. 1994. *Thick and thin: Moral argument at home and abroad.* Notre Dame: University of Notre Dame Press.

Wong, D.B. 1988. On flourishing and finding one's identity in community. *Midwest Studies in Philosophy* 13(1): 324–341. In *Ethical theory, character, and virtue*, ed. P. French. Notre Dame: University of Notre Dame Press.

Wrong, D. 1994. *The problem of order.* New York: Simon and Schuster.

Part IV
Moral Issues Raised by Individual Rights

Chapter 8
Free Speech Versus Safe Space

The comedian allowed himself to tell an old joke about "homos." The audience groaned. He stretched his index finger as far as he could and shouted "First Amendment!" There followed several lame jokes –one about a Rabbi, Minister and Priest who went into a bar. This time the audience responded with an ice silence. The comedian one more time shrieked: "First Amendment!" During the intermission that followed I asked a young couple sitting opposite me, in the cramped night club table, what they thought about his declaration that he was merely exercising his First Amendment rights. "Well, I see that he has right to say all these things; still, I wish…" He trailed off, wondering on what grounds he could object to such loaded, biased commentary about protected groups. His girlfriend had a solution: "We should, like all other civilized nations, ban hate speech."

All three of them, I mean the comedian and the young couple, like most Americans, seem more infused with popular culture versions of the law—than with elementary communitarian concepts. These suggest a crucial difference between the right to say the most God awful things—use the N word, deny the Holocaust, advocate ISIS—and the rightness of saying these things. A difference between a legal right to speech—and what we consider morally appropriate speech. We are not only citizens, with a whole array of rights; we are also members of various communities (where we reside, work, pray and socialize). These communities, in effect, tell us that if you must engage in offensive speech—granted, which is your right—we in turn may express our dismay, never wish to visit with you again, let alone lend you a cup of sugar in a time of need. In other words, there is nothing in the First Amendment that promises you that free speech will be cost-free.

Better yet: as a society, America has found a way to have our cake and eat it too. We make room for unpopular speech, which is vital for a free society, for dissent, for innovation, for a vigorous civic life. But we also seek to ensure that you do not offend lightly, because there will be consequences. Call it a communitarian balance

This chapter draws on a segment of an article previously published as "Right Does Not Make it Right" in *The American Scholar,* September 29, 2015.

A. Etzioni, *Happiness is the Wrong Metric*, Library of Public Policy and Public Administration 11, https://doi.org/10.1007/978-3-319-69623-2_8

between individual rights and social responsibility. For example, when Larry Summers, serving as president of Harvard, was understood to have stated that that women's underrepresentation in the sciences somehow reflects their shortcomings, a storm of protest ensued (See, e.g., Dooe 2015). It led him to explain that he was misunderstood, tried to make amends, but in the end was one of the reasons he resigned. When then-candidate Donald Trump made several comments women found insulting, including a particularly vulgar comment about a Fox News reporter, he was disinvited from speaking at the Conservative RedState Gathering—a group that had considered him one of its heroes. Journalist Chris Hedges was disinvited from a lecture at the University of Pennsylvania after publishing an article arguing that the "terrorism," "ethnic cleansing," and "religious fundamentalism" of the Islamic State "mirrors the quest for a Jewish state eventually carved out of Palestine in 1948." Beer giant Budweiser apologized after many on social media criticized its advertisement of "The perfect beer for removing 'no' from your vocabulary for the night" at a time when women's rights advocates were pushing for a "yes means yes" policy on affirmative sexual consent. U.S. Representative Todd Akin, who led in the election polls for a U.S. Senate seat for Missouri, was roundly criticized and lost the election decisively after stating that women who are victims of "legitimate rape" rarely get pregnant. Several sports commentators and athletes have had to learn to live with the consequences of offensive speech. ESPN refused to rehire commentator Craig James after he said homosexuals "are going to have to answer to the Lord for their actions" during a failed Senate campaign (Bonesteel 2015), and the NFL fined player Riley Cooper for using a racial slur at a concert (Hanzus 2013) and suspended referee Roy Ellison for cursing at a player during a game (ESPN 2013). Moreover, these consequences do not apply only to public figures in the media spotlight. For example, the *New Yorker* reported that after a DJ continued to play "Blurred Lines" against the request of a female patron who felt it promoted "rape culture"— and the bar in question was criticized on social media—the radio station announced it would never invite him back (Sanneh 2015). After Bill Maher used a racial epithet in a live interview on his HBO late-night show, he was widely criticized; the network called Maher's words "completely inexcusable and tasteless" and Senator Al Franken cancelled his upcoming guest appearance on Maher's show because of the offensive remark. Maher apologized for what he said (Itzkoff 2017). An Uber board member resigned after making a sexist comment at a meeting that angered employees (Isaac and Chira 2017). These types of incidents demonstrate that society has ways to contain inappropriate and offensive speech without making it illegal.

As a result, for everyone so chastised, thousands of others say to themselves: I know I have the right to say it, but is it the right thing to say? Which is dandy, because free speech does not presume shooting from the hip, and is best deliberate rather than wanton. I am not arguing that we have found the perfect balance. Those on the left these days seek more limits on speech (more about this soon) and libertarians hold that free speech is endangered. Each has some choice examples of their own. However, if you look at them together, as the examples cited above illustrate, public figures and the mainstream media seem quite well balanced; that is, speaking up without being unduly and wantonly offensive. And when one does offend, they hear plenty, which is the way society keeps the communitarian balance between the right to speak and keeping the community's sensibilities intact.

8.1 Reflecting a Profound Societal Design

The communitarian setup of free speech, combining a legal right to speak freely with social norms that curb offensive speech, is merely the tip of a much larger iceberg, a reflection of a deep communitarian social structure often overlooked by those who focus on the difference between the private sector and the government, as so much of public discourse does. To outline this structure requires a brief digression into human nature. I first wrote about it in a book that later earned me tenure at Columbia University two years after a got my PhD. I tell you this not to boast about my achievement (well, just a bit) but to suggest that the idea was really well received. I showed, as you recall from Chap. 4, that there are only three ways to motivate people to engage in behavior that they would not engage in otherwise: force them (if you park in the hospital fire lane, you will be towed); pay them (as they are in offices and factories); and convince them of the merit of doing what must be done (e.g. call for volunteers). People who are coerced resent the imposition and tend to do as little as they can get away with it. People who are paid would still rather be doing something else. However, people who are convinced—do their new chores happily; they want to do them! True, they may not be pure altruists. They often simply heed the voice of the community because they are social creatures who crave the approval of others, and try to avoid their disapproval. What most people overlook is the huge amount of social business that is carried out in this third way: the community sets norms of conduct, that define what we are expected to do, and undergirds them by little else than a stream of kudos and appreciation as well as mild digs and snide remarks. Thus most of what people do for their children, their elders, their friends and neighbors, for their community, is not coerced nor paid for but fueled by communal norms and informal social controls.

Prohibition was a prime example: it was largely coercive, failed to achieve its goals, and vastly damaged America's law enforcement system and even its societal fiber; in contrast, the ban on smoking in public, which is based on convictions that this smoking harms others and should be prohibited, is 99.9999% self-enforcing, i.e. based on norms and informal social controls and a smashing success.

This is what observers refer to when they point to peer pressure and informal social controls. True, these can become oppressive, especially in more traditional societies and traditional parts of our society, but increasingly in modern societies they have become quite moderate. When Jonathan Rauch, one of our most seminal authors and a dedicated libertarian, came across this communitarian design, he wrote an enthusiastic oft-cited essay about this design in which he declared himself a soft communitarian, because "soft communitarianism is less oppressive, usually much less so, than the real-world alternatives. Shame is valuable not because it is pleasant or fair or good but because it is the least onerous of all means of social regulation, and because social regulation is inevitable" (Rauch 2000). All this is behind the social structure that legally allows people to say what they want—but makes them think twice before they use this privilege.

8.1.1   Not Soft Censorship

When faced with the community's voice, in effect a kind of counter speech, free speech advocates complain about it, calling it soft censorship or outright censorship. For example, users of social media site Reddit called on the site to fire its CEO for "censorship" after five forums (out of thousands) were deleted for racial or other harassment (Dewey 2015). Facebook has been criticized and even sued for "censorship" due to its policy of banning those who display pictures of women's breasts and genitalia (Bouton n.d.) Twitter was criticized for introducing content filters and temporary account suspensions for "abusive messages" and "indirect threats of violence," (Hern 2015) in what one user said "can only be described as heavy-handed censorship" (Fagioli n.d.) And in response to a Harris poll showing that 71% of Americans want a ratings system for books to protect children from inappropriate content, as exists for movies and games, free speech campaigners likewise argued that such a proposal would "raise serious concerns about censorship" (Flood 2015).

These champions of free speech, unwittingly or deliberately, use the horror the term censorship evokes to object to social reactions to their offensive speech. They would like to be able to say outrageous things—and be appreciated for doing so. But in the process, they are delegitimizing social pressure, which is the foundation of all communities. Censorship occurs when the government exercises its coercive powers to prevent speech, by jailing dissenters, closing newspapers, taking over TV stations, and so on. Social pressures merely ensure that before you speak, you ask yourself whether what you have to say justifies the hurt you will cause, often to people who have already been hurt plenty.

But do not a bookstore that refuses to sell *Mein Kampf*, a symphony orchestra that refuses to play Wagner, a cinema that refuses to show *Gone with the Wind*, a library that bans *Fifty Shades of Grey*, a video hosting site that bans "hateful content," a comedy club or television channel that bans an offensive comedian, a film studio that refuses to work with Mel Gibson, or an online retailer that refuses to sell Confederate flag merchandise, engage in censorship? Only if they truly prevent speech. *Free speech requires that everyone will have a Hyde Park corner, a place one can freely state whatever the person seeks to state—but not that every corner be a Hyde Park.* If all the bookstores in town, Amazon, and Barnes and Noble and the publishers of e-books refuse to carry a given book, if you could not download it— that would come close to censorship, even if the government was not involved. But this is hardly ever the case, especially since the advent of social media, which provides a large number of alternative platforms such that it is hard to stop any utterance even if we all agree it ought to, like in the case of bullying.

8.1.2 Ban Hate Speech?

What about the suggestion of the young lady that we should outlaw hate speech? Most democracies do. And we already ban some speech; libel and child pornography for example. The main difficulty is with defining what hate speech is, without banning much of public discourse and art and literature. For instance, would we have to ban *Huckleberry Finn* because it includes the N word? The book is seen as required reading by some educators, while others argue that the teaching of a book with racist language is unacceptable (Roberts 2003; Holmes 2014). Historically, the list of authors frequently banned or challenged from libraries not only includes purveyors of hate or even dirty language, but also Orwell (for being "pro-communist"), Whitman (for "homoerotic themes"), and Darwin (for promoting the theory of evolution). Moreover, if you ban hate speech, you do very little to eradicate it, you just drive it underground. We would be better off being aware of when, where, and by whom hate speech is made, and respond with counter-speech, than leaving it simmering and unaddressed. In addition, from a communitarian viewpoint, banning hate speech is trying to solve a problem by law, instead by drawing on the community's informal social controls.

8.1.3 Microaggressions and "Check Your Privilege"

Informal social controls can be taken too far, as is the case with the campaign against "microaggressions." This term was coined in the 1970s and refers to "brief, everyday exchanges that send denigrating messages to certain individuals because of their group membership," whether as "people of color, women, [or] lesbian, gay, bisexual, or transgender (LGBT)" people (Granger 2012). Microaggressions have also been referred to as "subtle forms of racial bias" that are "so deeply embedded in societal values and practices that they lie outside the consciousness of many well-intentioned White people who may genuinely consider themselves to be nonracist." Note you cannot be micro-aggressive against white males by this widely followed definition; they are aggressors but cannot be aggrieved.

Those concerned with microaggression frown on statements such as, "There is only one race, the human race;" "America is a melting pot;" and "When I look at you, I don't see color"—for "denying the significance of a person of color's racial/ethnic experience" and sending the message that they should "assimilate/acculturate to the dominant culture" (Examples of Racial Microaggressions n.d.). "I believe the most qualified person should get the job" is interpreted to promoting a myth of meritocracy and suggest that people of color and women are lazy (Tool: Recognizing Microaggressions n.d.). Likewise, scrutinizing a thirty-something woman's hand, looking for a wedding band is interpreted as a microaggression communicating that "women should be married during child-bearing ages because that is their primary purpose." And the act of asking a non-white person where they are from is interpreted as micro-aggressively suggesting someone is "exotic" or not a "true American" (Tool: Recognizing Microaggressions n.d.). A guide to "interrupting Microaggressions" in turn recommends that the victim respond to such questions by asking, "I'm wondering what message this is sending [...] Do you think you would have said this to a white male?" Or "How might we examine our implicit bias to ensure that gender plays no part in this?" (Tool: Interrupting Microaggressions n.d.).

I had the following exchange with a microaggression antagonist. I started by noting that I understood concerns about hidden, subtle aggressions, though I was concerned that one is defenseless against being charged with such speech. One is always subject to the argument that "you are unaware of your bias," that others determine if you are aggressive, and that there is no way to appeal such judgments. The line "check your privilege" seemed to me particularly to cross a line. This expression is increasingly used online and on college campuses to demand that a speaker consider the unearned advantages that result from their race or gender before expressing their opinion on an issue. It basically implies that white males should mince their words, listen rather than talk.

The antagonist suggested that "one should know where one is coming from." I replied, "That is true for one and all, even those who come with a chip on their shoulder from the inner city, but this is not the way this line is used; it addresses one group and seek to curb one group."

Antagonist: "Well, if there is a space set aside for, say, Latinos to find their voice, and white males keep occupying the space with their voices..." I agreed that this is indeed an open and shut case of robbery. But when whites speak in a common place, like a class room, and their views are dismissed as biased on the face of it, we are taking social pressures a step or more too far.

I found that concern with microaggressions is held not merely by some far out college kids. Some years back I was asked to address the General Assembly of the Unitarian Universalist Association. I felt I did not know enough about the group and hence spent some days sitting in on meetings and listening. I was surprised to learn that several local chapters resolved that anyone (means white) who did not acknowledge that he or she has racist and homophobic feelings, should be encouraged to dig deeper. That one could not start on a journey of exorcising these feelings unless one first acknowledged that one had them. I had a hard time with such statements; there is no way to clear yourself. Whatever you feel or say—whether you accept the statement that you are profoundly biased—or refused to own up to your alleged feelings—is considered prima facie evidence that your view was profoundly warped.

I learned since that one can never be too much on one's guard. Thus, to reveal and overcome homophobic feelings, for instance, is far from enough. A truly sensitive person would acknowledge that he is "transphobic" and be aware that he maintains different biases not just for gays, lesbians, bisexuals, and transgender people, but also for people of mixed genders or no gender and still others. On his way to curing his phobias, I am told, a person seeking to free himself from hidden biases would avoid the titles of Mr., Mrs., and Ms., and sign Mx.

In short, the movement to overcome microaggressions is part naïve idealism, part slightly disguised anti-elite rhetoric, part theater of the absurd. Above all, it draws reforming energy into micro issues in a world full of macro ones. It leads people to worry about wording in a world where ISIS fighters burn people alive, behead others because they are Christians, and sell young girls as sex slaves. A world in which—still!—hundreds of black men are shot by the police in the US, often without any reason. In which gang warfare turns blocks of cities into war zones—year after year after year. And, in which Citizens United is turning democracy into plutocracy—one dollar, one vote—by claiming that bribery is a form of free speech.

An old children's rhyme says it very simply but best: "Sticks and stones will break my bones, but words will never hurt me." If words do hurt you, you have a right to speak up, but see if you cannot find some sticks and stones whose removal commands much greater attention.

References

Bonesteel, M. 2015, August 4. Craig James sues Fox Sports, alleging religious discrimination. *The Washington Post*.

Bouton, E. n.d. Breasts on facebook: Stop the censorship, Mark Zuckerberg! *The World Post*.

Dewey, C. 2014, October 31. Pianist asks The Washington Post to remove a concert review under the E.U.'s 'right to be forgotten' ruling. *The Washington Post*.

Dooe, M. 2015, January 31. Larry Summers 'may have done a service to women' with his sexist remarks. *PRI*.

ESPN. 2013, November 23. Roy Ellison suspended 1 game.

Examples of Racial Microaggressions. n.d. University of Minnesota. http://sph.umn.edu/site/docs/hewg/microaggressions.pdf. Accessed 14 July 2017.

Fagioli, B. n.d. Twitter begins heavy-handed censorship – will force users to delete tweets. *Betanews*.

Flood, A. 2015, August 7. Are Americans falling in love with censorship? *The Guardian*.

Granger, N. 2012, October. Microaggressions and their effects on the therapeutic process. *Society for Humanistic Psychology Newsletter*.

Hanzus, D. 2013, July 31. Eagles fine Riley Cooper for insensitive comment. *NFL*.

Hern, A. 2015, April 21. Twitter announces crackdown on abuse with new filter and tighter rules. *The Guardian*.

Holmes, L. 2014, December 30. In 'Huckleberry Finn,' a history in echoes. *NPR*.

Isaac, M., and S. Chira. 2017, June 13. David Bonderman resigns from Uber board after sexist remark. *The New York Times*.

Itzkoff, D. 2017. Al Franken cancels appearance on 'Real Time with Bill Maher.' *The New York Times*.

Rauch, J. 2000. Conventional wisdom: Rediscovering the social norms that stand between law and libertinism

Roberts, G. 2003, November 25. 'Huck Finn' a masterpiece – or an insult. *Seattle Post-Intelligencer*.

Sanneh, K. 2015. The hell you say. *The New Yorker*.

Tool: Interrupting Microaggressions. n.d. http://academicaffairs.ucsc.edu/events/documents/Microaggressions_InterruptHO_2014_11_182v5.pdf. Accessed 14 July 2017.

Tool: Recognizing Microaggressions and the Messages They Send. n.d. https://academicaffairs.ucsc.edu/events/documents/Microaggressions_Examples_Arial_2014_11_12.pdf. Accessed 14 July 2017.

Chapter 9
The Right to Be Forgotten

9.1 Second Chances

A young man in upstate New York drinks too much and gets a little rowdy, picks a fight, smashes up the bar, and is arrested. When he gets into trouble again a short time later, the judge sends him to jail for a week. After his release, he gets fired and cannot find a new job because he has a record. The local newspaper carries a story about his misconduct. The merchants on Main Street refuse to sell him anything on credit. The young women gossip about him and refuse to date him. One day, he has had enough. He packs his meager belongings, leaves without a good-bye, and moves to a small town in Oregon. Here, he gains a new start. Nobody knows about his rowdy past, and he has learned his lesson. He drinks less, avoids fights, works in a lumberyard, and soon marries a nice local woman, has three kids, and lives happily ever after. Cue the choir of angels singing in the background.

The idea that people deserve a second chance is an important American value. Perhaps it grows out of America's history as a nation of immigrants who moved to the United States to start new lives. And as the American West was settled, many Easterners and Midwesterners found a place there for a second beginning. More profoundly, the belief in a new beginning is a tenet of Christianity, which allows sinners to repent and be fully redeemed, to be reborn. In a similar vein, the secular, progressive, optimistic, therapeutic culture of today's America rejects the notion that there are inherently bad people. As individuals, Americans seek insights into their failings so they can learn to overcome them and achieve a new start. From a sociological perspective, people are thrown off course by their social conditions—because they are poor, for instance, and subject to discrimination. But these conditions can be altered, and then these people will be able to lead good lives. Under the right conditions, criminals can pay their debt to society and be rehabilitated, sex

This chapter draws on "Second Chances, Social Forgiveness, and the Internet" in *The American Scholar*, (Spring 2009). This article was co-authored by Radhika Bhat, a research and outreach assistant at the Institute for Communitarian Policy Studies at The George Washington University.

© The Author(s) 2018
A. Etzioni, *Happiness is the Wrong Metric*, Library of Public Policy and Public Administration 11, https://doi.org/10.1007/978-3-319-69623-2_9

offenders can be reformed, and others who have flunked out can pass another test. Just give them a second chance.

Today, a wide variety of public figures call for giving everyone a second chance. Texas Governor and former presidential candidate Rick Perry said, "The idea that we lock people up, throw them away, and never give them a chance of redemption is not what America is about [...] Being able to give someone a second chance is very important" (Izad and Wald 2014). New York Representative Charles Rangel is "a firm believer that upon release, ex-offenders should be afforded a second chance to become productive citizens by providing rehabilitation and education that will help them join the workforce" (Rangel 2013). Former Secretary of State Hillary Clinton frequently asserts that "everyone deserves a second chance, a third chance to keep going and to make something of themselves [...] That was one of the most important lessons of my life" (Merica 2014). Famous singer and former drug addict El DeBarge called for "the world to know that everybody deserves a second chance" (El DeBarge Debuts 2010). Rabbi Bernard Barsky asked, "How could a Jewish community not be committed to giving ex-felons a second chance? Our entire faith is based on stories of second chances" (Barsky 2013). And even church leader the Reverend Glenn Grayson, whose 18-year-old son was shot and killed, said that "if [God] can give us a second chance, [...] there are things you have to atone for, but you deserve a second chance" (Gibb 2010).

The internet poses a great technological challenge to social forgiveness. By indexing digital versions of local public records, the internet acts as a bright light that casts people's shadows much further than ever before: criminal or otherwise debilitating records now follow people wherever they go. True, arrest records, criminal sentences, bankruptcy filings, and even divorce records were accessible to the public long before being digitized. Some were listed in blotters kept in police stations, others in courthouses; anyone who wished to take the trouble could go there and read them. But most people did not. Above all, there was no way for people in distant communities to find these damning facts without going to inordinate lengths.

Making records at least inconvenient to attain was sensible because the American legal system has never been quick to wipe offenders' slates clean. In her book *Ctrl+Z: The Right to be Forgotten*, Meg Leta Jones outlines the system's criteria for expungement and concludes, "Legal forgiveness is not offered lightly in the U.S" (Jones 2016, p. 141). Indeed, certain crimes—especially sexual offenses—are not considered forgivable, so we maintain public offender registries and protracted statutes of limitations. For most crimes, however, "the U.S. legal system acknowledges that punishment should not necessarily be eternal and that limiting the use of information about an individual can be a form of relief" (Jones 2016, p. 144).

Yet for those citizens whose misdeeds the legal system has elected to forgive and forget, the ever-expanding, interminable memory of the internet undermines the possibility of redemption by dismantling any information monopoly once held by government records and careful journalistic accounts. In fact, several companies have started compiling criminal records and making them available to everyone in the country and, indeed, the world. For instance, in 2008, PeopleFinders, a company based in Sacramento, introduced CriminalSearches.com, a free service to access public criminal records, which draws data from local courthouses (Stone 2008). Similar services provide access to many other types of public records that range from birth records to divorces. As long as the aggregated information is accurate, one has scant opportunity for legal recourse to salvage his reputation. According to the National Association of Criminal Defense Lawyers, this "growing obsession with background checking and commercial exploitation of arrest and conviction records makes it all but impossible for someone with a criminal record to leave the past behind" (Zimmerman and Stringer 2004). This is particularly apparent in the United States due to its level of technological development and strong protections of free speech.

These developments disturb privacy advocates and anyone who is keen to ensure that people have the opportunity for a new start. Beth Givens, director of the Privacy Rights Clearinghouse, says that internet databases cause a "loss of 'social forgiveness" (Givens 1995). For instance, a person's "conviction of graffiti vandalism at age 19 will still be there at age 29 when [he's] a solid citizen trying to get a job and raise a family"—and the conviction will be there for anyone to see (Givens 1995). Furthermore, as companies "rely on background checks to screen workers, [they] risk imposing unfair barriers to rehabilitated criminals," wrote reporters Zimmerman and Stringer (2004) in *The Wall Street Journal*. Eric Posner argues that "[p]rivacy allows us to experiment, make mistakes, and start afresh if we mess up [… it] is this potential for rehabilitation, for second chances, that is under assault from Google" (Powles 2014). In short, as journalist Brad Stone (2008) wrote in *The New York Times*, by allowing database producers to remove "the obstacles to getting criminal information," Americans are losing "a valuable, ignorance-fueled civil peace." Moreover, many arrestees "who have never faced charges, or have had charges dropped, find that a lingering arrest record can ruin their chance to secure employment, loans and housing" (Fields and Emshwiller 2014).

In a study conducted by Sarah Esther Lageson (2017) of digital records and expungement in the U.S., a subject who had spent one night in jail after an altercation with her partner—which resulted in no charges—found her mugshot in a search engine alongside erroneous information about her legal brush-up: "I've never been charged with assault, and now I see assault on my record." Even for those subjects whose records were published accurately, Lageson concluded, "The public reposting of these data left interviewees both incredulous and exhausted at the prospect of attempting to clear their digital trail." As one subject lamented, "It's just not good for someone that's really trying to get their life together. It just keeps dragging on" (Lageson 2017).

In response to this dilemma, some have advocated a "right to be forgotten," which entails allowing a person to delete or otherwise remove from public view information relating to them on the Internet. One of the leading intellectual advocates of online "forgiving and forgetting" is Viktor Mayer-Schönberger, a professor of Internet Governance and Regulation at Oxford. In his 2009 book *Delete: The Virtue of Forgetting in the Digital Age*, Mayer-Schönberger notes that Europeans have greater concern for privacy than have Americans; this characteristic dates back to World War II, when Nazi Germany used the Netherlands' comprehensive population registry to facilitate the Holocaust, as well as to the East German surveillance state during the Cold War. Yet he argues that privacy fares even worse in the digital age than under the Stasi because online storage and transfer is far more efficient than using paper records. According to Mayer-Schönberger, society has traditionally accepted "that human beings evolve over time, that we have the capacity to learn from past experiences and adjust our behavior," with the fallibility of human memory and limits of record-keeping techniques allowing "societal forgetting" (Mayer-Schönberger 2009, p. 13). However, the internet, which may "forever tether us to all our past actions," threatens to make it "impossible, in practice, to escape them," with the result that, "without some form of forgetting, forgiving becomes a difficult undertaking" (Mayer-Schönberger 2009, p. 125). For example, Mayer-Schönberger notes that, for a woman who had spent time in prison a decade ago, having her mug shot posted online effectively renewed her punishment, as her neighbors began to scorn her: "Digital memory, in reminding us of who she was more than 10 years ago, denied her the chance to evolve and change" (Mayer-Schönberger 2009, p. 203). As a result, he advocates greater capacity for individuals to purge their personal information from the web.

But is the internet age really destroying second chances, making us less forgiving, and hindering the possibility for rehabilitation and even redemption? The sad fact is that most convicted criminals in the pre-digital age did not use the second chance that their obscurity gave them, nor did they use their third or fourth chances. Convincing information shows that most criminal offenders—especially those that committed violent crimes—are not rehabilitated; they commit new crimes. Many commit numerous crimes before they are caught again. Thus, while obscurity may well help give a second chance to a small percentage of criminals, it helps a large percentage of them strike again.

Take the case of James Webb (not the former United States Senator from Virginia of the same name). He had served 20 years in prison for raping six women when, on August 16, 1995, he was released on parole. Rather than look for a new start, he raped another woman the day after he was released. He raped three more women in the next few months. He was re-arrested in December 1995, after he committed the fourth rape (New York Times 1995). Or consider the case of James Richardson, a New York resident who served 20 years of a life term for raping and murdering a 10-year-old girl. After he was paroled in 1992, he committed three bank robberies before being re-incarcerated ("Metro News Briefs…" 1998). Both cases happened before the advent of databanks of criminal convictions.

These two are typical cases. In its most recent study on recidivism in the United States, the Justice Department's Bureau of Justice Statistics tracked a large sample of the 405,000 prisoners released in 30 states in 2005. It found that within 3 years of their release, 45% of them were convicted for a new offense, and within 5 years 55% had been convicted again (Bureau of Justice Statistics 2014). These results were similar to a survey of prisoners released in 1994 (Bureau of Justice Statistics 2002).[1] In short, most people who commit crimes are more likely to commit crimes in the

---

[1] Unlike the 2005 study, this study only looked at prisoners in 15 states, in a 3-year window after their release.

future than to make good use of a second chance. This was true long before the digitization of criminal data and the loss of obscurity. Moreover, one cannot assume that the prisoners who were not convicted of new offenses did not commit any crimes. Many crimes are not reported, and of those that are, many are never solved and their perpetrators never caught (Gramlich 2017). Studies found that the majority of rapists and child molesters are convicted more than once for a sexual assault—and commit numerous offenses before they are caught again. On average, these offenders admit to having committed *two to five times* as many sex crimes than were officially documented (See Groth et al. 1982). That is, not only did they fail to use their second chances to start a new life, they used obscurity to their advantage. Overall, allowing offenders a measure of obscurity is likely to do more harm than good.

In short, the image of a young person who goes astray and who would return to the straight and narrow life if he were only given a second chance does not fit most offenders. Indeed, prisons are considered colleges for crime; they harden those sentenced to spend time in them and make them *more* disposed to future criminal behavior upon release. Social scientists differ about whom to blame for the limited success of rehabilitation. Some fault "the system," or poor social conditions, or lack of job training. Others place more blame on the character of those involved. In any case, obscurity hardly serves to overcome strong factors that agitate against rehabilitation.

Medical malpractice is a good example. Online databases display the records of physicians who do not live up to the Hippocratic Oath. The National Practitioner Data Bank allows state licensing boards, hospitals, and other health-care entities to find out whether a doctor's license has been revoked recently in another state or if the doctor has been disciplined. Doctors' licenses are generally revoked only if they commit very serious offenses, such as repeated gross negligence, criminal felonies, or practicing while under the influence of drugs or alcohol.

If these databases had been used as intended in the late 1990s and early 2000s, they could have tracked Pamela L. Johnson, a physician who was forced to leave Duke University Medical Center after many of her patients suffered from unusual complications. In response, Johnson moved to New Mexico and lied about her professional history in order to obtain a medical license there and continue practicing. After three patients in New Mexico filed lawsuits alleging that she was negligent or had botched surgical procedures, she moved again and set up shop in Michigan (Thompson 2005b).

Similarly, Joseph S. Hayes, a medical doctor licensed in Tennessee, was convicted of drug abuse and assault, including choking a patient, which resulted in the revocation of his Tennessee license in 1991. But his license was reinstated in 1993. When he was charged with fondling a female patient in 1999, he simply moved to South Carolina to continue practicing medicine (Thompson 2005a). Likewise, Michael Skolnik died in Colorado in 2001 after what has been reported to be unnecessary brain surgery, which led his mother to become an advocate for medical transparency. The surgeon involved had recently moved from Georgia, where he had lost a malpractice suit of which no record existed in Colorado databases (Allen

2010). Similar cases involve many scores of other doctors, especially those who acted while on the influence of controlled substances or alcohol. Yet the National Practitioner Data Bank is not open to members of the general public, who may request only that data that does not identify any particular individual or organization. Even that access was temporarily cut off in 2011 by the Department of Health and Human Services at the request of a Kansas doctor with a history of malpractice suits (Wang 2011). Thanks to the rise of the internet, the public has some chance, through a web search or through a detailed search of state licensing board websites, of uncovering such information that has leaked out into the public sphere, but the lack of a more reliable or accessible option gives some poorly performing doctors their own right to be forgotten—to the detriment of the public.

Beyond the fact that internet databases do little harm to those who are not likely to reform themselves, the widespread dissemination of information about wrongdoers has real benefits for potential victims. Hospitals hire few doctors these days without first checking them through digitized data sources. Before you hire an accountant, such data makes it possible to discover whether he or she has a record of embezzlement. A community can find out if a new school nurse is a sex offender. Employers may direct ex-offenders to other jobs, or they may still hire them but provide extra oversight, or just decide that they are willing to take the risk. But they do so well-informed—and thus warned—rather than ignorant of the sad facts.

Registration and notification laws for sex offenders provide a good case in point. The Washington State Institute for Public Policy conducted a study in 2005 that evaluated the effectiveness of the state's community notification laws. In 1990, Washington passed the Community Protection Act, a law that requires sex offenders to register with their county sheriff and authorizes law enforcement to release information to the public. The study found that the recidivism rate among felony sex offenders in the state had dropped, and "the influence of community notification laws cannot be ruled out" (Drake and Barnoski 2006). In addition, a separate study found that "[o]ffenders who were subjects of community notification were arrested for new crimes much more quickly than comparable offenders who were released without notification (Schram and Milloy 1995, p. 3).

The advocates for second chances and an opportunity to start anew without being dogged by one's record tend to call for a generic right. That is, they favor the same basic right for killers and political extremists, rapists and those who were merely arrested but not convicted. This is the case for both normative and practical reasons. Normatively, there is a moral case to be made for giving *everyone* a chance to redeem themselves. A practical reason is that when information only existed on paper, as most of it did until 1980 or so, information about all these different categories of people was difficult to access and distribute. However, as I just tried to show, such a generic right to be forgotten fails the liberal communitarian test, because it causes a great deal of harm to the common good and only limited benefit to personal good. A person truly out to redeem himself had best start by acknowledging his wrongdoing, expressing true remorse, making amends, and showing that he has restructured his life, not by attempting to erase his past (See Etzioni and Carney 1997; Etzioni 1999).

9.2   A Hedged Right to Be Forgotten

What is needed is a mixture of technological and legal means to ensure a hedged right to be forgotten that is differentiated according to the scope of the harm done by the initial act, the extent to which the person has rehabilitated himself, and the scope of privacy that will be granted.

For example, where the inefficiency of paper records once ensured that information would not travel far, the digitized world now requires restrictions if certain kinds of information are to be kept isolated. Formerly, in smaller communities, if a person was arrested his neighbors would learn whether he had been exonerated or convicted. The community might even have had a sense of whether a person who was released had in fact committed the crime, or whether the arrest was unjustified. These days, it is possible to access an arrest record across the globe, but it may be difficult to find out if the arrest was justified. Either arrest records should not be made public (although they might be made available to police in other jurisdictions), or they should be accompanied by information about the outcome of the case.

In addition, a criminal record could be sealed both locally and in online databases after a set period of time, for example after 7 years, if the person has not committed any new crime. Considerable precedent for such a move exists. For instance, information about juvenile offenders and presentations to grand juries are often sealed.

One other major concern is that lawbreakers who have paid their debt to society will face hiring and housing discrimination. Protections against such discrimination are already in place, but others could be added. For instance, employers cannot, as a general rule, legally maintain a policy of refusing to hire people merely because they are ex-cons, whether the employer gets this information from a police blotter or from a computer. Internet databases should be held accountable for the information they provide. If they rely on public records, then they should be required to keep up with the changes in these records. They should also provide mechanisms for filing complaints if the online data are erroneous, and they should make proper corrections in a timely fashion, the way those who keep tabs on credit records are expected to do.

These are a few examples of measures that provide obscurity equivalents in the digital age. Still, it is important to remember the importance of gossip fueled by public records. As a rule, people care deeply about the approval of others. In most communities, being arrested is a major source of humiliation, and people will go to great pains to avoid ending up in jail. In such cases, the social system does not work if the information is not publicly available. This holds true for the digitized world, where the need for a much wider-ranging "informal social communication," as sociologists call gossip, applies not merely to criminals, sexual predators, and disgraced physicians. It holds for people who trade on eBay, sell used books on Amazon, or distribute loans from e-banks. These people are also eager to maintain their reputations—not just locally but globally. Stripping cyberspace of measures to punish those who deceive and cheat will severely set back the utility of the internet for travel, trade, investment, and much more.

This need is served in part by user-generated feedback and ratings, which inform others who may do business via the internet—much like traditional community gossip would. The ability of people to obscure their past in the pre-internet days made it all too easy for charlatans, quacks, and criminal offenders to hurt more people by simply switching locations. The new, digitized transparency is one major means of facilitating deals between people who do not know each other. With enough effort, its undesirable side effects can be curbed, and people can still gain a second chance. It may also be useful to provide people with greater control over their online presence more broadly, although difficult to implement in a balanced way.

The European Union's evolving privacy legislation is making a major move in this direction. Since 2014, the European Union's data protection rules have explicitly incorporated the "right to be forgotten." According to Jeffrey Rosen, this legislation has its intellectual roots "in French law, which recognizes *le droit à l'oubli*—or the 'right of oblivion'—allowing a convicted criminal who has served his time and been rehabilitated to object to the publication of the facts of his conviction and incarceration" (Rosen 2012, p. 88). At the time of its announcement, commentators disputed the implications of this ruling. Where the EU Justice Commissioner Viviane Reding (2012) asserted that this right to be forgotten was merely a limited right for people "to withdraw their consent to the processing of the personal data they have given out themselves," Jeffrey Rosen (2012, p. 88) warned that it represented "the biggest threat to free speech on the Internet in the coming decade." On the other hand, John Hendel (2012) asserted that the right "shouldn't worry proponents of free speech," but only those "companies whose profits rely on mined, invasive data abuses."

The practical implications of this law began to emerge in 2014, when the European Court of Justice, the highest appeals court in matters of EU-wide law, ruled on a case in which a Spanish citizen demanded that a Spanish newspaper remove an outdated story relating to his previous indebtedness, as well as that Google remove the relevant search results (Toobin 2014). The EU court upheld the Spanish Data Protection Agency's decision, which allowed the newspaper to leave the story posted, but forced Google to take down links to the story from the results of searches *that related to the citizen's name* (as opposed to *all* searches). More broadly, the EU court reaffirmed the broader "right to be forgotten," interpreted as the individual right to ask "search engines to remove links with personal information about them" that is "inaccurate, inadequate, irrelevant, or excessive"–but only under "certain conditions." The court stated this right was "not absolute," but rather "to be balanced against other fundamental rights, such as the freedom of expression and of the media" based on a "case-by-case assessment." According to the European Commission (n.d.), "The right to be forgotten is certainly not about making prominent people less prominent or making criminals less criminal."

At this point, it is too early to say what effect the EU's "right to be forgotten" will have on the balance among privacy, free speech, and security. While the decision clearly affirms that a person may remove material that he or she posted directly, it remains to be seen to what extent the right will apply to material the person posted that then has been copied by others, or to material that was created by others but relates to the person and which that person finds offensive. Given the vagueness and subjectivity of terms such as "inadequate, irrelevant, or excessive," it is plausible that the third type of information applies as well, with negative implications for free speech and even public safety. For example, Croatian pianist Dejan Lazic requested in October 2014 that *The Washington Post* remove a negative review of one of his performances, which "has marred the first page of his Google results for years" (Dewey 2014). Caitlin Dewey, a *Post* reporter, wrote:

> Leaving aside the fact that Lazic's request is misdirected, under the ruling—it applies to search engines, not publishers, and only within the E.U.—its implications are kind of terrifying. We ought to live in a world, Lazic argues, where everyone—not only artists and performers but also politicians and public officials—should be able to edit the record according to their personal opinions and tastes. (Dewey 2014)

But, as Kieron O'Hara et al. point out, "[i]n the judgment, 'forgetting' does not involve deletion, and so a right to be forgotten is distinct from a right to erasure" (O'Hara et al. 2016, p. 7).

It is also important to note that the first line of decision for balancing privacy and other values in such cases is not the EU court system, but Google. It is a company that has lobbied for free speech and limited regulation in the United States. Some scholars have pointed out that this is less than ideal as a long-term system, especially given the lack of transparency that private companies tend to exercise (O'Hara 2015, p. 77).

Since 2014, Google has faced ever more stringent demands from France to remove content from all Google search domains, regardless of location (Hern 2015). According to a company spokesperson, Google "disagree[s] with the idea that a national data protection authority can assert global authority to control the content that people can access around the world" (Hern 2015). There is concern that yielding to such a requirement could be the start of a slippery slope. As Kent Walker, general counsel for Google, said: "We comply with the laws of the countries in which we operate. But if French law applies globally, how long will it be until other countries—perhaps less open and democratic—start demanding that their laws regulating information likewise have global reach?" (Hern 2016). France's data protection authority (CNIL) maintains that "in order to be effective, delisting must be carried out on all extensions of the search engine" (Hern 2016).

Luciano Floridi, professor at Oxford University and member of Google's Advisory Council on the Right to be Forgotten believes that delinking at a European level strikes a "fair balance," although for practical purposes he favors delinking at a national level, as "[m]ost users never leave their local search engines" (Floridi 2015, p. 26). O'Hara, writing before the Google Spain judgment, was also of the opinion that applying the law to European Google domains, but not Google.com, was a "reasonable balance" (O'Hara 2015, p. 75). He noted that "getting to Google.com is an obstacle; it's not much of an obstacle, but it weeds out a large number of speculative searches, without hindering a serious, interested inquiry. And that's okay…" (O'Hara 2015, pp. 75–76).

In March 2016, Google announced that it was changing its approach to delisting URLs under the EU's right to be forgotten, "as a result of specific discussions that [they] had with EU data protection regulators in recent months" (Fleischer 2016). Previously, if Google approved a delisting request, it removed the URL from all European versions of Google's search engine (e.g. google.co.uk, google.fr). Now, however, it would also remove it from any Google search domain for a search origi- nating in the country the delisting request came from. Peter Fleischer, Global Privacy Counsel for Google explains what this means:

> So for example, let's say we delist a URL as a result of a request from John Smith in the United Kingdom. Users in the UK would not see the URL in search results for queries containing [John Smith] when searching on any Google Search domain, including google. com. Users outside of the UK could see the URL in search results when they search for [John Smith] on any non-European Google Search domain. (Fleischer 2016)

This is something Google initially refused to do when pressed by a working group of European data regulators in 2014 (Toobin 2014).

The EU mandate poses a "real, if manageable" (Toobin 2014) burden for Google, which by 2017 received more than 700,000 takedown requests and has evaluated over two million URLs; of these URLs, Google removed roughly 43% (Google Transparency Report 2017). Google accepted a request "to remove five-year-old stories about exoneration in a child porn case," but refused a "request from a public official to remove a news article about child pornography accusations," as well as "to remove a 2013 link to a report of an acquittal in a criminal case, on the ground [*sic*] that it was very recent." As long as Google takes such a careful approach to takedown requests, one may expect the "right to be forgotten" to pose relatively little danger to public safety or free speech—however, as Jeffrey Toobin points out, the proliferation of such laws may lead search companies "to tailor their search results in order to offend the fewest countries" as the costs of compliance (or risks of noncompliance) increase the burden on them.

As for the risk to public safety, under its current practice, Google has asserted that it will "also weigh whether or not there's a public interest in the information remaining in our search results—for example, if it relates to financial scams, profes- sional malpractice, criminal convictions or your public conduct as a government official (elected or unelected) [… whether] it relate[s] to a criminal charge that resulted in a later conviction or was dismissed" (Kravets 2014).

Paul Bernal has advocated a qualified right to be forgotten, with five categories of cases where an individual would not be able to delete information about them. These include "paternalistic reasons," "communitarian reasons," "administrative or economic reasons," "archival reasons," and "security reasons" (Kravets 2014). As the EU faces more cases, where these lines are drawn will be tested and, hopefully as a result, clarified.

Until then, what this newly minted EU right to be forgotten entails remains opaque. What, however, is clear is that it provides a key example of a hedged right rather than a generic one. Whether one would hedge differently is less important than realizing from the outset that a generic right fails the liberal communitarian test, because of the great harm to the common good—while the hedged one can be recalibrated to meet the test and to take into account changing historical conditions and new technological developments.

References

Allen, M. 2010, September 19. Colorado transparency unique. *Las Vegas Sun*.

Barsky, B. 2013, April 26. A second chance. *The Dayton Jewish Observer*.

Bureau of Justice Statistics. 2002, June. *Recidivism of Prisoners Released in 1994*.

———. 2014, April 22. *3 in 4 former prisoners in 30 states arrested within 5 years of release*.

Dewey, C. 2014, October 31. Pianist asks The Washington Post to remove a concert review under the E.U.'s 'right to be forgotten' ruling. *The Washington Post*.

Drake, E., and R. Barnoski. 2006. *Sex offenders in Washington State: Key findings and trends*. Olympia: Washington State Institute for Public Policy. Document No. 06–03- 1201.

El DeBarge debuts music from new album 'second chance' on 'bet awards' show. 2010, June 27. *eurweb*.

Etzioni, A., ed. 1999. *Civic repentance*. Lanham: Rowman & Littlefield.

Etzioni, A., and D. Carney, eds. 1997. *Repentance: A comparative perspective*. Lanham: Rowman & Littlefield.

European Commission. n.d.. Factsheet on the 'Right to be forgotten' ruling http://ec.europa.eu/justice/data-protection/files/factsheets/factsheet_data_protection_en.pdf.

Fields, G., and Emshwiller, J.R. 2014, August 18. As arrest records rise, Americans find consequences can last a lifetime. *The Wall Street Journal*.

Fleischer, P. 2016, March 4. Adapting our approach to the European right to be forgotten. *Google*. https://blog.google/topics/google-europe/adapting-our-approach-to-european-rig/.

Floridi, L. 2015. Should you have the right to be forgotten on Google? Nationally, yes. globally, no. *New Perspectives Quarterly* 32: 24–29.

Gibb, E. 2010, October 30. Program supports convicts and helps them after prison. *Pittsburgh Post-Gazette*.

Givens, B. 1995, September 23. Public records in a computerized network environment: Privacy implications. Speech presented at First Amendment Coalition Conference, Oakland, CA.

Google Transparency Report. 2017, May 12. European privacy requests for search removals. https://www.google.com/transparencyreport/removals/europeprivacy/.

Gramlich, J. 2017, March 1. Most violent and property crimes in the U.S. go unsolved. *Pew Research Center*.

Groth, A.N., R.E. Longo, and J.B. McFadin. 1982. Undetected recidivism in rapists and child molesters. *Crime and Delinquency* 28 (3): 450–458.

Hendel, J. 2012, January 25. Why journalists shouldn't fear Europe's 'right to be forgotten.' *The Atlantic*.

Hern, A. 2015, July 30. Google says non to French demand to expand right to be forgotten. *The Guardian*.

———. 2016, May 19. Google takes right to be forgotten battle to France's highest court. *The Guardian*.

Izad, E. & Wald, A.S. 2014, March 7. Criminal-justice reform, brought to you by CPAC. *National Journal*.

Jones, M.L. 2016. *Ctrl Z: The right to be forgotten*. New York: New York University Press.

Kravets, D. 2014, October 10. Google has removed 170,000-plus URLs under "right to be forgotten" edict. *Ars Technica*.

Lageson, S.E. 2017. Crime data, the internet, and free speech: An evolving legal consciousness. *Law & Society Review* 51 (1): 8–41.

Mayer-Schönberger, V. 2009. *Delete: The virtue of forgetting in the digital age*. Princeton: Princeton University Press.

Merica, D. 2014, October 28. Things Hillary Clinton says at almost every speech. *CNN*.

New York Times. 1995, December 7. Man charged with 4 rapes was on parole.

O'Hara, K. 2015. The right to be forgotten: The good, the bad, and the ugly. *The Digital Citizen* 19: 73–79.

O'Hara, K., Shadbolt, N. & Hall, W. 2016. A pragmatic approach to the right to be forgotten. *Global Commission on Internet Governance*.

Powles, J. 2014, May 21. What did the media miss with the 'right to be forgotten' coverage? *The Guardian*.

Rangel, C. 2013, April 4. Advancing the dream through education. *The Huffington Post*.

Reding, V. 2012, January 22. The EU data protection reform 2012: Making Europe the standard setter for modern data protection rules in the digital age. Speech presented at *Innovation Conference, Digital, Life, Design*, Munich.

Rosen, J. 2012. The right to be forgotten. *Stanford Law Review Online* 64: 88–92.

Schram, D.D. & Milloy, C.D. 1995, October. Community notification: A study of offender characteristics and recidivism. Prepared for the *Washington State Institute for Public Policy*. http://www.wsipp.wa.gov/ReportFile/1208.

Stone, B. 2008, August 3. If you run a red light, will everyone know? *The New York Times*.

Thompson, C.W. 2005a, April 12. Multiple state licenses helped shield history. *The Washington Post*.

———. 2005b, April 12. Poor performance records are easily outdistanced. *The Washington Post*.

Toobin, J. 2014, September 29. The solace of oblivion. *The New Yorker*.

Wang, M. 2011, November 10. How complaints from a single doctor caused the gov't to take down a public database. *ProPublica*.

Zimmerman, A. & Stringer, K. 2004, August 26. As background checks proliferate, ex-cons face a lock on jobs. *The Wall Street Journal*.

Chapter 10
Back to the Pillory?

Young drug dealers, caught for the first time peddling, should be sent home with their heads shaved and without their pants instead of being jailed, was a suggestion I cautiously floated. My liberal friends rolled their eyes and stared at me with open dismay. When I tried to explain that if the same youngsters are jailed they are likely to graduate more hardened criminals than when they entered the stockades, that rehabilitation in prisons is practically unknown, and young people are often abused in jails, one of my friends stated that the next thing I would suggest would be to mark people with scarlet letters. The others changed the subject.

A few weeks after this dinner conversation, a tragedy brought the merit of shaming back into public and scholarly discussion. I was a member of a panel of lawyers and academics who were asked by National Public Radio to discuss the rape and murder of a 7-year-old girl in a women's bathroom in a Las Vegas casino (NPR 1998). The media attention this time was not focused on the father, who left his child roaming the casino at 3:30 a.m., or on the rapist-assassin Jeremy Strohmeyer, but on a friend of the murderer named David Cash (Booth 2001). He accompanied Strohmeyer to the lady's room but did nothing to try to stop the savaging of Sherrice Iverson or to inform the police after the act.

In reaction, outraged Representative Nicholas Lampson drafted a Good Samaritan Act, which imposes severe punishments on those who do not stop a sexual crime against a child when they could do so at little risk to themselves, or who do not report such offenses to public authorities. UCLA law professor Peter Aranella, who joined the NPR conversation, argued that the punishment was too severe and suggested instead that a shorter jail sentence should suffice. Elizabeth Semil from the National Association of Criminal Defense Lawyers, also on the panel, was even more critical of the Good Samaritan draft act. She pointed out: "…Punitive legislation, criminal legislation, isn't the proper response." She also wondered out loud "whether making it criminal to fail to act is good public policy. In other words, is it

---

This chapter draws on "Back to the Pillory?" in *The American Scholar* 68 (3), (Summer 1999): 43–50.

© The Author(s) 2018

A. Etzioni, *Happiness is the Wrong Metric*, Library of Public Policy and Public Administration 11, https://doi.org/10.1007/978-3-319-69623-2_10

going to assist in solving the problem? And my response to that is: absolutely not" (NPR 1998). A typical letter to the editor of the *Sacramento Bee* opined, "I realize this is a popular issue, but the consequences of a law of this nature are terrifying … Americans would be required to function as part of the government apparatus … Maybe you know someone who takes cash in their business, but doesn't necessarily tell the IRS. You may go to jail for not turning that person in" (Sacramento Bee 1998). A commentator in Bergen, New Jersey's *Record* holds forth, "As much as I'd like to encourage compassion and community, I think it's too late to legislate such morality" (Sjoerdsma 1997).

I, too, wondered if Americans should and could be turned into a nation of police informers, a role often despised not merely by their fellow citizens but even by the police themselves. And yet there is a strong sense that Mr. Cash behaved poorly (or worse) and others must do better. One looks for ways Good Samaritans may be fostered but in some less punitive way, ideally one that entails no jail terms.

I suggested shaming. Instead of jailing future Cashes, the law should require that the names of *bad* Samaritans be posted on a website and in advertisements (paid for by the offenders) in key newspapers. Such posting would remove any remaining ambiguities concerning what society expects from people who can help others when there is no serious risk to their well-being. And those with a weak conscience or civic sense will be nudged to do that which is right by fearing that their names will be added to the list of bad Samaritans, their friends and families will chide them, and their neighbors will snicker (NPR 1998).[1]

While there are no statistics on the matter, judges seem recently to be trying shaming more often than a decade or two ago, as a middle course between jailing offenders and allowing them to walk off scot free. Those convicted of driving under the influence of alcohol in Fort Bend County, Texas, must place "DUI" bumper stickers on their cars (Kahan 1996). A child molester in Port St. Lucie, Florida was ordered by a judge to mark his property with a sign warning away children. The same judge ordered a woman convicted of purchasing drugs in front of her children to place a notice in the local newspaper detailing her offense (Hoffman 1997, p. A1). Stephen K. Germershausen was ordered to place a 4 × 6 in. ad in his local Rhode Island newspaper, accompanied by his photo, reading, "I am Stephen Germershausen, I am 29 years old … I was convicted of child molestation … If you are a child molester, get professional help immediately, or you may find your picture and name in the paper…" (Massaro 1991). A Tennessee judge sentenced a convicted defendant to confess his crime of aiding in the sale of a stolen vehicle before a church congregation (Massaro 1991). Syracuse puts embarrassing signs in front of buildings owned by slum lords, and Des Moines publishes their names in newspapers (Belluck 1998, pp. A4–A5).

Far from being widely hailed as a more humane and just way of punishing offenders and deterring others, judicial shaming has raised waves of criticism that

---

[1] The larger sociological issues of shaming and juvenile crime, and the need for alternative punishments and the use of *social* instead of legal controls, are explored throughout Etzioni 2003.

put to shame my friends' reaction to my proposals. Nadine Strossen, president of the American Civil Liberties Union (ACLU) was rather gentle: "I'm very skeptical when criminologists and sociologists say that the best way to rehabilitate someone is to isolate him and put some sort of scarlet letter on him. We need to integrate criminals back into our community"(CQ Researcher 1997, p. 252). The ACLU's Mark Kappelhoff states that "Gratuitous humiliation of the individual serves no societal purpose at all ... and there's been no research to suggest it's been effective in reducing crime" (Allen-Mills 1997). Judge Politan, U.S. District Court (N.J.), wrote similarly that:

> [S]ocieties have often used branding or close equivalents thereto as means of making certain persons or groups of persons easily identifiable and thus, easily ostracized or set apart ... A clear example of such branding, justified by a social purpose wrongfully deemed acceptable by the populace, was the requirement in Nazi Germany that Jews wear the Star of David on their sleeve so that they might easily be identified ... This Court must determine whether Megan's Law and its attendant notification provisions amount to a branding of registrants with a 'Mark of Cain' or a 'Scarlet Letter,' thus rendering them subject to perpetual public animus (American Civil Liberties Union 1996).

Law professor Evan Cherminsky is also concerned about shaming, claiming, "The real measure of how civilized we are is the way we choose to punish people. It's not civilized to tell somebody 'you're going to sit in the stocks and we're going to throw stones at you'" (American Civil Liberties Union 1996).[2] Carl F. Horowitz, Washington correspondent for *Investor's Business Daily*, attacks shaming, which he writes includes public hanging, beheading of drug dealers, blacklisting, and boycotts (Horowitz 1997, p. 71).

When I faced similar challenges from a class I teach at The George Washington University, I suggested an examination of shaming suffers if one labels all punitive measures one disapproves of and seeks to shun as shaming. True or pure shaming entails only *symbolic acts* that communicate censure, ranging from relatively gentle acts such as according a student a C+ or sending a disruptive kid to stand in the classroom's corner, to such severe measures as marking the cars of convicted repeat drunk-drivers with glow-in-the-dark "DUI" bumper stickers. Shaming differs sharply from many other modes of punishment—public flogging, Singapore style, for instance—in that the latter inflict bodily harm, rather than being limited to psychic discomfort. While shaming has some untoward consequences of its own, it is relatively light punishment, especially if one takes into account that most other penalties shame in addition to inflicting their designated hurt.

I also stressed that shaming is morally appropriate or justified only when those being shamed are acting out of free will. To the extent that people act in ways that the law or prevailing mores consider inappropriate, but cannot help themselves from doing so (such as when those with mental illnesses defecate in the streets or scream

---

[2] See also: ACLU 1999 ("Notification laws will not prevent sex offenders from committing crimes, the ACLU said but rather will victimize rehabilitated ex-offenders and their families. Those in stable environments have the highest likelihood of staying out of trouble. Attacking the family unit by publicizing this information will only make ex-offenders more likely to reoffend."); McAlinden 2007, pp. 42–46.

their head off at 3 a.m.), chiding them is highly inappropriate. They are to be helped, removed if need be, but hardly shamed.

When I tried to advance similar arguments on NPR, Ms. Semil would not have any of it; she instead would rely on education, celebrating those who conduct themselves as Good Samaritans rather than punishing those who do not:

> Instead of thinking about ways in which we can shame people, let's think about ways in which we can honor or hold up examples of the many heroes that we read about every week who risk their lives to save others; in other words, teaching by positive example children and adults that, indeed, this kind of behavior is rewarded and respected and admired (NPR 1998).

Such suggestions show that one's assessment of shaming is highly colored by one's assumption of human nature. Ms. Semil belongs to the sanguine camp that believes that people can be convinced to conduct themselves in a virtuous manner solely by means of praise, approbations, and words of encouragement, or by drawing on non-judgmental responses, allowing the goodness of people to unfold. For those who share this view, shaming is not merely cruel but also unnecessary punishment; indeed, punishment in general is anti-social. Many of those who hold this view of human nature tend also to believe that people are good by nature; if they misbehave—either the demands imposed on them are unjust or their behavior reflects distorting forces which they neither caused nor are able to control (for instance, that they were abused by their own parents).

I file with those who hold that a world of only positive reinforcements, while in theory very commendable, is not within human reach, and that hence a society must—however reluctantly—also employ some forms of punishment. Granted, we should first determine if the social demands are fair and reasonable, and to what extent we can rely upon positive inducements in given situations. But, at the end of the day, some form of disincentive—hopefully sparing and mostly of the gentle kind—cannot be avoided. Or, as Judge Ted Poe, a strong proponent of shaming penalties, puts it, "...a little shame goes a long way. Some folks say everyone should have high self-esteem, but that's not the real world. Sometimes people should feel bad" (Massaro 1991, pp. 1880, 1883).

An often overlooked feature of shaming, I should add, is that it is deeply democratic. Shaming reflects the community's values, and hence cannot be imposed by the authorities per se against a people. Thus, if being sent to the principal's office is a badge of honor in a person's peer culture, no shaming will occur in that situation. A yellow star, imposed to mark and shame Jews in Nazi Germany, is worn as a matter of pride in Israel. Thus, people are better protected from shaming that reflects values that are not shared by the community than from other forms of punishment, punishment that can be imposed by authorities without the specific consent of those who are governed.

Critics are quick to turn the communitarian tables on those who seek to use community to shame offenders by pointing out that communitarians have shown that communities are waning. Legal scholar Toni M. Massaro argues in the *Michigan Law Review* (1991, p. 1921) that shaming will be cogent and productive only if five conditions coexist.

First, the potential offenders must be members of an identifiable group, such as a close-knit religious or ethnic community. Second, the legal sanctions must actually compromise potential offenders' group social standing. That is, the affected group must concur with the legal decisionmaker's estimation of what is, or should be, humiliating to group members. Third, the shaming must be communicated to the group and the group must withdraw from the offender—shun her—physically, emotionally, financially, or otherwise. Fourth, the shamed person must fear withdrawal by the group. Finally, the shamed person must be afforded some means of regaining community esteem, unless the misdeed is so grave that the offender must be permanently exiled or demoted.

But, Massaro adds, the "cultural conditions of effective shaming seem weakly present, at best, in many contemporary American cities." While granting that it is unfair to say that "Americans have no commonly shared instincts about crime or about shame," Massaro believes that "American subculturism, or cultural pluralism, is pronounced enough to make broad conclusions about our moral coherence suspect, and thus to undermine the likely effectiveness of widespread government attempts to shame offenders, absent significant decentralization of criminal law authority and the delivery of formal norm enforcement power to the local subcultures" (Massaro 1991, p. 1923; see also Markel 2007, p. 1385).

Massaro and others who draw on communitarians' arguments do not take into account that while communities clearly are much weaker now than they were in, for instance, colonial days, they are not powerless, especially in smaller towns and in what have been called urban villages, numerous ethnic concentrations in big cities that form rather strong communities—Chinatown in New York City, for instance. Otherwise shaming would be no punishment at all. People are, however, very reluctant—ashamed—to drive around with a DUI marker on their car or to take ads in their town newspaper that contain their picture, apologizing for their offenses. Indeed, an accountant, who was sentenced to stand in his neighborhood with a sign "I embezzled funds" seemed deeply distraught when interviewed, and mused that he might have been better off if he had instead accepted a jail sentence.

Hardly indifference. A woman convicted of welfare fraud in Eau Claire, Wisconsin preferred to be jailed than wear a sign admitting, "I stole food from poor people." In arguing about these matters with liberal criminologists, I picked up a useful distinction between two kinds of shaming, one that isolates and is to be avoided, and one that reintegrates offenders into communities and is to be preferred. Liberal criminologists worry that once a person is shamed, he will be cut off from his community and withdraw into himself or worse, into a criminal subculture, and hence will be unlikely to be rehabilitated. Instead, criminologists suggest dealing with crimes in a way that restores people to good standing in their communities. The measures they favor include face-to-face meetings of the offenders and the victims, "facilitated" by community members; the offenders making amends (for instance, rebuilding a fence their car demolished); and closure, a ritual of reconciliation and forgiveness, all of which restore the offender to full membership in the community. David Karp (1998, p. 292), a criminologist, adds, "These efforts may be through social services or local economic efforts to change the social conditions of the offender's neighborhood."

Reintegrative shaming may well be the best shaming there is, although the jury is out on whether it can be made to work, especially for offenders who are members of different communities than their victims, such as gang members. In effect, any kind of shaming will work only if it is couched in the reference terms of the community of the offenders—or if these terms can be changed as shaming occurs.

Our history offers some lessons on the working of shaming, mainly what happens to a good thing when it is driven too far, much too far. Most importantly, history teaches us the significance of the particular context. In colonial America shaming was very common, not merely one tool of punishment among others but a major one. Indeed, historians report it often worked so well, no prisons were deemed necessary in some colonies, for instance, in South Carolina. (Reference is only to white folks; slaves were savagely treated.)

One reason shaming was so powerful is that it took place in communities that were much smaller, tightly knit, and moralistic than any known to us today on these shores. Historian Lawrence M. Friedman (1994, pp. 36–37) describes them as "little worlds on their own, cut off from each other…" and "…small-town life [was] at its most communal—inbred and extremely gossipy." Another historian, Roger Thompson, writes about Massachusetts that its communities were "well stocked with moral monitors who did not miss much in the goldfish-bowl existence of daily life" (Friedman 1994, p. 37). Single people who moved into colonies were required to board with someone, so that the community could better keep an eye on them.

In contrast, today many Americans are members of two or more communities (for instance, at work and where they reside) and psychologically can shift much of their ego involvement from a community that unduly chastens them to another. While it was not practical for most individuals to escape from one community to another during colonial times, today the average American moves about once every 5 years, and in the process chooses to which community he or she is willing to subject himself. Moreover, privacy at home is much greater, and the moral agenda of most communities is almost incomparably shorter.

In short, the colonial era shows us how little we now seek to shame about and how limited our ability to shame actually is. (Amy Gutmann, a liberal philosopher and former professor at Princeton University, once quipped that "communitarians seek Salem without witches," which the communitarians took as a scorching criticism. As I see it, we communitarians should, shamelessly, plead guilty as charged. We do favor communities in which moral mores are upheld without witch hunts, and maintain that in our kind of society this is possible.)

The purest form of shaming was 'admonition.' Law professor Adam Hirsch (1982, pp. 1179, 1224) described it as follows:

> Faced with a community member who had committed a serious offense, the magistrates or clergymen would lecture him privately to elicit his repentance and a resolution to reform. The offender would then be brought into open court for formal admonition by the magistrate, a public confession of wrongdoing, and a pronouncement of sentence, wholly or partially suspended to symbolize the community's forgiveness.

"The aim was not just to punish, but to teach a lesson, so that the sinful sheep would want to be back to the flock," writes Friedman (1994, p. 37).

The emphasis on reintegrative justice should appeal to the progressive criminologists who seek to restore it, although for others it may evoke the image of a Soviet or Chinese trial. Having witnessed one of these, what offended me most was not the shaming per se but the kind of matters people were shamed for, having conceived a second child and listened to the BBC.

While pure (merely symbolic) shaming was employed in the colonial era and long thereafter, often it was mixed with other forms of punishment such as fines, whipping, and worse.

Stocks and pillories combined holding people up for public ridicule, with confining their movements, exposing them to the elements, and at least a measure of physical discomfort.

Friedman describes another common shaming measure, which was to make the culprit (a thief) wear for 6 months a "Roman T, not less than four inches long and one inch wide, of a scarlet colour, on the outside of the outermost garment, upon the back, between the shoulders, so that all times to be fully exposed to view, for a badge of his or her crime." A robber had to wear a scarlet R; and a forger, a scarlet F "at least six inches long and two inches wide" (Friedman 1994, p. 75).

But, unlike the DUI signs today, wearing of these insignia was preceded by a public whipping in a considerable number of cases.

All said and done it is easy to see why shaming as practiced in earlier periods or in other kinds of societies has left it in ill-repute. We best think about shaming in terms of how different our much more liberal and tolerant society may adapt it to our needs rather than be swayed by an anachronistic image.

Most important, one must not evaluate any social policy in itself but must compare it to others. The existing criminal justice system jails millions of people, about half of them for non-violent crimes mainly dealing in controlled substances. Offenders are incarcerated for ever longer periods, in harsher conditions, with fewer opportunities for parole. Still, the system rehabilitates very few, and the recidivism rate is very high, all while imposing high charges on the taxpayers. A year in jail costs the public about the same as a year at one of our nation's most costly colleges (see Schmitt et al. 2010). Ergo, society is keen to find some new, more effective, more humane, and less costly modes of deterrence. Whether it works, and for which kinds of offenders, we are about to find out, that is, if our well-meaning progressive friends will allow us to proceed.

References

Allen-Mills, T. 1997. American criminals sentenced to shame. *Sunday Times*.
American Civil Liberties Union. 1996. *ACLU answers: Megan's law*.
———. 1999. *Megan's law prompts fairness question in online notification of sex offenders*.
Belluck, P. 1998. Forget prisons: Americans cry out for the pillory. *The New York Times*.

Booth, C. 2001. The bad Samaritan. *TIME*.

CQ Researcher. 1997. Sentencing lawbreakers to a dose of shame.

Etzioni, A. 2003. *The monochrome society*. Princeton: Princeton University Press.

Friedman, L.M. 1994. *Crime and punishment in American history*. New York: Basic Books.

Hirsch, A.J. 1982. From pillory to penitentiary: The rise of criminal incarceration in early Massachusetts. *Michigan Law Review* 80: 1179.

Hoffman, J. 1997. Crime and punishment: Shame gains popularity. *The New York Times*.

Horowitz, C.F. 1997. The shaming sham. *The American Prospect*.

Kahan, D.M. 1996. What do alternative sanctions mean? *University of Chicago Law Review* 63: 591–653.

Karp, D.R. 1998. The judicial and judicious use of shame penalties. *Crime and Delinquency* 44 (2): 277.

Markel, D. 2007. Wrong turns on the road to alternative sanctions: Reflections on the future of shaming punishments and restorative justice. *Texas Law Review* 85: 1385.

Massaro, T.M. 1991. Shame, culture, and American criminal law. *Michigan Law Review* 89 (7): 1880.

McAlinden, A.M. 2007. *The shaming of sexual offenders: Risk, retribution, and reintegration*. Portland: Hart Publishing.

NPR. 1998. *Good Samaritan laws*, Transcript #98100102-211.

Sacramento Bee. 1998. Letter to the editor, F4.

Schmitt, J., K. Warner, and S. Gupta. 2010. *The high budgetary cost of incarceration*. Washington, DC: Center for Economic and Policy Research.

Sjoerdsma, A. 1997. *Is America too dangerous for a 'Good Samaritan Law'?* Bergen: The Record.

Chapter 11
Moral Triage

One of the main elements of soft power is the expression of moral condemnation or approval. Although a realist may argue that nations act to promote their self-interest and are moved by factors such as the size of another nation's military, economy, or other such "real" factors, nations in effect *do* respond to the moral voices of other states, non-state entities, and the "international community." Thus, even totalitarian and authoritarian states do not simply ignore criticisms of their human rights records, but rather seek to justify their actions by arguing that socioeconomic rights are more important than legal or civil ones. Alternately, they argue that their human rights records are better than outside observers claim, or that they will attend to legal or civil rights once they have achieved a higher level of economic development. Nor do these same states hesitate to criticize liberal democracies; for example, Russia's President Vladimir Putin chastised the United States for its human rights record (Grove 2012).

Nations are inclined to raise their moral voices, even if the impact on other nations is limited, because many local and transnational groups expect it. It serves the domestic politics of those in power. As a result, nations and non-state actors raise their moral voices readily and quite often. However, such overexposure undermines the moral voice and squanders the moral capital states have; nations and the world would be much better served if they raised their moral voices much more sparingly—and in particular if they focused on those situations in which they can do most good. In short, *moral triage* is called for (Etzioni 2007).

The term triage is usually used in the context of emergency medicine to describe standard operating procedure when a medical team is faced with a number of injured people that far outstrips the team's resources. Simple triage calls for sorting the injured into three categories: those who will likely die regardless of immediate treatment; those whose injuries seem comparatively light; and those whose injuries are severe but are likely to survive and recover if treated rapidly. This last group gets first attention. (The ratio of those treated to those neglected depends on the resources available and the number of people who would greatly benefit from immediate intervention.)

This chapter draws on "Moral Triage" in *Providence*, 6 (Winter 2017): 38–42.

The same should hold for moral triage. At any given point, a state could readily chastise scores of other nations for one reason or another—or, more often, for several reasons. However, if a nation issues scores of condemnations, they quickly lose their effect. This is particularly true if states or non-state actors that ignore moral condemnations do not face concrete consequences for their continued abuses.

Because moral triage is a new concept, it is not possible to point to an agent that has applied this approach in the past. Nor do there seem to be states or other actors that have applied policies that generally correspond to its basic tenets. Instead, there follows three cases in which a moral voice was applied, with good effect, to situations that seem to fit the triage criteria. This is followed by a study of a scattergram approach. I cannot stress enough that in each case factors other than the moral voice were at play, but nevertheless it seemed to have played a role in the first three cases, and hardly in the others.

11.1   Out of the Boats

The United Nations has called the Rohingya "the most persecuted minority in the world" and at risk of genocide (Ibrahim 2015). To flee this violence and persecution, as many as 20,000 Rohingya, or one in ten (Holmes 2015), have fled Myanmar in small boats and are now living on the waters of the Andaman Sea (Maule 2015; Stoakes and Kelly 2015). In May 2015, Indonesia stated that it would deny Rohingya people the ability to land on its territory (Al Jazeera 2015), as did Thailand (Wescott 2015). In response, the international community urged other countries in Myanmar's immediate vicinity to accept the Rohingya people as refugees (Reuters 2015). The United Nations' human rights chief said he was "appalled" at the news that Thailand, Indonesia, and Malaysia had refused to allow Rohingya refugees to land their boats (Maule 2015), and non-governmental organizations such as the Arakan Project also expressed grave concern (Al Jazeera 2015). A spokesperson for the United States Department of State called the situation an "emergency" and "urged" regional states to offer the Rohingya shelter (Reuters 2015). The United States offered to settle about 1000 Rohingya refugees. Gambia offered to shelter all of the Rohingya boat people, saying, "As human beings, more so fellow Muslims, it is a sacred duty to help alleviate the untold hardships and sufferings these fellow human beings are confronted with" (Tiffin 2015). Pope Francis also chided Southeast Asia for its inaction (Harris 2015).

In specific response to this international outcry, Indonesia and Malaysia extended assistance and temporary shelter to 7000 of the nationless refugees (Scott 2015), with Malaysia also offering its navy and coast guard for rescue operations (Deutsche Welle 2015a). Thailand announced that it would stop preventing boats carrying Rohingya refugees from landing on its shores (Wescott 2015), and Bangladesh, Australia, and the Philippines also offered to temporarily settle some of the remaining refugees (Deutsche Welle 2015b). This especially represented "a shift in policy" for Malaysia and Indonesia (Guardian 2015). The United Nations then praised these efforts as "an important first step in the search for solutions" (Wescott 2015).

11.2 Exodus for a Chinese Activist

The international community's moral voice was critical to the outcome of the diplomatic crisis precipitated by reproductive rights activist Chen Guangcheng's flight from house arrest to the United States embassy in Beijing in April 2012 (Branigan and MacAskill 2012; Sagalyn 2012; Jacobs and Ansfield 2012; Lee 2012). Chen is known for fighting against forced sterilization and forced abortion in China. There was considerable concern that China would prevent Chen from leaving, keeping him in effect locked in the American embassy.

The international community quickly responded by urging China to permit Chen to leave or allow Chen and his family to obtain the passports they would need to legally leave the country (Liu 2012). And in the wake of allegations that the United States had "abandoned" Chen, human rights activists, nongovernmental organizations, and politicians such as US Representative Ileana Ros-Lehtinen (R-FL) vocally called on the United States to assist Chen to the greatest extent possible (Myers and Jacobs 2012).

In response, in early May 2012, the United States pressured China to clear Chen to travel abroad to study at American University (Branigan and MacAskill 2012). By May 19, New York University had offered Chen a special student position at its law school, and Chen had been allowed to leave China for the United States (Fujita et al. 2012).

11.3 Squandering the Moral Voice

Considerable debate has centered on whether the United States should or does act as the world's policeman. The US sees itself as the guarantor of major international norms; for example, it assertively enforces the freedom of maritime navigation. However, the US often overextends itself and applies its moral voice without consideration for its likely effectiveness. In many cases, the United States behaves much like a grouchy, retired uncle who sits at the edge of a playground and snipes at the children playing there by telling them to run less, clean up their language, play nice, and so on, all while being roundly ignored.

A critic on a previous draft posited that "the primary problem here [is] not the moral censure—assuming that the uncle's complaints are in fact legitimate—but that there is no force backing up the words" and that "ignoring the children[]... is not the same thing as saying nothing about ISIS beheading someone." It is important to note in response that the scope of this chapter is limited to moral censure; it does not encompass an analysis of any other action or the lack thereof. Furthermore, the purpose of this chapter is to highlight why moral censure should be used sparingly. Indeed, the US and the international community should condemn brutal acts by ISIS. However, if it will issue similar condemnations on a frequent basis on other acts of terrorism—all of which are deserving of such comments—there will be a declining marginal utility of the effect of such condemnations.

Burundi President Pierre Nkurunziza's April 2015 announcement that he would seek reelection sparked a failed coup, months of protests, and government brutality against protesters (Smith 2015). The United States called on the Burundian government to "condemn and stop the use of violence by the police and the ruling party's Imbonerakure youth militias" and demanded that all who used violence to intimidate protesters "be held accountable" (Rathke 2015). It also issued a statement urging all parties to the fighting to "commit themselves to a constructive dialogue" and condemning any attempts to gain power through violence or other extraconstitutional mechanisms (Kirby 2015). The American ambassador-at-large for war crimes issues additionally condemned reports that peaceful protesters were being shot by members of the ruling party's youth militia, saying, "We are sending [the] strongest message we can that those that commit them [acts of violence]—in particular, those that incite them, order them, arm and deploy the forces that are committing these crimes—will be held to account" (Rwema 2015). All to no effect.

At this point one may ask: "Is the brutality to be simply ignored? Is there no kind of moral censure that falls short of making demands?" To use a musical analogy, moral outrage can be expressed in different registers. In particular, the higher registers (i.e. more severe) should be used sparingly.

Shortly thereafter, the United States issued one more criticism on the development in Sudan, which was barely noted. It was followed by an expression of moral outrage by the US about the acts of Boko Haram. Before and after, there were several critical statements by various American authorities about human rights abuses in Russia, China, and elsewhere in the world. Most to little effect.

A comment on a previous draft pondered "a situation where we don't publically condemn an action because it won't directly cause behavioral change (like China building artificial islands with military installations), but then we must react militarily because that actor did cross a red line. How could they ever know we might react militarily (or with economic sanctions) if we said nothing?" This concern is not directly related to the concept of moral outrage. A distinction can be made between moral censure and the drawing of a red line, which comes into play especially when the national interest is at stake. Limiting moral censure would not limit, for example, the United States' ability to make its interests known, or its intended method of recourse should those interests be compromised. In other words, public condemnations are not the only way for other nations to enforce red lines.

One may ask: "Isn't there something less than [the issuing of red-lines we do not mean to enforce]—a public condemnation that doesn't carry demands but still makes a moral proclamation and, if so, isn't that kind of thing valuable? Wasn't there power in Reagan's declaration of the Soviet Union as an 'evil empire'?" In response I note that I am not arguing that moral outrage has no effect but that it needs to be sharply focused. President Reagan used the term in reference to one country. (Vice President Cheney referred to three nations as parts of the axis of evil.) If instead that characterization would be made of all the countries that violate human rights—several scores—the label is likely to lose much of its effect.

The use of highly evocative terms, such as evil, raises another issue, which is beyond the scope of this chapter but deserves brief discussion. One does not deal or negotiate with evil; one seeks to vanquish it. Hence, once the leaders of one nation characterize another nation as evil, and that nation is not subject to regime change or major reforms, it is difficult to work with it, yet doing so is often unavoidable. Thus Reagan sat down with Gorbachev and made a very important arms deal long before Russia was truly reformed (it still is not), and John Kerry arranged the removal of a major pile of chemical weapons from a war zone, in which they were employed, by negotiating with an 'evil' nation. I suggest that it would be morally more appropriate and politically savvier to follow the line of hating the sin but loving the sinner, of criticizing policies but not nations, and of assuming that all are redeemable.

What would a triage-based approach look like? A state such as the United States should say little about the moral conduct of states and non-state actors, such as North Korea or ISIS, that are extremely unlikely to be affected by its censure or its approbation. It should also refrain from chastising the occasional missteps of states that by and large maintain a high standard of human rights. Instead, it should focus its moral voice on those nations it is most likely to affect and whose moral violations are serious, and choose areas in which the voice might carry. For instance, China is much more likely to take into account criticism of its treatment of the environment than of limitations in free speech.

The United States took such an approach toward Germany and other members of the Eurozone over the Greek debt crisis. In February 2015, President Obama called for reasonable leniency, saying, "You cannot keep on squeezing countries that are in the midst of depression" (Ackerman 2015). Meanwhile, other American officials called for compromise from both Greece and the other members of the Eurozone (Marans 2015). In July 2015, the White House reiterated its position that Germany must compromise with Greece in order to salvage the latter's position in the Eurozone and offer opportunities for Greek economic growth (Marans 2015). On July 17, the German parliament voted in favor of a proposal to negotiate a bailout with Greece (BBC News 2015; Ellyatt 2015). The United States asserted its position, but has refrained from issuing moral condemnations against any of the parties involved; instead, it has preferred to comment only when necessary and in more utilitarian terms.

This does not mean that nations assigned a low priority should be ignored. The United States might well continue to issue annual reports on human rights conditions in each country, as the Department of State does. However, most of the United States' effort should focus on the visible, active, and high-powered application of its moral voice to the latter category. Most importantly, when nations ignore the United States' moral voice, they should anticipate that the United States will subject them to additional measures beyond mere declarations by White House or State Department spokespeople.

To mix the metaphors: the moral voice has a currency. If it is raised too often, against targets that are unyielding or engaged in minor violations of what is considered proper conduct, it will be largely squandered. If it is applied selectively, in places of significant concern and where it might have an effect, it will be more effective when it is raised.

References

Ackerman, A. 2015, February 1. Obama expresses sympathy for new Greek government. *The Wall Street Journal*.
BBC News. 2015. *Greece debt crisis: German MPs vote 'yes' to bailout talks*.
Branigan, T., and MacAskill, E. 2012, May 4. US expects China to allow dissident Chen Guangcheng to travel abroad. *The Guardian*.

Deutsche Welle. 2015a, May 21. *Malaysian prime minister orders rescue operations to save migrants at sea.*

———. 2015b, June 24. *Thailand charges 72 in human trafficking crackdown.*

Ellyatt, H. 2015, August 17. Strings attached to German vote on Greek bailout? *CNBC.*

Etzioni, A. 2007. *Security first.* New Haven: Yale University Press.

Fujita, A., Dover, E., Schabner, D. 2012, May 19. Chen Guangcheng: Chinese dissident arrives US. *ABC.*

Grove, T. 2012, October 22. Russia condemns America's human rights record. *Huffington Post.*

Harris, E. 2015, May 19. Pope Francis: Are you ready for your final goodbye? *Catholic News Agency.*

Holmes, O. 2015, July 20. Burma's Rohingya: One woman's journey to marriage on a smuggling boat. *The Guardian.*

Ibrahim, A. 2015, July 16. Who is instigating the violence against the Rohingya in Myanmar? *The Huffington Post.*

Jacobs, A. & Ansfield, J. 2012, April 27. Challenge for U.S. After escape by China activist. *The New York Times.*

Jazeera, Al. 2010, May 12. *Indonesia to 'turn back Rohingya' boats.*

Kirby, J. 2015, July 10. *U.S. condemns violence in Burundi.* Washington, DC: United States Department of State Press Statement.

Lee, J. 2012, April 30. How the Chen Guangcheng case will test U.S.-China Relations. *Time.*

Liu, M. 2012, May 2. Activist Chen Guangcheng: Let me leave China on Hillary Clinton's plane. *The Daily Beast.*

Marans, D. 2015, July 6. U.S. At odds with Germany over Greek debt crisis. *Huffington Post.*

Maule, A. 2015, May 16. State department: Rohingya refugee crisis an emergency. *MSNBC News.*

Myers, S.L., and Jacobs, A. 2012, April 30. On a tightrope, President Obama prods China on rights. *The New York Times.*

Rathke, J. 2015, May 15. *United States warns against violence in Burundi.* United States Department of State.

Reuters. 2015, May 15. *Kerry discusses shelter for Rohingya with Thai minister.*

Rwema, E. 2015, July 8. US envoy warns Burundi leaders could face prosecution. *Voice of America.*

Sagalyn, D. 2012, April 30. Who is Chinese activist Chen Guangcheng? *PBS.*

Scott, A. 2015, May 21. US, Myanmar officials discuss treatment of Rohingya. *Voice of America.*

Smith, D. 2015, May 7. Burundi protesters set man ablaze in apparent revenge attack. *The Guardian.*

Stoakes, E., and Kelly, C. 2015, May 28. Asian refugee crisis: Trafficked migrants held off Thailand in vast 'camp boats.' *The Guardian.*

The Guardian. 2015, May 20. Indonesia and Malaysia agree to offer 7,000 migrants temporary shelter.

Tiffin, F. 2015. There's no chance that the Rohingya people will end up in the Gambia. *Vice News.*

Wescott, L. 2015, May 20. Indonesia and Malaysia agree to take Rohingya and Bangladeshi Boat Migrants. *Newsweek.*

Part V
A Global Dimension

Chapter 12
Talking with the Muslim World

12.1 One Challenge, Wrapped in a Bigger One

The struggle against terrorism in the Middle East has led to a quest to find ways to counter the normative appeal[1] of violent extremists, especially the so-called Islamic State of Iraq and Syria (ISIS). There is widespread recognition that ISIS has a very effective normative position as indicated by the fact that it (a) strongly motivates its rank and file; (b) has persuaded many thousands of young Muslims from around the world to join its ranks; and (c) has considerable appeal in parts of the Muslim world. Several analyses of ISIS' normative appeal focus on its ability to exploit social media; however, much of ISIS' appeal derives not just from the tools and platforms it leverages but from the underlying message that it broadcasts. Boaz Ganor, the executive director of the International Policy Institute for Counter-Terrorism writes: "[ISIS] captivates these young people, not only by virally disseminating its messages of victory and barbarism, but also, and perhaps mainly, by inviting them to join an alternative conceptual system" (Ganor 2015). Psychologist John Horgan finds that ISIS recruits typically feel a "a very, very strong moral pull…this passionate need to right some perceived wrong, to address some sort of injustice, to restore honor to those from whom it's been taken" (Singal 2014). Although the vast majority of the Muslim world opposes ISIS, there are significant minorities in several very disparate countries that seem to support ISIS. A Pew Global Attitudes Survey in Spring 2015 found that 20% of Nigerian Muslims and 12% of Malaysian Muslims had "favorable" opinions of ISIS while the percentages for Pakistan and Senegal

---

This chapter draws on: "Talking to the Muslim World: How, and with Whom?" in *International Affairs* 92 (6), (2016): 1361–1379. I am indebted to David Kroeker-Maus for extensive research assistance on this paper. Amelia Arsenault, Shahira Fahmy and Nick Cull provided thoughtful comments and insights on a previous draft of this chapter.

[1] I use the term normative as a reference to value-based conceptions and communications. Other terms such as "ideology," "propaganda" or "messaging" are prejudicial and tend to assume posturing rather than that the advocacy of a true believer.

© The Author(s) 2018
A. Etzioni, *Happiness is the Wrong Metric*, Library of Public Policy and Public Administration 11, https://doi.org/10.1007/978-3-319-69623-2_12

were 9% and 11% respectively (Poushter 2015). Although a small minority, these percentages represent millions of Muslims around the world who support ISIS at least to some extent.

The US lacks a compelling normative response to ISIS' appeal in the Muslim world. Charlie Winter (2015) writes "This war [against ISIS] cannot be won through military and political means alone; it is as much a war of information and propaganda as anything else and, currently, it is fatally imbalanced to the advantage of Islamic State." Christina Schori Liang, a senior fellow at the Geneva Center for Security Policy, put it more simply: "We need a compelling story that makes our story better than theirs, and so far their story is trumping ours" (Geller 2016).

The challenge posed by ISIS' normative positions is part of a much greater challenge concerning how the West should speak to and with the Muslim world, a world in which, it is generally agreed, the US has not found an effective way to "win hearts and minds."[2] The Chicago Council on Global Affairs noted in a 2010 report that ongoing theological debates within several religions, including Islam, will have profound foreign policy consequences, but warned that "the United States often lacks the capacity to understand even the broad contours of such debates, much less the subtleties and nuances of religious history, theological argument, and cultural context" (Appleby et al. 2010).

Amr and Singer (2007) of the Brookings Institute pointed out:

> By any measure, America's efforts at communicating with Muslim-majority nations since 9/11 have not been successful. The efforts have lacked energy, focus, and an overarching, integrated strategy. Instead, the efforts have relied on informational programming that has lacked priority or been misdirected, lacked nuance in dealing with diverse and sensitive issues, and not reached out to the key "swing" audiences necessary to marginalize and root out violent extremists.[3]

Freud argued that there are no accidents; when people act in ways that seem ineffectual or illogical, there are often underlying causes that drive such behavior. I suggest the same holds for governments and nations. The reason the US is doing so poorly in countering the message of ISIS and in communicating with the Muslim world is not because the people at the State Department are witless or undedicated. There are deep underlying issues that explain why they are bound to fail.

Once these are better understood—the subject of the next section—we might be better positioned to suggest what might be done and by whom.

---

[2] The often repeated phrase entered into popular use following the release in 2003 of the Report of the State Department's Advisory Group on Public Diplomacy for the Arab and Muslim World, often called the Djerejian Report. See Djerejian 2003.

[3] Steven Kull notes that US Diplomats are particularly ill-equipped to understand this conflict, as they are pre-disposed to view conflicts as primarily between organized groups. See Kull 2014.

12.2 Components of US Normative Strategy

The US' normative position toward the Islamic world draws on three basic elements:

1. The value of keeping religious life limited to the private sphere and out of politics (typically referred to as separation of church or mosque and state), and the value of a rational secular approach to nature, society, and the self.
2. The value of free markets and capitalism as a means of achieving the good life. This life is often viewed as requiring a high level of economic growth in order to provide millions of people with a large variety of consumer goods and services— in short, an affluent life.
3. The virtues of human rights and democracy, often referred to as liberal democracy.

The three positions differ in the ways they are promoted within the Muslim world: Liberal democracy is most explicitly promoted by the US government through a variety of agencies, including the State Department, the National Endowment for Democracy, publicly-funded broadcasters like Voice of America and Radio Sawa, and various NGOs—and in several key cases by the US military and the CIA, including in effecting regime changes. Secularism is promoted much more implicitly, we shall see, but by the same agencies and NGOs. Capitalism is promoted by various agencies and divisions within the State Department and Department of Commerce, by private lobbies such as the US Chamber of Commerce, and by the World Bank and IMF (in which the US plays a leadership role).[4] Above all, the view of what Americans consider the good life, and believe others could gain if they work hard, is promoted very effectively through American movies and TV programs and by tourists. According to Northwestern University in Qatar's 2016 "Media in the Middle East" study, at least half of respondents in Lebanon, Qatar, and the UAE said they watch American movies, and in Egypt, there were more respondents who said they watch American movies than those who watch movies from Arab countries (Northwestern University in Qatar 2016). One may say that Americans "ooze" the conception of affluent life as a good life in a way that supplements, and in many ways eclipses, the US government's explicit messaging.

12.2.1 The Precariousness of Secularism

David Hume wrote in *The Natural History of Religion* in 1757 that "the primary religion of mankind arises chiefly from an anxious fear of future events; and what ideas will naturally be entertained of invisible, unknown powers, while men lie

---

[4]Rajiv Chandresakaran gives a particularly striking view of the US' attempts to promote capitalism immediately after the invasions of Iraq and Afghanistan. See Chandresakaran 2007, 2012.

under dismal apprehensions of any kind, may easily be conceived" (Hume 1757). This Enlightenment view of religion as a vestige of an earlier, more primitive age, akin to witchcraft, alchemy, and sorcery—influenced the founders of the United States, as did their experience with the powerful, established Anglican Church in Great Britain. These factors, as well as the quest for tolerance from groups that practiced different versions of Christianity, led the founders to enshrine the separation of church and state into the US Constitution.

The anthropological view of religion in turn held that humans would ultimately evolve out of religion. Anthropologist Anthony Wallace wrote in 1966 that "belief in supernatural beings and in supernatural forces that affect nature without obeying nature's laws will erode and become only an interesting historical memory" (Wallace 1966). And although Americans privately were and are more religious than the citizens of most (if not all) other developed nations, only a minority support establishing an official state religion.[5]

The same core idea guides US foreign policy. Sheherazade (2007) writes:

> This incomplete understanding [by government officials] of such a powerful socio-cultural force stems in part from the historical Western assumption that secularism naturally follows modernism, and will eventually catch on across the world as other countries develop. Today, the U.S. tradition of separation between church and state is so central to its national identity that many government officials express discomfort with having anything to do with the topic of religion.

Conversely, Shadi Hamid (2016) writes in his book *Islamic Exeptionalism:*

> Because the relationship between Islam and politics is distinctive, a replay of the Western model— Protestant Reformation followed by an enlightenment in which religion is gradually pushed into the private realm—is unlikely. That Islam—a completely different religion with a completely different founding and evolution—should follow a similar course as Christianity is itself an odd presumption.

Thus, in its dealings with Muslim-majority countries, the US keeps looking for allies that are secular and seeks to ensure that they too will separate state and religion. John Kerry stated in 2015, "We all agree that it's imperative to save the state of Syria and the institutions on which it is built and preserve a united and **secular** Syria [emphasis added]" (Kerry 2015). When Hosni Mubarak was swept from office by the 2011 Tahrir Square protests, Rep. Howard Berman, then the ranking member of the House Foreign Affairs Committee, stated, "As this change takes hold, we must keep firmly in mind that our goals include an Egypt that supports close relations with the United States; supports the welfare of the Egyptian people, including democracy and universal human rights; [and] is **secular** in orientation [emphasis added]" (Berman 2011). In Iraq, USAID contractors tasked with reforming the education system sought to remove religious references from textbooks (Etzioni 2007).

---

[5] In recent years, various polls have consistently found the percentage of respondents who support making Christianity the official religion to be in the low 30s. See for example, http://big.assets. huffingtonpost.com/toplines_churchstate_0403042013.pdf and http://www.publicpolicypolling. com/pdf/2015/ReligionPollingResults.pdf

The strong preference for secular forces and the quest to enshrine separation of state and religion in the Muslim world ignores the fact that, far from fading, religion is actually growing and playing a much greater role in many regions of the world—especially among Muslims. Polls show that the majority of Muslims want religion to play a *greater* role in public life, and want a state that is *more* influenced by Islam, not less. After decades in which communist governments used the educational system, cultural products, and the media to suppress religion—communism has faded but churches are full in Russia; in 2014, 72% of Russians identified as Orthodox Christian, up from 31% when the Soviet Union disbanded in 1991 (Pew Research Center 2014). In China, the number of Protestants alone has grown by 10% per year since 1979, and China may well soon have a larger Christian population than any other country in the world (Albert 2015). Hinduism has always had, and continues to have a key role in India, a fact highlighted by the election of the current Hindu nationalist government; meanwhile, the number of Muslims and Christians in India is also growing. In Latin America and Africa, the Catholic and Anglican churches have long held sway over politics, but are currently being challenged by the rise, not of secularism, but of Evangelical and Pentecostal churches. Polling indicates that a majority of Muslims in many countries would like to see Islam and, specifically, Islamic law, play a **greater** role in their lives. A Pew Research Center survey asked Muslims in 2015 whether they want Islamic law (or Sharia) to be the official law of the land in their country. Nearly all Muslims in Afghanistan (99%) and most in Iraq (91%) and Pakistan (84%) support Sharia as official law. In the largest Muslim-majority countries in the world, there is significant support for making Sharia official: In Indonesia, 72% were in favor; in Bangladesh, 84%; in Nigeria, 71% and in Egypt, 74% (Lipka 2015). Polling data from the Arab Barometer Surveys found that, across seven different Arab countries, 34% of respondents said they preferred Sharia without democracy, and 41% said they supported both. Only a small minority (14%) said they supported democracy without Sharia (Ciftci 2012).[6] The role of Islam is growing significantly in countries where it was once thought to be weakening, such as in Turkey and Tunisia (see Hirschl 2011). The rise of political Islam should not be too surprising, as "secularism" is an extremely fraught concept in the Islamic world; in many countries, secularism is synonymous with repression, from "Kemalist" Turkey to Bourguiba's Tunisia (Al-Ghannouchi 2000).

Given the resurgence of religion as a political force globally and the particular antipathy toward secularism in much of the Muslim world, the US government is swimming against very powerful historical currents when it seeks to find and ally

---

[6]The Arab Youth Survey conducted by ASDA'A Burson-Marsteller asked 3500 young Arabs in 16 different countries whether they agreed with the statement "Religion plays too big a role in the Middle East," and found that majorities or pluralities said "yes." However, the text of the question is much more ambiguous than the one asked by Pew (asking about the "Middle East" rather than the respondents' particular countries and leaving "role" open to interpretation by the respondent rather than asking specifically about implementation of Sharia law). Moreover, the Arab Youth Survey asked the question about the role of religion in the context of Sunni-Shia conflict in the region. See http://www.arabyouthsurvey.com/

itself with secular groups in the Muslim world and to promote separation of mosque and state.[7]

12.2.2 Promoting the Good Life

Arguing that the prevailing American normative message to the Muslim world entails extolling consumerism as a means to attaining the good life may seem unsupported and overly critical. However, the US government has advocated and pressured other countries to open up markets to foreign investment, privatize state-owned corporations, deregulate their industries, and otherwise embrace neoliberal capitalism. These moves are justified on the grounds that they would lead to higher economic growth, which will enable the nations involved to provide their people with more goods and services, with a growing measure of the kind of affluence that Americans enjoy.

The US "oozes" this message via the ways that American life is displayed in the movies and television programs that are viewed by significant portions of the Muslim world. American pop culture remains popular even where American foreign policy is decidedly not: A Pew poll in 2013 found that only 7% of Shia Muslims in Lebanon had a favorable overall view of the US, but nevertheless, half had a favorable opinion of American pop culture (Wike 2013). Muslims also learn about the American consumerist lifestyle from observing tourists and business travelers who frequent their countries. In addition, the US government contracts PR and communications firms to portray the allure of capitalist affluence abroad.[8]

The promotion of the American conception of the good life—and what constitutes a "higher standard of living"—is explicitly favored by the US government as way to counter the appeal of radical extremist Islam, and to 'drain the swamp' in which terrorism festers. For example, in 2014, Secretary of State John Kerry stated, "We have a huge common interest in dealing with this issue of poverty, which in many cases is the root cause of terrorism" (Kerry 2014).

Others, including former Secretary of State Hillary Clinton, have called for a "Marshall Plan for the Middle East," to develop the region economically and politically (Clinton 2011). True, these drives are favored not merely as way to prevent terrorism but also to alleviate human suffering. However, the good intentions do not make them more realistic.

---

[7]A discussion of the lack of causal links between religiosity and violence is well beyond the scope of this paper. Jocelyne Cesari has examined the supposed exceptionalism of religiously-motivated violence, and demonstrated that the most extreme cases of religious violence since the inception of the nation-state have been instantiated by the politicization of religion initiated by "secular" state actors. See Cesari 2015.

[8]For example, in Kazakhstan, USAID hired Burson-Marsteller, the world's PR firm, to develop a soap opera to sell capitalism and privatization to the people, as told in (Chua 2004).

This element of American normative messaging fails on several grounds. First, the data consistently fail to show a link between material deprivation and terrorism. For example, political scientist James Piazza's study of terrorist incidents in 96 different countries between 1986 and 2002 found no statistically significant correlation between any measures of economic development and terrorism (Piazza 2006). Peter Bergen and Swati Pandey's research undermines the putative link between inaccessibility to higher education and terrorism, as their study of 79 terrorists found that 54% had a university degree or at least some college education (compared to 52% of Americans with the same level of education). Bergen and Pandey (2006) conclude that "History has taught that terrorism has been a largely bourgeois endeavor."

Last but not least, many devout Muslims believe that Americans worship at the altar of consumer goods rather than that of God. They view their own conception of the good life—living by the dictates of the Qur'an (and Hadith)—as morally superior to a life of Western "hedonist materialism."

12.2.3 Promoting Liberal Democracy

Attempts to promote democracy and human rights around the world have a long history as a major element of American diplomacy, going back at least as far as Woodrow Wilson. Wilson envisioned the League of Nations as the centerpiece of a global order that would be based on democratic principles as well as promoting liberal regimes in the nations of the world. More recently, neoconservatives championed exporting democracy to foreign lands. After the collapse of the USSR, whose former members were assumed to be rushing toward forming liberal democracies, the neoconservatives assumed that authoritarian rulers were the last barriers preventing a world of flourishing democracy. Francis Fukuyama asserted in *The End of History* that Western liberal democracy was the final stage of evolution toward which all political regimes were converging.

If authoritarian regimes did not crumble under their own weight, neocons held that the US was called upon to use its might to topple such regimes, allowing their freed peoples to establish democracies in their wake.[9]

US experiences in Afghanistan and Iraq have demonstrated that democratic institutions cannot function without certain necessary underlying sociological conditions. Moreover, as Hamid (2016) notes, liberalism and democracy coincided for much of Western history, and thus have been conflated; however, they are in fact two very different concepts, and even in the West, liberalism had to precede democracy. These conditions are absent in large parts of the Muslim (and especially Arab) world. Oftentimes, the advocates for democratic regime change in the Middle East point to the example of post-World War II Germany and Japan as evidence that

---

[9] Robert Kagan and William Kristol wrote that the possibility of the US using its power to usher in democratic regime change from Iraq to China was "eminently realistic. See Kagan and Kristol 2000, 20.

democratic institutions can be successfully imported by outsiders. Even a cursory review of what happened in these two nations illustrates a lack of parallels to the present case. Both Japan and Germany had a strong national identity and sense of national unity—in contrast, many Middle Eastern countries whose borders were arbitrarily drawn by colonial powers are riven by internal strife and sectarian loyalties. In both Germany and Japan, the foreign occupation was widely viewed as legitimate; and both had solid economic fundamentals, such as a highly educated workforce and established infrastructure. Above all, democracy building started only after all opposing forces were defeated and all hostilities ceased.

In recent years, the US as well as the World Bank have scaled back their political development programs. They now tend to favor "merely" state building rather than nation building. They are looking for stable states, and to make governments more effective and less corrupt rather than necessarily liberal and democratic. However, it seems that often the conditions for implementing even these much less ambitious missions are missing, at least in Iraq, Afghanistan, Yemen, Pakistan, Syria, Libya, and several other African countries.

12.3 Working with Islam to Address Islam

We have seen so far that three major elements of the US' normative appeal to Muslim nations face inherent major difficulties. The US advocates separation of religion and state, while the majority of Muslims seek a *greater* role for religion in their *public* life; the US's characterization of the good life clashes with that of devout Muslims, and raises expectations that cannot be met; and the US's promotion of liberal democracy disregards that the foundations needed for such regimes to thrive are missing in most Muslim-majority states and cannot be externally imposed or introduced via long distance social engineering.

To form a sounder approach, one must acknowledge an observation that has been often overlooked or obscured: that there are two fundamentally different interpretations of Islam, *both* of which are supported by a close reading of the Qur'an and major texts.[10]

On one hand, Islam has characterized as a peaceful religion that has been distorted by malicious radicals. On September 17, 2001, less than a week after the World Trade Center collapsed, President George W. Bush declared "The face of terror is not the true faith of Islam. That's not what Islam is all about. Islam is peace." That same year, Bush also said, "The Islam that we know is a faith devoted to the worship of one God, as revealed through The Holy Qur'an. It teaches the value and the importance of charity, mercy, and peace" (Backgrounder: The President's Quotes on Islam 2016). President Barack Obama stated that "We are at war with people who have perverted Islam" (Voice of America 2015). Others hold that terrorists and other violent extremists are not truly Muslims, such as the "You

---

[10] See (Etzioni 2007) specifically Part III, "The True Fault Line: Warriors vs. Preachers"

ain't no Muslim, bruv" social media campaign in Great Britain that Prime Minister David Cameron praised (Gayle 2015).

In contrast, others in the West view Islam as an inherently violent religion. This view has proven particularly popular among Republican presidential candidates. Mike Huckabee, a former governor of Arkansas and two-time Republican presidential candidate, said, "The Muslims will go to the mosque, and they will have their day of prayer, and they come out of there like uncorked animals—throwing rocks and burning cars" (Wing 2013).

Our extensive study shows that *both* views ignore that the Qur'an and Hadith—like Christian and Jewish texts—contain passages that justify violence and others that reject it (Etzioni 2007). Both are part of Islam. The Qur'an does include an exhortation to "Slay the idolaters wherever you find them," (Q 9:5) and says, "I will cast terror into the hearts of those who disbelieve. Therefore strike off their heads and strike off every fingertip of them" (Q 8:12). In the Hadith, one reads "I have been commanded to fight against people so long as they do not declare that there is no god but Allah" (Sahih Muslim 1.9.30) and, "Killing Unbelievers is a small matter to us" (Tabari 9:69). One may call them warriors[11]; "jihadists" seems closer to the common parlance.

One finds in the same texts, "And do not take any human being's life—that God willed to be sacred—other than in [the pursuit of] justice" (Q 17:33), and again, "The taking of one innocent life is like taking all of Mankind... and the saving of one life is like saving all of Mankind" (Q 5:33). There are also exhortations to peace and compassion in the Hadith: "Someone urged the Messenger of God, 'Call down a curse upon the idol-worshippers!' whereupon he said: 'I have not been sent to curse. I have been sent as compassion.'" (Muslim 6284). And again: "A strong person is not the person who throws his adversaries to the ground. A strong person is the one who contains himself when he is angry" (Al-Muwatta 47.12). These are the texts on which non-violent, moderate Islam draws. It should be noted here that the opposite of our definition of "moderate" Islam is not necessarily "conservative" or even "fundamentalist" Islam, but specifically violent Islam. Thus, the objective should not be to try to rebut entire branches or schools of Islam, but rather to specifically counter violent teachings. This is significant because most of the moderates we discuss below are still illiberal; that is, they abhor violence but do not necessarily embrace human rights, in particular women's rights and free speech. And when they state that they favor "democracy," they use the term rather differently than Americans do; for instance, one Tunisian leader explained that he favored democracy because it provides full employment.

A very telling example of the two iterations of Islam is the two views of "jihad," a term which literally means "struggle." It is interpreted by those who view Islam as

---

[11] Khaled Abou El Fadl identifies the schism within Islam as being between "moderates" and "puritans." This schema overlaps significantly with ours, but although El Fadl primarily identifies "puritans" as Wahabbists and Salafists, his criteria for delineation are the scope of application of religious texts that a particular version of Islam advocates, and the role of scholarly interpretation. See Abou El Fadl 2005.

legitimating violence as a holy war to convert or kill all infidels. In sharp contrast, for moderate Islam, "jihad" is a spiritual struggle of seeking self-improvement. In *A Metahistory of the Clash of Civilisation,* Arshin Adib-Moghaddam dismantles rather systematically what he calls the "clash regime," which perpetuates binary oppositions such as barbarian-civilized, Islam-Christianity, and West-Islam.[12] Significantly, Adib-Moghaddam (2010) notes that the advent of literalist Islam did not occur until after the siege of Baghdad by the Mongols in the thirteenth century; political Islam in this regard was borne in the context of existential crisis and external pressure.

This distinction between jihadist and moderate interpretations of Islam suggests that the most effective way to counter ISIS or other groups that draw inspiration from violent interpretations of Islam is not with secularism, the American version of the good life, or even liberal democracy, but rather with appeals based on moderate Islam. Simply put, Thomas Jefferson or John Locke will find little purchase among Muslims susceptible to the teachings of violent Islam; however, a dialogue could take as its point of departure the exhortations of clerics like Ali Sistani, the spiritual leader of Iraq's Shi'a Muslims; Egypt's Grand Mufti Shawqi Allam; the Arab League; the International Union of Muslim Scholars; and Mehmet Görmez, Turkey's highest-level cleric (Center for Research on Globalization 2014).

Speaking to Muslims about universal women's rights will be less persuasive than pointing out that the Prophet Muhammad's views on gender were rather egalitarian for his time, and that his wives were influential in political and military matters (Mernissi 1992). As the title of this paper suggests, the US must learn to communicate with the Muslim world using Islamic terms and ideas, rather than rely on liberal, Western ones. (This echoes a broader critique leveled by Hamid Dabashi 2015 in *Can Non-Europeans Think*, which explores the way that the "ethnographic gaze" marginalizes philosophies and "thinkers" operating outside the "European philosophical pedigree.")

One may respond that Jihadists are unlikely to be persuaded by appeals based on the nonviolent, moderate interpretations of Muslim texts. This may well be true. At the same time, those who already denounce violence hardly need such an appeal. The focus of efforts to dialogue with Muslims should be those in the middle, who are not yet committed to either side—what might be called the swing vote, a very large group (we shall see). If they were to join the ranks of those who are already committed moderates, jihadists would become an isolated minority and find it much more difficult to increase their ranks and replace those they lose to civil war and terrorism.

A full discussion on the nature of moral dialogues is beyond the scope of this chapter,[13] but several characteristics are important to highlight for our purposes

---

[12] Tariq Ramadan has also explored the historical context in which a polarized understanding of the world arose in Islam. See Ramadan 2004.

[13] For more extensive discussion, see Etzioni 1997, 1998, 2006. Additionally, Thomas Risse has explored arguing and truth-seeking as communicative action in International Relations, and suggests that the preconditions for "argumentative rationality" are more common in International Relations than is usually assumed. See Risse 2000, 2004.

here. First, moral dialogues differ both from deliberations—which attempt to isolate "reason" from "passion"—and from culture wars, which turn differences into total opposition. Secondly, moral dialogues are necessarily normative, and are not mere discussions of fact or logic; they often appeal to some overarching value shared by all participants.

The swing vote needs to be addressed using the language of non-violent interpretations of Islam, rather than in terms of appeals based on liberal democracy because many who support moderation do not necessarily support human rights, especially in cases where it conflicts with Sharia. They are, thus, properly referred to as "illiberal moderates." Evidence indicates that this group comprises the majority of Muslims worldwide. Pew polling found that in 2015, majorities in most Muslim countries thought suicide bombing was rarely/never justified: In both Iraq and Indonesia, over 90% responded thusly, and at least 80% said the same in Tunisia, Jordan and Pakistan. Even in Afghanistan, 58% of respondents said suicide bombing was rarely or never justified (Lipka 2015). As we have noted above, these same countries also had significant majorities that supported making Sharia official; it follows that the vast majority of moderates (in the sense of opposing violence) are also illiberal. For example, the Pew Research Center (2013) found that, across all Muslim countries, fewer than 10% of Muslims think that homosexuality is morally acceptable, including only 1% of respondents in such relatively liberal Muslim countries as Senegal and Indonesia. Similarly, in many Muslim countries, such as Pakistan, Iraq, Malaysia, and a handful of sub-Saharan African countries, a higher percentage of respondents thought polygamy was morally acceptable than thought divorce was morally acceptable (Pew Research Center 2013). Dedicated proponents of secularism fail to recognize granularity on the spectrum of religious involvement in politics. There are numerous groups who want Islam to play a greater role in public life, but do not favor coercive enforcement of religion. One would hardly fear a Caliphate headed by moderate Quakers or Reformed Jews; neither should one be troubled by an Islamic state if it follows one of the most oft-quoted lines from the Koran: "There should be no compulsion in religion" (Q 2:256).

This strategic position is similar to the one the US adopted during the Cold War. John Esposito (2007) observes that countering communism was premised on the thesis that the most effective way to counter violent socialism—communism—was to draw on the values of moderate socialism, on social democrat values rather than on those of groups at the opposite end of the normative spectrum, i.e. the conservatives.

12.4 In Conclusion

ISIS has crafted a compelling narrative that has lured Muslim recruits from all over the world. ISIS may be defeated militarily, but so long as the normative positions that it espouses remain relevant, other groups are likely to draw on them to support attacks on free societies, their allies, and moderate Muslims. Thus far, US "counter-messaging" has been ineffective; it has failed to articulate a normative position that is responsive to the deeply-held beliefs of the majority of the world's Muslims. The US strongly holds that religion should be a private affair; it continually seeks to ally itself with secular forces in the Muslim world and to promote them. These often turn out to be the weakest groups because the overwhelming majority of Muslims, data show, seek more religion in public life, not less. The US is promoting capitalism and hence in effect the affluent way of life associated with it. To many devout Muslims, it seems that Americans worship consumer goods instead of God, and others are further alienated to the point that they cannot find a job or are poorly paid and thus cannot gain even a piece of the life portrayed on American TV and in movies. Promising them economic development or a "Marshall Fund for the Middle East," which cannot be delivered, just adds to their frustration. Promoting liberal democracy ignores the evidence that many of the nations involved have not yet developed the sociological foundations necessary for such a regime to take hold. The US—whether dealing with ISIS or other such groups or in addressing the much larger Muslim world—needs to appeal to different values than secularism, capitalism and democracy. The answer may be found in the fact that there are basically two different iterations of Islam. One legitimates violence, for instance in the call to kill all infidels. The other abhors violence and holds, for instance, that there ought to be no compulsion in religion. A very large part of the Muslim world, data show, subscribes to the moderate iterations of Islam. However, many of these do not accept secularism or liberalism. Hence, they are best called "illiberal moderates." One can appeal to them in terms of rejecting terrorism and violence but much less so if one seeks to convince them to embrace other values that Americans hold dear.

For fairly obvious reasons, official US agencies are not well-suited to promote moderate Islam as the best antidote to violent Islam. Rather, the best messengers for this message can be found in the Muslim world; they are already in place, but their reach must be significantly expanded. And their message of moderation must not be undermined by seeking to graft onto it values other than doing good without using force.

References

Abou El Fadl, K. 2005. *The great theft: Wrestling Islam from the extremists*. New York: Harper San Francisco.

Adib-Moghaddam, A. 2010. *A metahistory of the clash of civilisations: Us and them beyond orientalism*. London: Columbia University Press.

Albert, E. (2015). Christianity in China. *Council on Foreign Relations*.

Al-Ghannouchi, R. 2000. Secularism in the Arab Maghreb. In *Islam and secularism in the Middle East*, ed. A. Tamimi and J.L. Esposito, 97–124. New York: New York University Press.

Amr, H., and P.W. Singer. 2007. Engaging the muslim world: A communication strategy to win the war of ideas. *The Brookings Institution*.

Appleby, R.S., Cizik, R., Wright, T. (2010). Engaging religious communities abroad: A new imperative for US policy: Report of the task force on religion and the making of US foreign policy. *Chicago Council on Global Affairs*.

Backgrounder: The President's Quotes on Islam. 2016. http://georgewbush-whitehouse.archives. gov/infocus/ramadan/islam.html. Accessed 25 Apr 2016.

Bergen, P., and S. Pandey. 2006. The madrassa scapegoat. *The Washington Quarterly* 29 (2): 115–125.

Berman, H. 2011, February 9. Recent developments in Egypt and Lebanon: Implications for U.S. policy and allies in the broader Middle East, Part I. *US House of Representatives, Committee on Foreign Affairs.*

Center for Research on Globalization. 2014, August 24. *Muslim Leaders Worldwide Condemn.*

Cesari, J. 2015. Religion and politics: What does God have to do with it? *Religions* 6 (4): 1330–1344.

Chandresakaran, R. 2007. *Imperial life in the Emerald city: Inside Iraq's green zone.* New York: Vintage Books.

———. 2012. *Little America: The war within the war for Afghanistan.* New York: Alfred A. Knopf.

Chua, A. 2004. *World on fire: How exporting free market democracy breeds ethnic hatred and global instability.* New York: Anchor.

Ciftci, S. 2012. Secular-Islamist cleavage, values, and support for democracy and shari'a in the Arab world. *Political Research Quarterly* 66: 781.

Clinton, H.R. 2011, June 2. *Secretary Clinton Receives the 2011 George C. Marshall Foundation Award.*

Dabashi, H. 2015. *Can non-Europeans think?* London: Zed Books.

Djerejian, E. 2003, October 1. Changing minds winning peace. *Report of the advisory group on public diplomacy for the Arab and Muslim world,* submitted to the Committee on Appropriations, US House of Representatives.

Esposito, J. (2007). It's the policy, stupid: Political Islam and US foreign policy. *Harvard International Review* 2.

Etzioni, A. 1997. Deliberations, culture wars, and moral dialogues. *The Good Society* 7 (1): 34–38.

———. 1998. *The new golden rule: Community and morality in a democratic society.* New York: Basic Books.

———. 2006. Transnational moral dialogues. *Society* 43 (3): 45–49.

———. 2007. *Security first: For a muscular, moral foreign policy.* New Haven: Yale University Press.

Ganor, B. 2015. Four questions on: A 'Trend' analysis of the Islamic State. *Perspectives on Terrorism* 9 (3): 56–64.

Gayle, D. (2015, December 7). David Cameron praises 'You ain't no Muslim, bruv' remark. *The Guardian.*

Geller, E. (2016, March 29). Why ISIS is winning the online propaganda war. *The Daily Dot.*

Hamid, S. 2016. *Islamic exceptionalism: How the struggle over Islam is reshaping the world.* New York: St. Martin's Press.

Hirschl, R. 2011. *Constitutional theocracy.* Cambridge: Harvard University Press.

Hume, D. (1757). *Four dissertations: I. The natural history of religion. II. Of the passions. III. Of tragedy. IV. Of the standard of taste. No. 7.* A. Millar.

Kagan, R., and W. Kristol. 2000. *Present dangers: Crisis and opportunity in American foreign and defense policy.* San Francisco: Encounter Books.

Kerry, J. 2014, January 14. *Remarks after meeting with Secretary of State of the Holy See Pietro Parolin.*

———. 2015, October 28. *Remarks at the carnegie endowment for international peace.*

Kull, S. 2014. The inner clash of civilizations within the Muslim ummah. In *Engaging the other: Public policy and Western-Muslim intersections,* ed. K.H. Karim and M. Eid, 133–150. New York: Palgrave Macmillan.

Lipka, M. 2015, December 7. Muslims and Islam: Key findings in the US and around the world. *Pew Research Center.*

Mernissi, F. 1992. *The veil and the male elite: A feminist interpretation of women's rights in Islam.* New York: Basic Books.

Northwestern University in Qatar. 2016. Media use in the Middle East 2016, a six nation survey.
Pew Research Center. 2013, April 30. The World's Muslims: Religion, politics and society. The Pew Forum on Religion and Public Life.
———. 2014, February 10. *Russians return to religion, But Not to Church.*
Piazza, J.A. 2006. Rooted in poverty?: Terrorism, poor economic development, and social cleavages. *Terrorism and Political Violence* 18 (1): 159–177.
Poushter, J. 2015, November 17. In nations with significant Muslim populations, much disdain for. *Pew Research Center.*
Ramadan, T. 2004. *Western Muslims and the future of Islam.* New York: Oxford University Press.
Risse, T. 2000. "Let's argue!": Communicative action in world politics. *International Organization* 54 (1): 1–39.
———. 2004. Global governance and communicative action. *Government and Opposition* 39 (2): 288–313.
Sheherazade, J. 2007. Local religious peacemakers: An untapped resource in US foreign policy. *Journal of International Affairs* 61 (1): 111–130.
Singal, J. 2014, August 18. Why ISIS is so terrifyingly effective at seducing new recruits. *New York Magazine.*
Voice of America. 2015, February 19. *Obama: 'Ugly Lie' that west is at war with Islam.*
Wallace, A. 1966. *Religion: An anthropological view.* New York: Random.
Wike, R. 2013, February 22. *American star power still rules the globe.* Washington, DC: Pew Research Center.
Wing, N. 2013, August 8. Mike Huckabee: Muslims depart mosques like 'uncorked animals,' throwing rocks, burning cars. *Huffington Post.*
Winter, C. 2015. The virtual 'Caliphate': Understanding Islamic state's propaganda strategy. *Quilliam.*

Chapter 13
Defining Down Sovereignty

"Defining down sovereignty" refers to the normative thesis that sovereignty should not grant a state absolute protection against armed intervention in their internal affairs by other states, and that instead the international community should condition such immunity on states living up to particular standards. This essay suggests two modifications to this thesis. First, the international community should spell out the kinds of failures to protect civilians that can justify armed interventions by other states, as well as which agency has the authority to determine when such failures have occurred. In other words, the international community should determine how low to set the bar for intervention, and who rules. Second, the international community needs to establish an additional international responsibility, namely a responsibility to prevent international terrorism. The essay treats both of these modifications as shared international normative understandings; it does not attempt to translate these changes into international law.

The essay first briefly reviews the normative assumptions about state sovereignty that form the foundation of the international order. The next section holds that state sovereignty has never been considered absolute. The third section briefly reviews the well-known drive to define down state sovereignty by discussing the normative conception of the "responsibility to protect" (RtoP). The fourth section identifies a need to spell out the conditions under which the international community would judge that a state has failed to fulfill its responsibility to protect its civilians and that, thus, armed intervention is justified, as well as which specific authority would make such a ruling. In other words, even if one agrees that defining down sovereignty is fully justified, one still must determine how low the bar for armed interventions should be set, and which body should make the determination. The final part of the essay suggests that a new responsibility to prevent international terrorism should exist and that a state's failure to discharge it—whether because the state is unwilling or unable to act—justifies armed intervention by other states.

This chapter draws on a segment of an article published as "Defining Down Sovereignty" in *Ethics and International Affairs* 30 (1), (Spring 2016).

13.1   Sovereignty as a Keystone

Both modifications proposed by this essay concern changes to what many hold to be the most profound foundation of the international order (Ikenberry 2011b), the concept of state sovereignty, which in contemporary thought and practice has been largely understood in association with the Westphalian principle that forbids armed interference by one state in the internal affairs of another.[1] Respect for international borders is a crucial part of this order. They are the markers that separate that which is fully legitimate and that which most assuredly is not. If the troops of a given state are positioned within its boundaries, the international community considers them to be a legitimate part of an orderly world composed of states. The international community holds that the same troops crossing a border with hostile intentions is a severe violation of the agreed-upon world order; the international order and the invaded state are inclined to respond violently. The news regularly reports that people in very different parts of the world feel personally aggrieved, insulted, and humiliated when they learn that their state's sovereignty has been violated, even if another state's troops merely crossed a minor, vague line in the shifting sands (see Guha and Spegele 2013). That millions of people have shown that they are willing to die to protect their state's sovereignty is an indication of the depth of their commitment to this precept. Indeed, even when a state violates another's sovereignty to bring aid to the latter's population, strong loyalty to the sovereignty paradigm persists. As Francis Deng (1996, p. xvi) notes:

> Whether international involvement in a domestic problem is strategically motivated or driven by humanitarian concerns, it nearly always evokes a reaction that is both appreciative of assistance and hostile to foreign intervention. It could indeed be conjectured that when the state fails to honor the responsibilities of national sovereignty, the people will retain their consciousness of pride, honor, and independence, despite their need for external help.

The same normative idea is also tied to the strongly-held precepts of self-determination that played a key role in dismantling colonial empires and establishing independent nation-states. The right to state sovereignty is trumpeted by the governments and citizens of both autocracies and democracies—all of which tend to decry foreign intervention into their affairs on nationalist grounds. The respect for sovereignty[2] is ensconced in a slew of international laws and institutions, such as the International Criminal Court (ICC) and most notably the Charter of the United Nations (Philpott 2010; see also Goldsmith and Levinson 2009, p. 1844).

---

[1] The historical question whether this conception of sovereignty arose out of the Treaty of Westphalia is the subject of significant debate within the literature. For a concurring view, *see* Philpott 2001, 76. For dissenting views, see Nexon (1999) and Krasner (1999, 20–25).

[2] Some scholars (e.g. John Ikenberry) hold that the international order centered on Westphalian sovereignty is a decidedly liberal order, while others (e.g. Anne-Marie Slaughter) associate the Westphalian model of sovereignty with realism as distinct from a liberal notion of sovereignty under which states have responsibilities, especially to protect their citizens, as well as rights. For Ikenberry's view, see: Ikenberry (2011a). For Slaughter's see: Slaughter (2004) and Slaughter (2011).

For example, the Preamble as well as Articles 17 and 53 of the Rome Statute, which established the ICC, identify the Court's jurisdiction as complementary to the jurisdiction of its member states, which means that the ICC may only pursue cases that states are unable or unwilling to prosecute themselves (United Nations 2000). Article 2 of the United Nations Charter (1945), meanwhile, states that the United Nations is based "on the principle of the sovereign equality of all its Members."

13.1.1 Sovereignty Was Never Absolute

Many criticized the Westphalian sovereignty paradigm from the start. The idea faced criticism, both from those who considered claims of sovereignty to be a form of idolatry and from those who saw the paradigm as a shield for tyrants' abuses (Philpott 2010). For example, political philosopher Jacques Maritain contends that the concept of sovereignty is intrinsically faulty, as it both separates the will of the nation from that of the body politic and creates insurmountable complications for international law (Maritain 1951). Others like Stephen Krasner have characterized sovereignty as "organized hypocrisy," criticizing it on the grounds that it is universally recognized but, at the same time, widely violated. Specifically, Krasner (1999, pp. 85–86, 108, 163–175, 180–182, 202–217) holds that leaders endorse sovereignty when the paradigm helps them maintain their positions of power and ignore it when it is politically expedient to do so.

Other scholars insist that sovereignty has never been considered absolute. Bertrand de Jouvenel (1957), for example, argues that people often understand the sovereign will as being an absolute authority, but that it is itself subject to constraints of morality that are independent of it. According to this view, sovereignty rests upon a further moral framework that serves to justify the paradigm—but that can also justify deviations from and exceptions to the paradigm.

Furthermore, there have always been pragmatic and principled exceptions to the self-determination component of sovereignty. For example, international law has long restricted states from carrying out "acts wholly within one state which cause damage to another state," such as using a disproportionate amount of a water source shared by other states or injuring foreign nationals and diplomats (Hannum 1990, p. 20).

In addition, the Charter of the United Nations may be taken to treat sovereignty as instrumental. As has been previously noted: "The Charter of the United Nations seeks to protect all States, not because they are intrinsically good but because they are necessary to achieve the dignity, justice, worth and safety of their citizens"—the implication being that states might forfeit their sovereignty if they fail to achieve the ends that justify state sovereignty (United Nations Department of Public Information 2004, p. 17). In the wake of World War II, a majority of states drafted and signed the 1948 Universal Declaration of Human Rights (UDHR), thereby codifying the obligation of states to uphold their citizens' rights to be free from mass atrocity crimes and human rights abuses. Although this declaration did not include enforcement mechanisms, it gave voice to the growing normative consensus that states have an obligation to respect human rights—an obligation that is simultaneous with, and perhaps even overrides, the right to sovereignty.[3] Indeed, many scholars have contended that not only does the UDHR allow violations of sovereignty norms (e.g. humanitarian intervention), but also that the UDHR is "fundamentally at odds with state sovereignty" (Bobbitt 2009, pp. 453–454). Similarly, the 1948 Convention on the Prevention and Punishment of the Crime of Genocide ("Genocide Convention") obliges states both to refrain from and work to punish genocide; two additional covenants, one on civil and political rights, the other on economic and cultural rights, followed the Genocide Convention in the mid-1960s (Philpott 2010). Michael W. Doyle (2012, p. 617) adds that the United Nations Charter hampers unbridled state sovereignty in a host of ways, including in issues of international security and budget authority.

13.1.2   Defining Down Sovereignty: The Responsibility to Protect

Proponents of sovereignty as responsibility (RtoP) sought to fundamentally shift the role played by the international community in the internal affairs of states by establishing an *a priori* category of conditions that, if met, would cause states to forfeit their sovereignty. As such, states that called for armed humanitarian intervention would not need to justify interventions in principle, but rather would need merely to show that a state had not fulfilled its responsibilities. States that manifestly neglect their responsibilities to prevent mass atrocity crimes forfeit their sovereignty, and the international community has the responsibility to intervene with coercive measures, including military intervention.

Contemporary international theory and practice is largely departing from the view that sovereignty is absolute and is instead adopting the idea of conditional sovereignty—that is, that sovereignty is contingent upon states fulfilling certain domestic and international obligations. This is largely a communitarian approach, and it is one built on a communitarian notion of citizenship. In other words, it recognizes that states (like individuals) have not only rights but also responsibilities; they are entitled to self-determination and self-government, but must also demonstrate their commitment to the common good by protecting the environment, promoting peace, and refraining from harming their population.[4] Recent humanitarian crises have further called into question the inviolability of sovereignty. The international community widely accepts that states have a responsibility to refrain from

---

[3] Bobbitt calls the notion of sovereignty practiced by the UN "translucent" sovereignty and describes it as a form of sovereignty that is afforded to states *unless* the Security Council says otherwise (Bobbitt 2009, p. 454).

[4] One might observe a certain similarity between this view and the Kantian view proposed in the article "Perpetual Peace."

committing (or allowing) mass atrocities against their citizens (for example, geno-cide), and that in failing to uphold such responsibilities they forfeit their sover-eignty. This understanding is manifested in RtoP (United Nations General Assembly 2005). Francis Deng and his associates, in a 1996 book entitled *Sovereignty as Responsibility*, argued that when states do not conduct their domestic affairs in ways that meet internationally recognized standards, other states have not only a right but also a duty to intervene (Deng et al. 1996). Deng forcefully stated this modification of the Westphalian norm and, at great length, defended his thesis that

> [t]he sovereign state's responsibility and accountability to both domestic and external con-stituencies must be affirmed as interconnected principles of the national and international order. Such a normative code is anchored in the assumption that in order to be legitimate sovereignty must demonstrate responsibility. At the very least that means providing for the basic needs of its people. (Deng et al. 1996)

The International Commission on Intervention and State Sovereignty (ICISS, or the Evans-Sahnoun Commission) further developed the idea in its 2001 report *The Responsibility to Protect*, and centered its proposals on sovereignty as responsibil-ity. It held that:

> The Charter of the UN is itself an example of an international obligation voluntarily accepted by member states. On the one hand, in granting membership of the UN, the inter-national community welcomes the signatory state as a responsible member of the commu-nity of nations. On the other hand, the state itself, in signing the Charter, accepts the responsibilities of membership flowing from that signature. There is no transfer or dilution of state sovereignty. But there is a necessary re-characterization involved: from sovereignty as control to sovereignty as responsibility in both internal functions and external duties. (Evans et al. 2001, p. 13)

In 2004 the UN Secretary General's High-Level Panel on Threats, Challenges, and Change (the "High-Level Panel") advanced this view in its report, "A More Secure World—Our Shared Responsibility," which argues that:

> Whatever perceptions may have prevailed when the Westphalian system first gave rise to the notion of State sovereignty, today it clearly carries with it the obligation of a State to protect the welfare of its own peoples and meet its obligations to the wider international community. (United Nations Department of Public Information 2004, p. 17)

Here, again, the report implies that a state's willingness and capacity to fulfill its basic responsibilities and obligations preconditions its sovereignty. RtoP reaches even further; it not only holds that states must fulfill their obligations to protect their citi-zens from mass atrocity crimes in order to maintain their sovereignty—but also holds that *other states* have the *obligation to intervene* if a state fails to uphold its responsi-bility to protect (United Nations Department of Public Information 2004, p. 17).

The United Nations Security Council previously authorized interventions, in states such as Somalia and Haiti, rarely and on an ad hoc basis; before the advent of RtoP, it had not developed a general case for downgrading state sovereignty. RtoP codified a specific set of criteria that would justify violating a state's sovereignty—and thus significantly "walked back" the Westphalian norm. The United Nations General Assembly endorsed RtoP unanimously in 2006 (United Nations Security

Council 2006). Since then, "numerous resolutions by the Security Council and General Assembly" have referenced RtoP, which has ascended to a place of prominence in the international debate and has been invoked by a wide range of state and nonstate actors (Glanville 2012, p. 1). (However, RtoP has also suffered setbacks; the employment of RtoP as the rationale for the 2003 invasion of Iraq and the NATO intervention in Libya during 2011 caused the concept to lose support) (Ackerman 2011; Norton-Taylor 2012). Accordingly, some of RtoP's normative grounding—namely conditional sovereignty—has been similarly eroded.

13.1.3   How Far Is "Down"?

While considerable international consensus exists about RtoP, much less agreement exists about the point at which a state's neglect of its responsibilities justifies armed intervention by other states, and about which authority should determine that this point has been reached. Deng, who is credited with coining the concept of sovereignty as responsibility, holds that in order to avoid being stripped of its sovereignty a state must maintain good governance and provide for the "general welfare of its citizens and those under its jurisdiction" (Glanville 2011a). In his 1996 book *Sovereignty as Responsibility: Conflict Management in Africa*, Deng and his colleagues wrote that the only states exempt from potential intervention are those with governments that "under normal circumstances, strive to ensure for their people an effective governance that guarantees a just system of law and order, democratic freedoms, respect for fundamental rights, and general welfare" (Deng et al. 1996, p. 223). This formula sets the bar very low; very few states would be safe from armed intervention if the international community were to adopt Deng's guidelines. Deng does not spell out which authority should judge whether intervention is justified—the tenor of his writing suggests he intends the United Nations Security Council or, possibly, General Assembly to fill the role.

In the early 1990s, French diplomat Bernard Kouchner and his colleagues coined the term "le droit d'ingérence," which seems to aim to establish a principle that France has a right to support its nongovernmental entities in their attempts to end atrocities (Martin 2011, p. 160). Because this right seems to be grounded in nongovernmental organizations' assessments of whether they have a moral duty to offer assistance in humanitarian crises (Garigue 1993, p. 672), the circumstances under which it would hold that France has a right to support humanitarian aid would seem to hinge on the assessment of private organizations. Arguably, this set the bar even lower than Deng did. However, this principle never gained traction. Indeed, it is only very rarely mentioned in the literature.

In 1995 the Commission on Global Governance recommended that the United Nations craft legal opportunities for armed humanitarian intervention under specific circumstances. In the Commission's holding, the "acceptable basis for humanitarian action"—which it grounded in the fundamental principle that "all states have an obligation to protect [the right of all people to a secure existence]"—is extraordinarily vague: "The line separating a domestic affair from a global one [that is, one validating intervention] cannot be drawn in the sand, but all will know when it has been crossed" (Commission on Global Governance 1995). Earlier in the document, it proposed "restricting [the scope of a new Charter amendment] to cases that constitute a violation of the security of the people so gross and extreme that it requires an international response." This report set the bar higher than did Deng and specified which authority would render the ruling that a state has not lived up to its responsibilities.

Another approach to the conditions under which armed humanitarian intervention may be undertaken is derived from international law. It holds that armed humanitarian intervention, as authorized by the Security Council, should be undertaken whenever a humanitarian crisis escalates to the point that it poses a "threat to international peace and security" (Rogers 2004, p. 728). This is the justification that supported the intervention in Libya in 2011(for example, the establishment of a no-fly zone); in March 2011, Security Council Resolution 1973 "act[ed] under Chapter VII of the Charter" (which empowers the Security Council to "determine the existence of any threat to the peace" and to authorize collective action) and authorized "Member States that have notified the Secretary-General, acting nationally or through regional organizations or arrangements, and acting in cooperation with the Secretary-General, to take all necessary measures … to protect civilians and civilian populated areas under threat of attack…while excluding a foreign occupation force" (United Nations Department of Public Information 2011). This approach focuses more on determining which agency has the authority to rule on the necessity of an intervention than on determining the degree of harm done to a population that justifies an intervention. Indeed, one scholar holds that the Security Council's "discretion to determine the existence of threats to or breaches of international peace and security is virtually absolute" (Chimni 2002, p. 107).

The 2001 report drafted by the International Commission on Intervention and State Sovereignty, chaired by Gareth Evans and Mohamed Sahnoun, spells out where to "draw the line in determining when military intervention is, prima facie, defensible" (Evans et al. 2001, p. 31). It offers two "threshold criteria" that constitute just cause for humanitarian intervention: "large scale loss of life, actual or apprehended, with genocidal intent or not, which is the product either of deliberate state action, or state neglect or inability to act, or a failed state situation; or large scale 'ethnic cleansing,' actual or apprehended, whether carried out by killing, forced expulsion, acts of terror or rape" (Evans et al. 2001, p. 32). This is by far the clearest set of criteria and does not set the bar so low that any state can claim justification for humanitarian intervention.

Several scholars agree that RtoP as adopted at the United Nations World Summit in 2005 holds states responsible for protecting their people from four "mass atrocity" crimes (Piiparinen 2012, p. 410). Paragraph 138 of the Outcome Document specifically lists "genocide, war crimes, ethnic cleansing and crimes against humanity" as the four moral atrocity crimes against which a state is responsible for protecting its population (Glanville 2011b, p. 234). When states fail to live up to their responsibility to protect their civilians from mass atrocities, other states become collectively responsible for taking coercive measures to end the mass atrocities; these include political, economic, and juridical measures, and only in "extreme" circumstances may states resort to military intervention. Adrian Gallagher attempts to further specify these conditions by pointing out the Outcome Document's term "manifestly failing to protect their populations." He holds that the term, which replaced "unable or unwilling" in the final Outcome Document for reasons unknown, is highly ambiguous; he then proposes that the international community arrive at consensus about indicators of "manifest failing," which he suggests should be "government intentions[,] the types of weapons used[,] the death toll[,] the number of people displaced[, and evidence of] intentional targeting of civilians, especially women, children and the elderly" (Gallagher 2014).

Louise Arbour, former UN High Commissioner for Human Rights, meanwhile offered a very similar set of guidelines, grounded not in the United Nations Charter but rather in the Convention on the Prevention and Punishment of the Crime of Genocide, the Rome Statute of the International Criminal Court, and various war crimes tribunals. She advanced the notion that the international community should be responsible for intervening in cases of genocide ("a crime under international law which [States] undertake to prevent and to punish"), and offers a set of guidelines for determining whether a state has fulfilled this responsibility based on the rulings of the International Criminal Court (Arbour 2008, p. 450–452). Namely, the state must essentially exercise due diligence to prevent genocide, and whether the state has exercised due diligence is, in turn, based on factors such as but not limited to its influence over the actors likely to commit genocide (Arbour 2008, p. 450–452). Arbour's is a relatively detailed set of guidelines.

In short, if the international community authorizes the United Nations to determine whether the conditions have been met for humanitarian intervention—conditions that draw on the specific criteria outlined above, which avoid excessively lowering the standard for intervention—the challenge of answering the dual question of who should judge a state's fulfilment of its duties and the specific content of those responsibilities has been met.

13.1.4 No Coercive Regime Change

By contrast, intervention for the purpose of regime change and nation-building should be limited to non-coercive means and should exclude the use of force. Neither adding to the set of responsibilities a state must fulfill to guarantee its sovereignty nor demanding a certain form of government at the threat of armed intervention is justified; these matters should be the purview of the people of the states involved, and intervention over these issues often results not in a free regime, but rather in new forms of authoritarianism, anarchy, or civil war (Etzioni 2015b). Pushing beyond RtoP toward regime change threatens the possibility of a new international consensus regarding changes to the international paradigm. Russia and China—both states that have, in the past, strongly endorsed the Westphalian norm (Ikenberry 2011a, b, p. 250)—have in part come to accept armed interventions for humanitarian purposes provided that those interventions do not advance other causes.[5] For example, in 2006, China's then-ambassador to the United Nations endorsed RtoP as it pertains to "genocide, war crimes, ethnic cleansing and crimes against humanity," but insisted that "it is not appropriate to expand, willfully to interpret or even abuse this concept" (Thakur 2010). Pushing for too expansive a challenge to sovereignty might, thus, sour China on the more limited responsibilities outlined above. Moreover, although ambiguity in the responsibility to protect worried some states and observers who were concerned that states would use RtoP as a smokescreen to justify the pursuit of their national interests,[6] as Alex J. Bellamy (2010) points out, recent invocations of the responsibility to protect have worked as planned.

13.1.5   The Duty to Prevent Transnational Terrorism

It may seem obvious that if terrorists based in one nation attack the people of another nation, the forces of the attacked nation should have the right to use force against these terrorists. However, many view acts such as the use of unmanned aerial vehicles (UAVs) or Special Forces to strike transnational terrorists (i.e. terrorists based in one nation attacking people in another) as violations of state sovereignty. Hence, when the United States conducted UAV strikes in Pakistan or Yemen, it typically notified the Pakistani and Yemeni governments (albeit "concurrently") (Khan 2011) or stressed that the United States' actions had the governments' "tacit consent" (O'Connell 2010; see also Priest 2005) in a show of respect for the norm of state sovereignty. The international community criticized the United States in the name of state sovereignty for its clear violation of the sovereignty of Pakistan when American Special Forces killed Osama bin Laden in Abbottabad (Woods 2012).

Mary Ellen O'Connell (2005, p. 5), an international law scholar at the University of Notre Dame, argues that "international law has a definition of war [that] refers to places where intense, protracted, organized inter-group fighting occurs. It does not refer to places merely where terrorist suspects are found." She further argues that outside of the narrowly defined theaters of war, spelled out in declarations of war by the nations involved, the "law of peace" should guide counterterrorist efforts.[7]

---

[5] For example, both China and Russia have endorsed the "Responsibility to Protect," and the two nations (reluctantly) permitted the intervention in Libya by declining to veto the United Nations Security Council's authorization of the use of force in the country. See Bilefsky and Landler (2011).

[6] An ICISS report found, for example, that "in the ten cases where humanitarian claims were made for intervention prior to 1999 'the rhetoric of humanitarianism had been used most stridently in cases where the humanitarian motive was weakest.'" See Hehir (2010, p. 224).

[7] This assumes sovereignty in the Westphalian sense. In an influential book, Stephen Krasner identifies three further notions of sovereignty: international legal sovereignty, which is a property of independent territorial entities that have rights, like entering into contracts; interdependence sovereignty; and domestic sovereignty. On Krasner's view, Westphalian sovereignty captures the idea

Along similar lines, other scholars maintain that it is never permissible, according to the United Nations Charter, to militarily infringe upon another state's territorial sovereignty in order to deal with a non-state threat.[8]

Moreover, until the late 1980s, terrorist acts were considered to be outside of the jurisdiction of the Security Council, meaning that states had little recourse in responding to transnational terrorism within the purview of international law. Still, the Security Council and General Assembly condemned the Israeli attack on the Palestine Liberation Organization headquarters in 1985 (United Nations Security Council 1985) and the American strike against Libyan targets in 1986 (United Nations General Assembly 1986). Both of these responses to transnational terrorism (past and expected) were deemed violations of the international norms of state sovereignty. In 2004, United Nations Security Council Resolution 1566 addressed the issue of terrorism as criminal activity, hence a matter to be handled by local law enforcement authorities, rather than as conduct associated with war (United Nations Security Council 2004). And in 2006, the United Nations adopted a Global Counter-Terrorism Strategy to combat terrorism using a criminal law model (United Nations General Assembly 2006). The United Nations thus undermines "the possibility that states could lawfully resort to forcible measures against terrorists based in another country" (Tams 2009).

As I see it, from a normative standpoint, however, there are strong grounds to add the responsibility to prevent transnational terrorism (RtoPT) to norms nations are expected to uphold. If a state fails to honor this responsibility, it seems morally appropriate for the attacked nation to respond with counterterrorism measures within the territory of a state used as a base and launching pad by the attackers.[9] That is, sovereignty should be defined down one more notch; nations should add one more responsibility to maintaining their status as good citizens of the nascent global community.

Behind the arguments that follow in support of the RtoPT is the rather basic moral intuition that if terrorists do not respect international borders (by attacking across them), those who respond to their attacks need not do so either. This intuition is supported here by a new application of a very widely respected normative principle, the golden rule. It holds that you should expect others to treat you the same way you treat them. To test this intuition, I suggest one should apply what

---

that states can organize their domestic affairs any way they wish and other states may not intervene in these domestic affairs, which he considers a misnomer and argues has never truly been practiced in international relations. See Krasner (1999).

[8] It is important to note that the Rome Statute of international criminal law authorizes the ICC to prosecute individuals of non-state, but state-like entities who commit crimes against humanity. Because the ICC does not have a police force, but relies on states to apprehend and arrest individuals suspected of such crimes, this practice does not raise concerns with violations of territorial sovereignty.

[9] A Justice Department white paper states that targeted killings in a foreign nation are "consistent with legal principles of sovereignty and neutrality if it were conducted, for example, with the consent of the host nation's government or after a determination that the host nation is unable or unwilling to suppress the threat posed by the individual targeted" (Department of Justice).

might be called the "uniform test." If the military of a given nation crossed a border and attacked and terrorized the people of another nation, very few would hold that these troops can hide behind claims of sovereignty for the nation from which the attack stemmed to be spared from counter attacks. If these troops took off their uniforms but engaged in the same kind of attacks, that is hardly a reason for them to be spared. Indeed, as I see it, they are entitled to fewer rights than uniformed fighters. In other words, terrorists have a lower standing than soldiers.

The main reason for this lower standing is that terrorists are violating one of the most profound rules of all armed conflicts, the rule of distinction. The rule of distinction holds that combatants should make special efforts to spare civilians when engaging in armed confrontations (Etzioni 2013, p. 356). It is for this reason that the majority of US military aircrafts involved in the fight against the ISIS are returning to their base without dropping their bombs or after dropping them on low-value targets. This is the case because as they close in on their original targets, they often find that civilians would be hurt (Schmitt 2015). Responding forces often cannot effectively eliminate combatants who masquerade as civilians and hide among them without killing some innocent civilians. One of the major reasons the US military did so poorly in Afghanistan and Iraq was terrorists' violation of said rule of distinction (Etzioni 2015a). The US military has a five-page single-spaced list of targets that may not be hit or may be hit only after consultations with high-ranking officials, or even the White House. At various points, American commanders denied artillery support or close air support to beleaguered American troops over concerns that civilians may be hit. In addition, they have ordered American soldiers not to fire until they are hit first (Etzioni 2014). True, there has nevertheless been considerable "collateral damage." However, a close examination of these cases would show that the main culprits are the terrorists, who masquerade as civilians, use unmarked vehicles, and fire from civilians' homes, mosques, and schools. Indeed, there can be little doubt that if terrorists abided by the rule of distinction—separating themselves from the civilian population and marking themselves, their encampments, and their vehicles—there would be very little collateral damage. In short, terrorists are entitled to less protection than soldiers, because they are violating a very basic role of armed conflicts. In this case, there seems no reason to accord terrorists any special privileges.

The main counterargument to the RtoPT is that armies are under the control of the government of a given nation and hence can be held accountable for their acts but that is not the case for terrorists. Hence, the sovereignty of the nations from which terrorists attack should be respected. However, one should note that there are basically two different situations: one in which nations in effect have considerable control over the terrorists and one in which the terrorists act from ungoverned, under-governed, or ill-governed parts of a country (hereafter ungoverned).

True, nations rarely admit that the terrorists they launch are their agents. However, in quite a few cases, there is considerable evidence that governments help finance terrorists; provide them with intelligence, arms, and other equipment; and, above all, signal which targets to attack and when, as well as when and where to refrain from attacking. In short, to a large extent, these governments control the terrorists. Iran and Hezbollah function in this way, as do Pakistan and Lashkar-e-Taiba with attacks on India. The United States' support of the Mujahideen during the Soviet War in Afghanistan can also be characterized this way. In other cases, the connection is weaker and less evident (see De Nevers 2007; Byman 2005, p. 119). The varying degrees of control and involvement by nations in support of terrorism suggest that the response should be similarly graded. The less clear it is whether a given nation is indeed in charge, i.e. whether the terrorists are state agents, the more warning said nation should be given and the more limited counterstrikes should be. For instance, the use of drones might be used in place of Special Forces because their involvement is considered a greater violation of sovereignty. Granting concurrent notification might also be considered in such cases.

Indeed, the United States (and several other nations) designates select nations as terrorist-sponsoring states. As determined by the secretary of state, the United States currently recognizes Iran, Sudan, and Syria as "[c]ountries determined [...] to have repeatedly provided support for acts of international terrorism" (US Department of State) pursuant to Section 6(j) of the Export Administration Act, which states that support for acts of international terrorism includes the recurring use of the land, waters, and airspace of the country as a sanctuary for terrorists (for training, financing, and recruitment) or as a transit point (Cornell University Law School). The government must also expressly consent to, or with knowledge, allow, tolerate, or disregard such use. As a result of this determination, these countries are subject to restrictions on US foreign assistance, a ban on defense exports and sales, certain controls over exports of dual-use items, and miscellaneous financial and other restrictions. What I am calling for is simply taking a next step: legitimizing armed responses when the measures already listed do not suffice to stop attacks.

One may argue that this step is not needed because as of 2012, there were 13 international conventions and protocols that required state parties to criminalize a particular manifestation of international terrorism under domestic law, cooperate in the prevention of terrorist acts, and take action to ensure that offenders are held responsible for their crimes (Trapp 2012). However, the enforcement of these conventions relies on international courts, which raises numerous issues that cannot be explored here. Suffice it to say, there have been no signs that this approach could curb transnational terrorism; hence, this task is left to the assaulted nations.

What about terrorists who are based and launch their attacks from ungoverned parts of a country? The United States does not include these nations on the list of state sponsors of terrorism. According to the United States' Country Reports on Terrorism 2014, terrorist safe havens include "ungoverned, under-governed, or ill governed physical areas" where terrorists can "organize, plan, raise funds, communicate, recruit, train, transit, and operate in relative security because of inadequate governance capacity, political will, or both" (US Department of State 2015). The report goes on to exclude such territories from the determination of a state as a sponsor of terrorism. This makes sense in one way but not in another. If a nation is not in control of a given area that serves as a base for terrorists, it should not be held responsible for what is happening in this area. Thus, the US surely should not impose sanctions or cut aid to Pakistan if it tried in good faith to gain control of the parts of Waziristan but failed. However, it does not follow that one ought to spare terrorists in such areas. Attacking terrorists in ungoverned areas is not violating a nation's sovereignty because a national government forfeits such claims by being unable or unwilling to govern these. (Sovereignty is defined as having a commanding control of a given territory. If an area is ungoverned, for practical and normative purposes, it is not encompassed in the sovereignty of the government of the nation at issue, though I grant that this position is not reflected in current understanding of international law. However, these laws were changed before and ought to be changed accordingly).

In short, nations should be expected to prevent terrorists from using their territories. If they do not or cannot live up to this responsibility, they give up the relevant part of their sovereignty claims. Hence, the international community and, if it fails, the nations attacked by terrorists act legitimately when they respond to terrorists with force, regardless of what side of the border these terrorists are found.

References

Ackerman, B. 2011. Obama's unconstitutional war. *Foreign Policy*.

Arbour, L. 2008. The responsibility to protect as a duty of care in international law and practice. *Review of International Studies* 34 (3): 445–445.

Bellamy, A.J. 2010. The responsibility to protect—five years on. *Ethics and International Affairs* 24 (2): 143–169.

Bilefsky, D., and Landler, M. 2011. As U.N. backs military action in Libya, U.S. role is unclear. *The New York Times*.

Bobbitt, P. 2009. *Terror and consent: The wars for the twenty-first century*. New York: Anchor.

Byman, B. 2005. Passive sponsors of terrorism. *Survival* 47 (4): 117–144.

Chimni, B.S. 2002. Forum replies: A new humanitarian council for humanitarian interventions? *The International Journal of Human Rights* 6 (1): 103–112.

Commission on Global Governance. 1995. *Our global neighborhood: Report of the commission on global governance*. New York: Oxford University Press.

Cornell University Law School. n.d. *Section 2405 foreign policy controls*. Accessed 18 Jul 2017. https://www.law.cornell.edu/uscode/html/uscode50a/usc_sec_50a_00002405----000-.html.

de Jouvenel, B. 1957. *Sovereignty: An inquiry into the political good*. Cambridge, UK: Cambridge University Press.

De Nevers, R. 2007. Sovereignty and ethical argument in the struggle against state sponsors of terrorism. *Journal of Military Ethics* 6 (1): 1–18.

Deng, F.M. 1996. *Sovereignty as responsibility: Conflict management in Africa*. Washington, DC: The Brookings Institution.

Deng, F.M., S. Kimaro, T. Lyons, D. Rothchild, and I.W. Zartman. 1996. *Sovereignty as responsibility: Conflict management in Africa*. Washington, DC: Brookings Institution Press.

Department of Justice. n.d. *Lawfulness of a lethal operation directed against a U.S. citizen who is a senior operational leader of Al-Qa'ida or an associated force*. Washington, DC: DOJ Memo.

Doyle, M.W. 2012. Dialectics of a global constitution: The struggle over the UN Charter. *European Journal of International Relations* 18 (4): 601–624.

Etzioni, A. 2013. A liberal communitarian paradigm for counterterrorism. *Stanford Journal of International Law* 49 (2): 330–370.

———. 2014. Rules of engagement and abusive citizens. *Prism* 4 (4): 87–102.

———. 2015a. COIN: A study of strategic illusion. *Small Wars & Insurgencies* 26 (3): 345–376.

———. 2015b. The democratization mirage. *Survival: Global Politics and Strategy* 57 (4): 139–156.

Evans, G., M. Sahnoun, et al. 2001. *The responsibility to protect: Report of the International Commission on Intervention and State Sovereignty.* Ottawa: International Development Research Centre.

Gallagher, A. 2014. What constitutes a 'Manifest Failing'? Ambiguous and inconsistent terminology in the responsibility to protect. *International Relations* 28 (4): 428–444.

Garigue, P. 1993. Intervention-sanction and droit d'ingerence in international humanitarian law. *International Journal* 48 (4): 668–686.

Glanville, L. 2011a. Darfur and the responsibilities of sovereignty. *The International Journal of Human Rights* 15 (30): 462–480.

———. 2011b. The antecedents of 'sovereignty as responsibility'. *European Journal of International Relations* 17 (2): 233–255.

———. 2012. The responsibility to protect beyond borders. *Human Rights Law Review* 12 (1): 1–32.

Goldsmith, J., and D. Levinson. 2009. Law for states: International law constitutional law, public law. *Harvard Law Review* 122 (7): 1792–1868.

Guha, R., and Spegele, B. 2013. China-India border tensions rise. *The Wall Street Journal.*

Hannum, H. 1990. *Autonomy, sovereignty, and self-determination: The accommodation of conflicting rights.* Philadelphia: University of Pennsylvania Press.

Hehir, A. 2010. The responsibility to protect: 'Sound and Fury Signifying Nothing'? *International Relations* 24 (2): 218–239.

Ikenberry, G.J. 2011a. *Liberal leviathan.* Princeton: Princeton University Press.

———. 2011b. The future of the liberal world order. *Foreign Affairs.*

Khan, A.N. 2011. Legality of targeted killings by drone attacks in Pakistan. *Pak Institute for Peace Studies* 1, pp. 3–4.

Krasner, S. 1999. *Sovereignty: Organized hypocrisy.* Princeton: Princeton University Press.

Maritain, J. 1951. *Man and the state.* Chicago: University of Chicago Press.

Martin, S. 2011. Sovereignty and the responsibility to protect: Mutually exclusive or codependent? *Griffith Law Review* 20 (1): 153–187.

Nexon, D. 1999. Zeitgeist? Neo-idealism and international political change. *Review of International Political Economy* 12: 700–719.

Norton-Taylor, R. 2012. Libya campaign 'Has made UN missions to protect civilians less likely.' *The Guardian.*

O'Connell, M.E. 2005. When is a war not a war? The myth of the global war on terror. *ILSA Journal of International, and Comparative Law* 12: 535–573.

———. 2010. *Rise of the drones II: Examining the legacy of unmanned targeting: Hearing before the subcommittee on National Security and Foreign Affairs, United States House of Representatives,* 111th Congress. Statement of Mary Ellen O'Connell, Robert and Marion Short Chair in Law, University of Notre Dame, South Bend, IN.

Philpott, D. 2001. *Revolutions in sovereignty: How ideas shaped modern international relations.* Princeton: Princeton University Press.

———. 2010. Sovereignty. In *The Stanford encyclopedia of philosophy,* ed. E. N. Zalta. Summer 2010. http://plato.stanford.edu/cgi-bin/encyclopedia/archinfo.cgi?entry=sovereignty

Piiparinen, T. 2012. Sovereignty-building: Three images of positive sovereignty projected through responsibility to protect. *Global Change, Peace and Security* 24 (3): 405–424.

Priest, D. 2005. Foreign network at front of CIA's terror fight. *The Washington Post.*

Rogers, A.P.V. 2004. Humanitarian intervention and international law. *Harvard Journal of Law and Policy* 27 (3).

Schmitt, E. 2015. U.S. caution in strikes gives ISIS an edge, many Iraqis say. *The New York Times.*

Slaughter, A.M. 2004. Sovereignty and power in a networked world order. *Stanford Law Review* 40: 283–329.

———. 2011. Intervention, Libya, and the future of sovereignty. *The Atlantic.*

Tams, C.J. 2009. The use of force against terrorists. *European Journal of International Law* 20 (2): 359–397.

Thakur, R. 2010. Law, legitimacy and United Nations. *Melbourne Journal of International Law* 11.

Trapp, K.N. 2012. Holding states responsible for terrorism before the International Court of Justice. *Journal of International Dispute Settlement* 3 (2): 279–298.

United Nations. 1945. *Charter of the United Nations*.

———. 2000. *The Rome statute of the International Criminal Court*.

United Nations Department of Public Information. 2004. *A more secure world: Our shared responsibility*. New York: United Nations.

United Nations, Department of Public Information. 2011. Security Council approves 'No-Fly Zone' over Libya, authorizing 'All Necessary Measures' to protect civilians, by vote of 10 in favour with 5 abstentions, SC/10200.

United Nations General Assembly. 1986. General Assembly Resolution 41/38, A/RES/41/38.

———. 2005. 2005 World Summit Outcome (Draft resolution referred to the High-level Plenary Meeting of the General Assembly by the General Assembly at its fifty-ninth session).

———. 2006. General Assembly Resolution 60/288, A/RES/60/288.

United Nations Security Council. 1985. Security Council Resolution 573, S/RES/573.

———. 2004. Security Council Resolution 1566, S/RES/1566.

———. 2006. Security Council Resolution 1674, S/RES/1674.

United States Department of State. 2015. Country reports on terrorism 121. http://www.state.gov/documents/organization/239631.pdf.

———. n.d. *State sponsors of terrorism*. Accessed 19 Sept 2015. http://www.state.gov/j/ct/list/c14151.htm.

Woods, C. 2012. .CIA drone strikes violate Pakistan's sovereignty, says senior diplomat. *The Guardian*.

Chapter 14
The Case for Decoupled Armed Interventions

There is growing opposition, both in the US and among its allies, to armed intervention in the internal affairs of other nations, unless vital core national interests are at stake. Even when governments engage in massive abuse of their citizens, for instance in Syria and before that in Iran, the nations of the world are increasingly reluctant to act. Indeed, the normative baseline, the default position for the international order, continues to be the Westphalian norm, strongly supported by China and Russia, and large parts of the third world. The high level of casualties and mounting costs of the longest war the US. has ever been engaged in, in Afghanistan, as well as the lack of certainty that the results will ultimately vindicate this intervention, further reinforce the argument against armed intervention. True, the Libyan campaign has been deemed a success, but those involved are quick to stress that it does not set a precedent for such interventions in the future. The economic austerity regimes that the US and many of its allies are facing, as they seek to draw down their debt and reinvigorate their economies, further agitate against the expenditures involved in such interventions. As President Obama put it in the middle of 2011: "America, it is time to focus on *nation-building* here at *home*" (Obama 2011b).

This chapter suggests that if the humanitarian goals of armed interventions—stopping genocides, ethnic cleansing, and other massive abuses of civilian populations by their own governments—are decoupled from coerced regime change (e.g. democratization) and from nation-building, these interventions can be carried out effectively and at rather low costs. Hence, they need not be avoided in the future. In addition to decoupling, the standard for justifying a humanitarian intervention must be set at a high level (to be specified below). We shall see that this high level is justified by strong normative reasons and not merely prudential ones.

This chapter draws on "The Case for Decoupled Armed Interventions" in *Global Policy* 3 (1), (February 2012): 85–93. I am indebted to Julia Milton and Courtney Kennedy for research assistance on a previous draft of this chapter.

The thesis for narrowly crafted armed humanitarian intervention is supported in the following pages by showing that a mixture of idealism and hubris has driven the West to assume that it can achieve much more than stopping massive abuse of a people by their government, and that the West's repeated failure to accomplish these expansive goals is a root cause for calls to avoid armed interventions altogether—including those missions whose normative standing is strong and which can be carried out effectively. (The following examination focuses on the US because it played a leading role in the matters at hand; however, the points made also apply to other NATO members, as well as other democracies such as Australia, South Korea, and Japan.)

14.1 The Idealism, Right and Left

Several armed interventions in the recent past sought much more than the Responsibility to Protect calls for ending massive humanitarian abuse—or interpreted it in a very expansive way. They often started with relatively narrowly crafted goals, but soon expanded these goals to include coerced regime change and nation-building, both because the US and its allies held that their democratic values call for such expanded missions, and because they believed that they could successfully transform other nations in a relatively short time and without undue outlays.

President Bush entered office in 2001 after strongly criticizing, indeed mocking, nation-building. In fact, in the second presidential debate against Al Gore, he claimed, "I just don't think it's the role of the United States to walk into a country and say, we do it this way, so should you" (Bush 2000). His subsequent policies, however, did not align with his original position, as was demonstrated three years later when he authorized the invasion of Iraq. The reasons behind his decision to invade Iraq in 2003 are reported to include intelligence reports that Iraq was amassing weapons of mass destruction, claims that Iraq had links to al-Qaeda, and—according to some—a response to attempts by the Iraqi government to kill his father. While all these attributed motives have been contested, there is little doubt that neoconservative normative arguments, which call for coerced regime change, played a key role in justifying the intervention in Iraq. Following the collapse of the Soviet Union in 1990, neoconservatives championed "The Freedom Agenda," which assumed that the nations of the world were moving toward liberal democratic regimes, and that the West was duty-bound to help lagging nations catch up with history by bringing them freedom, by force if necessary. In this vein, Iraq was not to be liberated merely for its own sake, but also to "flip" other autocratic regimes throughout the Middle East (Tanenhaus 2003).

President Obama entered office in 2009 committed to avoiding such coerced regime change interventions. His position was first laid out during his inaugural speech, in which he stated: "To those who cling to power through corruption and deceit and the silencing of dissent, know that you are on the wrong side of history; but that we will extend a hand if you are willing to unclench your fist" (Obama 2009a). This short quote deserves a careful reading. The first half of the sentence, in effect, announces that the United States will not seek to change regimes that violate human rights. The second half lays out a condition: such intervention will be avoided as long as these illiberal nations do not use force. This is a sharp break from the Fukuyama-neoconservative-Bush position that, in order to secure peace, nations must have democratic regimes (Kristol 2006, p. 9; Fukuyama 1992).

Obama elaborated his position in what was framed as a major foreign policy speech in Cairo. He explicitly tied U.S. military intervention to security—and to no other goals:

> We do not want to keep our troops in Afghanistan. We see no military—we seek no military bases there. [...] We would gladly bring every single one of our troops home if we could be confident that there were not violent extremists in Afghanistan and now Pakistan determined to kill as many Americans as they possibly can. But that is not yet the case. (2009b)

Later in the speech, when Obama did turn to discuss democracy, he stated: "I know there has been controversy about the promotion of democracy in recent years, and much of this controversy is connected to the war in Iraq. So let me be clear: no system of government can or should be imposed upon one nation by any other" (2009b).

And he stated, "Each nation gives life to this principle in its own way, grounded in the traditions of its own people. America does not presume to know what is best for everyone, just as we would not presume to pick the outcome of a peaceful election" (2009b).

As time passed, President Obama came under withering normative criticism from both the right and the left, not merely for not interfering to stop violations of the Responsibility to Protect, but also for not promoting human rights and democracy more vigorously and explicitly (Malinowski 2009; Wasserstrom 2009). Of Obama's trip to China, Phelim Kine, a spokesman for Human Rights Watch, said, "It was a missed opportunity. He failed to address some of the most specific and visceral human rights abuses going on in China" (Mosk 2009, p. A3). Larry Cox, Executive Director of Amnesty International USA, stated that Obama "has created a false choice between having to speak out forcefully on human rights or being pragmatic and getting results on other issues" (Colvin 2009). Bret Stephens, a columnist at the *Wall Street Journal*, wrote that Obama's time in office has "[treated] human rights as something that 'interferes' with America's purposes in the world…" (Stephens 2009, p. A19).

Obama's response to the 2009 Iranian protests were initially subdued, and he faced considerable criticism as a result (Obama 2009c, 2009d). Obama initially stated only that he was "deeply troubled by the violence that [he'd] been seeing on television," but that the US would continue to seek to dialogue with Iran. Obama's reaction was widely criticized. "Obama's posture has been very equivocal, without a clear message," said Representative Eric Cantor, then House minority whip. "Now is the time for us to show our support with the Iranian people. I would like to see a strong statement from him that has moral clarity" (Cooper and Landler 2009, p. A16). Steven Clemons, director of the American Strategy Program at the New America Foundation, said, "For Barack Obama, this was a serious misstep... It's right for the administration to be cautious, but it's extremely bad for him to narrow the peephole into an area in which we're looking at what's happening just through the lens of the nuclear program" (Cooper and Landler 2009, p. A16).

The same pattern unfolded in the first weeks of the 2011 uprising in the Middle East. President Obama was at first rather circumspect in his comments, but, under criticism from both the right and the left, spoke out more strongly in support of democratic forces in Tunisia and Egypt. And in 2011, an armed intervention in Libya that started as a humanitarian intervention quickly morphed into a forced regime change drive. And before too long, several leading voices called for massive nation-building by introducing a Marshall Plan for the Middle East. Former U.S. National Security Advisor and NATO Supreme Allied Commander General James Jones has explained, "We learned that lesson after World War II—you know, we rebuilt Europe, we rebuilt Japan. That was an example of an enlightened view of things. The Marshall Plan, I am told, wasn't very popular in this country, but we went ahead and did it" (Jones 2011). Secretary of State Hillary Clinton believes "as the Arab Spring unfolds across the Middle East and North Africa, some principles of the [Marshall] Plan apply again, especially in Egypt and Tunisia. As Marshall did in 1947, we must understand that the roots of the revolution and the problems that it sought to address are not just political but profoundly economic as well" (Clinton 2011a). Two professors at Columbia Business School, Glenn Hubbard (who was also Chairman of the Council of Economic Advisors under George W. Bush) and Bill Duggan, argued that a Middle East Marshall Plan would "limit the spread of Islamic extremism" in the region (Hubbard and Duggan 2011). Senator John Kerry argued that "we are again in desperate need of a Marshall Plan for the Middle East" (Kerry 2011). Senator John McCain also expressed support for such a plan. And in *Prospect*, MP and former foreign office minister David Davis calls for a British Marshall Plan in the Middle East, arguing that such a plan "is one of the best ways to consolidate and support the Arab Spring as it stands, [and] could spark reform in other Arab Gulf countries too" (Davis 2011).

Some realists and conspiracy theorists may well deconstruct these normative appeals and the reactions to them and point to other motives instead (access to oil being one often cited). However, I suggest that analysis of these rationales (not carried out in the confines of this chapter) would show that normative considerations, which had "real" effects because of their resonance with opinion makers and voters in the United States and in other nations, did play a significant role in the repeated transformation of foreign policy from a position that was antagonistic to forced regime change and nation-building—to one that sought to carry them out. (Some may argue that averting humanitarian crises requires expanding the mission to unseating tyrants and building civil society and stable governments. For my response, see below.)

One serious difficulty the expansive approach to armed intervention encounters, as a normative principle, is that it has not been (and we shall see cannot be) consistently applied. In earlier ages, nations could act with limited concern for public opinion. However, as the masses became more educated and paid closer attention to public affairs (facilitated by greater access to information via the media), governments recognized the necessity of justifying their actions; they were now forced to provide a normative rationale for them. They would be held accountable. Fulfilling such a responsibility requires a measure of consistency. This is, of course, what is meant when one states that the Goddess of Justice is blind: she treats all comers in the same way, and it is in large part that consistency that legitimates her role as ultimate arbiter. Inconsistency is associated with arbitrariness, a failing of which the

American public is not tolerant, but which has, unfortunately, dogged US foreign policy in the matters at hand.

Throughout the Cold War, the US positioned itself as the champion of freedom, yet it supported military dictatorships in South America, Asia, and elsewhere. During the recent uprisings in the Middle East, the US fought to oust Qaddafi, but merely urged Mubarak to step down in Egypt; it cheered the departure of Tunisia's Ben Ali, while at the same time making few, delayed, and muted pleas for Saleh to step down in Yemen (LaFranchi 2011). It waffled on Syria and the Green Movement in Iran and, in effect, supported the autocrats of Saudi Arabia and Bahrain. Even as Bahrain was violently suppressing protests, and just before Saudi Arabia sent its troops to help, Secretary Clinton commended King Hamad for engaging in "meaningful outreach and efforts to try to bring about the change that will be in line with the needs of the people" (Clinton 2011c).

American leaders tried to explain away these gross inconsistencies. Most notably, Secretary Clinton, in a speech asserting US commitment to "sustained democracies" in the region, argued that diverse approaches were called for given such a "fluid" situation and that "a one-size-fits-all approach doesn't make sense" (Clinton 2011b). In his speech at the National Defense University justifying the Libyan intervention, President Obama took pains to emphasize that it was geared only toward that particular country, rather than representing a broader doctrine (Obama 2011). These arguments, however, have persuaded neither critics abroad nor those at home—again, because they are inconsistent. Critics cannot help but notice that the US lectures Russia and China about human rights, but provides equipment and training to the secret police of Saudi Arabia, Egypt, Yemen, and previously propped up the dictators of Argentina, Chile, and Indonesia, among others. It intervened in Libya but not in Syria, where there were more casualties even though the rising groups were composed of peaceful civilians rather than armed rebels.

Consistency does not require relying only on one criterion. As President Obama pointed out, if US vital interests are directly affected—say, a foreign power is blocking the shipment of oil through the Strait of Hormuz—the US will act, based on interest considerations and not necessarily what other nations consider the right foreign policy. There may well be other grounds for differential treatment of nations that seem to engage in similar violations of human rights, but these must be articulated. Otherwise, instead of adding to the legitimacy of one's action, the rationale provided raises doubts and opposition, as has often been the case in the past. Indeed, when a nation cannot provide a consistent rationale for its armed interventions in the internal affairs of other nations, this ought to be one reason such acts are avoided.

14.1.1   The Hubris

Foreign policies that favor coerced regime changes as well as those that call for long-distance nation-building (that is, nation-building by one country in some other country, often on the other side of the ocean), draw not merely on the conviction that it is the role of the West to bring its light to those who have not found it, on idealism, but also on the assumption that the West can transform other nations into liberal democracies, or at least help stabilize their government, prevent civil war, shape law and order (what is called state-building, which is less demanding than nation-building), and develop modern economies (which key advocates hold mainly requires freeing the nations from the old regimes that rely heavily on government interventions in the marketplace). That is, these transformations are not merely worthy ideals, but ideals that can be advanced, and in relatively short order, without unduly taxing the involved Western nations. This attitude reflects a mixture of a Western sense of exceptionality, superiority, positive thinking, and faith in social engineering. The result is what Peter Beinart calls "the beautiful lie": a hubristic sense that the US can accomplish anything and thus needs no limits, and that US interests are wedded to international military domination (Beinart 2010, pp. 378–380).

Actually, the record of such interventions is very poor. The United States, for instance, after WWII, engaged in coerced regime changes in sixteen nations, eleven of which failed to establish a functioning democracy. True, Germany and Japan are exceptions (Pei and Kasper 2003). However, even a cursory examination of the conditions that existed in these nations shows that these conditions do not exist in the Middle East, which is the reason a Marshall Plan here cannot be effectively introduced (Etzioni 2007).

Germany and Japan had surrendered after decisive defeat in a war and fully submitted to occupation. That is, new regimes were installed only after hostilities had completely ceased. There were no terrorists and no insurgencies.

While the German and Japanese reconstructions were very much hands-on projects, following the experience in Iraq and Afghanistan, few, if any, give serious consideration to the possibility that the West will occupy more lands in the Middle East or attempt to manage their transformation. The post-Arab Spring attempts at reconstruction that are currently underway amount to long-distance social engineering, with the West providing funds and advice, but primarily leaving the execution to the locals. That is, no boots on the ground—and no managers to advance either political or economic development. Such engineering is much more difficult to carry out.

One further notes that even before WWII, German and Japanese citizens strongly identified with their nations and were willing to make major sacrifices for them. And this nationalistic sentiment and corresponding willingness endured throughout the reconstruction period. The first loyalty of many citizens of Middle Eastern nations-many of which are, in reality, tribal societies that have been superficially cobbled together by Western countries, is to their ethnic or confessional group. They tend to look at the nation as a source of spoils for their tribe and fight for their share rather than make sacrifices for the national whole. Deep ethnic and confessional hostilities, such as those between the Shi'a and the Sunnis, among the Pashtun and the Tajik, the Hazara and the Kuchi, and various tribes in other nations, either gridlock the national polities (e.g. in Iraq and Afghanistan), lead to large-scale violence (e.g. in Yemen, Bahrain, and Sudan), result in massive oppression and armed conflicts (e.g. in Libya and Syria), or otherwise hinder political and economic development.

Max Weber established the importance of differences in core values when he demonstrated that Protestants were more imbued than Catholics with the values essential for modern capitalistic economies. Indeed, economic developments in Catholic countries (such as those in Southern Europe and Latin America) lagged behind the Protestant Anglo-Saxon nations and those in Northwest Europe. Weber also pointed to the difference between Confucian and Muslim values, thus, in effect, predicting the striking difference between the very high rates of economic development among the South Asian 'tigers'—China, Hong Kong, Taiwan, Singapore, and South Korea—and the low rates of Muslim states. These differences in core values are the major reason foreign aid played very little role in the strong takeoff in 'Confucian' societies, and the reason for the poor record of foreign aid in Muslim ones. These values can change overtime, but hardly at the urging of the West, on its schedule.

One must also take into account the fact that Germany and Japan were developed nations before WWII, with strong industrial bases, strong infrastructure, educated populations, and strong support for science and technology, corporations, business and commerce. Hence, they, in effect, required reconstruction. In contrast, many Middle Eastern states lack many of these assets, institutions, and traditions, and therefore cannot be reconstructed but must be constructed in the first place—a much taller order. This is most obvious in Afghanistan, Yemen, Sudan, and Libya. It is also a major issue in nations that have drawn on one commodity, oil, to keep their economy going, but have not developed the bases for a modern economy—especially Saudi Arabia and Bahrain. Other nations, such as Tunisia, Pakistan, Morocco, Syria, and Egypt, have better prepared populations and resources, but still score poorly on all these grounds compared to post-WWII Germany and Japan.

Germany and Japan also had competent government personnel and relatively low levels of corruption. In many nations in the Middle East, corruption is endemic, pervasive, and very difficult to scale back to levels sufficient for a functional government. Thus, one must take into account that a significant proportion of whatever resources are made available to Middle Eastern nations will be siphoned off to private overseas bank accounts, allocated on nepotistic bases to cronies and supporters, and that a good part of the funds will be wasted and not accounted for.

Also often overlooked is the fact that the Marshall Plan entailed much larger outlays than have been dedicated in recent decades to foreign aid that seeks to stimulate economic development (not to be conflated with military aid). In 1948, the first year of the Marshall Plan, it consumed 13% of the US budget. In comparison, the United States currently spends less than 1% of its budget on foreign aid.

Moreover, the US and its allies are entering a protracted period of budget retrenchments in which many domestic programs will be scaled back—including aid for the unemployed and poor, and for education and health care—as well as military outlays. It is a context in which the kinds of funds a Marshall Plan would require are extremely unlikely to be available.

In short, even if there were no normative reasons to question the expansive missions of armed interventions, there are prudential reasons to minimize them, namely that they tend not to yield the hoped-for results. Moreover, they squander scarce resources (both economic and political capital) and backfire, because the disappointing outcomes agitate against future interventions, even those that are normatively compelling and can be accomplished.

Critics may argue that to avert massive humanitarian abuse, regimes must be toppled and nation-building must take place, i.e. that these goals cannot be decoupled. However, there are clear instances in which such decoupling did succeed. Serbian ethnic cleansing in Kosovo was stopped without KFOR imposing any regime or engaging in significant nation-building. True, in the years that followed the UN engaged in a major nation-building drive, even seeking to build a multiethnic society. However, this drive has not succeeded (Jordan 2004). In other major humanitarian crises, such as Rwanda and Cambodia, Samantha Power showed in fine detail that the regimes first "tested the waters" to determine what the Western reaction was going to be. Only when the West was or at least seemed indifferent, did the genocide take place (Power 2002). That is, it seems that had the West made it clear that it would not tolerate gross violations of the Responsibility to Protect, this may well have been sufficient. In Libya in April 2011, as the rebels gained some momentum, Qaddafi suggested a ceasefire to be followed by a negotiation between the rebels and his government. Such a ceasefire could have been reinforced by a threat of renewed NATO airstrikes if the agreement was violated or by positioning UN peace keeping forces. The result it seems would have been no major humanitarian abuses in western Libya, but retention of power by Qaddafi's regime in the eastern parts. However, NATO rejected this offer out of hand, ruling that Qaddafi must go, i.e. forcing a regime change. Whether this expansive approach was justified in this case will be determined by what happens in the future. If it leads to a stable representative government in all of Libya, overthrowing Qaddafi will seem much more justified than if the future entails tribal strife, unstable governance, possibly some kind of a new tyrant and, above all, numerous civilian casualties, as we have seen in liberated Iraq and Afghanistan.

14.2   Criteria for Interventions

The quest for criteria for interventions that can be justified and that can be carried out effectively may start with the Responsibility to Protect. There has been considerable difference of opinion as to what it specifically entails (Evans 2004; Feinstein and Slaughter 2004). Francis Deng and his associates, who were the first to write about "Sovereignty as Responsibility," defined nations in which outside powers should intervene by defining the opposite: nations in which intervention would be impermissible. They determined that these were limited to nations whose governments "… strive to ensure for their people an effective governance that guarantees a just system of law and order, democratic freedoms, respect for fundamental rights, and general welfare" (Deng 1996). With the bar set so low and defined so vaguely, there are few nations that would not be vulnerable to intervention (Holzgrefe and Keohane 2003).

As we have seen, a substantially more limiting criteria were proposed by the Evans-Sahnoun Commission, which was established by the Canadian government as an attempt to resolve a dilemma crystallized by then UN Secretary General Kofi Annan. Annan had posed the question, "If humanitarian intervention is, indeed, an unacceptable assault on sovereignty, how should we respond to a Rwanda, to a Srebrenica- to gross and systematic violations of human rights that affect every precept of our common humanity?" (Annan 2000) The commission, named the International Commission on Intervention and State Sovereignty (ICISS), suggested a resolution that relied on a recharacterization of sovereignty. ICISS pointed to the Charter of the UN as "an example of an international obligation voluntarily accepted by member states," and recommended that a similar conceptualization be applied to sovereignty, such that "sovereignty as responsibility" replaced "sovereignty as control." Recall the ICISS threshold criteria for intervention: "(a) large-scale loss of life, actual or apprehended, with genocidal intent or not, which is the product either of deliberate state action, or state neglect or inability to act, or a failed state situation; or (b) large-scale 'ethnic cleansing,' actual or apprehended, whether carried out by killing, forced expulsion, acts of terror or rape" (International Commission on Intervention and State Sovereignty 2001). Moreover, both the Commission and the High-Level Panel assert that any intervention must be based on exclusively humanitarian intentions, be taken as a last resort, use only the minimum force necessary to complete the mission, and have reasonable prospects of success. That is, to achieve the large-scale saving of lives, not to force regime change and most assuredly not for nation-building.

Setting the bar for interventions along the lines the Commission suggested is supported by the tragic but inescapable fact that the political capital and economic resources needed for advancing human rights on the international level by the use of force are in very short supply. This is evidenced by the observation that many rights are often violated, and no actions are taken by foreign powers (Udombana 2004). Even stopping genocides has been, so far, beyond the international community's abilities, as has stopping the bloodshed in numerous civil and international conflicts still smoldering in several parts of the world. This harsh reality is in sharp contrast to the vision that, following economic development and the toppling of despotic regimes, rights will flourish in one country after another. These great difficulties point to the need to set a high bar for interventions and to the importance of examining which rights should be promoted first and foremost.

A major reason it is morally appropriate to recognize the paramount standing of the right to life is that all other rights are contingent on this one, while the right to life is not contingent on the others.[1] It seems all too simple to state that dead people cannot exercise their rights, yet it bears repeating because the implications of this observation are often ignored: When the right to life is violated because basic security is not provided, all other rights are undermined—but not vice versa.

The supreme standing of the right to life is also supported by the finding that when basic security is provided, the public support for non-security (e.g. civil and political) rights increases, but not the other way around. A review of public opinion polls concerning attitudes towards civil liberties after 9/11 revealed that shortly after the attacks, nearly 70% of Americans were strongly inclined to give up various

[1] For earlier discussion, see Shue (1996).

constitutionally protected rights in order to prevent more attacks. However, as no new attacks occurred on the American homeland and the sense of security returned (as measured by the return of passengers to air travel), support for rights was restored. By 2004–2005, about 70% of Americans were more concerned with protecting rights than with enhancing security (Etzioni 2004, pp. 38–39). Hence, the principal reasons for employing the US and international community's limited intervention capital to save lives, along the lines specified by the commission, should be considered before armed intervention to promote other goals.

14.2.1   A Mental Experiment

To highlight the issue, the following minor mental experiment may serve. Assume that the Taliban in Afghanistan offers the US the following deal: The Taliban will commit itself to preventing Afghanistan from being used as a base for terrorists. Indeed, it offers to chase the remaining al-Qaeda members out of Afghanistan or turn them over to the United States and its allies if caught. In turn, it expects that the coalition forces will allow the Taliban to contend with other Afghan groups, and if it prevails, to govern Afghanistan the way it prefers, namely by imposing *sharia*. The Taliban would close schools for girls; require women to stay home unless accompanied by a husband or relative; force religious observances; eliminate voting rights, free speech, assembly; and so on. (The Taliban further suggests that the US could keep troops on some military bases out of populated areas for years to come so they would be readily available if the Taliban did not live up to its commitments, and the Taliban also understands that it would be severely bombed under such circumstances.

The US would thus face a stark choice between narrowly crafted security goals and the promotion of human rights beyond the right to life. Strong human rights advocates would reject such a deal. If the preceding analysis is valid, the US should accept it, on the grounds that even if many more lives of Americans, of other NATO members, and of Afghans were sacrificed, the Afghan people would still have to work out their own form of government and economy.

14.2.2   Which Means?

To argue that force—armed interventions—should be employed rarely, when the rationale that supports them can clear the high bar outlined above, is not to suggest that other means cannot be employed more liberally in the support of a much more extensive array of human rights.

Regarding normative means, national leaders can often chastise other nations for not respecting human rights and express their approval when such nations improve their human rights record. There are many instances where the lives of dissenters were spared, or they were released from prisons or house arrest, because of drum-beats of criticisms from the international community—without armed interventions. Even general changes in policy have taken place. For instance, since the firestorm of criticisms China received following the Tiananmen Square massacre, China has exercised more restraint in its handling of opposition. Indeed, while China used to maintain that human rights are Western bourgeois values, it now holds that it respects them and is merely delaying the implementation of political rights until socio-economic ones are better advanced. Other Southeast Asian nations—Singapore, for instance—have similarly learned to at least show respect for these rights and have moved to violate them less often. Critics argue that by publically exhorting other nations, one merely insults their sensibilities and stiffens their rejection. Indeed, in some cases private presentations by one national leader to another may be the preferred way to proceed. However, by and large, other nations have shown little reluctance to voice their criticism of the West, and the West should as a rule articulate in normative terms the case not just for the right to life but for all the others.

The imposition of economic sanctions to advance human rights has a much more mixed record. They often result in imposing more suffering on the people than on the regime, as was the case in Saddam's Iraq. Rarely have they brought down a regime, as one notes after a generation of sanctions on Cuba. "Smart" sanctions—those focused on leaders and specific industries—may be more effective, but unless these are very widely supported by other nations, they rarely produce significant concessions (Pape 1997).

The observation that nations can employ non-lethal (normative and economic) means to promote human rights and democracy further supports the thesis that the use of force should be limited to preventing massive abuse of human lives and should not be allowed to morph into coerced regime change, not to mention into futile attempts at nation-building. For as we have seen, such expansive drives often succeed mainly in wrecking the prevailing regime but not in building a stable, representative new one. They cost numerous lives, both of the local population and those of Americans and their allies, and require a very large-scale commitment of resources in an era in which those are particularly short. At the same time, the record suggests that if the goals of armed interventions are limited to preventing massive human abuses, they can be successfully implemented. Hence, rather than giving up on all armed interventions that do not directly serve the vital interests of the nations involved, decoupled humanitarian missions can be justified—even in the era of grand austerity.

References

Annan, K. 2000. *We the peoples: The role of the United Nations in the 21st century.* New York: United Nations.
Beinart, P. 2010. *The Icarus syndrome: A history of American hubris.* New York: HarperCollins.

Bush, G.W. 2000. Second presidential debate. http://www.fas.org/news/usa/2000/usa-001011.htm. Accessed 14 July 2011.

Clinton, H. 2011a. Secretary of State Hillary Rodham Clinton's remarks on receiving the George C. Marshall Foundation award. http://www.marshallfoundation.org/SecretaryClintonremarksJune22011.htm. Accessed 14 July 2011.

———. 2011b. Senator Clinton's remarks at the U.S. Islamic World Forum.

———. 2011c. Secretary Clinton on Libya. at Andrews Air Force Base 27 February.

Colvin, R. 2009. Obama rights record questioned ahead of Nobel prize. *Reuters*.

Cooper, H., and Landler, M. 2009. For Obama, pressure to strike firmer tone. *New York Times*.

Davis, D. 2011. A 21st century Marshall Plan. *Prospect*, July, 12–13.

Deng, F. 1996. *Sovereignty as responsibility: Conflict management in Africa*. Washington, DC: Brookings Institution.

Etzioni, A. 2004. *How patriotic is the Patriot Act?* New York: Routledge.

———. 2007. *Security first: For a muscular, moral foreign policy*. New Haven: Yale University Press.

Evans, G. 2004. *Uneasy bedfellows: 'The responsibility to protect' and Feinstein-Slaughter's 'duty to prevent.'* Commentary presented at the American Society of International Law Conference, Washington, DC.

Feinstein, L., and A.M. Slaughter. 2004. A duty to prevent. *Foreign Affairs* 83 (20): 136–150.

Fukuyama, F. 1992. *End of history and the last man*. New York: Free Press.

Holzgrefe, J.L., and R.O. Keohane. 2003. *Humanitarian intervention: Ethical, legal, and political dilemmas*. Cambridge: Cambridge University Press.

Hubbard, G., Duggan, B. 2011. A Marshall Plan for the Middle East? *The Huffington Post*.

International Commission on Intervention and State Sovereignty. 2001. Responsibility to protect: Report of the international commission on intervention and state sovereignty.

Jones, J. 2011. Comment of General James Jones at Stimson Center Chairman's forum on international security issues.

Jordan, M. 2004. Even in eager Kosovo, nation-building stalls. *The Christian Science Monitor*.

Kerry, J. 2011. Senator John Kerry addresses the Fletcher School graduating class of 2011. *The Fletcher School*.

Kristol, W. 2006. The long war. *The Weekly Standard* 11 (24): 9.

LaFranchi, H. 2011. Why Obama isn't pushing for Yemen president to go: Al Qaeda. *Christian Science Monitor*.

Malinowski, T. 2009. Overly cautious. In *Obama's Soft Approach on Human Rights*, ed. K. Roberts, T. Tang, S. Ellingwood, and F. Zhang.

Merriam-Webster Online Dictionary. 2010. *Democracy*. http://www.merriam-webster.com/dictionary/Democracy. Accessed 14 Jan 2010.

Mosk, M. 2009. Obama too polite in Shanghai for some rights defenders see forum as a key 'missed opportunity.' *Washington Times*.

Obama, B. 2009a. *Inaugural address*. http://www.whitehouse.gov/blog/inaugural-address/. Accessed 10 Jan 2010.

———. 2009b. *Remarks by the president on a new beginning*. http://www.whitehouse.gov/the_press_office/Remarks-by-the-President-at-Cairo- University-6-04-09/. Accessed 10 Jan 2010.

———. 2009c. *Statement by the president on the attempted attack on Christmas Day and recent violence in Iran*. http://www.whitehouse.gov/the-press-office/statement-president-attempted-attack-christmas-day-and-recent-violence-iran. Accessed 10 Jan 2010.

———. 2009d. *The president's opening remarks on Iran*. http://www.whitehouse.gov/blog/The-Presidents-Opening-Remarks-on-Iran-with- Persian-Translation/. Accessed 10 Jan 2010.

———. 2011a. President Obama on Libya. *The White House*.

———. 2011b. *Remarks by the president on the way forward in Afghanistan*. http://www.whitehouse.gov/the-press-office/2011/06/22/remarks-president-way-forward-afghanistan. Accessed 13 Jul 2011.

Pape, R. 1997. Why economic sanctions do not work. *International Security* 22 (2): 90–136.

Pei, M., Kasper, S. 2003. *Lessons from the past: The American record on nation-building.* Carnegie Endowment Policy Brief No. 24.

Power, S. 2002. *A problem from hell: America and the age of genocide.* New York: Basic Books.

Shue, H. 1996. *Basic rights: Subsistence, affluence, and U.S. foreign policy.* Princeton: Princeton University Press.

Stephens, B. 2009. Does Obama believe in human rights? *Wall Street Journal.*

Tanenhaus, S. 2003. The world: From Vietnam to Iraq; The rise and fall and rise of the domino theory. *New York Times.*

Udombana, N.J. 2004. When neutrality is a sin: The Darfur crisis and the crisis of humanitarian intervention in Sudan. *Human Rights Quarterly* 27 (4): 1149–1199.

Wasserstrom, J. M. 2009. Oratory for lawyers. In *Obama's soft approach on human rights,* ed. K. Roberts, T. Tang, S. Ellingwood, and F. Zhang.

Part VI
Science and Technology

Chapter 15
Incorporating Ethics into Artificial Intelligence (with Oren Etzioni)

Driverless cars, which have already travelled several million miles,[1] are equipped with artificial intelligence (AI) that, according to reports, enable these cars to make autonomous decisions. These decisions have moral and social implications, especially because cars may cause considerable harm. Indeed, in May of 2016, a Tesla car traveling in autopilot mode crashed, and the passenger was killed (Levin and Woolf 2016). Wallach and Allen (2009, p. 3) are among those who hold that the world is on the verge of "the creation of robots whose independence from direct human oversight and whose potential impact on human well-being is the stuff of science fiction." Hence, the question arises: how is one to ensure that the decisions of these cars will be rendered ethically? The same question stands for other autonomous machines: weapons that choose their own targets; robotic surgeons; robots that provide child, elder, and health care; as well as quite a few others.

Several scholars have addressed this new challenge by suggesting that driverless cars (and other autonomous machines) be programmed to be able to render moral decisions on their own. (Like many other articles, this chapter treats the terms *ethical* and *moral* as synonyms.) This chapter attempts to show that such a course is, at best, enormously taxing; the notion that autonomous machines can be made to render ethical decisions is based on a conflation of several misconceptions, including what criteria are required of a moral agent, and about the fundamental nature of human decision-making. This line of criticism, in turn, leads to a suggestion that we require a much more 'traditional' (i.e. in line with the world before machines became autonomous) solution to the ethical challenges posed by these machines.

Specifically, this chapter (a) provides a brief overview of the reasons that scholars hold that these machines will be able to make ethical decisions, and enumerates the very considerable difficulties this approach faces. (b) It shows that the way the

---

This chapter draws on "Incorporating Ethics into Artificial Intelligence" in *The Journal of Ethics*, 21 (4), (2017): 403–418.

[1] As of July 2016 Google alone reports that its driverless cars have logged 1.5 million miles. See https://www.google.com/selfdrivingcar/

A. Etzioni, *Happiness is the Wrong Metric*, Library of Public Policy and Public Administration 11, https://doi.org/10.1007/978-3-319-69623-2_15

term "autonomous" is commonly applied to these machines is misleading, and that it leads to invalid conclusions about the kinds of AI used in these machines. The chapter's most important claim is that (c) a very significant part of the challenge posed by these AI-equipped machines can be addressed by two rather different forms of ethical guidance: law enforcement and personal choices, both used by human beings for millennia. Ergo, there is little need to teach machines ethics even if this could be done in the first place. (d) The chapter then points out that it is a grievous error to draw on extreme outlier scenarios as a basis for conceptualizing the issues at hand, and that one reaches radically different conclusions once the extreme nature of these examples (associated with the Trolley Problem) is recognized.

15.1 Smart Machines, Harm, and Ethical Self-Guidance

15.1.1 Reasons Smart Machines Are Said to Need Ethics

Driverless cars, viewed as the archetypal autonomous machines, are learning machines. They are programmed to collect information, process it, draw conclusions, and change their behavior accordingly, without human intervention or guidance. Thus, such a car may set out with a program that includes an instruction not to exceed the speed limit, only to learn that other cars exceed these limits and conclude that it can and should speed too.

Given that vehicles may cause harm, scholars argue that driverless cars need to be able to differentiate between "wrong" and "right" decisions. In other words, computers should be made into or become "explicit moral reasoners" (Wallach and Allen 2009, p. 6). Susan Leigh Anderson and Michael Anderson (2011, p. 1) argue, "Ideally, we would like to be able to trust autonomous machines to make correct ethical decisions on their own, and this requires that we create an ethic for machines." Many AI researchers seem to hold that if these machines can make thousands of information-driven, cognitive decisions on their own—when to slow down, when to stop, when to yield, and so on—they should also be able to make ethical decisions. This assumption is particularly plausible to those who see no fundamental difference between deliberating about factual matters and moral issues, because they view both as mental processes driven by reason.[2] As John Stuart Mill (1859/2008) famously wrote, "our moral faculty is a branch of our reason."

Much attention has been paid to the need for these cars (and other AI-equipped, so-called "smart" machines) to choose between two harms in cases of unavoidable harm. These discussions often begin with an adaptation of the Trolley Problem, wherein the car is unable to brake in time and is forced to choose between continu-

---

[2] Granted, 'is' statements and 'ought' statements bleed into each other, but they still differ significantly. Compare a statement against the death penalty that pointed out that data show it does not deter killers, and one that holds that the state should never deliberately take a person's life. See e.g. McDermott (2011).

ing in its lane and hitting a pedestrian, or swerving into oncoming traffic in an opposite lane (Bonnefon et al. 2016). Another variant is that of a child running across the road just before the entrance to a one-lane tunnel, forcing the car to choose between continuing and hitting the child or swerving into the side of the tunnel and killing the passenger (Millar 2014).

15.1.2 Two Ways to Enable 'Smart' Cars to Render Ethical Decisions

Two overarching approaches have been suggested as a means of enabling driverless cars and other smart machines to render moral choices on their own: top-down and bottom-up. In the top-down approach, ethical principles are programmed into the car's guidance system. These could be Asimov's Three Laws of Robotics, the Ten Commandments, or other religious precepts—or a general moral philosophy, such as Kant's categorical imperative, utilitarianism, or another form of consequentialism. The main point is that rather than a programmer instructing the car to proceed under specific conditions in the most ethical way, the car will be able to make such ethical choices based on the moral philosophy that it was granted or acquired (Wallach and Allen 2009, p. 16).

Critics of the top-down approach (as well as some proponents) recognize the inherent difficulties in adhering to any particular moral philosophy, given that any one of them will, at some point or another, lead to actions and outcomes that some will find morally unacceptable. To take but two familiar examples: Benjamin Constant points out that the categorical imperative would obligate someone to tell a murderer the location of his prey, because of the prohibition on lying under any circumstances (Constant 1797). As for consequentialism, if a car's instruction is to minimize the amount of damage it causes in a situation where damage is inevitable, it may calculate that it would be preferable to crash into the less expensive of two cars in the adjacent lanes, which would raise obvious concerns about discrimination (Goodall 2014).

True, these (and other) moral philosophies have developed variants that attempt to address such 'flaws.' Still, among and within these schools of ethics, there are significant debates that highlight the difficulties faced in drawing on particular philosophies to serve as moral guidance systems for machines. For instance, there is well-known and significant disagreement over whether and how "utility" can be quantified, with Bentham and Mill disagreeing over whether there are different levels of utility (Mill's "higher" and "lower" pleasures). Consequentialists continue to face these challenges; for example, estimating long-term consequences and determining for whom consequences should be taken into account. Most of the Trolley Problem thought experiments assume that a body is a body, and hence killing five is obviously worse than one. However, people do not attach the same value to terminally ill senior citizens as to children in kindergarten, or to Mother Teresa as to a convicted felon.

There is no need to rehash here the significant back and forth among various ethical schools. It suffices to suggest that, given these differences, it is very difficult to program a machine that is able to render moral decisions on its own, whether using one or a combination of these moral philosophies. But one might ask, "If humans can do it, why not smart machines?" In response, one first notes that humans are able to cope with nuance, deal with fuzzy decisions while computer programmers find such decisions particularly taxing. Moreover, while one can argue that individuals make moral choices on the basis of this or that philosophy, actually humans first acquire moral values from those who raise them, and then modify these values as they are exposed to various inputs from new groups, cultures, and subcultures, gradually developing their own personal moral mix. Moreover, these values are influenced by particular societal principles that are not confined to any one moral philosophy. In short, the top-down approach is highly implausible.

In the second approach to machine ethics, the bottom-up approach, machines are expected to learn how to render ethical decisions through observation of human behavior in actual situations, without being taught any formal rules or being equipped with any particular moral philosophy. This approach has been applied to non-ethical aspects of driverless cars' learning. For example, an early autonomous vehicle created by researchers at Carnegie Mellon University was able to navigate on the highway after 2–3 min of training from a human driver; its capacity for generalization allowed it to drive on four-lane roads, even though it was only trained on one- or two-lane roads (Batavia et al. 1996). Machine learning has also been used by several researchers to improve a car's pedestrian detection ability (See Hsu 2016; Harris 2015). And a team from NVIDIA Corporation recently demonstrated a driverless car that used "end-to-end" machine learning, which was able to drive on its own after observing only 72 h of human driving data (Bojarski et al. 2016).

However, to view these as precedents for learning ethical conduct is to presume that there is no significant difference between learning to respond differently to green, red, and yellow traffic lights and learning to understand and appreciate the imperative to take special care not to hit a bicyclist traveling in the same lane as the car, let alone not to harass or deliberately hit the cyclist out of road rage (McDermott 2011). But this parallel between cognitive and ethical decision-making is far from self-evident. Some AI mavens believe that cars could learn ethics like children do, gradually improving their ability to engage in moral reasoning, along the Kohlberg stages. We shall see that cars may be able to follow specific moral positions, but not necessarily to engage in moral reasoning.

Moreover, the kinds of moral questions the cars are asked to address—who to kill or injure in a situation where a crash is inevitable—are actually very rare; according to data from the US Department of Transportation, there were only 77 injuries and 1.09 fatalities per 100 million miles driven in 2013 (National Highway Traffic Safety Administration 2013). And each such challenging situation is different from the next: sometimes it is a kitten that causes the accident, sometimes a school bus, and so on. A driverless car would have to follow a person for several lifetimes to learn ethics in this way. It has hence been suggested that driverless cars could learn from the ethical decisions of millions of human drivers, through some kind of aggregation system, as a sort of group think or drawing on the wisdom of the crowds. Note, however, that this may well lead cars to acquire some rather unethical preferences, as it is far from clear that the majority of drivers would set a standard worthy of emulation by the new autonomous cars. If they learn what many people do, smart cars may well speed, tailgate, and engage in road rage. One must also note that people may draw on automatic responses when faced with the kind of choices posed by the Trolley Problem rather than on ethical deliberations and decision-making. That is, observing people will not teach these machines what is ethical—but what is common.

This concern is supported by an experiment conducted by Jean-François Bonnefon et al. (2016), who tested participants' attitudes about whether driverless cars should make utilitarian moral decisions, even when that would mean sacrificing the passenger's life in order to save a greater number of pedestrians. They found that most respondents want driverless cars to make utilitarian decisions, but they themselves desire cars that will prioritize their own well-being at the cost of others. Philosopher Patrick Lin put it that, "No one wants a car that looks after the greater good. They want a car that looks after them" (Metz 2016). This is hardly a way for Google, Tesla, or any other car manufacturer to program ethical cars. They'd best not heed the masses' voice.

In short, both the top-down and the bottom-up approaches face very serious difficulties. These difficulties are not of a mechanical sort, but concern the inner structures of ethical philosophies used by humans. Even so, these difficulties pale in comparison to those posed by the question of whether or not smart machines can be turned into moral agents in the first place.

15.1.3 Can Smart Machines Be Made into Moral Agents?

Both the top-down and bottom-up approaches to machine ethics presume that machines can be made into or become moral agents. Moral agency is understood to be the ability to make decisions based on some conception of morality, and to act in a manner that can be judged as either "right" or "wrong." (If a printer malfunctions, for example, one does not consider it to have done something "wrong.") To be a moral agent requires a specific set of attributes. Drawing on the work of Eugene Hargrove (1992) and of Luciano Floridi and J.W. Sanders (2004), we suggest that at least the following attributes are essential: (a) Self-consciousness. If the agent is not aware of itself in any given situation, and of the alternative courses that might be followed, then no moral decisions can be rendered. (b) The agent must be aware that she can affect the situation. (c) The agent must be able to understand the moral principles to be employed in arriving at a particular moral choice. (d) The agent must have a motive to act morally. This involves having passions, as otherwise moral preferences are merely intellectual preferences with nothing to fuel the moral action.[3] (e) Some scholars add that a will or intention is required (see Coeckelbergh 2009; Himma 2009).

One notes that autonomous machines do not have the attributes required for them to be able to act as moral agents. We are hardly the first or the only ones to make this crucial observation. Domingos (2015, p. 283) writes "Unlike humans, computers don't have a will of their own. They're products of engineering, not evolution. Even an infinitely powerful computer would still be only an extension of our will." Deborah Johnson (2006) argues that while computer systems can in fact have intentionality and thus should not be dismissed from the realm of morality, because they do not possess mental states, they cannot be considered moral agents. Patrick Chisan Hew (2014) holds that a central issue in establishing moral agency is responsibility, but any machine will have its rules for behavior supplied externally by humans, thus denying it moral agency.

Moreover, intelligence and intentionality may go together in humans, but cars can only have the first, not the second. Pedro Domingos (2015) observes:

> It's natural to worry about intelligent machines taking over because the only intelligent entities we know are humans and other animals, and they definitely have a will of their own. But there is no necessary connection between intelligence and autonomous will; or rather intelligence and will may not inhabit the same body, provided there is a line of control between them.

Some scholars tried to deal with this challenge by arguing that although cars cannot be made into "full ethical agents," they can be "ethical impact agents" or "implicit ethical agents" (Moor 2011). The first is defined as agents that have a moral impact, even if unintended and not a result of any moral deliberation. By this definition, falling rocks, runaway fires, and hurricanes are ethical impact agents. The second is defined as agents that are designed with some sort of virtue in mind; for example, ATM machines that protect privacy. But of course, the ATM's virtues are fully implanted by humans. These two definitions seem to stretch exceedingly the concept of moral agency because they do not entail machines that are engaging in moral deliberations and acting on their conclusions.

Other valiant efforts to support machine ethics leads Susan Leigh Anderson (2011) to argue that cars' lack of emotions (and therefore empathy) would not necessarily be a weakness, as humans often get "carried away" by their emotions and thus behave immorally or unethically. Others go much further. Joseph Emilie Nadeau (2006) contends that an action can only be said to have been taken freely if it is the product of a strictly logical, fully reasoned decision-making process. Humans lack this capacity, but robots will be explicitly programmed this way, and thus could be the first truly moral agents. Blay Whitby (2011) wonders, "Is humanity ready or willing to accept machines as moral advisors?" Still others believe that emotions implanted into machines could allow them to become moral agents, but these thinkers are concerned that such a move would mean smart machines would be capable

---

[3] John-Stewart Gordon (2016) paraphrases this Aristotelian viewpoint as follows: "The fine or the noble and the just require the virtuous person to do or refrain from doing certain things, for example, not to murder (in particular, not to kill one's parents), not to commit adultery, and not to commit theft."

of suffering, thus increasing the cumulative amount of suffering in the world (Scheutz 2012). To crown it all, David J. Calverley (2011) holds that machines could be granted legal rights in the same way that corporations and other non-human entities currently are. The government of South Korea is developing a Robot Ethics Charter which aims to protect humans from abuse by robots—and vice versa (BBC 2007).x

As we see it, machines are indeed increasingly intelligent, but do not currently have (nor will they gain, at least in the foreseeable future) the attributes essential for becoming moral agents. Calls to either implant in these machines a moral philosophy that enables specific moral decisions (the top-down approach) or to let them learn from humans which ethics to follow (the bottom-up approach) presume that machines are or can be made into moral agents. However, machines are not moral agents and there is no indication that they can be made into such agents.

15.2   "Autonomous Machines," A Highly Misleading Term

15.2.1   How Autonomous Are Smart Machines?

In many discussions of the ethical challenges posed by driverless cars, and smart machines generally, they are referred to as "autonomous." To begin with, one must recall that not every scholar is willing to take it for granted that even human beings act autonomously. Some hold that everything that happens is caused by sufficient antecedent conditions which make it impossible for said thing to happen differently (or to not happen); such causal determinism renders it impossible to assign moral responsibility (see for example van Inwagen 2003; Harris 2011). There is no need here to repeat the arguments against this position, and it suffices to note that we file with those who take it for granted that human beings have some measure of free will, though much of their lives may indeed be determined by forces beyond their understanding and control (Frankfurt 1969).

However, it does not follow that the same holds for machines, however smart they are. Indeed, a colleague who read a previous draft of this chapter argued that it only *seems* like smart machines make decisions on their own—in actuality, changes in how these machines conduct themselves merely reflect external forces. One could say, he pointed out, that a missile diverted from its original course by a strong gush of wind "decided" to change direction, but this would be merely a misperception, an illusion.

As we see it, autonomy is a variable that exists along a continuum. Some tools have no autonomy; one can fully account for their behavior by forces external to them. A hammer hitting a nail has no autonomy even when it misses because one can show that the miss was due to the inexperience of the person using it, poor eyesight, or some other such external factor. A rudimentary GPS system may be said to have a very small measure of autonomy, because when asked the best way to get from point a to point b, it compares several options and recommends one, but its recommendation is based on a human-made algorithm that calculates the shortest route, or that which will take the least amount of time to travel, or some other such criteria. A significant amount of autonomy occurs when the machine is given a large number of guidelines, some that conflict with each other, and is ordered to draw on information it acquires as it proceeds, to draw conclusions on its own—such as a more advanced GPS system, which identifies upcoming traffic, or an accident, and reroutes accordingly. Machines equipped with AI are held to be able to act much more autonomously than those not so equipped.

Monica Rozenfield (2016) writes:

Deep learning is a relatively new form of artificial intelligence that gives an old technology—a neural network—a twist made possible by big data, supercomputing, and advanced algorithms. Data lines possessed by each neuron of the network communicate with one another.

It would be impossible to write code for an unlimited number of situations. And without correct code, a machine would not know what to do. With deep learning, however, the system is able to figure things out on its own. The technique lets the network form neural relationships most relevant to each new situation.

A group of computer scientists from Carnegie Mellon University notes that "Machine-learning algorithms increasingly make decisions about credit, medical diagnoses, personalized recommendations, advertising and job opportunities, among other things, but exactly how usually remains a mystery" (Spice 2016).

Some believe that machines can command full autonomy. For instance, weapon systems that choose their own targets, without human intervention, excluding even the ability to abort the mission. In fact, even these machines are limited to the missions set for them by a human, and they are only 'free' to choose their targets because a human programmed them that way. Their autonomy is second hand. Military ethicist George Lucas Jr. (2013) notes that debates about machine ethics are often obfuscated by the confusion of machine autonomy with moral autonomy; the Roomba vacuum cleaner and Patriot missile are both autonomous in the sense that they perform their missions, adapting and responding to unforeseen circumstances with minimal human oversight, but not in the sense that they can change or abort their mission if they have moral objections. Domingos (2015, p. 283) writes:

They can vary what they do, even come up with surprising plans, but only in service of the goals we set for them. A robot whose programmed goal is "make a good dinner" may decide to cook a steak, a bouillabaisse, or even a delicious new dish of its own creation, but it can't decide to murder its owner any more than a car can decide to fly away.

Brad Templeton put it well when he stated that a robot would be autonomous the day it is instructed to go to work and it instead goes to the beach (Markoff 2015, p. 333).

For the sake of the following discussion, we shall assume that smart machines have a significantly greater capability of rendering their own cognitive choices than old fashioned ones; e.g. deciding on their own how much to slow down when the roads are slick without a programmed instruction that covers such a condition. Given this measure of autonomous volition, these cars are potentially more likely to be able to choose to cause harm, and therefore require ethical guidance, all the while not necessarily having an ability to make ethical choices autonomously, as we shall see. Machines are ultimately tools of the human beings who design and manufacture them. If humans fail to include sufficient controls in the construction of machines with AI, then these humans must bear the responsibility of any ill effects— just as if an owner of a poorly trained bulldog cuts his leash, he is responsible for any havoc then wreaked.

15.2.2 When Smart Machines Stray

So far we have referred to smart machines as many AI scholars do, as autonomous machines. However, "autonomous" is a highly loaded term because in liberal democracies it is associated with liberty, self-government, and individual rights. To violate someone's autonomy is considered a serious ethical offense (although one acknowledges that there are some extenuating circumstances). Indeed, bioethicists consider autonomy as a leading principle: physicians and other health care personnel should first and foremost heed the preference of the patient. However, cars and other machines are not emotional beings that experience pain, but unfeeling tools made to serve humans. *There is nothing morally objectionable about overriding their choices, or making them toe the line.* One does not violate their dignity by forcing them to make choices within the boundaries set by their programmers. While we would be horrified if one rewired the brain of an autonomous person, there is no ethical reason to object to reprogramming a smart machine that is causing harm to human beings.

A basic change in the way these machines are conceptualized serves to highlight our point: if a car that decided on its own to speed or tailgate was considered a rule-breaking offender or a deviant (i.e. an agent that deviated from the prevailing norms), one would ask how to reprogram that car in order for it to "behave" better. One would not ask—as one does about an autonomous person—how to help that car acquire the moral values that would allow it to make ethical decisions. (How machines can be reined in is discussed below.) To push the point: human beings— even if they have a highly developed sense of right and wrong and score high on the various attributes that make them moral agents—occasionally misbehave. And when they do, society tries to draw out their good nature and improve their character by moral suasion and reeducation—but often, society will also set new limits on them (curfew for teenagers, jail for repeat drug offenders). There seems no reason to treat cars any differently. Indeed, since a malfunctioning smart car is not "autonomous" in the way people are, there appear to be no moral injunctions against implementing extensive constraints on a smart car's behavior. Quite simply, the car is a malfunctioning tool that should be dealt with accordingly.

15.2.3 Partners, Not Free Standing Agents

Another major source of the misconception that seems to underlie much of the discussion is to be found in public discussions of AI, even among academics: The assumption that there is essentially one kind of program that makes machines much more effective and efficient ('smarter')—a guidance system that draws on artificial intelligence. Actually, there are two different kinds of AI. The first involves software that seeks to reason and form cognitive decisions the way people do (if not better), and thus aspires to be able to replace humans. It seeks to reproduce in the digital realm the processes in which human brains engage when they deliberate and render decisions. The famous Turing test deals with this kind of AI; it deems that a program qualifies as "intelligent" if its reactions are indistinguishable from that of a person. One could call this kind of AI, *AI minds*.

The other kind of AI merely seeks to provide smart assistance to human actors; call it, *AI partners*. This kind of AI only requires that the machines be better at rendering decisions in some matters than humans, and that they do so effectively within parameters set by humans or under their full supervision. For instance, AI caregivers engage in childcare in conjunction with parents, taking care of the children for short periods of time, or while parents are working nearby within the home (Sharkey and Sharkey 2010, 2012).

Those who seek to call attention to the key difference under discussion have used a wide variety of other terms. Some refer to AI minds as "strong AI" (Encyclopaedia Britannica 2016). AI partners have been called Intelligence Augmentation (IA) (Markoff 2015), "intelligence amplification," "cognitive augmentation," or "machine augmented intelligence" (DMello 2015). (John Markoff dedicates much of his book *Machines of Loving Grace: The Quest for Common Ground Between Humans and Robots* to the difference between these two camps, their major figures, and the relations between them.) Many AI mavens hold that the reason they pay little attention to the difference between the two AIs is that the work they do applies equally to both kinds of AI. However, often—at least in public discourse—the difference is significant. For instance, the threat that AI will make machines so smart that they could dominate humans[4] applies mainly to AI minds but not AI partners.

In terms of cars, Google is developing a completely driverless car, going so far as to remove the steering wheel and brake pedals from its recent models; this is an example of AI minds. Tesla merely seeks (at least initially) to provide human drivers with AI features that make driving safer. Passengers are warned that even when the car is in autopilot mode, they must keep their hands on the wheel at all times, and be an alert partner driver. True, as AI partners become more advanced, the difference between the two kinds of AI could shrink and one day disappear. For now the opposite problem prevails: namely, that AI partners with rather limited capabilities are expected to act (or evoke fears) as if they were AI minds.

All of this is pertinent because if smart machines are going to have minds, replace humans, and act truly on their own—and if humans are to be removed from the loop (e.g. in killing machines that cannot be recalled or retargeted once they are launched)—then smart machines will indeed have to be able to render moral decisions on their own. As their volition increases, smart machines will have to be treated as if they were moral agents and assume at least some responsibility for their

---

[4]This is, of course, a popular theme in science fiction, but for a serious treatment of the threat (Joy 2000).

acts. One could no longer consider only the programmers, manufacturers, and owners (from here on, the term also refers to users) as the moral agents. Under this condition, the question of who or what to ticket when a driverless car speeds becomes an acute one.

However, there seem to be very strong reasons to treat smart machines as partners, rather than as commanding a mind that allows them to function on their own. A major reason is that while even the smartest machine is very good at carrying out some functions that humans used to perform (e.g. memorizing), it remains very poor at others (e.g. caring about those they serve and others). Thus, elder care robots are good at reminding patients to take their medications, but not at comforting them when they grieve or feel fear.

In particular, at least for the foreseeable future, a division of labor between smart machines and their human partners calls for the latter to act as the moral agent. Human beings have the basic attributes needed for moral agency, attributes that smart machines do not have and which are very difficult to implant into any machine. The chapter turns next to examine how humans can provide moral guidance to smart machines, despite the fact that they are learning machines and hence have a strong tendency to stray from the instructions originally programmed into them.

15.3 The Main Ethical Implementing Factors: Legal and Personal

How can driverless cars and other such machines follow the ethical preferences of humans if these machines are not provided a capacity to make ethical decisions on their own? In answering this question, one must first consider the two different ways that moral and social values are implemented in the human world; then, how these values might be introduced into the realm of the new machines.

The primary ways moral and social values are implemented in society are through legal enforcement and personal choices (although these choices are socially fostered). Many moral and social values are embodied in laws and regulations; those who do not heed these values are physically prevented from continuing (e.g. their cars are towed if they park illegally), penalized (e.g. issued tickets), or jailed (e.g. drunken drivers). Other values are fostered through informal social controls. Those who violate these values are shamed or chastised away, while those who abide by them are commended and appreciated. Stopping to help stranded motorists is a case in point. Thus, while Good Samaritan acts are required by law in France, in the US they are merely encouraged. Other personal choices include whether one buys environmentally-friendly gasoline or the cheapest available; purchases cars that pollute less than others; stops for hitchhikers; and allows friends to use one's car.

The distinction between the two modes of implementing social and moral values—between legal enforcement and informal social controls—is critical because the *many values* that are implemented through laws enacted by legislatures, interpreted by courts, and enforced by the state—*are in principle not subject to individual deliberations and choice!* They are subject to communal deliberation and decisions. Society does not leave it to each individual to decide if he or she holds that it is morally appropriate not to speed nor tailgate, pass only on the left (usually), refrain from running though stoplights, pollute, throw trash out of the window, wear a seat belt, leave the scene of a crash, drive intoxicated, or drive under the legal age, among many other decisions. Hence, the notion that smart machines need to be able to render moral decisions does not take into account that in these many important matters, *what cars ought to do is not up to them any more than it is up to their owners*. (True, people may judge the state-imposed rules as unethical and engage in civil disobedience. We take it for granted that, for the time being, we need not concern ourselves with whether cars should or should not be programmed to be able to rebel.) In contrast, there are relatively few important ethical decisions not enshrined in law and are left to individuals to make, at least when one deals with cars, robotic surgeons, and killing machines.

By treating all these choices as "ethical" in nature (which they are), but disregarding the many facets of human behavior and decision-making that are not subject to individual deliberation and decision, the advocates of machine ethics see a much greater realm of decision-making for the AI-equipped machine than actually exists. Driverless cars will have to obey the law like all other cars and there is no need for them to be able to deliberate if they consider it ethical to speed, pollute, and so on. True, these laws may be adapted to take into account the special features of these cars; e.g. allowing them to proceed at a higher speed than other cars, in their own lane. Still, driverless cars will need to obey the laws, collectively agreed upon, like all other cars, or else be taken off the road. Their owners, programmers, and manufacturers will need to be held liable for any harm done.

A leading AI researcher pointed out that some of these legal measures are not as sharply edged as those listed above, comparing the yield sign to the stop sign. The ambiguity, he argued, leaves room and need for ethical judgments—and hence for cars to be able to make ethical judgments even in cases where there is legal prescription. There is no denying that the law does not define yield signs as precisely as stop signs (which makes programming the car more difficult). Moreover, as Noel Goodall points out, people have a sense of judgment as to when to abide by the spirit of the law rather than its letter, e.g. when to cross a double yellow line when they face an object in their lane and the adjacent one is empty (Goodall 2016). Driverless cars might barrel ahead or else stop suddenly. However, given that computers have been programmed to play chess—which entails taking into account moves by others and responding to these moves—it seems reasonable that cars can be programmed to deal with issues much more complex than those posed by yield signs and other ambiguities in the law. Or, they may be programmed to deal with such situations with less flexibility than humans; say, always wait until other cars are at least five car lengths away (at a given speed) and more—if the speed is higher.

There remain those ethical decisions that are not prescribed by law and which thus must be rendered by an individual or—their car. We already have seen that seeking to program these cars to be able to make these decisions on their own is, at best, a very difficult task. What can be done? One answer is for individuals to instruct the car they own or use to follow their value preferences. To a limited extent, this can be achieved through setting options. For instance, Tesla enables owners to set the distance their car maintains from the car in front of it (Gibbs 2015). However, data show that people tend not to engage in such decision-making if they must make more than a few choices. Numerous studies of human behavior, ranging from retirement contributions (see Beshears et al. 2009; Benartzi and Thaler 2013) to organ donations (Johnson and Goldstein 2003, pp. 1338–9) to consumer technology (Shah and Sandvig 2008) reveal that the majority of people will simply choose the default setting, even if the options available to them are straightforward and binary (e.g. opt-in versus opt-out). This is not to suggest that customization should be excluded but to acknowledge that it cannot take care of most of the personal choices that must be made.

To proceed, we suggest that enhanced moral guidance to smart machines should draw on a new AI program that will "read" the owner's moral preferences and then instruct these machines to heed them. We call it an *ethics bot*. An ethics bot is an AI program that analyzes many thousands of items of information (not only information publicly available on the internet but also information gleaned from a person's own computers) about the acts of a particular individual in order to determine that person's moral preferences. *Essentially, what ethics bots do for moral choices is rather similar to what many AI programs do for ferreting out consumer preferences and targeting advertising to them accordingly, except that in this case, the AI program is used to guide instruments that are owned and operated by the person, in line with their values,* rather than by those of some marketing company or political campaign seeking to advance their own goals. For instance, an ethics bot may conclude that a person places high value on environmental protection if it finds that said person purchases recycled paper, drives a Prius, contributes to the Sierra Club, prefers local food, and never buys Styrofoam cups. It would then instruct that person's driverless car to refuel using only environmentally friendly gas, to turn on the air conditioning only if the temperature is high, and to turn off the engine at stops. Note that this program does not seek to teach the car an ethical system that will allow it (and other smart machines) to deliberate and then form their own moral conclusions. Rather, it extracts specific ethical preferences from an owner and subsequently applies these preferences to the operations of the owner's machine.

To illustrate: Nest constructed a very simple ethics bot, which has already been used by more than a million people. Nest built a smart thermostat which first "observes" the behavior of the people in their households for a week, noting their preferences on how cool or warm they want their home to be. The smart thermostat then uses a motion-detecting sensor to determine whether anyone is at home. When the house is empty, the smart thermostat enters into a high energy saving mode; when people are at home, the thermostat adjusts the temperature to fit their preferences. This thermostat clearly meets the two requirements of an ethics bot, albeit a very simple one: it assesses people's preferences and imposes them on the controls of the heating and cooling system. One may ask what this has to do with social and moral values. This thermostat enables people with differing values to have the temperature settings they prefer—to be either more environmentally conscious or less so (Lohr 2015).

A more advanced ethics bot could be used to monitor the behavior of smart machines and rein them in if need be. For instance, we noted that a smart car might originally be instructed not to exceed speed limits, but being a learning machine, stray from these instructions when it imitates other cars that do exceed the speed limit. An ethics bot would monitor the performance of the car, and if the car learned to speed, the bot would reset the car's speed controls, alert its owner, and if necessary, "patch" the car's program. That is, instead of treating the AI world as if it were one unitary field, one should view AI along the same lines as the rest of the world, which is managed in two (or more) layers. Workers have supervisors, teachers have principals, and businesses have auditors as a second layer. This serves to ensure that the performance of the first layer stays within the boundaries of whatever program is required by the mission or undertaking to be carried out, including its ethical standards. (In the human world one recognizes that these supervisors themselves may stray or act unethically, and thus require additional layers of guidance or counterbalancing forces.)

The same structure is now needed for AI: the ever-growing number of smart instruments needs a second line of AI programs to act as supervisors, auditors, accountants—as ethics bots—of the first line AI programs to keep them from straying (See Etzioni and Etzioni 2016a, b).

One may say that ethics bots are very much like the bottom-up approach we viewed as visionary. However, the ethics bot approach does not require that the machines learn to adopt any kind of ethics or have any of the attributes of moral agents. The ethics bot simply takes the moral positions of the human owner and instills them in the machine. One may wonder, what if these preferences are harmful? Say the ethics bot orders the car to speed in a school zone because that is what the owner would do. This question and similar ones do not take into account the major point we cannot stress enough: that the ethical decisions left to the individual are only those which the society ruled—rightly or wrongly—are not truly harmful, and hence remain without regulation or attending legislation.

We have seen so far that implanting or teaching machines ethics is at best a very taxing undertaking. We pointed out that many of the ethical decisions that smart machines are said to have to make need not and should not be made by them because they are entrenched in laws and regulations. These choices are made for the machines by the community, using legislatures and courts. Many of the remaining ethical decisions can be made by ethics bots, which align the cars' 'conduct' with the moral preferences of the owners. Granted, neither the law nor ethics bots can cover extreme outlier situations. These are discussed next.

Legally enforced   Personal choices

15.4   The Outlier Fallacy

A surprisingly great amount of attention has been paid to the applications of Trolley narratives to driverless cars. The media frequently uses these tales as a way to frame the discussion of the issues at hand, as do a fair number of scholars. The Trolley narratives are not without merits. Like other mental experiments, they make for an effective dialogue starter, and they can be used as an effective didactic tool, for instance to illustrate the difference between consequentialism and deontology. However, such tales are particularly counterproductive as a model for decision-making by smart machines and their human partners. The Trolley tales are extremely contrived. They typically leave the actor with only two options; neither of these options nor any of the other conditions can be modified, making the outcome of each option knowable with 100% accuracy. For example, the choice is framed as either killing a child or causing a devastating pile up. To further simplify the scenario, it assumes that killing two people is "obviously" worse than one, disregarding that most people value different people's lives very differently; compare a 95-year-old person with terminal cancer to a 25-year-old war veteran, or to a child, for example. James O'Connor (2012) adds significantly:

> What is wrong with trolley theorizing is that by design it implicitly, but nonetheless with unmistakable dogmatism, stipulates that the rescuer is not in a position, or does not have the disposition, to really help, only to act by selecting one or other of a Spartan range of choices, all of them morally repugnant, that the trolley philosopher has pre-programmed into the scenario. The trolley method, by this token, is premised on a highly impoverished view of human nature.

Barbara Fried (2012) suggests that the "intellectual hegemony" of trolley-ology has encouraged some philosophers to focus more on "an oddball set of cases at the margins" than on the majority of real-life cases where the risk of accidental harm to others actually occurs.

An important adage in legal scholarship is that "hard cases make bad law;" cases that attract attention because of particularly extreme circumstances tend to result in laws or decisions that address the exception but make for poor rules. The same holds for ethics. Thus, the "Ticking Time Bomb" scenario is used to argue that utilitarian ethics justifies torture (Luban 2005). And, just because someone may prostitute themselves if promised that in exchange their spouse's life will be spared, that does not mean that everyone has a price, or that everyone is willing to prostitute themselves.

To reiterate, most of the time, smart machines can be kept in line through legal means. In other situations, they will abide by their owners' ethical preferences (both assisted by second order, supervisory AI programs). Granted, these human guidance modalities will leave "uncovered" the once-in-a-million-miles situations (each unique and often unpredictable). Indeed, one must assume that such events will be even less likely for smart cars because they can respond much more quickly than humans, and thus, for instance, determine if there is enough space between the child and the cars in the adjacent lane to squeeze by. If instead, one made the cars egoistical (always acting to maximize the safety of the passenger), society is sure to condemn those who make them and drive them, if not ban them altogether. If cars are made to be always altruistic and self-sacrificing, very few would purchase them. However, there will always be some incidents that cannot be foreseen and programmed; this happened, for instance, when a metal balloon flew right in front of a driverless car and confused it. In these cases, the choice is best left to be made randomly with regards to which party will be harmed (covered by no-fault insurance). If these situations are repeated, the programs will need to be updated by humans.

All said and done, it seems that one need not, and most likely cannot, implant ethics into machines, nor can machines pick up ethics as children do, such that they are able to render moral decisions on their own. The community can set legal limits on what these machines do in most cases; their owners and users can provide them with ethical guidance in other situations, employing ethics bots to keep AI equipped machines in line; and collectively, we can leave be the one-in-a-million situation, without neglecting to cover the harm.

Those concerned with these matters might give the Trolley cases a rest and focus instead on ethical issues raised by the proliferation of smart machines that are almost immeasurably more consequential, such as the number of lives saved by the accelerated development of driverless cars of the partner kind. Also, the issues raised by a particular subset of "autonomous" machines—such as killing machines or smart weapons—that should not be allowed to become driven by AI minds but only by AI partners, thereby always keeping a human in the loop who can abort missions and otherwise keep smart machines within bounds.

References

Anderson, S.L. 2011. Philosophical concerns with machine ethics. In *Machine ethics*, ed. Michael Anderson and Susan Leigh Anderson, 162–167. Cambridge: Cambridge University Press.

Anderson, M., and S.L. Anderson, eds. 2011. *Machine ethics*. Cambridge: Cambridge University Press.

Batavia, P.H., D.A. Pomerleau, and C.E. Thorpe. 1996. *Applying advanced learning algorithms to ALVINN*. Pittsburgh: Carnegie Mellon University, The Robotics Institute.

BBC News. 2007, March 7. Robotic age poses ethical dilemma.

Benartzi, S., and R.H. Thaler. 2013. Behavioral economics and the retirement savings crisis. *Science* 339 (6124): 1152–1153.

Beshears, J., J.J. Choi, D. Laibson, and B.C. Madrian. 2009. The importance of default options for retirement saving outcomes: Evidence from the United States. In *Social security policy in a changing environment*, 167–195. Chicago: University of Chicago Press.

Bojarski, M. et al. 2016. End to end learning for self-driving cars.

Bonnefon, J.F., A. Shariff, and I. Rahwan. 2016. The social dilemma of autonomous vehicles. *Science* 352 (6293): 1573–1576.

Calverley, D.J. 2011. Legal rights for machines: Some fundamental concepts. In *Machine ethics*, ed. M. Anderson and S.L. Anderson, 213–227. Cambridge: Cambridge University Press.

Coeckelbergh, M. 2009. Virtual moral agency, virtual moral responsibility: On the moral significance of the appearance, perception, and performance of artificial agents. *AI & Society* 24 (2): 181–189.

Constant, B. 1797. Des réactions politiques. *Oeuvres complètes* 1: 1774–1799.

DMello, A. 2015. Rise of the humans: Intelligence amplification will make us as smart as the machines. *The Conversation.*

Domingos, P. 2015. *The master algorithm: How the quest for the ultimate learning machine will remake our world.* New York: Basic Books.

Encyclopaedia Britannica. 2016. "Artificial Intelligence (AI)."

Etzioni, A., and O. Oren Etzioni. 2016a. AI assisted ethics. *Ethics and Information Technology* 18 (2): 149–156.

———. 2016b. Keeping AI legal. *Vanderbilt Journal of Entertainment & Technology Law* 19 (1): 133–146.

Frankfurt, H.G. 1969. Alternate possibilities and moral responsibility. *The Journal of Philosophy* 66 (23): 829–839.

Fried, B.H. 2012. What does matter? The case for killing the trolley problem (or letting it die). *The Philosophical Quarterly* 62 (248): 505–529.

Gibbs, S. 2015. What's it like to drive with Tesla's Autopilot and how does it work? *The Guardian.*

Goodall, N. 2014. Ethical decision making during automated vehicle crashes. *Transportation Research Record: Journal of the Transportation Research Board* 2424: 58–65.

Goodall, N.J. 2016. Can you program ethics into a self-driving car? *IEEE Spectrum* 53 (6): 28–58.

Gordon, J.S. 2016. Modern morality and ancient ethics. *Internet Encyclopedia of Philosophy.*

Hargrove, E.C. 1992. *The animal rights/environmental ethics debate: The environmental perspective.* Albany: SUNY Press.

Harris, S. 2011. *The moral landscape: How science can determine human values.* New York: Simon and Schuster.

Harris, M. 2015. New pedestrian detector from Google could make self-driving cars cheaper. *IEEE Spectrum.*

Hew, P.C. 2014. Artificial moral agents are infeasible with foreseeable technologies. *Ethics and Information Technology* 16 (3): 197–206.

Himma, K.E. 2009. Artificial agency, consciousness, and the criteria for moral agency: What properties must an artificial agent have to be a moral agent? *Ethics and Information Technology* 11 (1): 19–29.

Hsu, J. 2016. Deep learning makes driverless cars better at spotting pedestrians. *IEEE Spectrum.*

Johnson, D.G. 2006. Computer systems: Moral entities but not moral agents. *Ethics and Information Technology* 8 (4): 195–204.

Johnson, E.J., and D. Goldstein. 2003. Do defaults save lives? *Science* 302 (5649): 1338–1339.

Joy, B. 2000. Why the future doesn't need us. *WIRED* 8: 238.

Levin, S., and N. Woolf. 2016. Tesla driver killed while using autopilot was watching Harry Potter, witness says. *The Guardian.*

Lohr, S. 2015. Homes try to reach smart switch. *New York Times.*

Luban, D. 2005. Liberalism, torture, and the ticking bomb. *Virginia Law Review* 91: 1425–1461.

Lucas, G.R., Jr. 2013. Engineering, ethics and industry: The moral challenges of lethal autonomy. In *Killing by remote control: The ethics of an unmanned military,* ed. B.J. Strawser, 211–228. New York: Oxford University Press.

Luciano, F., and J.W. Sanders. 2004. On the morality of artificial agents. *Minds and Machines* 14 (3): 349–379.

Markoff, J. 2015. *Machines of loving grace: The quest for common ground between humans and robots.* New York: ECCO.

McDermott, D. 2011. What matters to a machine. In *Machine ethics,* ed. M. Anderson and S.L. Anderson, 88–114. Cambridge: Cambridge University Press. 88–114.

Metz, C. 2016. Self-driving cars will teach themselves to save lives—But also take them. *The Atlantic.*

Mill, J.S. 2008. *On liberty and other essays* (originally published in 1859). Oxford: Oxford University Press.

Millar, J. 2014. You should have a say in your robot car's code of ethics. *WIRED.*

Moor, J. 2011. The nature, importance and difficulty of machine ethics. In *Machine ethics*, ed. M. Anderson and S.L. Anderson, 13–20. Cambridge: Cambridge University Press.

Nadeau, J.E. 2006. Only androids can be ethical. In *Thinking about android epistemology*, ed. K. Ford and C. Glymour, 241–248. Cambridge, MA: MIT Press.

National Highway Traffic Safety Administration. 2013. *Traffic safety facts 2013: A compilation of motor vehicle crash data from the fatality analysis reporting system and the general estimates system*. US Department of Transportation.

O'Connor, J. 2012. The trolley method of moral philosophy. *Essays in Philosophy* 13 (1): 242–255.

Rozenfield, M. 2016. The next step for artificial intelligence is machines that get smarter on their own. *The Institute*.

Scheutz, M. 2012. The affect dilemma for artificial agents: Should we develop affective artificial agents? *IEEE Transactions on Affective Computing* 3 (4): 424–433.

Shah, R.C., and C. Sandvig. 2008. Software defaults as de facto regulation the case of the wireless Internet. *Information, Community & Society* 11 (1): 25–46.

Sharkey, N., and A. Sharkey. 2010. The crying shame of robot nannies: An ethical appraisal. *Interaction Studies* 11 (2): 161–190.

Sharkey, A., and N. Sharkey. 2012. Granny and the robots: Ethical issues in robot care for the elderly. *Ethics and Information Technology* 14 (1): 27–40.

Spice, B. 2016. *Carnegie Mellon transparency reports make AI decision-making accountable*. Carnegie Mellon Computer University School of Computer Science.

van Inwagen, P. 2003. Fischer on moral responsibility. *The Philosophical Quarterly* 47 (188): 373–381.

Wallach, W., and C. Allen. 2009. *Moral machines: Teaching robots right from wrong*. New York: Oxford University Press.

Whitby, B. 2011. On computable morality: An examination of machines. In *Machine ethics*, ed. M. Anderson and S.L. Anderson, 138–150. Cambridge: Cambridge University Press.

Chapter 16
Pros and Cons of Autonomous Weapons Systems (with Oren Etzioni)

Autonomous weapons systems (AWS) and military robots are progressing from science fiction movies to designer's drawing boards, to engineering laboratories, and to the battlefield. These machines have prompted a debate among military planners, roboticists, and ethicists about the development and deployment of weapons that are able to perform increasingly advanced functions, including targeting and application of force, with little or no human oversight. Some military experts hold that these autonomous weapons systems not only confer significant strategic and tactical advantages in the battleground, but that they are also are preferable to the use of human combatants, on moral grounds. In contrast, critics hold that these weapons should be curbed, if not banned altogether, for a variety of moral and legal reasons. The chapter reviews first the arguments by those who favor AWS, then those who oppose them, and closes with a policy suggestion.

16.1 In Support of AWS

16.1.1 Military Advantages

Those who call for further development and deployment of autonomous weapons systems generally point to several advantages. (a) Autonomous weapons systems act as a "force multiplier;" that is, fewer soldiers are needed for a given mission, and the efficacy of each soldier is greater. (b) Autonomous weapons systems expand the battlefield, allowing combat to reach into areas that were previously inaccessible. And (c) Autonomous weapons systems reduce casualties by removing human soldiers from dangerous missions (Marchant et al. 2011, pp. 272–276).

This chapter draws on "Pros and Cons of Autonomous Weapons Systems" in *Military Review*, (May-June 2017): 72–80.

© The Author(s) 2018

A. Etzioni, *Happiness is the Wrong Metric*, Library of Public Policy and Public Administration 11, https://doi.org/10.1007/978-3-319-69623-2_16

The Pentagon's *Unmanned Systems Roadmap 2007–2032* provides additional motivations for pursuing AWS. These include that robots are better suited than humans for "dull," "dangerous," and "dirty" missions. Examples given for each respective category of mission include long sorties, bomb disposal, and operating in nuclear clouds or areas with high radioactivity (Clapper et al. 2007). Jeffrey S. Thurnher of the US Naval War College adds that "LARs [Lethal Autonomous Robots] have the unique potential to operate at a tempo faster than humans can possibly achieve and to lethally strike even when communications links have been severed" (Thurnher 2012, p. 83).

The long-term savings that could be achieved through fielding an army of military robots have also been highlighted. *The Fiscal Times* notes that each US soldier in Afghanistan costs the Pentagon roughly $850,000 per year (some estimate the cost to be over $1 million per soldier per year), which does not include the long-term costs of providing health care to veterans. Conversely, the TALON robot—a small, armed robot—can be built for only $230,000 and is relatively cheap to maintain (Francis 2013). Gen. Robert Cone, head of the Army's Training and Doctrine Command, suggested in 2014 that by relying more on "support robots," the Army could reduce the size of a brigade from 4000 to 3000 soldiers without a concomitant reduction in effectiveness (Ackerman 2014).

Major Jason DeSon, writing in the *Air Force Law Review*, notes the potential advantages of autonomous aerial weapons systems. The physical strain of high-g maneuvers and the intense mental concentration and situational awareness required of fighter pilots makes them very prone to fatigue and exhaustion; robot pilots, on the other hand, would not be subject to these physiological and mental constraints. Moreover, fully autonomous planes could be programmed to take genuinely random and unpredictable action, which could confuse an opponent (DeSon 2015). More striking still, US Air Force Captain Michael Byrnes predicts that a single Unmanned Aerial Vehicle (UAV) with machine-controlled maneuvering and accuracy could, with a few hundred rounds of ammunition and sufficient fuel reserves, take out an entire fleet of aircraft with human pilots (Byrnes 2014).

In guiding future research in AWS, the Defense Science Board at the Pentagon has identified six areas where advances in autonomy would be of significant benefit to current systems:

Perception, which includes not just new hardware (the actual sensors) but also software (algorithms for sensing).

Planning, which includes "the algorithms needed to make decisions about action (provide autonomy) in situations in which humans are not in the environment (e.g. space, the ocean)" (DSB 2012, p. 39).

Learning. The DSB report states the advantages of machine learning over manual software engineering, but notes that machine learning approaches to autonomous vehicles have thus far mostly been applied to ground vehicles and robots, and not yet air and marine vehicles.

Human-Robot Interaction (HRI). Robots are quite different from other computers or tools because they are physically situated agents, and thus elicit different responses from human users. Hence HRI research needs to span a number of domains well beyond engineering, including psychology, cognitive science, and communications, among others.

Natural language. The authors of the DSB report hold that "Natural language is the most normal and intuitive way for humans to instruct autonomous systems; it allows them to provide diverse, high-level goals and strategies rather than detailed teleoperation" (DSB 2012, p. 49). Hence, further development of the ability of autonomous weapons systems to respond to commands in a natural language is necessary.

Multi-Agent Coordination refers to the distribution of tasks among multiple robots, with either centrally planned or directly negotiated synchronization. This sort of collaboration goes beyond mere cooperation because "it assumes that the agents have a cognitive understanding of each other's capabilities, can monitor progress towards the goal, and engage in more human-like teamwork" (DSB 2012, p. 50).

16.1.2   Moral Justifications

Several military experts and roboticists have argued that autonomous weapons systems should not only be regarded as morally acceptable, but that they would in fact be ethically preferable to human fighters. Roboticist Ronald Arkin believes that autonomous robots in the future will be able to act more "humanely" on the battlefield for a number of reasons: For one, they do not need to be programmed with a self-preservation instinct, thus potentially eliminating the need for a "shoot-first, ask questions later" attitude. The judgments of autonomous weapons systems will not be clouded by emotions like fear or hysteria, and they will be able to process much more incoming sensory information than humans, without discarding or distorting it to fit preconceived notions. Finally, in teams comprised of human and robot soldiers, the robots could be more relied upon to report ethical infractions that they observe than would a team of humans who might close ranks (Arkin 2010).

Lieutenant Colonel Douglas A. Pryer of the US Army adds that there might be ethical advantages to removing humans from high-stress combat zones in favor of robots. He points to neuroscience research which suggests that the neural circuits responsible for conscious self-control can shut down when overloaded with stress, leading to sexual assaults and other crimes that soldiers would otherwise be less likely to commit. But Pryer (2013) sets aside the question of whether or not waging war via robots is ethical in the abstract and suggests that because it sparks so much moral outrage among the populations from which the US most needs support, robot warfare has serious strategic disadvantages and is helping to fuel the cycle of perpetual warfare.

16.2   Opposition to AWS

16.2.1   Opposition on Moral Grounds

In July of 2015, an open letter calling for a ban on autonomous weapons was released at an International Joint Conference on Artificial Intelligence. The letter warns: "Artificial Intelligence (AI) technology has reached a point where the deployment of such systems is—practically if not legally—feasible within years, not decades, and the stakes are high: autonomous weapons have been described as the third revolution in warfare, after gunpowder and nuclear arms" (Autonomous Weapons 2015). The letter also notes that AI has the potential to benefit humanity, but that if a military AI arms race ensues, its reputation could be tarnished and a public backlash might curtail future benefits of AI. The letter has an impressive list of signatories, including Elon Musk (inventor and founder of Tesla), Steve Wozniak (co-founder of Apple), physicist Stephen Hawking (University of Cambridge), and Noam Chomsky (MIT), among others. Over 3000 AI and Robotics researchers have also signed the letter. The open letter simply calls for "a ban on offensive autonomous weapons beyond meaningful human control." We note in passing that it is often unclear whether a weapon is offensive or defensive. Thus, many assume that an effective missile defense shield is defensive, but it can be extremely destabilizing, if it allows one nation to launch a nuclear strike against another without fear of retaliation.

Previously, in April of 2013, the UN's Special Rapporteur on extrajudicial, summary, and arbitrary executions presented a report to the UN's Human Rights Council recommending that member states should declare and implement moratoria on the testing, production, transfer, and deployment of Lethal Autonomous Robotics (LARs) until an internationally agreed upon framework for LARs has been established (Heyns 2013).

That same year, a group of engineers, AI and robotics experts, and other scientists and researchers from 37 countries issued the "Scientists' Call to Ban Autonomous Lethal Robots." The statement notes the lack of scientific evidence that robots could, in the foreseeable future, have "the functionality required for accurate target identification, situational awareness or decisions regarding the proportional use of force." Hence they may cause a high level of collateral damage. The statement ends by insisting that "Decisions about the application of violent force must not be delegated to machines" (ICRAC 2013).

Indeed, the delegation of life-or-death decision-making to non-human agents is a recurring concern of AWS' opponents. The most obvious manifestation of this concern relates to autonomous weapons systems that are capable of choosing their own targets. Thus, highly regarded computer scientist Noel Sharkey (2012) has called for a ban on "autonomous lethal targeting" because it violates the Principle of Distinction, considered one of the most important rules of armed conflict: autonomous weapons systems will find it very hard to determine who is a civilian and who is a combatant, which is difficult even for humans. Allowing AI to make decisions about targeting will most likely result in civilian casualties and unacceptable collateral damage.

Another major concern deals with the problem of accountability when autonomous weapons systems are deployed. Ethicist Robert Sparrow (2007) highlights this ethical issue by noting that a fundamental condition of international humanitarian law, or *jus in bello*, requires that someone must be able to be held responsible for civilian deaths. Any weapon or other means of war that makes it impossible to identify responsibility for the casualties it causes does not meet the requirements of *jus in bello*, and therefore should not be employed in war.

This issue arises because AI-equipped machines make decisions on their own, which makes it difficult to determine whether a flawed decision is due to flaws in the program or in the autonomous deliberations of the AI-equipped (so-called 'smart') machines. This problem was highlighted when a driverless car violated the speed limits by moving too slowly on a highway, and it was unclear to whom the ticket should be issued (For more, see Etzioni and Eztioni 2016). In situations where a human being makes the decision to use force against a target, there is a clear chain of accountability, stretching from whoever actually "pulled the trigger" to the commander who gave the orders. In the case of AWS, no such clarity exists. It is unclear who or what is to blame or bears liability.

What Sharkey, Sparrow, and the signatories of the open letter propose could be labelled "upstream regulation;" that is, a proposal for setting limits on the development of autonomous weapons systems technology and drawing red lines that future technological developments should not be allowed to cross. This kind of upstream approach tries to foresee the direction of technological development and pre-empt the dangers such developments would pose. Others prefer "downstream regulation," which takes a wait-and-see approach by developing regulations as new advances occur. Legal scholars Kenneth Anderson and Matthew Waxman, who advocate this approach, argue that regulation will have to emerge along with the technology because they believe that morality will co-evolve with technological development. Thus, arguments about the irreplaceability of human conscience and moral judgment may have to be revisited (Anderson and Waxman 2013a). They suggest that, as humans become more accustomed to machines performing functions with life-or-death implications/consequences—such as driving cars or performing surgeries—humans will most likely become more comfortable with AI technology's incorporation into weaponry. Thus, Anderson and Waxman propose what might be considered a communitarian solution, by suggesting that the United States should work on developing norms and principles (rather than binding legal rules) guiding and constraining research and development—and eventual deployment—of AWS. Those norms could help establish expectations about legally or ethically appropriate conduct. They write:

> To be successful, the United States government would have to resist two extreme instincts. It would have to resist its own instincts to hunker down behind secrecy and avoid discussing and defending even guiding principles. It would also have to refuse to cede the moral high ground to critics of autonomous lethal systems, opponents demanding some grand international treaty or multilateral regime to regulate or even prohibit them. (Anderson and Waxman 2013b, p. 46)

16.2.2   Counter Arguments

In response, some argue against any attempt to apply the language of morality that is applied to human agents, to robots. Military ethicist George Lucas Jr. (2013) points out, for example, that robots cannot feel anger or a desire to "get even" by seeking retaliation for harm done to their compatriots. Lucas holds that the debate thus far has been obfuscated by the confusion of machine autonomy with moral autonomy. The Roomba vacuum cleaner and Patriot missile "are both 'autonomous' in that they perform their assigned missions, including encountering and responding to obstacles, problems, and unforeseen circumstances with minimal human oversight," but not in the sense that they can change or abort their mission if they have "moral objections" (Lucas 2013, p. 218). Lucas thus holds that the primary concern of engineers and designers developing autonomous weapons systems should not be *ethics* but rather *safety* and *reliability*, which means taking due care to address the possible risks of malfunctions, mistakes or misuse that autonomous weapons systems will present. We note, though, that safety is of course a moral value as well.

Lieutenant Colonel Shane R. Reeves & Major William J. Johnson, Judge Advocates in the US Army, note that there are battlefields absent of civilians, such as underwater and in space, where autonomous weapons could reduce the possibility of suffering and death by eliminating the need for combatants (Reeves and Johnson 2014). We note that this valid observation does not agitate against a ban in other, in effect most, battlefields.

Michael N. Schmitt of the Naval War College makes a distinction between weapons that are illegal *per se* and the unlawful use of otherwise legal weapons. For example, a rifle is not prohibited under international law, but using it to shoot civilians would constitute an unlawful use. On the other hand, some weapons (e.g. biological weapons) are unlawful *per se*, even when used only against combatants. Thus, Schmitt grants that some autonomous weapons systems might contravene international law, but "it is categorically not the case that all such systems will do so" (Schmitt 2013, p. 8). Thus, even an autonomous system that is incapable of distinguishing between civilians and combatants should not necessarily be unlawful *per se*, as autonomous weapons systems could be used in situations where no civilians are present, such as against tank formations in the desert, or warships. Such a system could be *used* unlawfully though, if it were employed in contexts where civilians were present. We note that setting some limitations on such weapons should still be called for.

In their review of the debate, legal scholars Gregory Noone and Diana Noone conclude that everyone is in agreement that any autonomous weapons system would have to comply with the Law of Armed Conflict (LOAC), and thus be able to distinguish between combatants and noncombatants. They write, "No academic or practitioner is stating anything to the contrary; therefore, this part of any argument from either side must be ignored as a red herring. Simply put, no one would agree to any weapon that ignores LOAC obligations" (Noone and Noone 2015, p. 25).

16.2.3 Level of Autonomy

We take it for granted that no nation will agree to forswear the use of autonomous weapons systems unless its adversaries would do the same. At first blush, it may seem that it is not beyond the realm of possibility to obtain an international agreement to ban autonomous weapons systems or at least some kinds of them. One notes that a fair number of bans on one category or another of weapons exist and have been quite well honored and enforced. These include the Convention on the Prohibition of the Use, Stockpiling, Production and Transfer of Anti-Personnel Mines and on their Destruction; the Chemical Weapons Convention; and the Convention on the Prohibition of the Development, Production and Stockpiling of Bacteriological (Biological) and Toxin Weapons and on their Destruction. The record of the Treaty on the Non-Proliferation of Nuclear Weapons is more complicated, but it is credited with having stopped several nations from developing nuclear arms and causing at least one to give them up.

Some of the advocates of a ban on autonomous weapons systems seek to ban not merely production and deployment but also R&D and testing of these machines. This may well not be possible as autonomous weapons systems can be developed and tested in small workshops and do not leave a trail. Nor could one rely on satellites for inspection data, for the same reasons. We hence assume that if such a ban were possible, it would mainly focus on deployment and perhaps encompass mass production.

Even so, such a ban would face considerable difficulties. While it is possible to determine what is a chemical weapon and what is not (despite some disagreements at the margin, for example about law enforcement use of irritant chemical weapons Davidson 2009), and to clearly define nuclear arms or land mines, autonomous weapons systems come with very different levels of autonomy. A ban on all autonomous weapons would require foregoing many modern weapons, already mass produced and deployed.

16.2.4 Defining Autonomy

Different definitions have been attached to the word "autonomy" in different Department of Defense documents, and the resulting concepts suggest rather different views on the future of robotic warfare. One definition, used by the Defense Science Board Task Force views autonomy merely as high-end automation: "a capability (or a set of capabilities) that enables a particular action of a system to be automatic or, within programmed boundaries, 'self-governing'" (DSB 2012, p. 1). According to this definition, already existing capabilities, such as auto-pilot used in aircrafts, could qualify as "autonomous."

Another definition, used in the DoD's *Unmanned Systems Integrated Roadmap FY2011–2036*, suggests a qualitatively different view of autonomy: "an autonomous system is able to make a decision based on a set of rules and/or limitations. It is able to determine what information is important in making a decision" (DOD 2011, p. 43). In this view, autonomous systems are less predictable than merely automated ones, as the AI is not only performing a specified action, but also making decisions and thus potentially taking an action that a human did not order. A human is still responsible for programming the behavior of the autonomous system, and the actions the system takes would have to be consistent with the laws and strategies provided by humans, but no individual action would be completely predictable or preprogrammed. It is easy to find still other definitions of autonomy. The International Committee of the Red Cross defines autonomous weapons as those able to "independently select and attack targets, i.e. with autonomy in the 'critical functions' of acquiring, tracking, selecting and attacking targets" (ICRC 2014, p. 7).

We take autonomy to mean an ability to make decisions based on information gathered by a machine and to act on the basis of its own deliberations, beyond the instructions and parameters provided to the machine by its producers, programmers, and users.

It seems useful to consider three kinds or levels of autonomy:

Human-in-the-Loop Weapons: Robots that can select targets and deliver force only with a human command. Numerous examples of this type already exist and are in use. For example, Israel's Iron Dome system detects incoming rockets, predicts its trajectory and then sends this information to a human soldier who decides whether to launch an interceptor rocket (Marks 2012).

Human-on-the-Loop Weapons: Robots that can select targets and deliver force under the oversight of a human operator who can override the robots' actions.

Examples of Human-on-the-Loop weapons are either in development or have already been deployed. The SGR-A1 built by Samsung is a sentry robot placed by South Korea along the Demilitarized Zone (DMZ). It uses a low-light camera and pattern recognition software to detect intruders, and then issues a verbal warning. If the intruder does not surrender, the robot has a machine gun which can either be fired remotely by a soldier, who the robot has alerted, or by the robot itself if it is in fully-automatic mode (Lin et al. 2008).

The US also deploys Human-on-the-Loop weapons systems. For example, the MK 15-Phalanx Close-In Weapons System has been used on US Navy ships since the 1980s and is capable of detecting, evaluating, tracking, engaging, and using force against Anti-Ship Missiles and high-speed aircraft threats without any human commands (MK 15 n.d.). The Center for a New American Security estimates that at least 30 countries have deployed or are developing Human-on-the-Loop systems (Scharre and Horowitz 2015).

Human-out-of-the-Loop Weapons: Robots that are capable of selecting targets and delivering force without any human input or interaction (Docherty 2012). This kind of autonomous weapons system is the source of much concern about "killing machines." Military strategist Thomas K. Adams (2002) warned that, in the future, humans would be reduced to making only initial policy decisions about war and have mere symbolic authority over automated systems. Human Rights Watch, in its much discussed report *Losing Humanity: The Case against Killer*

Robots, warned, "By eliminating human involvement in the decision to use lethal force in armed conflict, fully autonomous weapons would undermine other, non-legal protections for civilians" (Docherty 2012). The authors believe that a repressive dictator could deploy emotionless robots to kill and instill fear among the population without having to worry about soldiers empathizing with their victims (who might be neighbors, acquaintances, or even family members) and turning against the dictator.

As we see it, it is hard to imagine nations agreeing to return to a world in which weapons have no measure of autonomy. On the contrary, development in AI leads one to expect that more and more machines and instruments of all kinds will become more autonomous. Bombers and fighter aircraft with no human pilot seem inevitable. Although it is true that any degree of autonomy entails, by definition, some loss of human control, this genie has left the bottle and we see no way to put it back again.

The most promising way to proceed is to determine whether one can obtain international agreement to ban fully autonomous weapons, whose missions cannot be aborted and that cannot be recalled once they are launched. If they malfunction and target civilian centers, there is no way to stop them. Like unexploded landmines, placed without marks, these weapons will continue to kill even after the sides settle their difference and make peace.

One may argue that gaining such an agreement should not be arduous because no rational policymaker will favor such a weapon. Indeed, the Pentagon has directed that "Autonomous and semi-autonomous weapon systems shall be designed to allow commanders and operators to exercise appropriate levels of human judgment over the use of force" (DOD 2012). One should note though that such Human-out-of-the-Loop arms are very effective in reinforcing a red line. Declaration by representatives of one nation that if another nation engages in a certain kind of hostile behavior, swift and severe retaliation will follow, are open to misinterpretation by the other side, even if backed up with deployment of troops or other military assets. Leaders, drawing on considerable historical experience, may bet that they be able to cross the red line and be spared because of one reason or another. Arms without a human in the loop make for much more credible red lines. (This is a form of the "pre-commitment strategy" discussed by Thomas Schelling (1966) in *Arms and Influence,* in which one party limits its own options by obligating itself to retaliate, thus making its deterrence more credible.)

We suggest that nations might be willing to forgo this advantage of fully autonomous arms in order to gain the assurance that once hostilities cease, they could avoid becoming entangled in new rounds of fighting because some bombers are still running loose and attacking the other side, or will malfunction and bomb civilian centers. Finally, if and when a ban on fully autonomous weapons is agreed upon and means of verification is developed, one may aspire to move toward limiting weapons with a high, but not full, measure of autonomy.

References

Ackerman, E. 2014. U.S. Army considers replacing thousands of soldiers with robots. *IEEE Spectrum*.

Adams, T.K. 2002. Future warfare and the decline of human decisionmaking. *Parameters* 31 (4): 57–71.

Anderson, K., and M. Waxman. 2013a. *Law and ethics for autonomous weapon systems: why a ban won't work and how the laws of war can.* Stanford University, Hoover Institution (Jean Perkins Task Force on National Security and Law Essay Series).

———. 2013b. Law and ethics for robot soldiers. *Policy Review*.

Arkin, R.C. 2010. The case for ethical autonomy in unmanned systems. *Journal of Military Ethics* 9 (4): 332–341.

Autonomous Weapons. 2015. An open letter from AI & robotics researchers. http://futureoflife. org/open-letter-autonomous-weapons/.

Byrnes, M. 2014. Nightfall: Machine autonomy in air-to-air combat. *Air and Space Power Journal* 28 (3): 48–75.

Clapper, J., J. Young, J. Cartwright, and J. Grimes. 2007. *Unmanned systems roadmap 2007–2032*. Office of the Secretary of Defense.

Davison, N. 2009. *'Non-lethal' weapons*. New York: Palgrave Macmillan.

DeSon, J.S. 2015. Automating the right stuff – the hidden ramifications of ensuring autonomous aerial weapon systems comply with international humanitarian law. *Air Force Law Review* 72: 85–122.

Docherty, B. 2012. Losing humanity: The case against killer robots. *Human Rights Watch*.

DOD (Department of Defense). 2011. Unmanned systems integrated roadmap FY2011–2036.

———. 2012. Directive number 3000.09, Subject: Autonomy in weapons systems.

DSB (Defense Science Board). 2012. Task force report: The role of autonomy in DoD systems.

Etzioni, A., and O. Etzioni. 2016. Keeping AI legal. *Vanderbilt Journal of Entertainment & Technology Law* 19 (1): 133–164.

Francis, D. 2013. How a new army of robots can cut the defense budget. *The Fiscal Times*.

Heyns, C. 2013. *Report of the special rapporteur on extrajudicial, summary or arbitrary executions*, U.N. Human Rights Council, U.N. Doc. A/HRC/23/47.

ICRAC (International Committee for Robot Arms Control). 2013. *Scientists' call to ban autonomous lethal robots*. https://icrac.net/call/.

ICRC (International Committee of the Red Cross). 2014. Autonomous weapons systems: technical, military, legal, and humanitarian aspects.

Lin, P., G. Bekey, K. Abney. 2008. *Autonomous military robotics: Risk, ethics, and design* (prepared for U.S. Department of Navy, Office of Naval Research), http://digitalcommons.calpoly. edu/cgi/viewcontent.cgi?article=1001&context=phil_fac.

Lucas, G.R., Jr. 2013. Engineering, ethics & industry: The moral challenges of lethal autonomy. In *Killing by remote control: The ethics of an unmanned military*, ed. B. Strawser, 211–228. Oxford: Oxford University Press.

Marchant, G.E., B. Allenby, R. Arkin, E.T. Barrett, J. Borenstein, L.M. Gaudet, et al. 2011. International governance of autonomous military robots. *Columbia Science & Technology Law Review* 12: 272–315.

Marks, P. 2012. Iron dome rocket smasher set to change Gaza conflict. *New Scientist*.

MK 15 – Phalanx close-in weapons system (CIWS). n.d.. *U.S. Navy fact sheet*. http://www.navy. mil/navydata/fact_print.asp?cid=2100&tid=487&ct=2&page=1.

Noone, G.P., and D.C. Noone. 2015. The debate over autonomous weapons systems. *Case Western Reserve Journal of International Law* 47 (1): 25–35.

Pryer, D.A. 2013. The rise of the machines: Why increasingly "perfect" weapons help perpetuate our wars and endanger our nation. *Military Review* 93 (2): 14–24.

Reeves, S., and W. Johnson. 2014. Autonomous weapons: Are you sure these are killer robots? Can we talk about it? *The Army Lawyer (April)*: 25–31.

Scharre, P., and M. Horowitz. 2015. *An introduction to autonomy in weapons systems* (Working Paper). Center for New American Security.

Schelling, T.C. 1966. *Arms and influence*. New Haven: Yale University Press.

Schmitt, M. 2013. Autonomous weapon systems and international humanitarian law: A reply to the critics. *Harvard National Security Journal Features*.

Sharkey, N. 2012. Saying 'no!' to lethal autonomous targeting. *Journal of Military Ethics* 9 (4): 369–383.

Sparrow, R. 2007. Killer robots. *Journal of Applied Philosophy* 24 (1): 62–77.

Thurnher, J. 2012. Legal implications of fully autonomous targeting. *Joint Force Quarterly* 67 (4): 77–84.

Chapter 17
Robotic Care of Children, the Elderly, and the Sick (with Oren Etzioni)

17.1 The Demand for Humanoid Robots

Humanoid robots are increasingly used in childcare, eldercare, in psychotherapy, and other kinds of medical care, and as tutors. They are also used as 'chat bots' by commercial enterprises. Despite studies that show they are quite effective, most of these kinds of robots are not currently in wide use, mainly because their costs are high. However, there are indications that these costs will decline, a trend familiar from the developments of many other technologies. Moreover, given the rapid aging of several major societies (e.g. Japan, China, and Germany) and their difficulties in retaining a sufficient number of qualified human caregivers, there is a great potential demand for robotic eldercare. Similarly, given the large number of working single parents and two-parent households where both parents work outside the home, there is a great potential demand for robotic childcare. The high cost of medical care also favors the use of robots.

Last but not least, after decades in which the development of AI swung from being overhyped to disappointing, AI seems currently ready for a major take-off. This is revealed by Watson beating masters of chess, Jeopardy, and even Go, and by driverless cars that have already traveled over one million miles in the US with very few incidents.

This chapter will focus on the use of AI caregivers. The chapter first explores several of the ethical concerns that are raised with respect to AI generally as well as to AI caregivers specifically. The chapter then provides an overview of current developments and applications of robotic caregivers, before distinguishing between different kinds of AI. The subsequent three sections consider standards for evaluating AI caregivers, frameworks for AI-human interaction in caregiving, and oversight systems for supervising AI caregivers.

This chapter draws on "The Ethics of Robotic Caregivers" in *Interaction Studies* 18 (2), (2017). The authors are indebted to Anne Jerome for research assistance on a previous draft of this chapter.

A. Etzioni, *Happiness is the Wrong Metric*, Library of Public Policy and Public Administration 11, https://doi.org/10.1007/978-3-319-69623-2_17

17.2   Challenges

The increased use of robots and their improving intelligence has raised major concerns, which has led several scholars to recommend that their use be regulated, and in some areas even avoided. Several uses, we shall see, are considered outright unethical.

One major line of concern is the fear that robots will outsmart humans and come to dominate humanity, if not destroy it (Bostrom 2014; Hawking et al. 2014). We examined these concerns elsewhere and suggested that while the threats were highly speculative, the human costs of slowing down work would be considerable. The benefits of AI—from car safety to robotic surgeries—are significant, real, and immediate (Etzioni and Etzioni 2016a, b). Hence, these fears are not explored here.

A rather different kind of concern has been raised by a number of social scientists; they apply way beyond robotic caregivers but, we shall see, apply especially to them. The main scholar who articulates this second line of concern is Sherry Turkle of MIT, who has long warned about the ill effects of computer-mediated interactions and relationships and the dark side of all matters concerning the internet. She is deeply concerned that technologies that increase human interactions with machines do so at the expense of human-to-human contact. Turkle explains: "[Sociable technology] promises friendship but can only deliver performances. Do we really want to be in the business of manufacturing friends that will never be friends?" (2010, p. 101). And: "Often, our new digital connections offer the illusion of companionship without the demands of friendship…We are not sure whom to count on. Virtual friendships and worlds offer connection with uncertain claims to commitment. We know this, and yet the emotional charge of the online world is very high" (Turkle 2011). Social scientists refer to this phenomenon as the false sense of community—"pseudo-*gemeinschaft*."

Moreover, humanoid robots can and do stray from what their programmers set out for them to do. Microsoft created Tay, a chat bot designed to learn through online conversations. Less than 24 h after being launched, however, Tay began supporting genocide, denying the holocaust (Price 2016), and agreeing with Hitler (Reese 2016). Microsoft had to rush to take the chat bot offline. According to the founder of Unanimous AI, Lois Rosenberg, "When Tay started training on patterns that were input by trolls online, it started using those patterns. This is really no different than a parrot in a seedy bar picking up bad words and repeating them back without knowing what they really mean" (Reese 2016). It is important to distinguish between a bug and a design flaw; Tay did not necessarily malfunction, but functioned according to the instructions given by Microsoft's programmers, who failed to properly design Tay's Natural Language Processing filters.

A third line of concerns—and the focus of this chapter—are raised about humanoid robots, those that care for the infirm, young, old, and many others. Some of the best articulations of these concerns are in the work of Noel Sharkey, who has both authored and co-authored with Amanda Sharkey several very carefully crafted and well-documented articles on the subject at hand.[1] They find that humanoid robots may violate privacy. "Sometimes conversations about issues concerning the parents, such as abuse or injustice, should be treated in confidence. A robot might not be able to keep such confidences from the parents before reporting the incident to the appropriate authorities" (Sharkey and Sharkey 2010). These robots are equipped "[w]ith massive memory hard drives," such that "it would be possible to record a child's entire life. This gives rise to concerns about …who will be allowed access to the recordings?" (Sharkey and Sharkey 2010). Authoritarianism is another concern. To illustrate, Sharkey and Sharkey posit an "extreme case" by asking readers to "imagine a child having doughnuts taken from her because the robot wanted to prevent her from becoming obese" (2010, p. 166). And they hold that it may well be unethical to create a machine that causes people to believe it is capable of genuine emotional engagement, though they note that "[i]t is difficult to take an absolutist ethical approach to questions about robots and deception" (2010, pp. 172–3). Other ethical concerns resulting from robotic eldercare raised by Sharkey and Sharkey include "feelings of objectification and loss of control," "loss of personal liberty," and "infantilisation" (2012).

Robert Sparrow, a professor at Monash University, and Linda Sparrow write that "robots are incapable of meeting" the elderly's "social and emotional needs," and that using robots to care for them would cause the elderly to experience a "decrease in the amount of human contact," which "would be detrimental to their well-being" (Sparrow and Sparrow 2006, p. 141). Furthermore, R. Sparrow asserts that robotic pets' lack of authenticity makes them unethical, and that "[i]t is perverse to respond to the fact that older persons are increasingly socially isolated with the invention of robot pets rather than by multiplying the opportunities for human contact…" (2002, p. 308).

The chapter from here on is dedicated to address the question of whether these humanoid robots should be used as caregivers; if yes—for what kinds of care, how they should be held accountable, and how they best relate to human caregivers. That is, it seeks to provide an ethical and legal evaluation of, and guidelines for, the use of these robots.

Specifically, the chapter first establishes the domain of the kind of robots that are at issue. The chapter next finds that several of the major concerns that apply to one kind of humanoid robot apply much less, if at all, to other kinds. The chapter then suggests that the wrong criteria have been used for the evaluation of these robots and that if properly evaluated they 'score' much more favorably. The chapter then specifies ways humanoid robots can be held accountable, both in legal and in ethical terms. The chapter closes with what arguably is the most important consideration for all the issues at hand, the relationship between robots that provide human services and humans who provide human services.

---

[1] For further reading, see: Sharkey and Sharkey 2006, 2010, 2012; Sharkey 2008.

17.3   Introducing AI Caregivers

One common attribute of many but far from all computerized caregivers that draw on AI programs is that they display simulated emotions.[2] This display is deemed necessary to cause bonding with human subjects, for them to become emotionally invested in these robots, to trust them, to feel that they are empathetic or sympathetic, and so on (see also Tanka et al. 2007; Turkley et al. 2006; Leyzberg et al. 2011; Gonsior et al. 2011). However, as van Wynsberghe points out, "There is no capability exclusive to all care robots" (2012, p. 409). Instead, care robots can differ in their capability for locomotion; voice, face and emotion recognition; and degree of autonomy. Coeckelbergh (2010) distinguishes between "shallow" and "deep" care: what distinguishes the latter from the former is the kind of *feelings* that accompany human care. He holds that AI can only provide shallow care because it does not actually care *about* the patient. Coeckelbergh notes that deep care is not guaranteed even from human caregivers, but that they are at least able to provide it.

The term humanoid robot, used to refer to this kind of caregiver, is misleading because it assumes that the computerized caregivers must have features that make them seem human, for instance simulated faces, legs, and arms. The Merriam-Webster dictionary defines the term humanoid as "having human form or characteristics" (Merriam Webster); masks from preliterate ages, for instance, were said to have humanoid features. In fact, many robots have no such features.

Moreover, evidence shows that human beings can become emotionally invested in inanimate objects that have no anthropomorphic features. An obvious example is a cuddly toy, such as a teddy bear (Sharkey and Sharkey 2010, pp. 161–190). One of our sons could not possibly go to sleep or to the playground without his 'gaki,' a well-worn small blanket, and another was attached to "Jack," a piece of fur he found, even more strongly than his father was attached to his dark blue, white top, convertible Sting Ray. The movie *Her* captures well the attachment one can form to a voice that emanates from a screen, basically a piece of software. In short, just as one can become addicted to anything (though some materials are more addictive than others), one can also become attached to anything (though if it displays affection, attachment is more likely to take place).

Many, indeed most, of the computerized caregivers are not robots—defined as "a machine that looks like a human being and performs various complex acts (as walking or talking) of a human being" (Merriam Webster). Many are merely software programs that can be made to work on any computer, tablet, or smart phone. For instance, programs that provide computerized psychotherapy (discussed below).

For this key reason we suggest that all AI-enriched programs that provide care and *seem affective to those they care for*, be included. To include both humanoid robots and the much larger number of these computer caregivers, we shall refer to them as AI caregivers.[3] Most have no visible human-like features, make no visible

---

[2] This is encompassed within "affective computing." *See, for example*, Picard 1997.

[3] Some refer to this as "Socially Assistive Robotics" See, for example: Feil-Seifer and Matarić 2011.

gestures, do not 'reach out and touch someone,' but instead use mainly their voices to convey affect. We choose our words carefully: We refer to the presentation of emotions that leads humans who interact with AI caregivers to believe that these machines have emotions. Without this feature, AI caregivers are unable to perform much of their care.

Following this definition has another major benefit: it excludes from the domain under study all programs that provide exclusively or mainly cognitive services. A prime example of these is Google Assistant. It provides answers to questions, gives customized suggestions to fit the user's preferences, and helps with tasks such as booking flights or making dinner reservations, among other things. Google Assistant presents no emotions; although people can find expression of emotions in anything, there is nothing in Google Assistant that fosters such projections. Other, mainly cognitive services by AI-driven software include Apple's Siri and Microsoft's Cortana, which have been designed to reveal a human touch, a rather limited sense of humor, but still do not qualify as AI caregivers because they are used mostly as a source of information. (In short, these programs are not caregivers and hence are not examined further here; online tutors are also mainly cognitive agents and are also not discussed.)

Chat bots constitute a somewhat more complicated case. There is no formal definition of what constitutes a chat bot. However, to the extent that these are mainly interactive, informative agents, they fall into the cognitive category and are not AI caregivers. This is true even if they are given some mannerisms to make them seem friendlier, such as greeting one by one's first name when one queries them, say, about the best place to have dinner. Other chat bots are designed to display emotions in order to manipulate those they interact with, acting like humans who work in sales.

An extreme position holds that all such interactive relationships between humans and AI caregivers are unethical because, by definition, AI caregivers display emotions that they do not have, and hence the relationships are "false" and "inauthentic." Robert Sparrow makes an applicable point about robot pets: "If robot pets are designed and manufactured with the intention that they should serve as companions for people, and so that those who interact with them are likely to develop an emotional attachment to them, on the basis of false beliefs about them, this is unethical" (2002). Sharkey and Sharkey offer a more nuanced view; they grant that illusion is a part of Artificial Intelligence, but draw a line between imagination, or a willing suspension of disbelief, and actual belief. Thus, they maintain that AI researchers must be honest and transparent about their designs in order to avoid deceit (2006, pp. 9–19). However, people are exposed to mild forms of ingratiation and false expressions of solicitude by many sales personnel, financial advisers, politicians, and others. The same is true about many people who read and apply the lessons of Dale Carnegie's *How to Win Friends and Influence People*. There seems no obvious reason to treat AI caregivers more strictly than humans.[4]

To the extent these kinds of manipulative AI caregivers (and humans) need to be restrained depends on whether or not they cause harm and the level of that harm, granted manipulation is never ethical. If the harm is minimal, it seems reasonable to

---

[4] A reviewer of a previous draft of this chapter noted that AI might merit stricter rules because we have a theory of mind for human caregivers and others, but not for AI agency.

rely here on "let the buyer (or listener) beware." If the harm is considerable, regulations set by law and ethical guidelines should apply to AI caregivers as they do to people (how this can be achieved is discussed below).

Finally, one should note that some manipulation by caregivers, like white lies, is carried out to help those cared for rather than for the benefits of the caregiver. For instance, in medical care when patients seek expressions of hope and are given reassurance, even when there is little hope left. Other cases in point are AI caregivers that cheer on people who lost weight, did more steps than before, or repeated exercises during physical therapy, with quite a bit more enthusiasm than a precision instrument would call for. These are all cases in which a measure of manipulation should be tolerated, as with all white lies.

In summary: any form of deception violates a key ethical precept. Kantians would ban it. Utilitarians would measure the size of the harm it causes versus the size of the gain and find that many AI caregivers score quite well from the viewpoint of those they care for.

17.4   Substitute vs Partner?

As we see it, many deliberations of the ethical issues raised by AI caregivers suffer from a common flaw that one encounters in public discussions of AI and even in several academic ones: These deliberations tend to presume that there is basically one kind of program that is made much more effective and efficient ('smarter') because it draws on Artificial Intelligence. Actually there are two very different kinds of AI. One seeks to design software that will reason and form decisions the way people do and better, and thus be able to replace them. The other AI merely seeks to provide smart assistants to human actors. We called them *AI: the Partner*.

One could instead talk about full versus partial human substitutes, rather than *the Mind* and *the Partner*. The rationale for using the term 'mind' draws on the fact that several leading AI researchers are trying to build computers that would act like human minds. For instance, in *Machines of Loving Grace*, John Markoff reports about endeavors such as the Human Brain Project, which used "deep learning neural network techniques" to produce a system able to assemble images similar to the way the brain's visual cortex functions (2015, p. 153). Henry Markram received one billion euros from the EU for his project to simulate a human brain (Markoff 2015, p. 155). Books such as *How to Create a Mind*, by Ray Kurzweil (2012), and *On Intelligence* (2004), by Jeff Hawkins and Sandra Blakeslee, also deal with these efforts. They all seek to duplicate the brain or mind in full, so that the robot will be able to make decisions on its own rather than partner with a human.

When AI caregivers engage in eldercare, they work in conjunction with human personnel, carrying out some tasks on their own (e.g. reminding patients of the time to take medication and chatting with them when they are lonely) but alert the human staff in response to many other conditions (e.g. patient leaving the room). (Molly reminds patients to take their medications, encourages them to stick to their diet, asks them how they are feeling, offers voice support, and, if need be, alerts a physician (Al Jazeera 2014).)

Many, though by no means all, of the ethical concerns raised by AI caregivers emanate from treating them as if they were to be substitute care rather than a partner in providing it. Hence, if one compares, say, an AI caregiver for the elderly to a human nurse, one indeed will find all kind of limitations. One must not seek to rely on an AI caregiver nanny in a crisis—a child breaks a leg, starts a fire, cannot stop the bathtub from overflowing and so on. These nannies ought to be programmed to alert a human for help rather than deal with such situations, and many others that may arise, on their own.

At first, AI caregivers that provide psychotherapy may seem to be a major exception. These AI caregivers have been reported to be widely used and very successful. In the 1960s, MIT professor Joseph Weizenbaum developed a computer program called ELIZA, designed to simulate conversation with a human. The user would type something on a typewriter connected to the computer, and the program would formulate a response and type it back. After the initial version of ELIZA, Weizenbaum made a new version known as DOCTOR after a meeting with Kenneth Colby, a psychiatrist who wanted to use computers in his study of psychotherapy. While Weizenbaum was troubled by the fact that people were quite willing to share their intimate thoughts with a machine, Colby held that people could begin using "computer therapists" (Rheingold 1985, pp. 163–65).

Since then such programs have come a long way. Often cited is MoodGYM, which provides cognitive behavioral therapy online for people with anxiety, depression, and other conditions. According to Tina Rosenberg, "Scores of studies have found that online C.B.T. works as well as conventional face-to-face cognitive behavioral therapy – as long as there is occasional human support or coaching" (Rosenberg 2015). Online programs help people for whom cost, stigma, or access (due to location or time constraints) is a barrier to getting help. Britain, Sweden, and the Netherlands have online cognitive behavioral health programs, and MoodGYM is used by Australia's national health system. "About 100,000 Australians use it, as do people in 200 countries" (Rosenberg 2015). (Technically these programs may not qualify as AI caregivers but they have the same basic element: bonding with a computer and caregiving. Also, one must expect that in the near future such programs would incorporate AI, like the virtual therapist Ellie developed at the University of Southern California (Bohannon 2015, pp. 250–51).)

On further examination, though, one notes that these programs should not work on their own for a few key reasons. (a) Often when a person is presenting with one symptom (e.g. depression) he or she may have others that these programs are not equipped to deal with. (b) All such treatment ought to be preceded by a physical examination to rule out a physical cause of the patient's mental concerns (e.g. abnormal thyroid function). (c) Often these treatments work better if combined with medications, which these programs do not prescribe or administer. (d) All such programs should alert a human caregiver and/or authorities if the patients indicate that they may harm themselves or others. On all these important grounds, AI therapists are to be used as partners rather than as care substitutes.

One may point to situations in which for one reason or another only an AI caregiver is available. The human night nurse in a nursing home is dealing with a crisis, the patient might be unable to leave home because of a snow storm, or they are unable to find someone to take care of their children. However, in all these situations the AI caregivers are to act as temporary substitutes, as stand–ins, as partners rather than full substitutes for human caregivers. Sharkey and Sharkey are much more concerned about full-time robotic childcare than their use as part-time partners (Sharkey and Sharkey 2010, p. 185). They express concern that full-time care from robots might cause impaired development in children, which is why they see it only as a "last resort" in places such as Romanian orphanages. Yet they find the notion that "robots are better than nothing" to be dangerous, because it "could lead to a more widespread use of the technology in situations where there is a shortage of funding, and where what is actually needed is more staff and better regulation" (Sharkey and Sharkey 2010, pp. 179–180).

17.5   Goal vs. Comparative Evaluation

In evaluation of AI caregivers, one should draw on comparative and not goal evaluation, though the latter has its place. Goal evaluation compares a given program (whether formulated and executed by humans or by machines) to the one needed to accomplish the goal. Comparative evaluations compare available agents for carrying out the missions to one another. To illustrate the difference between these two kinds of evaluations, it serves to use light bulbs as an example. From a goal viewpoint one seeks a bulb that uses all the energy it receives to produce light and squanders none of it on producing heat. Examined from this viewpoint, all bulbs are dismal failures. Incandescent lamps produce about 2 W of light and 98 W of heat; halogen lamps 3.5 W of light and 96.5 W of heat, and fluorescent lamps produce between 6 and 8 W (MacCargar 2005). In contrast, while one seeks to develop better bulbs, it is evident that for now, there are no really "good" bulbs—instead, in comparing them to one another, one finds that some of them are much more efficient than others.

In the same vein, if one compares AI caregivers to an idealized version of a human caregiver, they all fail miserably. Thus, when Sharkey and Sharkey note that AI nannies may violate the privacy of the children in their care, turn authoritarian, and so on—they are correct. However, if one compared these caregivers to human ones, one notes that human nannies may also violate privacy, may turn authoritarian, and so on. Similarly, David Feil-Seifer and Maja Matarić discuss another ethical dilemma posed by humans becoming emotionally attached to robot caregivers, noting that "if the robot's effectiveness wanes, its scheduled course of therapy concludes, or it suffers from a hardware or software malfunction, it may be taken away from the user," causing "distress" as well as "possibly result[ing] in a loss of therapeutic benefits" (2011, p. 27). But human nurses, therapists, and caregivers are at least as likely to disappear from the lives of patients, and some courses of therapy will be scheduled to end regardless of whether they are conducted by a robot or a human.

Hence, instead of giving all caregivers a long list of demerits— while searching for ways of making both kinds better—one should tolerate wide use of AI caregivers as long as they are not inferior to whatever human caregivers are available, with reference to their specific tasks. We next ask how the weaknesses of AI caregivers can be mitigated by the humans they partner with, and vice versa.

17.6   Team Work

Most of the discussions of AI caregivers ask whether or not they could—or should—replace human caregivers. We already indicated that AI caregivers are best considered as partners rather than as substitutes. The next step is to bring to this field the kind of analysis often carried out in other areas, about human-machine interaction and collaboration (Nakajima et al. 2003). It is especially important to focus on how labor is best divided between the human and AI caregivers. For example, AI caregivers are obviously vastly superior to human caregivers when memory and retrieval of information are at issue. Therefore, they are best charged with recalling which medications a patient has taken and their interactions and side-effects. And they can encourage patients to take their medications, as patient noncompliance is a major issue (Shea 2006). AI caregivers can reward people in physical therapy for repeated exercises, and others for physical exercises to maintain or improve health. A study on assistive robots by Maja Matarić et al. found that "patient compliance with the rehabilitation routine was much higher during the experiments with the robot than under the control (no-robot, no prompting) condition" (Matarić et.al. 2007; see also Fasola and Matarić 2013). At the same time, human beings are better at reading between the lines, listening not just to what people say but the way they say it, their tone of voice, and at touching; patients are reported to benefit greatly from such contacts.

On many issues AI caregivers are best considered only as the first line of defense; humans are the main one. For example, if an Alzheimer's patient wandered out of the house or caused a fire on the stove, AI partners are to alert humans rather than—at least for the near future—be programmed to deal with them directly. It seems most of the work involving the details of partnering between human and AI caregivers has yet to be carried out.

17.7   AI Caregivers Need Supervision: Like Humans

Many of the concerns raised about AI caregivers can be handled by regulations and ethical guidelines. Some have suggested that the way to effectuate these controls is to include them in the AI programs that are embedded in the guidance systems of the computerized caregivers (Wallach and Allen 2009; Anderson and Anderson 2011; Winfield et al. 2014). However, AI caregivers' systems are learning systems that change their behavior based on new information and experiences. They may hence stray from their guidelines. Thus, AI caregivers instructed to alert a nurse when a patient complains about pain may "learn" that many patients frequently complain and/or nurses do not respond—and hence conclude that it is futile to alert the nurses and stop doing so. An AI caregiver nanny linked to the internet may be coaxed into sharing private information about the children in its care, circumventing whatever safeguards the original program provided. (Recall Microsoft's chat bot, Tay, whose online exposure led her to embrace Nazi sympathies.)

Indeed, such learning systems are widely considered to be 'autonomous.' John Sullins defines 'autonomous' systems as those "capable of making at least some of the major decisions about their actions using their own programming" (2011, p. 155). Robotic caregivers are hence frequently referred to as 'autonomous.' For instance, Michael Anderson and Susan Leigh Anderson refer to an eldercare robot as a "complex autonomous machine" (2011, p. 2). Noel Sharkey and Amanda Sharkey point out that "[f]or costly childcare robots to be attractive to consumers or institutions, they will need to have sufficient autonomous functioning to free the carer's time and call upon them only in unusual circumstances" (2010, p. 164). Aside from the chat bot Tay, another instance of machine learning gone wrong is Google's photo categorization system. In 2015, it "identified two African Americans as 'gorillas'" because "the data used to train the software relied too heavily on photos of white people, diminishing its ability to accurately identify images of people with different features," writes Jesse Emspak in the *Scientific American* article "How a Machine Learns Prejudice" (2016; see also Mayer- Schönberger and Cukier 2013).

To deal with the kind of situations we just cited, we advanced the thesis that to keep AI-equipped technologies from straying, legally and ethically, the AI community needs to develop a new slew of AI programs—oversight programs that can hold AI operations programs accountable (we called them AI Guardians) (Etzioni and Etzioni 2016a). All societies throughout history have had oversight systems. Workers have supervisors; businesses have accountants; school teachers have principals. That is, all these systems have hierarchies in the sense that the first-line operators are subject to oversight by a second layer and are expected to respond to corrective signals from the oversight systems (see also Etzioni and Etzioni 2016a).

The same point applies here. AI caregivers need oversight, to be provided by specialized AI programs. To give but one example: a program akin to audit trails could routinely determine whether or not AI caregivers released information about children or patients to unauthorized people, determine who these are, and alert the parents or the authorities. One may argue that this is a job a regular software program could accomplish. However, given that the operations of AI programs are opaque, complex, and learning systems (Mayer-Schönberger and Cukier 2013, p. 178), AI interrogation and enforcement programs will be needed.

When an AI-guided robot strays from its instructions, this can be due to programming mistakes, users' attempts to circumvent the instructions, or—as a result of the learning and deliberations of the computer. We asked several AI researchers if a human being, unassisted, could examine the algorithms used in AI-guided systems and determine who the 'culprit' is. They all agreed that this seems not possible. We hence suggested—as a needed research program—that AI systems should be developed to be able to interrogate other AI systems. This has not been done as far as we know, though some efforts can be understood as moving in this direction.

Until now, society has treated AI by and large as one field that encompasses many programs, ranging from IBM's Deep Blue to airplane autopilots and surgical robots. From here on, AI should be divided into two categories. The first category would consist of operational AI programs—the computerized "brains" that guide smart instruments. The second category would be composed of oversight AI programs that verify the first category's claims and keep them in line with the law. These oversight programs, which we call "AI Guardians," would include AI programs to interrogate, discover, supervise, audit, and guarantee the compliance of operational AI programs.

Thoughtful people have asked for centuries, "Who will guard the guardians?"[5] We have no new answer to this question, which has never been answered well. For now, the best we can hope for is that all smart instruments will be outfitted with a readily locatable off-switch to grant ultimate control to human agents over both operational and oversight AI programs.

17.8   Conclusion

There is a great need for 'smart' computerized caregivers that draw on AI, which we call AI caregivers. These are defined as programs that can display emotions, which is needed for bonding with humans, and without which caregiving will be woefully deficient. These AI caregivers raise a variety of ethical concerns. They clearly are inauthentic. However, if their inauthenticity either causes minimal harm—or benefits those that are cared for rather than those who give the care—it should be tolerated, as we do when we deal with human caregivers.

Other deficiencies of AI caregivers can be corrected or mitigated if they are used as care partners with humans rather than as substitutes. Much more work is needed to spell out the more effective divisions of labor and forms of cooperation between AI caregivers and humans. Last but not least, AI oversight programs need to be formed to ensure that AI caregivers will act legally and ethically—at least as ethically as human caregivers.

References

Al Jazeera. 2014. Robots for the elderly.

Anderson, M., and S.L. Anderson, eds. 2011. *Machine ethics*. New York: Cambridge University Press.

Bohannon, J. 2015. The synthetic therapist. *Science* 349(6247).

Bostrom, N. 2014. When machines outsmart humans. CNN.

Coeckelbergh, M. 2010. Health care, capabilities, and AI assistive technologies. *Ethical Theory and Moral Practice* 13 (2):181–190.

---

[5] The question "Quis custodiet ipsos custodes" was first posed by the Roman author Juvenal. See Juvenal 2014, p. 65.

Emspak, J. 2016. How a machine learns prejudice. *The Scientific American*.

Etzioni, A. and O. Etzioni. 2016a. Keeping AI legal. *Vanderbilt Journal of Entertainment and Technology Law* 19(1).

———. 2016b. Killer robots won't doom humanity, but our fears of AI might. *Quartz*.

Fasola, J., and M.J. Mataric. 2013. A socially assistive robot exercise coach for the elderly. *Journal of Human-Robot Interaction* 2 (2).

Feil-Seifer, D., and M. Matarić. 2011. Ethical principles for socially assistive robotics. *IEEE Robotics and Automation Magazine*, Special issue on Roboethics, Veruggio, J. Solis and M. Van der loos 18 (1): 24–31.

Gonsior, B., S. Sosnowski, C. Mayer, et al. 2011. Improving aspects of empathy and subjective performance for HRI through mirroring facial expressions. *Ro-Man* 2011: 350–356.

Hawking, S., M. Tegmark, F. Wilczek, and S. Russell. 2014. Transcending complacency on super-intelligent machines. *The Huffington Post*.

Hawkins, J., and S. Blakeslee. 2004. *On intelligence*. New York: Times Books.

Juvenal. 2014. Satire. In, ed. Lindsay Watson and Patricia Watson, 6th ed. Cambridge: Cambridge University Press.

Kurzweil, R. 2012. *How to create a mind: The secret of human thought revealed*. New York: Viking.

Leyzberg, D., E. Avruni, J. Liu, and B. Scassellati. 2011. Robots that express emotion elicit better human teaching. *Proceedings of the 6th international conference on human-robot interaction ACM* 347–354.

MacCargar, B. 2005. *Watts, heat and light: Measuring the heat output of different lamps*. January http://www.reptileuvinfo.com/html/watts-heat-lights-lamp-heat-output.html.

Markoff, J. 2015. *Machines of loving grace: The quest for common ground between humans and robots*. First ed. New York: ECCO.

Matarić, M.J., J. Eriksson, D.J. Feil-Seifer, and C.J. Winstein. 2007. Socially assistive robotics for post-stroke rehabilitation. *Journal of Neuroengineering and Rehabilitation* 4 (1): 5–5.

Mayer-Schönberger, V., and K. Cukier. 2013. *Big data: A revolution that will transform how we live, work, and think*. London: John Murray Publishers.

Merriam-Webster.com. n.d.-a. "Humanoid." Merriam-Webster.

———. n.d.-b. "Robot." Merriam-Webster.

Nakajima, H., R. Yamada, S. Brave, Y. Morishima, C. Nass, and S. Kawaji. 2003. The functionality of human-machine collaboration systems – mind model and social behavior. *SMC'03 Conference Proceedings. 2003 IEEE International Conference on Systems, Man and Cybernetics* 3:2381–2387.

Picard, R. 1997. *Affective computing*. Cambridge, MA: MIT Press.

Price, R. 2016. Microsoft is deleting its AI chatbot's incredibly racist tweets. *Business Insider*.

Reese, H. 2016. Why microsoft's Tay AI bot went wrong. *Tech Republic*.

Rheingold, H. 1985. *Tools for thought: The history and future of mind-expanding technology*. Cambridge, MA: MIT Press.

Rosenberg, T. 2015. Depressed? Try therapy without the therapist. *The New York Times*.

Sharkey, N. 2008. The ethical frontiers of robotics. *Science* 322: 1800–1801.

Sharkey, N., and A. Sharkey. 2006. Artificial intelligence and natural magic. *Artificial Intelligence Review* 25: 9–19.

———. 2010. The crying shame of robot nannies: An ethical appraisal. *Interaction Studies* 11 (2): 161–190.

Sharkey, A., and N. Sharkey. 2012. Granny and the robots: Ethical issues in robot care for the elderly. *Ethics and Information Technology* 14: 27–40.

Shea, S. 2006. *Improving medication adherence: How to talk with patients about their medications*. Philadelphia: Lippincott Williams & Wilkins.

Sparrow, R. 2002. The march of robot dogs. *Ethics and Information Technology* 4: 305–318.

Sparrow, R., and L. Sparrow. 2006. In the hands of machines? The future of aged care. *Minds and Machines*.

Sullins, J.P. 2011. When is a robot a moral agent? In *Machine ethics*, ed. M. Anderson and S.L. Anderson. Cambridge: Cambridge University Press.

Tanaka, F., A. Cicourel, and J.R. Movellan. 2007. Socialization between toddlers and robots at an early childhood education center. *Proceedings of the National Academy of Sciences* 104 (46): 17954–17958.

Turkle, S. 2010. *Alone together: Why we expect more from technology and less from each other.* New York: Basic Books.

———. 2011. The tethered self: Technology reinvents intimacy and solitude. *Continuing Higher Education Review* 75: 28–31.

Turkle, S., C. Breazeal, O. Dasté, and B. Scassellati. 2006. First encounters with Kismet and Cog: Children respond to relational artifacts. In *Digital media: Transformations in human communication*, ed. P. Messaris and L. Humphreys. New York: Peter Lang.

van Wynsberghe, A. 2012. Designing robots with care: Creating an ethical framework for the future design and implementation of care robots (doctoral dissertation).

Wallach, W., and A. Allen. 2009. *Moral machines: Teaching robots right from wrong.* New York: Oxford University Press.

Winfield, A.F., C. Blum, and W. Liu. 2014. Towards an ethical robot: Internal models, consequences and ethical action selection. In *Conference towards autonomous robotic systems*, 85–96. Springer International Publishing.

Chapter 18
Transforming the Active Orientation

Our ambitions are high. We have a long list of desiderata that in effect entail re-engineering much of the physical and social world around us, even the self. We Americans are keen to prevent the alarming deterioration of the environment, to attain higher rates of economic growth, to reduce inequality, to curtail the number of people incarcerated for nonviolent offenses while simultaneously reducing drug abuse, to end war and genocide, to foster human rights, to reform campaign finance, and to improve our knowledge, skills, and self-awareness (most recently through "mindfulness"). When then-President Bill Clinton was asked, on the eve of a new year, what he wished for his fellow Americans in the year to come, he responded: "Have all your dreams come true."

Sadly, a deep gap exists between our aspirations and our capabilities. We aspire to re-engineer much the world, but actually we are often buffeted by forces we neither understand nor control. Revisit the list of desiderata introduced above; it soon becomes clear that we have made little progress on most of these fronts, and we actually have fallen back on quite a few of them. All too often, we do not even agree about how to tackle these issues, nor do we command the know-how, resources, political will, or personal dedication to proceed successfully.

After conducting a review of the history of how we acquired these ambitions, and the role of science and technology in fostering them, I asked where we go from here. It seems obvious that either we must greatly scale back our ambitions, or we must double down and find more effective ways to proceed. Actually, it is likely that we will have to do both. Science and technology are seen by some as the most promising sources for finding ways to catch up, for controlling history rather than being subject to its vicissitudes. Others see science and technology as exacerbating the problem. Here, too, there might be a third way.

This chapter draws on "Transforming the Active Orientation" in *Issues in Science and Technology*, (Spring 2016): 79–85. I am indebted to Erin Syring for research assistance on a previous draft of this chapter.

© The Author(s) 2018

A. Etzioni, *Happiness is the Wrong Metric*, Library of Public Policy and Public Administration 11, https://doi.org/10.1007/978-3-319-69623-2_18

18.1   A Brief History of the Active Orientation

At the beginning, humans were passive. They largely accepted nature around them as a given, rather than seeking to recast it. They accepted their place in the social world as fixed rather than seeking to move up within or change their social structures or themselves. The Stoics of Ancient Greece, for example, held that our actions were orchestrated by forces beyond humans' control and that all events followed inherently from prior events dating back to the beginning of the universe. The philosophers Democritus, Heraclitus, and Aristotle held that "everything occurred by fate" (Miller and Reeve 2015, pp. 388–389). People accepted changes or lack thereof as God-given, or as being the result of spirits. True, passivity was not complete. People did make sacrifices and prayed, appealing to deities to intervene against natural disasters, illness, and war, but they did not believe that human beings could marshal the powers necessary to change the future.

When facing the social world, first Aristotle and then the Church told people to be the best they could be in whatever role in which they found themselves. Aristotle's virtue ethics dismissed hedonism and instead held that the good life was one that fully achieved or "perfected" the "final cause" or purpose inherent in one's nature (Lynch 2004). This purpose he referred to as a "telos." For example, the purpose of the flute is to be played well, not to be used as a knife. Each person should work to serve his or her purpose rather than seek to serve another goal—that is, people should not strive to be socially mobile.

The Catholic Church substantially incorporated Aristotelian teleology into its theology. Thomas Aquinas stated, "The Church [was] to teach the truth of God and to assist the faithful in fulfilling their God-given *telos*, individually and collectively" (Sheldon 2001, pp. 15–16). Thus, the nobleman should strive to be the best of his kind, and the serf should be the best possible serf. There was no place here for an active orientation toward the self or toward society by seeking reform.

This position dominated political thinking in Western societies in the Middle Ages, but it was not limited to the West. The Indian caste system, too, reflected a passive orientation toward society, what sociologists referred to as "status acceptance." Thus, Hinduism holds that: "If an individual respectfully accepts and carries out the duties of his or her caste, then he or she will live the next life in an elevated caste of society" (Johnson 2013, p. 159). Many other societies embraced similar values that promoted social and political passivity.

The active orientation, or the presumption that humans can re-engineer the world, was born as part of the Age of Reason, which originated in the 1600s and was characterized by according high value to rationality, science, and technology. (Some locate the origins of the relationship between ideas of progress and technology earlier, in the Renaissance [Bernat 2013].) Rationality presumed that individuals have clear and orderly ends; collect, process, and interpret information about ways of achieving those ends in an empirical and logical manner, and then act according to which means they judge to be the most efficient (Etzioni 1988). The "rational man" was free of the bondage of the superstition, prejudices, and biases that dominated earlier ages. Bigotry, belief, magic, and religion were treated by rational people as if they were one obsolete burden to be replaced by rational thinking and science, which were held to be the mainstays of an enlightened society. The era is widely credited with the birth of the modern approach to natural sciences, which in turn opened the world to be marshaled and used, allowing mankind to understand its place in the solar system, harvest electricity and radio waves, and create a host of other innovations that enabled the Industrial Revolution. At the same time, techno-logical breakthroughs and feats of engineering, such as the power loom and the steam engine, often played a much greater role than science, and science itself ben-efited from technological developments like the microscope, the telescope, and (eventually) computers. This chapter treats science and engineering as two forces that together empowered mankind to marshal nature and make it work for us. From here on, references to technology should be read as if referring to technology and science. Initially, the shift from a passive to an active orientation was associated with great benefit: the rise of affluence, the advent of modern health care and educa-tion, and free flow of information—essential for democratic politics, and celebrated by America's founders and by nineteenth century Americans, who typically viewed technical, human, and moral progress as strongly aligned.

Francis Bacon was one of the first philosophers to postulate that human beings could re-engineer the world around them and achieve mastery over nature. In his *The New Atlantis*, he foresaw a utopia in which technology would make life much less taxing and would empower humans to overcome natural limitations (Bernat 2013). Henry Brooks Adams wrote in 1906 that "the new American—the child of incalculable coal power, chemical power, electric power, and radiating energy, as well as new forces yet undetermined—must be a sort of God compared with any former creation of nature. At the rate of progress since 1800, every American who lived in the year 2000 would know how to control unlimited power" (Meakin n.d.). A thread of "technological utopianism," of which Edward Bellamy and Horatio Alger, Jr. were perhaps the greatest proponents, ran through much public culture from the late 1800s to the early 1900s (Segal 1985; see also Walden 1981).

Karl Marx extended the active orientation to re-engineering society. He envi-sioned a "classless society" brought about by the establishment of full communism, which would be characterized by "a co-operative union of free producers, who would be both owners of the means of production and workers." All people would labor together equally to satisfy the economic needs of all of the members of the community (New World Encyclopedia n.d.). Such a classless society would repre-sent the fulfilment of what Marx saw as humanity's "capacity for harmonious soci-ety with others and the capacity for free, conscious, and universal labor" (Coby 1986, p. 22). Technology developments were key to this societal transformation and to the achievement of a future utopia.

Sigmund Freud extended the active orientation to re-engineering ourselves. Freud and other psychoanalysts held that man is able, if only with great effort and pain, not only to understand himself but also to transform himself, to free himself from his own past, and to set a new course of action. Freud suggested that natural urges could be sublimated in favor of a more civilized social world.

The idea that mankind was progressing dominated. Robert Nisbet observed, "...
it is a notion of the European Enlightenment that thanks to scientific advances, [in
the future] all people would be united in an egalitarian commonwealth, freed by
machines from poverty and the necessity of toil, from disease and even death by
scientific medicine, and ennobled by the heights of civilizational achievement"
(Hughes 2012, p. 758). The idea that "civilization has moved, is moving, and will
move in a desirable direction" also was incorporated into major segments of the
social sciences (Ross 2001). Their core assumption is that we can recast the social
world in line with our values and ambitions. Thus, according to Keynesian economics, if one correctly sets interest rates and the rates at which people spend and save,
one can achieve high economic growth. Sociologists in the post-World War II era
held that Head Start, Medicaid, negative income tax, Social Security, and half a
dozen other such federal programs will allow us to close the gap between the races
and the classes. These were indeed heady, optimistic ages, captured in such mottos
as "where there is a will there is a way" and in assertions that "the richest nation of
the world should be able" to accomplish whatever was needed.

18.1.1   Rising Doubts

Historians of technology disagree about when people first noted that the active orientation had serious, negative side effects that people neither anticipated nor could
handle readily. Some hold that the idea that humanity inexorably progressed was
"dethroned" by the Great Depression and two World Wars, which collectively
"destroyed the sense of cumulative gain in civilization on which progress depended"
(Ross 2001). Others point to the dropping of the atomic bomb on Hiroshima and
Nagasaki as a major turning point. Literary scholar M. K. Booker finds that "[T]he
atomic bombing of Hiroshima and Nagasaki was not an entirely new departure so
much as it was a final straw that finally broke the back of the American national
narrative [about the merits of technology]" (Hall 2009). The world had to face the
fact that technological developments brought about a tool that incinerated cities
along with their hundreds of thousands of inhabitants and that threatened the whole
world. The pleading groups of scientists that recognized sooner than others the danger of the monster they had helped create were ignored. As the saying goes, you
cannot force toothpaste back into the tube.

Soon, other developments gave the champions of reason, science, and technology
additional pause. The development of hormonal birth control ("the pill") raised fears
of a population bomb. True, Malthusian fears about mass starvation due to overpopu-
lation did not come to pass, but the specter still lingered (Tierney 1990). There are very
familiar, growing concerns that humans' growing economic activities will exhaust the
world's resources; that the degradation of the environment will threaten human survival and that climate change will subject us to a whole series of calamities.

In the social realm, there are growing doubts that we can actually manage the
economy and an increasing sense that we are instead doomed to suffer recurring

major recessions beyond our control. Grave doubts emerged about the effectiveness of the talk therapy championed by Freud and other psychotherapy gurus. Marxian ideas about fashioning a better social world through central planning and command and control economies, and of reordering political life through a working class revolution, have been discredited.

A debate erupted in the United States in the late 1960s over the expansion of liberal social programs based on social science. It turned out that many of these programs failed to achieve their transformational goals, as neoconservatives stressed, while liberals held that given more money and more time, these programs could succeed. Most recently the rise of artificial intelligence and robots has raised great concerns about massive human unemployment and machines' domination of people.

Meanwhile, social scientists began to recognize that human beings are much less capable of the kind of rational thought that the active orientation takes for granted. In contrast to the innate rationality of behavior assumed by classical economics, other social science fields demonstrated the limits of rationality for individuals and for organizations. Decision scientists showed that more information did not add up to better decisions. Behavioral economics has demonstrated that human beings are constrained by innate, hardwired cognitive biases and that human intellectual capabilities are much more limited than they were previously assumed to be (See Kaustia and Perttula 2012, pp. 46–48).

"Muddling through" characterizes much of public policy success, while failure at "encompassing planning," especially of the central command-and-control kind, is well established (Lindblom 1959, p. 81). We increasingly give up on finding basic solutions for many of the major challenges we face, and instead seek to cope with the latest crisis—a much less active orientation. The terms arrogant and hubris versus humble begin to capture the difference between the sanguine active approach and the more accepting passive one. The political systems of most nations seem unable to cope with the growing list of problems societies and the international system face, raising the question of whether our aspirations are hyperactive and completely out of line with what we can achieve.

In short, it has become clear that the active orientation is not the panacea it once seemed to be—and, indeed, some hold that our hubris will destroy us. Increasingly, the whole idea of progress, which was a reflection of the active orientation, has been cast into doubt.

18.2 A Fork in the Road?

Nowhere is the question of whether humans should greatly scale back their ambitions more acute than in the debate between the advocates of greater economic growth (and the affluent society) and the three camps that advocate for scaling back economic activities and reliance on most technologies. One holds that without scaling back our activities, the world will run out of resources; the second holds that our activities degrade the environment; and the third holds that anthropogenic climate change endangers humans. (I refer to these hereafter as the triple challenges to the affluence society.) The growth and anti-growth positions come in radical and moderate versions, but all have very different views on the role of technologies in our future. The pro-growth champions hold that technological developments can empower humans to deal with the challenges that face humanity on the path to ever higher levels of affluence; the anti (or at least slower) growth champions hold that focusing on technological solutions exacerbates the triple challenge rather than offering a cure.

I turn to discuss the techno optimists and techno pessimists. Given that these positions are familiar, I treat them briefly, and close the chapter by outlining a third way.

18.2.1   Techno Optimism

According to a host of scientists and public leaders, technological progress can help us to end the ills that plague the human condition. For example, Bill Gates is convinced that "technology can fix everything" (Beyond handouts 2015). Gates thus announced plans to spend up to $2 billion on green technologies in the next 5 years (Visser 2015). Strong technological optimists believe technology "paves a clear and unyielding path to progress and the good life" (Florida 2013) and technology is "the means of bringing about utopia" (Sivek 2011, p. 189 quoting Segal 2005, p. 10). Professor Carroll Pursell (1994, p. 39) describes as very widespread "the notion [...] that a kind of invisible hand guides technology ever onward and upward, using individuals and organizations as vessels for its purposes but guided by a sort of divine plan for bringing the greatest good to the greatest number."

Technological optimists differ in how strongly they hold this position. Many recognize the magnitude of the challenges humanity faces and our resource limitations, including those on funding and political will. Some though are quite optimistic, believing that technology could make energy "free, much like unmetered air" (John von Neumann) and eliminate the need for human labor (Jeremy Rifkin) (Mokyr 2014). Other optimists claim that technological innovation itself is speeding up and becoming less costly, which will usher in a new era of prosperity and innovation (Mills 2012; Ridley 2014). Technological utopians even hold that society itself is akin to a large, exceptionally complex machine that scientists can engineer into perfection (Sivek 2011). Others are less sanguine about technology as a total panacea. Nonetheless, all technological optimists hold that the main way forward is to increase our investments in technology. This optimism is embraced by two-thirds of Americans who believe that technology will bring about a future in which people's lives are better than they are today (Peterson 2014).

Technological optimism takes continued economic growth as a sacred cow. Professor Ronald B. Mitchell notes, "Mainstream policy and scholarly discussions of climate change accept growth in population and affluence as a given and view *technological innovation as the only available policy lever* [emphasis added]" (Mitchell 2012, p. 25). Such optimists point to technological "fixes" such as geoengineering (Specter 2012), seeding the ocean with iron to stimulate phytoplankton, or even "sending a fleet of planes into the sky and spraying the atmosphere with sulfate-based aerosols" to cool the planet (Biba 2014).

18.2.2 Techno Pessimism

Technological pessimists, by contrast, refer to "the sense of disappointment, anxiety, even menace" engendered by technology (Marx 1994, p. 11). According to them, technology frequently if not always has unintended negative side effects that are worse than its contributions to dealing with the problem the technology purports to solve. The negative consequences of technology may be delayed, but never avoided (Huesemann and Huesemann 2011). Other scholars hold that such negative effects are inherent to the very nature of technology; according to Michael and Joyce Huesemann, "[g]iven that the second law of thermodynamics guarantees that for each unit of 'order' (neg-entropy) created in the human-based economy, more than one unit of 'disorder' (entropy) is created in the surrounding environment, it follows that all industrial activities must lead to unavoidable environmental disruptions" (2011, pp. 18–19). Professor Robert Gordon argues that most if not all truly revolutionary technological innovations have already been made (Krugman 2016). Scholars such as Nick Carr, Jonathan Zittrain, Sherry Turkle, and Jason Lanier hold that technology—especially technology associated with the media and with the internet—has had negative impacts on the ways human beings think and interact with each other (McAfee 2010).

Techno pessimists rarely see a technological fix that passes muster. For instance, they fear that geoengineering will increase acid rain, and is likely to reduce the urgency that is critical to mustering the political will to permanently address climate change (The Hidden Dangers of Geoengineering 2008; What is Geoengineering? 2011). (Early critics of geoengineering were so vehemently opposed to the idea that they left death threats on the voice machine of its most famous advocate, David Keith (Grolle 2013).) Others point out that although "only nuclear power can satisfy humanity's long-term energy needs while preserving the environment" (Hannum et al. 2005) nuclear reactors generate highly radioactive waste that is dangerous if not stored with the utmost care; reprocessing this waste is expensive and increases the possibility of the waste being accessed and used for malicious purposes (Fahey 2009).

Radical techno pessimists urge us to leave the high-growth pathway needed for the affluent society, a path that presumes ever-greater reliance on technological innovation, in favor of returning to a simpler life. Such a life would entail adapting to nature rather than seeking to exploit it. Less radical technological pessimists instead believe that we should focus on activities that add *less* to the triple challenge. Technological innovation, these moderate techno pessimists point out, has its place—as long as it first and foremost helps to ameliorate the harms already inflicted upon the earth by humans. For some, this entails greatly increased reliance on "alternative" sources of energy such as solar and wind; for others, it means increasing the energy efficiency of our buildings and cars. All, in effect, favor a less active, more adaptive world.

18.3   The Post-Affluence Society: A Third Way

I see great merit in shifting the focus of our actions from seeking ever-greater wealth to investing more of our time and resources in social lives, public action, and spiritual and intellectual activities—on communitarian pursuits. In small ways, this transformation is already underway: for example, a growing number of people choose to work less and to spend more time with their children, and people are increasingly voluntarily retiring early. Such a society has a much smaller ecological footprint than the affluence-chasing society and hence helps cope with the triple challenge.

The main merits of this society though lie elsewhere. The preponderance of the relevant evidence shows that as societies grow more affluent, the contentment of their members does not much increase. For example, between 1962 and 1987, the Japanese per capita income more than tripled, yet Japan's overall happiness remained constant over that period (Easterlin 2005). Similarly, in 1970, the average American income could buy over 60% more than it could in the 1940s, yet average happiness did not increase (Easterlin 1973). Gaining a good life through ever-higher levels of consumption is a Sisyphean activity. Only finding new sources of meaning in life can bring higher levels of contentment.

While at first blush such a major cultural shift is hard to imagine, one needs to recall that for most of history, work and commerce were not valorized; instead, devotion, learning, chivalry, and being involved in public affairs were. True, these were often historically only accessible to a sliver of the population, while the poor were shut out from such things and forced to work for those who led this chosen life. However, capping consumption now makes it possible for all the population to lead a less active economic life and a more active social, communal, and spiritual—i.e. communitarian—life.

Abraham Maslow, as we have discussed earlier, pointed out that humans have a hierarchy of needs. It follows that as long as the acquisition and consumption of goods satisfy basic creature comforts—safety, shelter, food, clothing, health care, and education—expanding the reach of those goods contributes to genuine human contentment. However, once consumption is used to satisfy Maslow's higher needs, it turns into consumerism—and consumerism becomes a social disease. Indeed, more and more consumption in affluent societies serves artificial needs manufactured by those who market the products in question. For instance, first women and then men were taught that they smelled bad and needed to purchase deodorants. Men, who used to wear white shirts and grey flannel suits, learned that they "had to" purchase a variety of shirts and suits, and that last year's clothing was not proper in the year that followed. Soon, it was not just suits but also cars, ties, handbags, sunglasses, watches, and numerous other products that had to be constantly replaced to keep up with the latest trends. The new post-affluence society would liberate people from these obsessions and encourage them to fulfill their higher needs once their baser needs have been satisfied. None of this entails dropping wholly out of economic or technological world. The shift to a less consumeristic society and a more communitarian one should not be used to call on the poor to enjoy their misery; everyone is entitled to a secure provision of their basic needs. Instead, those who have already "made it" would cap their focus on their economic activities.

18.3.1   The Triple Challenge and Social Justice

A society that combines capping consumption and work with dedication to communitarian pursuits would obviously be much less taxing on the environment, material resources and the climate than consumerism and the level of work that paying for it requires. Social activities (such as spending more time with one's children) require time and personal energy, but do not mandate large material or financial outlays. The same holds true for cultural and spiritual activities such as prayer, meditation, enjoying and making music and art, playing sports, and adult education. Playing chess with plastic pieces is as enjoyable as playing it with mahogany pieces. Reading Shakespeare in a paper bound edition made of recycled paper is as enlightening as reading his work in a leather-bound edition. And the Lord does not listen more to prayers from those who wear expensive garments than from those who wear a sack.

Less obvious are the ways a socially active society is more likely to advance social justice than the affluent society. Social justice entails transferring wealth from those disproportionally endowed to those who are underprivileged. A major reason such reallocation of wealth has been very limited in affluent societies is that those who command the "extra" assets tend also to be those who are politically powerful. Promoting social justice by organizing those with less and forcing those in power to yield has had limited success in democratic countries and led to massive bloodshed in others. However, if those in power embrace the capped culture and economy, they will have little reason to refuse to share their "surplus." This thesis is supported by the behavior of middle class people who are committed to the values of giving and attending to the least among us—values prescribed by many religions and by left liberalism.

18.4   In Conclusion

In shifting the active orientation from a society that seeks ever more affluence to one that caps its economic activity but is socially (widely understood) more active, technologies have three roles to play: (a) Keep the economy humming at a level that makes it possible to satisfy all the members' basic needs, for instance by making healthcare safer, higher quality and lower cost, as the introduction of hand sanitizers did. (b) Ameliorate the effects of the triple challenges, for instance by increasing the use of alternative sources of energy. (c) Allow for a more active communitarian life, for instance through technologies that facilitate group interactions versus those that isolate people, through technologies that make voting easier while helping to prevent fraud, and through technologies that enable parents to monitor the whereabouts of young children.

In the words of Pope Francis during his 2015 visit to Washington, DC, "We have the freedom needed to limit and direct technology to devise intelligent ways of developing and limiting our power, and to put technology at the service of another type of progress, one which is healthier, more human, more social, more integral" (Howard 2015).

References

Bernat, P. 2013. Technology, utopia, and dystopia: Modern technological change in early literary depictions. *Kultura i Wychowanie* 5(1).

Beyond handouts. 2015, September 17. *The Economist*, 55.

Biba, E. 2014, December 4. Planet reboot: Fighting climate change with geoengineering, *Newsweek*.

Coby, P. 1986. The utopian vision of Karl Marx. *Modern Age*.

Easterlin, R. 1973. Does money buy happiness? *The Public Interest* 30: 3–10.

———. 2005. Diminishing marginal utility of income? Caveat emptor. *Social Indicators Research* 70 (3): 243–255.

Etzioni, A. 1988. Normative-affective factors: Toward a new decision-making model. *Journal of Economic Psychology* 9 (1): 125–150.

Fahey, J. 2009, July 22. New fuel source: Nuclear waste? *Forbes*. http://www.forbes.com/2009/07/21/nuclear-waste-energy-technology-breakthroughs-nuclear.html.

Florida, R. 2013, March 29. *Robots aren't the problem: It's us. The Chronicle of Higher Education*.

Grolle, J. 2013, November 20. Cheap but imperfect: Can geoengineering slow climate change? *Der Spiegel*.

Hall, A.C.O. 2009. 'A way of revealing': Technology and utopianism in contemporary culture. *The Journal of Technology Studies* 35(1),

Hannum, W.H., Marsh, G.E., and Stanford, G.S. 2005, December. Smarter use of nuclear waste. *Scientific American*.

Howard, A. 2015, September 24. Pope wants technology to make us better humans. *The Huffington Post*.

Huesemann, M., and J. Huesemann. 2011. *Techno-fix: Why technology won't save us or the environment*. Gabriola Island: New Society Publishers.

Hughes, J.J. 2012. The politics of transhumanism and the techno-millennial imagination, 1626–2030. *Zygon* 47 (4): 757–776.

Johnson, L.A. 2013. Social stratification. *Biblical Theology Bulletin* 43 (3): 159.

Kaustia, M., and M. Perttula. 2012. Overconfidence and debiasing in the financial industry. *Review of Behavioral Finance* 4 (1): 46–62.

Krugman, P. 2016, January 25. Paul Krugman Reviews 'The Rise and Fall of American Growth' by Robert J. Gordon. *New York Times*.

Lindblom, C.E. 1959. The science of 'muddling through'. *Public Administration Review* 19 (2): 79–88.

Lynch, T.D. 2004. Virtue ethics, public administration, and telos. *Global Virtue Ethics Review* 5 (4): 32–49.

Marx, L. 1994. The idea of 'technology' and postmodern pessimism. In *Technology, pessimism, and postmodernism*, Sociology of the Sciences, ed. Y. Ezrahi, E. Mendelsohn, and H. Segal, vol. 17, 11–28. Dordrecht: Springer.

McAfee, A. 2010. Can technology optimists and pessimists get in the same room? *Harvard Business Review*.

Meakin, J. n.d. A 20th-century retrospective: Looking back at the age of extremes. *Vision*.

Miller, P.L., and C.D.C. Reeve, eds. 2015. *Introductory readings in Greek and Roman philosophy*. Indianapolis: Hackett Publishing Company.

Mills, M.P. 2012, August 25. *The next great growth cycle*. American Enterprise Institute.

Mitchell, R.B. 2012. Technology is not enough: Climate change, population, affluence, and consumption. *The Journal of Environment and Development* 21 (1): 24–27.

Mokyr, J. 2014. The next age of invention. *City Journal*.

New World Encyclopedia. n.d. Classless society. http://www.newworldencyclopedia.org/entry/Classless_society.

Peterson, A. 2014, April 18. One-third of Americans are pessimistic about tech – And they're more likely to be poor, less educated, and female. *The Washington Post*.

Pursell, C.W. 1994. *White heat: People and technology*. Berkeley: University of California Press.

Ridley, M. 2014, March 17. No need to fear the hi-tech jobs massacre. *The Times*.

Ross, D. 2001. Progress: History of the concept. In *International encyclopedia of the social and behavioral sciences*, ed. N.J. Smelser and P.B. Baltess. Amsterdam: Elsevier.

Scientific American. 2008, October 3. The hidden dangers of geoengineering.

Segal, H.P. 2005. *Technological utopianism in American culture*. 20th anniversary ed. Syracuse: Syracuse University Press.

———. 1985. *Technological utopianism in American culture*. Chicago: University of Chicago Press.

Sheldon, G.W. 2001. Aquinas, St. Thomas. In *Encyclopedia of political thought*, 15–16. New York: Facts on File, Inc.

Sivek, S.C. 2011. We need a showing of all hands: Technological utopianism in MAKE magazine. *Journal of Communication Inquiry* 35 (3): 187–209.

Specter, M. 2012, May 14. The climate fixers. *The New Yorker*.

Tierney, J. 1990, December 2. Betting on the Planet. *The New York Times*.

Visser, N. 2015, June 29. Bill Gates to help fight climate change by investing up to $2 billion in green technology. *The Huffington Post*.

Walden, D. 1981. The two faces of technological utopianism: Edward Bellamy and Horatio Alger, Jr. *The Journal of General Education* 33 (1): 26–30.

What is geoengineering? 2011, February 18. *The Guardian*.

Chapter 19
Communitarian Bioethics

Communitarianism is often viewed as the polar opposite of liberalism, as seeking to preempt individual choices by relying on communal normative criteria and authorities. Common good considerations are said to replace respect for autonomy. Accordingly, for example, people with infectious diseases are to be incarcerated, the way Cuba deals with those who contract HIV (Hansen and Groce 2003, p. 2875). Indeed, such authoritarian communitarianism has been championed by the leaders and some public intellectuals of East Asian nations, especially Singapore and Malaysia (Jiang 1998; Bell 1995). One major reason many, especially in the West, reject this kind of communitarianism is that they hold autonomy in high regard.

The same challenge does not apply to responsive (or liberal) communitarianism.[1] This communitarianism seeks to balance autonomy with concern for the common good, without a priori privileging either of these two core values. And it seeks to rely on society (informal social controls, persuasion, and education) to the greatest extent possible and to minimize the role of the state (law enforcement) in promoting compliance with the norms that flow from these values. Responsive communitarianism is often confused with, or treated as part and parcel of, authoritarian communitarianism, though the two differ as much as social democratic socialism differs from Soviet socialism.

Although responsive communitarianism's starting point is the recognition that the tense relationship between autonomy and the common good must be worked out rather than starting with the assumption that one of these core values trumps the other, it expects treatment to differ from one society to another and among different

---

This chapter draws on "On a Communitarian Approach to Bioethics" in *Theoretical Medicine and Bioethics* 32, (2011): 363–374.

[1] The responsive communitarian position was first articulated by a group of scholars and activists in the early 1990s, including William A. Galston, Mary Ann Glendon, Philip Selznik, Jean Bethke Elshtain, and Amitai Etzioni. They issued a platform (Communitarian Network 2010) that found many endorsers across much of the political spectrum.

© The Author(s) 2018

A. Etzioni, *Happiness is the Wrong Metric*, Library of Public Policy and Public Administration 11, https://doi.org/10.1007/978-3-319-69623-2_19

historical periods. Thus, in totalitarian societies and theocracies, such as those in Singapore and Iran, those who advocate the balance that responsive communitarianism favors would need to promote autonomy, while in societies in which individualism is rampant, such as the United States was in the 1980s, the advocates of responsive communitarianism would need to promote more attention to the common good. That is, societies often need to move in opposite directions from one another to achieve the same end balance.

19.1 Earlier Treatments of Communitarian Bioethics

Medicine is typically non-communitarian in the sense that it usually does not concern itself with the common good. The individual patient's good is at the center of nearly every discussion. Indeed, earlier communitarian examinations of bioethics focused on the observation that American bioethicists tend to err on the side of considering the patient as an individualistic being and view autonomy as the supreme value, according to which the patient's right to personal choice is paramount. Daniel Callahan quotes Joseph Fletcher, stating that bioethics is based on "the idea of personal choice as the highest moral value and the struggle against nature as medicine's most liberating mission" (Bell 1995). Ezekiel Emanuel, in his essay on the care of incompetent patients, points out that the understanding of the "best interests" of a patient in this individualist vision of health care is based upon the degree of pain a procedure would inflict on that person (Callahan 1994). Jeffrey Blustein explains this conception of autonomy in health care, stating, "It rests … on a picture of the person as a separate being, with a distinctive personal point of view and an interest in being able securely to pursue his or her own conception of the good" (Blustein 1993).

Communitarianism in these writings is often viewed as leaning in the authoritarian direction, at least in the sense that it is centered on the common good and not autonomy. For instance, Lawrence O. Gostin (2002) defines communitarianism as a tradition that "views individuals as part of social and political networks, with each individual reliant on others for health and security. Individuals, according to this tradition, gain value from being a part of a well-regulated society that seeks to prevent common risks". Similarly, Veena Das (1999) looks to a communitarian conception of bioethics to allow bioethicists to "find alternative anchoring concepts to those of patient autonomy." Ogunbanjo and van Bogaert (2005) define communitarianism as "a model of political organization that stresses ties of affection, kinship, and a sense of common purpose and tradition."

To illustrate briefly the generalizations introduced so far: a liberal bioethics may stress that patients should be free to instruct their physicians not to disclose their conditions to others (although exceptions may be recognized, such as when dealing with minors, infectious diseases, or attempts to commit homicide). The patient should also be free to argue for an order not to be resuscitated or refuse other treatments, disregarding the values and feelings of the patient's family and surely of his community. Communitarianism is then depicted as the opposite position, in which the family can instruct the physician not to disclose to the patient that his condition is terminal, can demand continued health care services, and so on. However, in the terms here employed, this second position is a form of authoritarian communitarianism, because it is centered on the values of the community and disregards the value of autonomy. Responsive communitarianism favors seeking to work out the conflict between the patient and the family and developing mechanisms for its resolution.

Some of the early writings by bioethicists about communitarianism do reveal recognition of the two, sometimes conflicting, core values—autonomy and the common good—although they do not employ these two terms. Thus, Callahan (1994) defines communitarian bioethics as seeking to "blend cultural judgment and personal judgment." Thomas H. Murray (1994, pp. 32–33) writes that many theorists believe "the solution is not to abandon autonomy.... But autonomy can only be a part of the story about how we are to live together, how we are to make families and communities that support the growth of love, enduring loyalties, and compassion."

Mark Kuczewski (2001, p. 136) recognizes explicitly that one is dealing here with two rather different kinds of communitarianism. He compares "whole tradition communitarians" with "liberal communitarians": the former requires an acceptance of the full cloth of a single tradition and does not allow for compromise or even significant communication across the borders of communities, while the latter stresses respectful "moral deliberation" as a way to communicate and coordinate moral expectations across traditional boundaries.

Before proceeding, I must explicate the term 'the common good.' It refers to those goods that serve the shared assets of a given community: for example, preserving national monuments, supporting "basic" scientific research, advancing national security, protecting the environment, and promoting public health. Contributions to the common good often offer no immediate benefits to any one individual, and it is often impossible to predict who will gain from them or to what extent, in the longer run. Often, investment in the common good is carried out because it is considered the right thing to do, by itself and for itself, not because we or our offspring will personally benefit from it.[2]

19.2 Society (Community) vs. State

Responsive communitarianism holds that the more one can rely on norms rather than laws and on public education, moral persuasion, and informal social controls rather than on law enforcement, the better the society. (I use 'better' to mean ethically preferred, in a non-consequentialist sense, rather than solely on the basis of cost-benefit analysis, although such an analysis can have ethical implications that should be taken into account). The main reason is that societal processes can change preferences and lead to truly voluntary compliance, while coercion leaves opposing

---

[2] For additional discussion, see Alex John London (2003), Kuczewski (2009), and Etzioni (2004).

preferences intact. It, hence, invites attempts to circumvent the law and tends to generate a sense of alienation (Etzioni 1975).

A telling example is the way Prohibition was introduced versus the way public smoking was banned. The enactment of Prohibition was not preceded by the building of a normative consensus and instead relied heavily on law enforcement. It failed to suppress the use of alcohol and greatly increased the corruption of the American legal and political system. Moreover, it is the only constitutional amendment that was ever repealed. In contrast, although it took some 25 years to build wide societal support to ban smoking in public spaces, once these laws were introduced, they served to lock in an already very well established norm, which is almost completely self-enforcing.

Similarly, responsive communitarianism would urge, for example, that long before one considers mandatory HIV testing, let alone forcefully isolating people who have contracted HIV, one is obligated to engage in public educational campaigns that encourage such testing and to work with the communities of those most at risk to encourage their members to be tested. And rather than open a market in human organs to incentivize more people to donate organs, which are in short supply (Erin and Harris 2003, pp. 137–138) one should appeal to people to make the gift of life. A colleague has suggested that the debate about how best to increase the supply of organs may be an instance of the debate between those who see the world through the eyes of rational choice and seek to reduce all conduct to self-interest, and those who hold—as I do—that people are indeed influenced by incentives and disincentives, but also by moral considerations, which change their preferences. It is not possible to deal with this debate here, and I have treated it extensively elsewhere (Etzioni 1988).

At the same time, responsive communitarianism does recognize that there are conditions under which the state must be involved, although it is best used as the last, rather than the first, resort. For instance, when people infected with a highly communicable disease that has fatal consequences do not heed calls to remain at home until they cease to be infectious, the state has an obligation to enforce their quarantine. Historically, this issue has arisen with regard to the treatment of people with leprosy, tuberculosis, and, more recently, severe adult respiratory syndrome (SARS) and H1N1 influenza.

Gostin (2002) provides a powerful case for a communitarian approach to similar issues, such as a bioterrorist attack or a severe medical emergency. He points out that excessive concern for autonomy and neglect of the common good have led to a focus on individualized achievements in health care at the cost of severely underfunding the public health infrastructure and ignoring the needed adaptations of public health laws. As a result, public health agencies do not have the capacity to "conduct essential public health services at a level of performance that matches the constantly evolving threats to the health of the public." At the same time, public health law has fallen off the radar and is now "highly antiquated, after many decades of neglect." Finally, the debate about the role of the government in providing health care, reignited in the United States by the Obama administration, has some strong communitarian dimensions, as does the reliance by insurers on community ratings versus "cherry picking" the healthy and the wealthy.

19.2.1 Which Community?

The term 'community' is often associated with small, traditional, residential communities, such as villages. However, in the modern era, communities are often non-residential and based on ethnicity, race, religious background, or a shared sexual orientation. Moreover, people are often members of more than one community. Finally, it is often productive to consider communities as nesting within more encompassing communities, such as local ones within a national one. People are hence subject not merely to tension between their personal preferences and the values and norms promoted by their community but are also subject to conflicting normative indications from various communities.

The family can be viewed as a small community. In bioethics, strong champions of autonomy, as well as some feminists, suggest that each adult member of the family should make her or his own choices and that other members of the family should have no status in these decisions (Blustein 1993). In contrast, discussions about severely ill neonates whose parents seek to allow the infant to die because it will benefit other siblings tend to attach considerable weight to the welfare of the family as a whole.

John Hardwig (1990) moves us toward a responsive communitarian position when he writes that "the interests of patients and family members are morally to be weighed equally" and "to be part of a family is to be morally required to make decisions on the basis of thinking about what is best for all concerned, not simply what is best for yourself." Hardwig adds, "That the patient's interests may often outweigh the conflicting interests of others in treatment decisions is no justification for failing to recognize that an attempt to balance or harmonize different, conflicting interests is often morally required." He leans somewhat in the authoritarian direction when at one point he claims that "considerations of fairness and, paradoxically, of autonomy therefore indicate that the *family* should make the treatment decision, with all competent family members whose lives will be affected participating." Thus, a less authoritarian position would suggest that, for instance, if nine out of ten family members agree that treatment should be stopped for a given member, but the member—who is competent—rejects this conclusion, the family's wishes should not carry. However, the person does owe the family members a careful consideration of their values, reasons, and needs.

Jeffrey Blustein (1993) also articulates a responsive communitarian position. He holds that while final decision-making authority ought to remain with the patient, medical personnel and society ought to focus on integrating family members into the decision-making process to support the patient's ability to determine the best option—taking into consideration the interests of those most important to him or her.

When bioethical communitarian considerations turn to more encompassing communities, especially to transnational ones, a whole host of additional issues arise. They often center on the question of which community's values should prevail. These issues have been debated with regard to numerous topics, ranging from female circumcision to the testing of new drugs overseas. Whether one can apply here the dual approach of combining respect for the cultural autonomy of various cultures and the concern for a global common good is a topic that must be left for another discussion. The same holds for the numerous inter-community issues that arise when a national culture, values, and laws conflict with the culture, values, and habits of various immigrant groups or confessional groups that are members of the same national society.

Ezekiel Emanuel (1987) points out that the various criteria for what is in the best interest of the patient are affected by what a given community considers "the good life." He writes, "This solution derives from communitarianism, a philosophy that incorporates the truths of utilitarianism and liberalism, but transcends both by arguing that ethical problems can be resolved only by accepting a public conception of the good life while rejecting the conception of the good particular to utilitarianism." Emanuel favors allowing each community to determine its own concept of the "good life" on the grounds that (a) it is impossible to answer this question on neutral grounds and (b) we are a pluralistic society, and hence, should respect the values of various member groups such as Orthodox Jews and the gay community. This position is very much in line with a communitarian position, but it raises the question of whether there is room for nationwide or even transnational communal criteria and policies.

As I see it, the answer lies in a position referred to as "diversity within unity." Accordingly, on some issues, it is clear that the most extensive community—often the nation, but increasingly also transnational communities such as the EU—should and do provide the normative criteria. On other matters, diversity of the kind Emanuel depicts is fully appropriate. And, in still a few other instances, one should expect that there will be room for disagreement about what "belongs" to the community at large and what to smaller, member ones. Examples of those that are best guided by the most encompassing communities are issues that concern basic rights (e.g. few would leave it to local communities to rule on whether gay patients or members of a given racial minority should be denied service) and the moral claims that urge people to donate organs, blood, and time. In contrast, allowing different groups to rely on faith healers up to a point is an example of local community values influencing biomedical decisions.

In the United States, an example of communities defining ethical care concerns the conditions under which parents can deny medical care for their children. Some states mandate treatment when it is a question of life and death, regardless of the parent's request to forego care, while others allow extreme latitude in the decision making options of parents, including choices made about lifesaving interventions. In contrast to this state-by-state determination of critical care decisions, there is a nationwide consensus that in matters less than life or death, parents should be allowed to refuse treatment for their children in order to maintain their personal perception of "the good life."

In short, diversity within unity[3] provides a responsive communitarian model of granting some discretion to member communities while also maintaining select values of the most encompassing conceptions of the common good. The fact that, in some matters, it is unclear which community should prevail does not obviate the merit of this design, which stands out when one compares the diversity within unity position to those that favor the national state and those that favor turning these matters into the domain of each member community.

19.2.2 Procedures and Criteria

Communitarians must concern themselves with procedures and criteria that allow one to work out personal decisions and public policies in the face of conflicting values. A major way to proceed is through moral dialogues. Examinations of actual processes of consensus building, especially when they concern normative matters, show that individual preferences and judgments are largely shaped through interactive communications about values—that is, through moral dialogues that combine passion with normative arguments and rely on processes of persuasion, education, and leadership. Moral dialogues focus more on values than on facts. Although passionate and without a clear starting and ending point, they often lead to new shared moral understandings. Such dialogues led to the formation of a new sense of duty to protect the environment, to reject racism and sexism, to oppose the war in Vietnam, and many other such society-wide shared understandings.

The redefinition of death that took place in the United States illustrates the ways in which moral dialogues work. In 1968, an ad hoc committee at the Harvard Medical School published a report that defined an irreversible coma as "brain death"—a new definition of death. The report, put together by academics and medical professionals, did little to redefine the public perception of death. However, in 1972, a young woman named Karen Ann Quinlan fell into a persistent vegetative state. After weeks of life support, her parents asked that she be taken off the machine and be allowed to die. The hospital refused, so the parents sued. Although Quinlan's case did not meet the definition of brain death, her case brought the issue to national attention (Jonsen 1998). There followed extensive and widespread dialogues in various communities spurred by the media, out of which gradually grew a consensus accepting brain death as a morally acceptable definition of end of life and substituted this definition for the previous belief that one ought to do "all one could" to keep one's loved ones alive.

Another way to work out the balance between autonomy and the common good as it applies to specific matters is to leave these issues to courts or to legislatures. Should people be required by law to vaccinate their children? Under what conditions may people be subjects of research? Can one require people who have been arrested—but not yet convicted—to yield their DNA, the way their fingerprints are

---

[3] For more discussion, see Etzioni (2003).

collected? These and many other bioethical considerations are best first subject to moral dialogues, assisted by bodies such as ethics committees in hospitals or the Presidential Commission for the Study of Bioethical Issues, but—especially given the growing volume of such policy matters—some ought to be worked out by courts and legislatures.

Finally, communitarian bioethics leads one to suggest criteria that moral dialogues, judges, and lawmakers may draw upon. One is the relative adverse impact on the two core conflicting values that flow from the adoption of a given policy. That is, when autonomy must be much curbed for minor gains to the common good, responsive communitarianism suggests autonomy should be given the right of way, while public policy should lean in the opposite direction if the gains to the common good are substantial and the sacrifice of autonomy is minimal (Etzioni 1999).

These criteria would help explain the position articulated by Tom L. Beauchamp (1994, pp. 18–19), who argues that society should switch its conceptions of the public and private good in terms of euthanasia and organ donation. Euthanasia, currently considered an issue where the public determines its application, ought to be a private matter, according to Beauchamp, because that is the logical conclusion of a culture that allows patients extreme latitude to determine their treatment up to (but currently not including) death, with the assumption that personal care choices have more impact on personal autonomy than they do on society at large. At the same time, organ donation, with its widespread implications for the well-being of the community, ought to be moved out of the realm of personal decision making and into the public arena, putting the focus on the public good, which is more impacted by organ donation decisions than is individual autonomy.

Other criteria indicate that one ought to find ways to absorb the side effects. For instance, if one introduces a policy that calls for testing newborn infants for HIV, special care must be taken to keep the results confidential, lest the mother lose her job, housing, or insurance.

19.2.3   Third Values

So far I have limited the discussion to two core values because these are the ones that define the main differences among liberals, authoritarian communitarians, and responsive communitarians. However, bioethical judgments obviously can and do draw on additional values, and the ways in which these can be treated in this context remain to be discussed. Much of this discussion must be deferred because it requires rather extensive deliberations. However, the main issue at hand can be illustrated by pointing to the four values often quoted by bioethicists, drawing on the influential work of Tom L. Beauchamp and James F. Childress, *Principles of Biomedical Ethics* (2008). These are respect for autonomy, nonmaleficence, beneficence, and justice.

Three of the four principles in this quartet focus on the individual. The meaning of autonomy in a bioethical context has already been covered in the first parts of this chapter. Nonmaleficence also focuses on the well-being of the individual patient: do no intentional harm. Beneficence, the third principle, is defined as an obligation to advance the healthcare interests and welfare of other individuals—because we have ourselves received benefits. Justice, the fourth principle, raises a host of complicated issues that so far have not been addressed extensively by communitarians.

19.2.4 Social Justice: A Case Study

One major place where the study of bioethics and social justice converge is in examining the normative criteria according to which scarce resources are allocated. For instance, when triage takes place, rationing is called for, and the argument is advanced that after a certain age, senior citizens should be granted only ameliorative care.

Here the focus is on questions raised in the United States, as well as in several other countries in the wake of the 2008–2009 great recession, by fears that the economy will continue to grow slowly and suffer from high levels of debt and a high rate of unemployment. Various public efforts were launched to reduce public outlays in general and those set aside for Medicare and Medicaid in particular. Indeed, it was argued that because "entitlements" command about 60% of the federal budget, and given that a good part of the remaining 40% is dedicated to defense and interest that must be paid, unless entitlements—and especially Medicaid and Medicare—were cut, it would be impossible for the United States to "put its fiscal house in order." Both legislators and media mavens argued that cutting into the social safety net was not merely necessary to reduce the deficit, but that it was mathematically inevitable. As Senator Michael Bennet (D-CO) put it, "We can't solve our budget crisis without dealing with our entitlements" (NPR 2010).

The "inevitable" need to cut into social safety nets is inevitable only if one refuses to collect additional revenues, such as through a carbon emissions tax, cap-and-trade system, or value-added tax. To give but one example, a carbon emissions tax of $10 per ton of carbon content could generate $50 billion a year and generate several other desirable outcomes. Whether or not one agrees with such revenue generating moves, they demonstrate that cutting entitlements is a matter of choice, not a mathematical necessity.

The normative case for social safety nets is often made on social justice grounds. These programs have lifted millions of Americans out of poverty, more than all other federal programs combined, and they transfer a modest amount of resources from more affluent Americans to those less endowed. They are also defended on social contract grounds. Senior citizens and those late in their careers have planned their whole lives around the assumption that the safety nets they paid into would be there when they retired or became infirm. To violate this contract is manifestly unfair. There is another moral argument to consider. If we must make cuts, we ought to first cut those budget items that in effect pay for harmful activities and then those without any discernable social benefits, before we even consider touching those that are beneficial—even if the benefits are limited and their costs are high. This is a sociological version of the medieval medical aphorism: first, do no harm.

In 2010, total Medicare spending was estimated to be over $500 billion (Congressional Budget Office 2010). This program was projected to run out of funds before Social Security—perhaps as early as 2029. In December 2010, the National Commission on Fiscal Responsibility and Reform issued a draft report that called for limiting what the nation could spend on Medicare, while others called for delaying the age at which one qualified for care (The National Commission on Fiscal Responsibility and Reform 2010). States moved to cut services in ways that were harmful to Medicaid patients. In Arizona, Governor Jan Brewer asked the Obama Administration for permission to remove 280,000 people from Medicaid rolls. In California, Governor Jerry Brown limited doctor visits and prescriptions for Medicare beneficiaries. In Georgia, Governor Nathan Deal proposed to end Medicaid coverage for adult dental, vision, and podiatry treatments, and South Carolina proposed to end hospice care. These and other such cuts seem morally unjustified as long as there are ways to fund these programs by curbing services that are harmful or have no proven benefit.

The United States spends twice as much on administrative costs for health care than do many other countries. One study found that U.S. administrative costs amount to $30 out of every $100 spent on health care, compared to $17 in Canada (Aaron 2003). There are many reasons the U.S. cannot match Canada's parsimonious ways, but if it could cut only part of the difference in administrative overhead, it would save a good part of what Medicare needs to remain financially solid. Some experts are skeptical when people argue that one can gain the needed funds by eliminating fraud and abuse. Yet one is duty-bound to increase the efforts to plug the leaky bucket before denying seniors the right to dip into it when they are ill. One report demonstrated that the Medicare fraud industry in South Florida by 2010 was larger than the cocaine industry, due to the relative ease of swindling Medicare: there was less risk of exposure and less risk of punishment if caught (60 Minutes 2009). Criminals buy patient lists and bill the government for expensive items ranging from scooters to prostheses, costing the government about $60 billion a year. Because Medicare is required by law to pay all bills within 30 days and has a small accounting staff, it often cannot vet claims before the checks go out. By the time Medicare authorities find out a storefront's bills are phony, the criminals have closed their operation and moved on. From a moral viewpoint, it seems wrong to cut anyone's benefits until the government triples its accounting staff and quadruples the number of such criminals in jail.

As much as $325 billion is spent every year in unnecessary treatments in the health care system. Cutting back on these procedures would reduce the deficit without denying benefits to anyone. An even stronger case can be made for increasing efforts to reduce the estimated 98,000 deaths caused every year by medical error.

All this is not to say that one should rule out adjusting benefits. However, it is morally wrong to deny benefits to those who retired or plan to retire or are ill and infirm before the nation greatly increases the number and prerogatives of those who seek to curb the billions siphoned off by criminals, wasted by bureaucrats, and squandered on useless medical interventions that can make people sicker—or even kill them.

19.2.5 Add the Common Good

Finally, it is important to note that even the nuanced and enriched set of normative principles developed by Beauchamp and Childress does not include a concept of the common good above and beyond the concept of justice. For instance, they do not discuss conditions under which individuals have to accept various sacrifices for the good of all. Thus, the kinds of concerns Gostin and communitarians more generally have about preventing the spread of infectious diseases, responding to bioterrorist attacks, protecting the environment, balancing preventive and acute medical treatments, and determining the extent to which one can foster or force limits on individual choices for the public good do not find a comfortable home in the most widely followed bioethical texts. Hence, concern for the common good, responsive communitarians would argue, should be added to the already existing core values on which bioethics draws.

References

60 Minutes. 2009. Medicare fraud: A $60 billion crime. *CBS News*.

Aaron, H.J. 2003. The costs of health care administration in the United States and Canada—A questionable answer to a questionable question. *New England Journal of Medicine* 349: 801–803.

Beauchamp, T.L. 1994. Reversing the protections. *Hastings Center Report* 24: 18–19.

Beauchamp, T.L., and J.F. Childress. 2008. *Principles of biomedical ethics*. 6th ed. Oxford: Oxford University Press.

Bell, D.A. 1995. A communitarian critique of authoritarianism. *Society* 32: 38–43.

Blustein, J. 1993. The family in medical decision making. *Hastings Center Report* 23: 6–13.

Callahan, D. 1994. Bioethics: Private choice and common good. *Hastings Center Report* 24: 28–31.

Communitarian Network. 2010. Responsive communitarian platform.

Congressional Budget Office. 2010. The budget and economic outlook: Fiscal years 2010 to 2020. Congressional Budget Office.

Das, V. 1999. Public good, ethics, and everyday life: Beyond the boundaries of bioethics. *Daedalus* 128: 99–133.

Emanuel, E. 1987. A communal vision of care for incompetent patients. *Hastings Center Report* 17: 15–20.

Erin, C.A., and J. Harris. 2003. An ethical market in human organs. *Journal of Medical Ethics* 29: 137–138.

Etzioni, A. 1975. *A comparative analysis of complex organizations*. Rev ed. New York: Free Press.

———. 1988. *The moral dimension: Toward a new economics*. New York: Free Press.

———. 1999. *The limits of privacy*. New York: Basic Books.

———. 2003. Diversity within unity. In *21st century opportunities and challenges: An age of destruction or an age or transformation*, ed. Howard F. Didsbury Jr., 316–323. Bethesda: World Future Society.

———. 2004. *The common good*. Cambridge, MA: Polity Press.

Gostin, L.O. 2002. Public health law in an age of terrorism: Rethinking individual rights and common goods. *Health Affairs* 21: 71–93.

Hansen, H., and N. Groce. 2003. Human immunodeficiency virus and quarantine in Cuba. *Journal of the American Medical Association* 290: 2875–2875.

Hardwig, J. 1990. What about the family? *Hastings Center Report* 20: 5–10.

Jiang, Y. 1998. *Asian values and communitarian democracy*. Paper presented at the International Workshop on Deliberating the Asian Value Debate, Taipei.

Jonsen, A.R. 1998. *The birth of bioethics*. New York: Oxford University Press.

Kuczewski, M. 2001. The epistemology of communitarian bioethics: Traditions in the public debate. *Theoretical Medicine and Bioethics* 22: 135–150.

———. 2009. The common morality in communitarian thought: Reflective consensus in public policy. *Theoretical Medicine and Bioethics* 30: 45–54.

London, A.J. 2003. Threats to the common good: Biochemical weapons and human subjects research. *Hastings Center Report* 33: 17–25.

Murray, T.H. 1994. Communities need more than autonomy. *Hastings Center Report* 24: 32–33.

NPR. 2010. Colorado's Senator Bennet on his narrow election win.

Ogunbanjo, G.A., and D.K. van Bogaert. 2005. Communitarianism and communitarian bioethics. *South African Family Practice Journal* 47: 51–53.

The National Commission on Fiscal Responsibility and Reform. 2010. The moment of truth: Report of the National Commission on Fiscal Responsibility and Reform.

Acknowledgements

Several chapters have not been published before. Other chapters, which draw on previous articles, as next indicated, have been extensively revised. The remaining chapters that draw on previously published articles have been updated and re-edited.[1]

Chapter 1: Happiness is the wrong metric
This chapter is published first here.

Chapter 2: Bring back the moral wrestler
This chapter is published first here.

Chapter 3: Crossing the Rubicon: This chapter draws on "Crossing the Rubicon: Including Preference Formation in Theories of Choice Behavior" in *Challenge* 57 (2), (March/April 2014): 65–79.

Chapter 4: Moral dialogues
This chapter is published first here.

Chapter 5: Moral effects of teaching economics: This chapter draws on "The Moral Effects of Economic Teaching" in *Sociological Forum* 30 (1), (March 2015): 228–233.

Chapter 6: Job collapse on the way to new Athens: This chapter draws on "Job Collapse on the Road to New Athens" in *Challenge* 60 (4), (2017): 327–346.

Chapter 7: Nationalist populism is not an enemy
This chapter is published first here.

Chapter 8: Free speech versus safe spaces: This chapter draws on a segment of an article previously published as "Right Does Not Make it Right" in *The American Scholar*, September 29, 2015.

Chapter 9: The right to be forgotten: This chapter draws on "Second Chances, Social Forgiveness, and the Internet" in *The American Scholar*, (Spring 2009).

Chapter 10: Back to the pillory?: This chapter draws on "Back to the Pillory?" in *The American Scholar* 68 (3), (Summer 1999): 43–50.

---

[1] Melissa Paul and Kevin Hudson helped put this book together.

© The Author(s) 2018
A. Etzioni, *Happiness is the Wrong Metric*, Library of Public Policy and Public Administration 11, https://doi.org/10.1007/978-3-319-69623-2

Chapter 11: Moral triage: This chapter draws on "Moral Triage" in *Providence*, 6 (Winter 2017): 38–42.

Chapter 12: Talking with the Muslim world: This chapter draws on "Talking to the Muslim World: How, and with Whom?" in *International Affairs* 92 (6), (2016): 1361–1379.

Chapter 13: Defining down sovereignty: This chapter draws on a segment of an article published as "Defining Down Sovereignty" in *Ethics and International Affairs* 30 (1), (Spring 2016).

Chapter 14: The case for decoupled armed interventions: This chapter draws on "The Case for Decoupled Armed Interventions" in *Global Policy* 3 (1), (February 2012): 85–93.

Chapter 15: Incorporating ethics into artificial intelligence (with Oren Etzioni): This chapter draws on "Incorporating Ethics into Artificial Intelligence" in *The Journal of Ethics* 21 (4), (2017): 403–418.

Chapter 16: Pros and cons of autonomous weapons systems (with Oren Etzioni): This chapter draws on "Pros and Cons of Autonomous Weapons Systems" in *Military Review*, (May-June 2017): 72–80.

Chapter 17: The ethics of robotic caregivers (with Oren Etzioni): This chapter draws on "The Ethics of Robotic Caregivers" in *Interaction Studies* 18 (2), (2017).

Chapter 18: Transforming the active orientation: This chapter draws on "Transforming the Active Orientation" in *Issues in Science and Technology*, (Spring 2016): 79–85.

Chapter 19: Communitarian bioethics: This chapter draws on "On a Communitarian Approach to Bioethics" in *Theoretical Medicine and Bioethics* 32, (2011): 363–374.